YOUNG ADULTS
AND PUBLIC LIBRARIES

Recent Titles in
The Greenwood Library Management Collection

Information Services for People with Developmental Disabilities
Linda Lucas Walling and Marilyn M. Irwin, editors

Public Library Planning: Case Studies for Management
Brett Sutton

Video Acquisitions and Cataloging: A Handbook
James C. Scholtz

Introducing and Managing Academic Library Automation Projects
John W. Head and Gerard B. McCabe, editors

The National Electronic Library: A Guide to the Future for Library Managers
Gary M. Pitkin, editor

Strategic Management for Public Libraries: A Handbook
Robert M. Hayes and Virginia A. Walter

Managing Business Collections in Libraries
Carolyn A. Sheehy, editor

Introduction to Health Sciences Librarianship: A Management Handbook
Frank R. Kellerman

Library Facility Siting and Location Handbook
Christine M. Koontz

Promoting Preservation Awareness in Libraries: A Sourcebook for Academic, Public, School, and Special Collections
Jeanne M. Drewes and Julie A. Page, editors

Serials Management in Academic Libraries: A Guide to Issues and Practices
Jean Walter Farrington

Creating the Agile Library: A Management Guide for Librarians
Lorraine J. Haricombe and T. J. Lusher, editors

Young Adults and Public Libraries

A HANDBOOK OF MATERIALS AND SERVICES

EDITED BY
Mary Anne Nichols and C. Allen Nichols

THE GREENWOOD LIBRARY MANAGEMENT COLLECTION
Gerard B. McCabe, *Series Adviser*

GREENWOOD PRESS
Westport, Connecticut • London

Library of Congress Cataloging-in-Publication Data

Young adults and public libraries : a handbook of materials and
  services / edited by Mary Anne Nichols and C. Allen Nichols.
      p. cm.—(The Greenwood library management collection, ISSN
  0894–2986)
    Includes bibliographical references and index.
    ISBN 0–313–30003–8 (alk. paper)
    1. Public libraries—Services to teenagers—United States.
  I. Nichols, Mary Anne, 1967– . II. Nichols, C. Allen.
  III. Series.
  Z718.5.Y66   1998
  027.62'6'0973—dc21   97–45649

British Library Cataloguing in Publication Data is available.

Library of Congress Catalog Card Number: 97–45649
ISBN: 0–313–30003–8
ISSN: 0894–2986

First published in 1998

Greenwood Press, 88 Post Road West, Westport, CT 06881
An imprint of Greenwood Publishing Group, Inc.

Printed in the United States of America

The paper used in this book complies with the
Permanent Paper Standard issued by the National
Information Standards Organization (Z39.48–1984).

10 9 8 7 6 5 4 3 2

Copyright Acknowledgments:

The following have generously given permission to reprint excerpts from their copyrighted works:

Extracts from: "What Makes a Good Review? Ten Experts Speak." *Top of the News*, 35 (Winter
1979): 146–52. REPRINTED WITH PERMISSION OF THE AMERICAN LIBRARY ASSOCIA-
TION FROM *TOP OF THE NEWS*, WINTER, 1979. COPYRIGHT © 1979.

Extract from: Carter, Betty. *Best Books for Young Adults: The History, the Selections, the Romance.*
Chicago: American Library Association, 1994. REPRINTED WITH PERMISSION OF THE
AMERICAN LIBRARY ASSOCIATION. COPYRIGHT © 1994.

Excerpted from *Booktalk! 4* Copyright © 1992 by Joni Richards Bodart. Reprinted by special
arrangement with The H.W. Wilson Company.

Tables 23.1–23.6 reprinted by permission of Cuyahoga County (OH) Public Library.

To Evan Luisi Nichols

Contents

Preface

Young adult (YA) services means a great deal for both of us. Not only is it something we have both been, or are, responsible for in our day-to-day job duties, but it is something that just makes plain sense. Since surveys have shown that YAs constitute around 25 percent of public libraries' patrons, customers, or whatever word you are using, we feel it is important to provide a targeted program of service to them. No business would systematically ignore 25 percent of its customer base, yet most libraries do when it comes to this age group.

We hope this book serves to benefit young adults in a number of ways:

- promote services in public libraries
- enhance existing services to teens
- assist library school students in gaining a better understanding of the meaning of YA services

We are extremely proud of the contributors who so graciously assisted with this work. You will find the names of some of YA services' best-known advocates, national leaders of the Young Adult Library Services Association (YALSA), a division of the American Library Association (ALA), past and present, and some new voices who we feel are proving themselves to be leaders as well. With the advance of technology, a number of the contributors have included World Wide Web addresses in their chapters. These addresses were current as of the time of publication; however, with the ever-changing Web, some may no longer exist or may have changed.

Many of the basic competencies required by YA librarians are focused upon in this book in one form or another, so use this as a continuing education tool. If for nothing else, use it to stimulate your curiosity and seek opportunities to learn more about a subject.

1

Adolescent Development: An Emotional Roller Coaster

Melanie Rapp

Knowledge of adolescent development is absolutely essential when working with young adults. This concept is an assumed expectation in young adult (YA) librarianship but is commonly overlooked and sometimes ignored. Just because one interacts with young adults does not mean that their development is understood. Knowledge of adolescent development may bring peace of mind to any individual coping with teenage subnormal behaviors. Young adult librarians need to be able to identify early, middle, and late adolescence as well as the identifying factors of physical, social, and cognitive developments related to the appropriate developmental area.

So what does this all mean to the "hipster librarian"? Why is knowledge of development so important to librarians? Have the times changed so much that as professionals we need to be reeducated? What can we do as librarians to groove with the changes within young adults? Can librarians help make growing up less painful? These questions have many answers, and within your own experiences you will find explanations and forever ponder new questions that arise when working with this specific age group. With background information and a different perspective, hopefully your daily journeys through adolescence will be a bit easier. There are numerous individual phases in adolescent development. It is difficult and almost unjust to place 12-year-olds in the same category as 18-year-olds. Physical, social, and cognitive differences prove that within this age span there needs to be some separation. Although there are many definitions and categories of adolescent development, the following will be referred to in this chapter. Early adolescence refers to individuals 12 to 14 years of age, middle adolescence involves 14 to 17 years, and late adolescence is 17 to 19.

Adolescent stages are distinct in nature, but many individuals will have their own unique experiences as a young adult. One cannot ignore that the whole adolescent experience is complicated to both the individual and the people surrounding him or her. As individuals, we are all unique, and despite popular belief, young adults are not an exception. This point may be challenged with occurrences that we observe as adults. How do we explain a group of 13-year-olds that look exactly alike, and even the rips in their jeans are identical? How can they be unique when all they want to do is look like everyone else? This is definitely a common response to a group of adolescents. As YA librarians, we need to be in sync with our adolescent mode so we can identify the aspects of surviving early adolescent years.

EARLY ADOLESCENCE

The early adolescent years are the beginning of the three momentous stages of adolescence. Peer groups blossom from seeds as quickly as telephones blossom from ears. Hand gestures are used as greetings, and parents become aliens. This is the time when girls typically mature at a more rapid pace than boys.

Scenario: You are sauntering through the YA area of the library, and something strange and drastic has just occurred. You stand there wondering what has overcome your body in such a debilitating way. Ah, you finally realize the problem: your senses have become temporarily disabled. The smell of bubble gum, strawberry lip gloss, and the combination of smelly sneakers and body odor could nauseate the strongest of librarians. A 13-year-old girl is flaunting shorts that you *know* she was not wearing when she left her house. A 12-year-old boy is strutting around in a T-shirt that says, "I'm Wearing This to Annoy You." Many four-letter words are being whispered, there is gossip of who's dating who, and page 115 of Judy Blume's book *Forever* is being recited by memory. You have just entered the puberty zone, otherwise known as "hormonal hell."

However, not all individuals struggling through early adolescence fall into the picture just portrayed. Many shy individuals do not want *any* attention at all. They easily go by unnoticed but deserving of as much attention as the MTV VJ wanna-be. Because of this, interacting with all young adults becomes even more important and more challenging. "A child may be physically mature but not emotionally mature. A twelve year old may look fifteen but act like a ten year old."[1] Individuals going through early adolescence are more likely to test limits to anyone representing authority. Insults are provided at request. A common conversation may sound like this:

Sylvester: Hey, where did you get the plastic coat? At K-Mart?
Luella: Ya, but at least I don't have a brain tumor zit on my face.

Translated, does this mean that the coat is (1) approved, (2) really ugly, or (3) neither? The only individual who knows the answer is the young adult who voiced his opinion. Try to figure it out? You can, but it may take a lifetime. Chances are that Sylvester and Luella are the best of friends. As librarians we need to be aware of this kind of communication and be able to handle similar efforts at communicating by teens in nonthreatening ways. This will always be an issue in degrees when there is a group of early adolescents in the library or participating in a program. The best approach is to encourage respect for everyone. Although these insults are acceptable between these two people, they may not be toward others around them. Obviously, not every individual will handle sweet insults like this in a positive way.

Like it or not, this is the stage of development when questions about sex run rampant. Young adults need to make educated and informed decisions that are right for them. "More than half of women and almost three quarters of men aged fifteen to nineteen have had sexual intercourse."[2] Because so many young adults are having sex by middle and late adolescence, early adolescence is an appropriate time to have information accessible for questions and curiosities.

The library should have materials available on abstinence, birth control, pregnancy, pregnancy alternatives, and sexually transmitted disease. These materials can vary from pamphlets, to displayed materials, to the well-read books hiding in the 612s. As librarians we need to observe how these materials are being used. For example, many sex books may not be heavily circulated but are read extensively. Weeding of the collection cannot be decided by circulation statistics alone. One can tell by the tattered edges and covers of these books how much they are being used, not to mention if they are found interfiled with the cookbooks.

What can we do as librarians to respect all young adults in early adolescensce? This is the perfect time to make sure that the tables and chairs in the young adult area are adult size. Many teens are growing and would feel much more comfortable at bigger tables, and chairs need to be more than three inches from the ground. Even though this has been said a myriad of times, the YA area needs to be separate in the library, not too close to the children's or adult areas, if possible. Young adults do not want adults staring at them and watching their actions, nor do they want to relive their childhood years that they so desperately want to ignore as teenagers. It is critical that young adults have the opportunity to gain a sense of physical boundaries and self-acceptance at this time. A sense of a specific space that is safe and comfortable will be a foundation for making young adults feel content with their surroundings.

Young adults need a place to hang out. Malls, record stores, and youth centers are all popular places. Additionally, the library should definitely be considered a place for young adults. However, this is not an accepted point of view. The phrase "hanging out" splatters red over all efforts to develop a positive environment and attitude. The presence of young adults in the library is not different from an adult's visiting the library to read the daily paper or a child's playing with puzzles in the toy area. The difference is that many libraries do not cater to young adults. Young adults should not be expected to be in "school mode" or "on task" at all times. The myth that young adults need to be "doing something" at all times needs to be reevaluated. The library welcome mat should be present for the individual patron, regardless of age.

Too many times adults become threatened when young adults hang out in groups. This is a library issue because the after-school crowd can end up being one big gang in the library. Strength comes in numbers, and this energy can be either negative or positive, depending on the approach taken by the individuals involved. Carol J. Eagle and Carol Colman's book *All That She Can Be* emphasizes why adolescent girls are attracted to groups. "During early adolescence, most girls feel too vulnerable to face the world alone and need the security of the group to provide strength. In addition, by observing the girls in the group, what they say and how they react to certain situations, a girl learns how to be an adolescent girl."[3] Many adults assume that teens hang out together just to make adults miserable. If only adults were that important!

Rules that apply to all patrons should apply to young adults. Too often a group of louder adolescents is confronted differently than adults or children are confronted. A common defense mechanism is asking the group to leave the building or becoming confrontational. Would you ask a group of adults visiting loudly to leave the library? What about a screaming child? Young adults need to be treated with respect and not automatically labeled as problems. Many potential discipline problems can be prevented by this approach.

Programming for adolescents in the early stage of development can be the most rewarding of all levels. If the librarian can interest a few young adults in an idea or activity, the enthusiasm can be contagious. Positive attitudes about the library can be demonstrated and encouraged in the hopes of encouraging lifelong library users. This is not an easy accomplishment, considering that many young adults in early adolescensce are not the easiest to communicate with. Books are rarely the sought-for materials; they are often an afterthought. The language needs to be spoken. Libraries need to provide materials of interest to this particular age group. Comic books, graphic novels, and music can rescue the librarian. Along with having these materials, the YA librarian must be familiar with them and what is popular. Popularity may change on a weekly basis and thus can make the aspect of being "with it" difficult. Interacting with YA patrons and asking for honest opinions may make life a little easier. Not only is it important for the librarian to listen to teens and to be knowledgeable of popular items, but having young adults review material can prove to be a valuable activity. Commonly, a young adult will accept a recommendation of a music CD more positively from a peer than from an adult.

Young adults need positive adult interaction, and the library is an ideal place for this to happen. Librarians do not have to be the grouch-spinster stereotype that young adults have nightmares about. There is not one rule book in the library field that requires a librarian to have a hair bun and wear sensible shoes.

There is no processed average teen, either. Strong young adult advocates are essential and can provide role models for other library staff and adult patrons who visit the library. The importance of interaction with teens cannot be ignored. Young adult advisory councils fall into this concept. Councils are not only a safe place to discuss thoughts and ideas and seek support, but also a place to interact with adults. Young adults can achieve positive relations with adults through volunteering, representation at an adult friend's group, or community involvement. Opportunities are endless when teens and adults are together in a positive environment.

The musical group the Indigo Girls views young adults in a manner that should be duplicated. These two musicians had a song lyric contest for high school students where the winner would receive a concert in his or her school. Why did Emily Saliers and Amy Ray approach this age group? A quote in the May 1997 issue of *Seventeen* explains, "We have a lot of faith in kids' ability to make positive changes in our world, and we want to experience that energy with them."[4] An attitude this definite should be adopted by not only librarians but anyone involved with young adults.

Young adults experiencing early adolescence are a great audience for programming and various activities. There is much importance in encouraging this crowd to frequent the library. Comfort in the library environment will be a significant help when young adults are presented with difficult assignments and life-involving questions when approaching middle adolescence.

MIDDLE ADOLESCENCE

The period of middle adolescence can be identified as the invisible years or the years of limbo. The discovery of one's inner self is a significant focus of this particular stage. Many internal and psychological changes are occurring. This is a time for late bloomers to catch up on puberty and the mature ones to deal with changes that have already occurred. Therefore, the search for balance between body and mind is introduced. This developmental stage affects most young adults when they are in high school. Academic and athletic expectations are increased. Performance and success are the pressure points. Relationships gain in importance and maturity.

Because there is so much going on in the young adult's life at this time, the library can easily be a low priority. Young adults may use the library for academic reasons but rarely for leisure. Therefore, it is critical that the librarian be available to provide help with school projects and research. Librarians must be sensitive to the immediate needs of the young adult patron. Young adults will come into the library the night before an assignment is due. This assignment may be minor or quite lengthy, but either way they need assistance. The last thing they are seeking is a lecture on why they didn't start earlier. A sense of humor and empathy will get the most irritated librarian through these recurrent situations.

There are also various items of importance between the ages of 14 and 17 that the library can focus upon in regard to programming. Dating, dances, and social events (including parties) top the list of activities for both male and female middle adolescents. The library can provide many special programs concerning the social butterfly and the "oh, I just can't" individuals. Fashion previews are a great approach to one of the most stressful events in high school—*prom!* Ideas on dresses, tuxedos, flowers, restaurants, and proper etiquette can either be presented in a program for both males and females or be displayed by a bulletin board or "help sheet." This would be a great opportunity to market the magazines in the YA area of the library. *Teen*, *Seventeen*, and *YM* have makeup tips and numerous preparations for the big evening. Contests or drawings for gift certificates to flower shops and car washes would prove popular for both sexes as well as encourage the use of the library.

Technology proves to be a reality and requires necessity of computer knowledge. Many libraries either have or are in the process of acquiring Internet access. Young adults are believed to know everything about computers. However, searching the Internet successfully and in an efficient manner may be another story. Because it is so easy to spend hours browsing, actual research may become frustrating and unsuccessful. The profusion of information available through library databases is overwhelming. The ease of use of and familiarity with selected databases that results through library-provided instruction would benefit the young adult greatly. Large and small group instruction along with one-on-one attention would provide the young adult with skills to complete assignments and research with the use of technology.

Proving oneself to be an independent individual can be the ultimate stress situation. Obtaining a learner's permit and obtaining a driver's license are perfect examples of the need for independence. The library can have driver's test materials available, as well as peer study sessions for the written test. This is an ideal opportunity to display statistics and information on safe and sober driving. A program on basic car knowledge and maintenance would prove appropriate for both interest and a foundation to establish responsibility for either borrowing the car or owning one.

Many young adults are unable to apply for their driver's license because of age, cost, and miscellaneous reasons. The importance of transportation and independence from parents is still significant. Alternative sources of getting around include rollerblades, skateboards, and mountain bikes. These forms of transportation require knowledge of miscellaneous accessories and repair. Programs displaying new car models and basic repair would be of high interest to the "oh, man, I don't want anyone seeing my mom drop me off at the mall" crowd. If public transportation is available, it may be attractive to the independent middle adolescent. Bus schedules should be available at the library in nonconspicuous places to deter the risk of attention.

The middle adolescent strives for independence, and conflicts with parents and authority figures become inevitable. A struggling parent may become a familiar sight in the library. Quite often parents are in the library doing home-work for their adolescent or finding books on how to deal with their adolescent's behavior. Sensitivity must be noticeable and sincere in the YA librarian. Parents' seeking your recommendation and assistance is extremely important. The YA librarian communicates and interacts with their child and therefore should have some influence when they need assistance. A program or pamphlet on parent–teen reading material would be useful. Cooperation with the adult librarian(s) in the building would encourage success. Materials on parenting should be in the adult area (one would not want a young adult to think that we are traitors).

Middle adolescence is also when an individual is ready to develop more mature relationships. The dating scene and the hype and interest in being in a serious "love bond" boom. YA librarians may have to break up a bonding situation in the back of the non-fiction area or on the public bench in front of the library. This behavior should not be labeled inappropriate or unacceptable but just dealt with in a suitable manner. Pulling the library staff to the window to watch or announcing possible mating activities is not the best way to handle these situations. The relationship between the young adults and the librarian should not be put at risk. The librarian should make the uncomfortable sepa-ration of two individuals as discreet as possible.

The increased interest in relationships may also bring questions about sexual orientation. "Some [teenagers] quickly realize that they are gay or lesbian. A few view themselves as mysteriously diseased. Others are merely confused, haunted by an attraction to members of the same sex that is looked upon with undisguised contempt by their own peers and society at large. And whatever the state of their sexual development, most lead troubled interior lives."[5] Providing guidance resources and support is the key factor in helping straight, gay, and lesbian teens and those who are questioning their sexual identity. This guidance results from knowing resources available in the community. Peer counseling, support groups, and organizations may be available in the community. The Cuy-ahoga County (Ohio) Public Library system publishes a booklet called *Teenage Survival Guide*.[6] This guide is to assist the YA patron who is searching for help or guidance on various issues. Names, addresses, telephone numbers, and brief descriptions are provided for each individual organization.

Middle adolescence is a time of discovering one's inner self, as well as build-ing relationships. Middle adolescence gives young adults the opportunity to test limits and build character. Attitudes and views of the world built at this time will affect the individual when he or she approaches late adolescence.

LATE ADOLESCENCE

Late adolescent years involve 17- through 19-year-olds. This stage contains a plethora of challenges and preparations for adulthood. Many adolescents choose varied and unique paths in life at this time. These paths can entail both temporary and long-term decisions. Opportunities and choices are endless to the late adolescent and may consist of college, trade school, the military, immediate employment, marriage, children, and so forth. An attentive and understanding support system would be ideal for the young adult during this stage of life. Unfortunately, this may not be the case for many, and even if it is, short-term and long-term decisions can still be difficult.

The times are changing. This phrase symbolizes the uncertainties of living in our everyday world. The reality that a college degree does not ensure employment or job security is blatant in today's world. Technology and job descriptions are continuously changing at a rapid and sometimes alarming pace. Elimination of certain positions and careers and the creation of others are daily occurrences. This can put the young adult through major turmoil when trying to decide on future plans. YA librarians need to be up-to-date with information on the job markets and areas of employment in their community, other areas of the United States, and international opportunities. A strong relationship with high school counselors would be ideal. Communication on programs offered, possibilities of cooperative efforts, and knowing how the librarian can fill the gaps would be positive for all individuals involved.

The issue of leaving home affects young adults in different ways. Anticipations of being on one's own can create a stressful abyss for some late adolescents. The fear of the unknown can bring up fears along with the insecurities and complex questions of life. On the other hand, some adolescents cannot wait to leave the confines of family life. Either way, the adolescent needs guidance, support, and the resources to build responsible decisions.

Programming on "your first apartment" and surviving dorm life could be presented by various community members consisting of young people and professionals. Teens are more likely to listen to individuals who have recently or are still going through late adolescence and who relay positive and negative facts on various ordeals. Roommate issues could also be approached on a candid and nonthreatening basis. Real-life challenges and experiences would prove to be educational as well as interesting. Assistance on how to search for an apartment and legal advice for interpreting lease agreements from community professionals could provide methods to prevent disasters.

Many unappealing details accompany the lifestyle into adulthood. Young adults will find out soon enough that visiting the grocery store is a necessity. Headaches may become a daily occurrence with a diet of Twinkies and Mountain Dew. Although programs on nutrition and buying healthy foods could easily be a "snore" (and therefore not attract many participants), the incentive for participating has to be enticing. An extra-credit opportunity with a high school teacher or great door prizes would attract late adolescents. Gift certificates and giveaways from local businesses are always an option for prizes. Grocery stores, department stores, legal services, tax help, and moving and cleaning services are just the beginning of sources that could be used as incentives. By cruising the yellow pages, you may find new businesses and services willing to participate in your programming.

Let us not forget the anguish of laundry duties. The excuse "I wanted all my wardrobe to be pink" doesn't work in any way, shape, or form. The embarrassing fact is whoever washed those clothes did not know how important the "color thing" is when separating clothes to be spin-cycle clean. The dreadful occurrence of a favorite sweater shrunk down to Cabbage Patch doll size could make an individual lose sleep for days. This may seem like a basic daily duty, but to many young adults it may be a new venture. Providing a do-and-don't guide and a display of laundry disasters may attract the attention of the curious mind.

Checking and savings accounts can appear and disappear in little or no time. Credit card applications with high credit limits and interest rates are temptations difficult to resist. Credit ratings can change from wonderful to nonexistent overnight. However, offers so enticing are difficult to refuse. Of course, a new stereo or wardrobe would be "to die for," but the realities of how much they cost when put on a credit card can be deceiving. Factual information needs to be available for the young adult when approaching these decisions. World Wide Web sites that include comparison charts on interest and incentives would prove useful. Financial books written especially for young adults should be accessible. Many times young adults shy away from financial books because of lack of interest or the serious, unappealing approach to money. Books on surviving college and adulthood may include sections with financial suggestions.

CONCLUSION

YA librarians are challenged daily with changes, attitudes, and bizarre happenings. Uncomfortable and negative situations can easily be taken personally by the librarian. Knowing that certain behaviors are associated with developmental levels may shed a different light. Young adults are being faced with more and more responsibilities and pressures to succeed. Certainly, trends and cool things will not be the same year to year or even tomorrow. As librarians, we are responsible for providing appropriate and up-to-date service to our patrons. Being able to communicate with early, middle, and late adolescents can be difficult, considering the varied stages and personalities involved. Knowledge of technology, music, and fashion can make communication with young adults possible and enjoyable. Knowledge of adolescent development enables the librarian to focus on services, programs, and material selection appropriate for the clientele served. The library can be a wonderful experience for all if the young adult is understood and respected.

NOTES

1. Elizabeth Fenwick and Tony Smith, *Adolescence: The Survival Guide for Parents and Teenagers* (New York: Dorling Kindersley, 1994), 18.

2. Debra Haffner, "Facing Facts: Sexual Health for America's Adolescents. The Re-

port of the National Commission on Adolescent Sexual Health," *SIECUS Report* (New York: Council of the United States Inc., August/September 1995), 10.

3. Carol J. Eagle and Carol Colman, *All That She Can Be* (New York: Simon and Schuster, 1993), 132–33.

4. Sophie Knight, "Indigo 101," *Seventeen* (May 1997): 108.

5. Barry Came, "Young, Gay, and Alone," *MacLean's* (February 22, 1993): 34.

6. The Cuyahoga County Public Library, 2111 Snow Road, Parma, OH 44134.

2

"I Want Another Book Like . . .": Young Adults and Genre Literature

Mary Arnold

Long summer days spent happily sleuthing with Trixie Belden or as an angel of mercy with Cherry Ames, student nurse, showed me that reading was fun, and when I'm looking for something to read "just for me," I still head to my current favorite detective or romance heroine. Being able to find and enjoy those books with just the right hook baited to reel us in time and again is the basis for genre reading. Escape, relaxation, vicarious experience—reading for pleasure is, in itself, a worthy activity, and promoting this idea is one of librarians' most important purposes. Betty Rosenberg, in her influential and useful book *Genreflecting*, reminds us that all reading tastes are created equal, a rallying cry echoed by genre readers everywhere.

The word "genre" is French for type or category, and so genres in literature are categories of writing that share common characteristics and patterns. Success depends on following conventions of plot, character, setting, tone, mood, and theme. Readers are hooked into a genre because all of these elements combine to appeal strongly—"I want another book just like . . ."—and far from breeding contempt, familiarity makes each genre read as satisfying as a favorite comfort food.

Genre fiction can suffer from a negative popular stereotype among nonreaders of that genre; but like any stereotype, this does not define the genre. While much can be found in library literature regarding the bias against collecting popular genre fiction and the onus many librarians feel to elevate the public's (including young adults') taste in literature, for our purposes we adhere to Betty

Rosenberg's first law of reading, "Never apologize for your reading taste."[1] If a book provides a satisfying and entertaining experience, then that's sufficient reason to find it in the YA collection.

Fortunately, much of genre literature already has one surefire factor for young adults, a paperback format. Usually, the covers and come-ons are designed to excite interest. Though genres can be somewhat arbitrary, and particular titles can have several elements of appeal that make them fluid as to genre classification, we will concentrate on the established genres with the most appeal for teen readers.

Although young adults read all over the map, there are genres with more built-in appeal. Romance is the successful pairing of a young couple, often with some kind of transformation taking place. Adventure stories are often quests with lots of action and excitement, culminating in something being accomplished. Science fiction and fantasy often seem to merge and overlap, since both can be called speculative fiction. Science fiction is grounded in the laws of science and nature as we know or postulate them and questions the potential future of humankind and the universe. Fantasy literature deals in the impossible—things that cannot happen caused by characters with superhuman powers in imaginary worlds, but worlds that, no matter how magical, must have a convincing reality of their own. Mystery/suspense books involve detection to solve a crime by following clues or, in the broader thrillers, to discover the true nature of a puzzling situation or character. There can be some crossover here to the ubiquitous horror genre. True horror must evoke fear—"be afraid, be very afraid." Books in the humor genre encourage us to laugh at ourselves and at human behavior and situations. Historical fiction can have a variety of stories but must re-create a time and place from the past as its setting. A specialized genre for young adults is the realistic fiction book in which teens read about "people like me." The popular sports novel falls into this category.

A little history—Patrick Jones points out the findings of a 1988 survey of young adult readers that showed how strongly genre reading appeals to teens. The most popular categories were romance and adventure/mystery, with science fiction/fantasy next. In 1991, the Young Adult Services Division (now YALSA) of the ALA hosted a preconference in Atlanta spotlighting genre fiction for young adults, and the Carnegie Reading List grant from ALA Publishing funded committees to determine criteria and prepare lists for rotating cycles of recommended genre lists designed to appeal to teen interests. Initially, Baker & Taylor provided multiple copies of the titles and bookmark lists in book dump tie-ins to promote the committee selections. Recent lists have been published in *Journal of Youth Services*, and a newly formed Popular Reading Committee will continue to produce lists of popular reading genre titles to encourage young adults to read and enjoy old favorites or explore new avenues.

Focusing on the popularity and importance of genre reading for young adults and providing selection and promotion tools to libraries serving teens have been important steps in the right direction for encouraging genre collections in the YA department. Let's build on that foundation.

ROMANCE

Romance novels essentially revolve around a relationship. The key plot action will be the pairing of a young couple, which readers hope will be successful, so romances require believable characters with whom readers can identify. A happy, daydream quality and more glamour, sophistication, and excitement than in everyday life are part of the appeal of a romance story; these same elements can be found in many television soap operas.

High interest in finding that special someone and heightened interest in sex, as well as young adults' supercharged emotions and youthful optimism, make these "wish fulfillment" stories popular. Longing for some kind of wonderful transformation that will put us at the prom, in a graduation cap and gown, planning a wedding, or maybe only walking down the school hallway or the beach hand in hand, we become our favorite Romeo or Juliet, sharing their hopes, dreams, and setbacks, as the course of true love seldom does run smoothly.

One of the early teen series success stories was the romance series. In the 1980s, young adult readers avidly followed the ups and downs of life at *Sweet Valley High (SVH)* much as they would the tangled lives of *Beverly Hills 90210* a few years later on television (which series spawned its own line of paperbacks in a profitable circle dance). The plethora of teen romance series that followed (*Sweet Dreams, Couples, Freshman Dorm*) now includes the Sweet Valley crowd's college years, but as Patrick Jones observed in his excellent *Connecting Young Adults and Libraries*, romance series are no longer the dominant force in the market they once were. Gradually, the underlying theme that boyfriend (or girlfriend) solves all problems began to shift toward more realism in style and content (*Hotline, Real Life, Boyfriends/Girlfriends*). These series have a more contemporary feel and an open, honest treatment of sex. Making decisions about social conventions is a key YA concern, and the characters in these series romances spend a lot of time thinking and talking about just that.

Criticism of the series romances centered on their insular qualities, depicting a white, middle-class suburban world where popularity is directly related to appearance and gender stereotypes abound, and on the elements not there— ethnicity, disabilities, sexuality, the poor, the elderly. While some of the series romances still focus on this narrow worldview, others have attempted to expand consciousness, although *18 Pine Street*, with its cast of African-American characters under the aegis of Walter Dean Myers, never seemed to achieve the name brand recognition *SVH* still has. But, after all, many of the romance series faithful devour each new title uncritically, secure that no matter how unrealistic it may be compared to the readers' own lives, there will be a happily-ever-after ending (maybe), but always a satisfying reading experience for them. Many of the romance titles that appear on the genre lists compiled by the YALSA committees are not happily ever after fantasies, though the key element is always the love relationship. In *Tell Me How the Wind Sounds* deafness complicates love; for Owl Tycho (*Owl in Love*) the complicating factor is her penchant to eat mice and perch in trees at night to watch her science teacher as he sleeps. We can have romantic suspense (*Silver Kiss*), romantic time travel (*Outlander*), historical romance (*Sweetgrass, Lily: A Love Story, Gift of Sarah Barker*), even humorous romance (*Probably Still Nick Swansen*). Social issues from today's headlines are the dark, secret sides to romance (incest in *Abby My Love*, abuse in *Dangerous Pursuit*, mental illness in *Saving Lenny*). Recently, more YA romances explore a much wider range of relationships in terms of gender and culture. Stories involving gay and lesbian couples (*Weetzie Bat, Annie on My Mind*), interracial love (*Crossing Blood*), love that challenges social stigmas (*Olivia and Jai, Children of the River*) have all appeared on recommended genre lists. Romances for today's young adults may not always follow the formula "boy meets girl, boy loses girl, boy gets girl," but as Weetzie Bat says, "I don't know about happily ever after . . . but I know about happily."[2]

SCIENCE FICTION AND FANTASY

Science fiction and fantasy stories deal with alternatives, a variety of possibilities for looking at reality; as such, these genres hold great appeal for young adults also juggling alternatives and choices in their own lives. While many libraries shelve these genres together, there is a distinction in focus between these two types of speculative fiction. Science fiction deals primarily with stories based on known scientific principles and possible outcomes of contemporary problems like pollution, population, politics, and sexual mores projected into the future for a new perspective. Fantasy creates an imagined world in which characters and events operate within established rules; no matter how imaginative, fantasy must have a convincing reality of its own in the midst of things that cannot happen to characters with superhuman powers in unreal worlds.

Often plot-driven, science fiction places greater emphasis on situations and solutions than on character development. But characters in science fiction often have great faith in human ingenuity, intelligence, and spirit. A sense of wonder in the plots may come from exotic backgrounds (alien worlds, the distant future), contemplation of the mysteries of the universe, or our ultimate destiny through sociological change or technology in service to humankind. Stories that imaginatively project possibilities or probabilities of current technology, hardware, and theories are sometimes designated "hard" science fiction. These can include space travel and galactic empires (Asimov's *Foundation* series, Sleator's *Interstellar Pig*); space opera (Adam's *Hitchhiker's Guide* series, Zahn's *Star Wars* continuation); media tie-ins (*Star Trek, X-Files*); time travel/time warp (Willis' *Doomsday Book*, Silverberg's *Project Pendulum*); interaction of man and machine through virtual reality, artificial intelligence, and robotics (McCaffrey's

Ship Who Sang); and cyberpunk, where human nature takes precedence, usually for the worse (Burgess' *Clockwork Orange*). Alien beings take myriad forms, but the emphasis is on the relationships between these "others" and the human characters. First-encounter stories range from the relatively gentle *ET* to the open warfare of Wells' *War of the Worlds*. Antiscience subthemes often reflect anti-intellectual distrust, where technology and scientific theory are uncontrolled monsters that will destroy humankind (Crichton's *Andromeda Strain*, Ure's *Plague*)—descendants of *Frankenstein* and that which man was not meant to know. Apocalyptic fiction, survival after man-made or natural mass destruction, relates the nature of the disaster, its effect, and the shape of the society that follows (Brin's *Postman*, Stervermyer's *River Rats*). Soft science fiction deals with disciplines like sociology and psychology. McCaffrey's *Pegasus* novels explore the nature of individuals with enhanced powers like ESP and telekinesis and their impact on the social order. Novels of social criticism like Keye's *Flowers for Algernon* and Bradbury's *Fahrenheit 451* give young adults the opportunity to question and ponder major issues and values. Closely linked are the dystopia/utopia stories, heavy with political and sociological overtones (Herbert's *Dune*, Lowry's *The Giver*, or Brooks' *No Kidding*); and alternative/parallel worlds that offer an opportunity to impose a new pattern on history (Avi's *Man Who Was Poe*, Willis' *Lincoln's Dreams*).

Much of the appeal of science fiction is in the excitement of the action, the appeal of the heroic character who is often an outsider in society, and the appeal to intellectual curiosity and abstract thinking.

FANTASY

Fantasy is another "otherworldly" reading experience that almost always involves magic or supernatural powers, a struggle of good and evil, characters that mature through trials or a test/quest, and, though good may prevail, the victory is usually transitory. Fantasy deals in polarities—good and evil, guilt and innocence, order and anarchy, truth and image—and appeals to young adult readers' own struggle with these absolutes. High fantasy is set in a complete secondary world filled with imaginary beings like fairies, dragons, and unicorns, with laws set by supernatural beings (Tolkien's *Middle-Earth*, Brooks' *Shannara*). Low fantasy is set in our more familiar world of natural laws in which nonrational happenings occur inexplicably (animal fantasy like *Watership Down*).

Some types of fantasy include sword and sorcery (Saberhagen's *Book of Swords*, Zelazny's *Amber* series, or Dungeons and Dragons offshoots like *Forgotten Realms* or *Lone Wolf*); Arthurian legend stories (Bradley's *Mists of Avalon*, Woolley's *Guinevere* series and T.H. White's trilogy); and parallel worlds (Card's *Alvin Maker*, King and Straub's *Talisman*), which often have young adult protagonists. The world of faery in the works of Charles DeLint, Ellen Kushner, and Josepha Sherman is a special kind of otherworld. Animal fantasy like Williams' *Tailchaser's Song*, Bell's *Ratha* books, or Jacque's popular *Red-*

wall saga follows in the tradition of Grahame's *Wind in the Willows* and Sewall's *Black Beauty*. Time travel tales can blur the lines between science fiction and fantasy through magic in *Playing Beattie Bow* or technology in *The Doomsday Book*. Science fiction and fantasy can be very gender-fair to women, as Linda Forrest points out in her article, with the heroes of both sexes escaping standard culture roles,[3] yet another part of the "what could be" aspect of the genres (see Pierce's *Lioness* series and McKinley's *Hero and the Crown*). More recently, dark fantasy that incorporates some horror elements has grown in popularity (Meredith Pierce's *Darkangel* trilogy, Krause's *Silver Kiss*).

Another factor with appeal for teens is that many of these books are reincarnated as films. Whether the theme is cautionary "what might happen if," optimistic "life goes on," or simply "what if, if only," reading science fiction and fantasy requires a willing suspension of disbelief, a questioning mind, and the desire for adventure.

HORROR/THRILLER

The most prevalent trend recently in genre popularity has been stories aimed at scaring the reader (often the cover seems to be the most gruesome part of the book). Legions of *Goosebumps* and *Fear Street* readers attest to this genre's "undying" (so far) appeal. Depending on the type of fear evoked, this genre is a continuum from thriller to chiller. Elements of darkness represent evil or menace (notice Lois Duncan's dark cover Dell reprints). The evil can be of human origin but beyond our comprehension or control (V.C. Andrews, Duncan) or supernatural (Anne Rice, Mary Downing Hahn, Margaret Mahy). Young adult fans of the horror genre are fascinated by the unknown, whether the occult, paranormal powers, supernatural beings, or "the evil that lurks in the hearts of men." These reads provide a fear/fun dual payoff—after the anarchy of evil, the OK factor of subsequent relief that's pleasurable, what Stephen King calls "not me, not yet, not this time."[4]

One of the conventions authors use to create this mood of fear and suspense can be physical setting and description, the old "dark and lonely night," although in some stories the very ordinariness of the setting, a world young adults already inhabit filled with brand names in familiar places like high school (Pike's *Monster*) or the mall (Yolen's *Vampires*), makes the horror even more tingling. A growing atmospheric evil and a looming threat that gradually encompasses the reader with an element of anticipation and edge-of-the-seat uneasiness all contribute to the appeal of the horror story. Again, the basic battle between the forces of good and evil may be the theme, but the gore continuum allows something for every stomach. For many of the current series, the appeal of a young protagonist prevailing over the things that go bump in the night gives young adult readers a feeling of control as they read. Short stories in the horror genre reflect a *Tales from the Crypt* appeal for a legion of television fans who love Jim Murphy's *Night Terrors*.

In the thriller, the suspense comes through the threat from character or situation, with a defining pattern similar to the mystery—an incident, process, climax, denouement. The focus can be on psychological suspense (Joan Lowery Nixon, Lois Duncan), narrator involvement, even victimization (Joe Cotton's *Quake*, Sleator's *Others See Us*), or the emotions and personal, private relationships of characters (V.C. Andrews, Robert Westall). The disaster subgenre, like Cooney's plane crashes and fires or the volcanic eruption in *Shark Callers*, have teenage characters as both victims and heroes.

Thriller/horror stories appeal to the emotions rather than the intellect, those dark forces beyond our control, the thing at the foot (or under) the bed. Whether through ghosts (the books by Richard Peck and Mary Downing Hahn), demonic possession (*Exorcist*), black magic (*Shadowland*), witches and warlocks (*Witching Hour*), vampires (Pike's *Last Vampire* trilogy), or werewolves (King, Tessier, Koontz), horror fiction presents threats to be faced, foes to be vanquished.

MYSTERY

Mysteries, those quick-moving, plot-driven detection stories, follow one inviolable rule—no unrevealed clues or hidden culprits. Teen mystery readers demand that the books "play fair" through the cycle of crime, trail of clues, investigation, solution, retribution, and restoration of order. One of the main appeals lies in the game element, solving a puzzle. Think of how popular the Clue-type mystery parties have been with all ages. In stories or series with a teen detective, it's interesting to have someone the reader identifies with who has authority and autonomy in the world of adults, picking up on and putting together details the adults miss. The elements of revenge and danger and an emphasis on action and dialogue can hook a reluctant teen reader. In Jay Bennett's wonderfully skinny mysteries or Lois Duncan's suspenseful reads, the teen protagonist often has some relation to the victim, and the process of investigating the murder is cathartic. While the amount of actual violence varies, depending on the type of crime, it's often on the edge or even outside the story in YA mysteries. Teens who enjoy critical thinking and using problem-solving abilities, finding the link between character and motive, are fans of this genre.

Teen mystery readers want things to happen fast—the puzzle, crime, and sleuth should appear at the earliest opportunity. The reader's identification with the character of the problem solver is a major hook, particularly important in continuing series like the ageless Nancy Drew and Hardy Boys. Whether sleuthing in separate books, teamed up on supermysteries, or updated in the more contemporary *River Heights* series, fans of these characters remain constant. Other more recent additions include Sylvia Smith Smith and T. Ernesto Bethancourt's Doris Fein. Adult mystery authors with some appeal to teens include Sue Grafton's Kinsey Milhone, Rita Mae Brown and her "partner," cat Sneaky Pie Brown, Tony Hillerman's Native American detectives, and the timeless Agatha Christie. The standard types of mysteries include the cozy, often British; the puzzle, an exercise in ingenuity; the private eye, more grim, cynical, and violent; the police procedural that relies on forensic and scientific methods; and the thriller, often espionage. But the amateur detective story, the often altruistic, well-meaning teen sleuth caught in an unexpected situation and determined to "get to the bottom of things," is the type of mystery many teens prefer.

ADVENTURE

In adventure stories, action is one of the key elements that challenge the main character's resourcefulness: survival, exploration, a quest for accomplishment worked out through plot twists, cliff-hangers, and increasing difficulty and danger—the narrative may emphasize action over description but needs enough realistic details to anchor the action. The challenge can come by accident or choice and can be person against person, person versus nature, or an individual in conflict with self, but the outcome is always uncertain. The young adult reader identifies with the main character, the heroic qualities and, often, the aura of the outsider that lends itself to teen recognition. If the antagonist is wily and dangerous, the appeal of going against the odds and winning is magnified. Adventure stories are exciting and involve the intelligence, abstract thinking, and curiosity of the reader.

Westerns are a subgenre of adventure, the quintessential American experience of the challenge of the frontier. The general adventure elements of individual accomplishment, competence, and self-reliance make up the Western's characters, but the emphasis on self-definition outside the restrictions of social conventions, the escape and freedom many young adult readers crave, is the hallmark of the Western. While we may critique the often black-and-white resolutions to conflicts, there is appeal in the simple life and simple values presented.

HUMOR

Laughter is appealing to most of us and can be a less intimidating reading experience for many reluctant teen readers, demanding less emotional commitment, allowing distance from character and situation. Books in this genre can be expected to end happily, as we laugh at common human foibles and behaviors and recognize the universal nature of some of the adolescent difficulties that can seem so particular in our own experience. While the style of humorous writing can vary from simple to sophisticated, the tone is the essential element here, light and playful. Some of the popular humor reading for teens veers into satire or parody (witness the enduring popularity of *Mad Magazine*) as young adults enjoy poking fun at sacred cows. The sources of humor in these books can stem from situation, style, dialogue, irony, or exaggeration. In the same way that situation comedy television shows are popular with teens, the entertaining side of daily life can be a soothing reminder that we're all in this together.

HISTORICAL FICTION

Those readers curious about other times, places, and people are the often more specialized audience for historical fiction. While the plot may combine elements of mystery, suspense, or adventure, the re-creation of a specific time and place is the essential focus. Accurate details conjure a sense of what it was like to be alive in a past time, especially references to actual persons and events from history. Historical fiction transports us and at the same time allows us to make connections with the universal human emotions that link us through years and changes. There is appeal in stories about how things came to be the way they are through the values portrayed in characters living through their own time and place in history. Young fans of *American Girls* may find young adult series like Scholastic's *Dear American* and Aladdin's *American Diaries* becoming new favorites. Historical fiction reminds us that it's people who make history, then and now.

REALISTIC FICTION

The genre of realistic fiction, sometimes called the problem novel, became nearly synonymous with YA fiction in the 1970s, with its focus on "people like me." In the standard model, a teenage character has a problem or comes to realize there is a problem complicating his or her life (as if being a teenager isn't enough) and seeks to solve said problem. The appeal is the interpersonal action, self-definition, and self-reliance that develop. The problems encountered run the full range of modern life—sex, substance abuse, headline issues like date rape, incest, homelessness, racism, violence, health issues, relationships, death, and growing up. Although commentators point out that problem novels tend to focus more on "hot button" topics than on character,[5] in the 1970s this was truly groundbreaking fiction for young adults. In our world of 900 numbers, explicit personal ads, outrageous talk shows, and bumper stickers and T-shirts that shy away from nothing, young adult realistic fiction seems to have less shock value. Recent titles reflect more balance, complexity, and diversity of worldview and greater realism in setting, plot, and character, especially the adult figures. Many of the contemporary realistic fiction stories have open-ended resolutions (Voight's *When She Hollered*, Tamar's *Fair Game*, Arrington's *What You Don't Know Can Kill You*).

SPORTS

Whether from participant or spectator focus, sports stories are generally youth-oriented, a powerful identification factor for young adult readers as they vicariously participate with, or as, the protagonist. The story may focus on athletic action, highlighting the game and rules, but in most of the successful sports genre stories, the emphasis is on sport as a framework for character. The young athlete builds, or fails to develop, character, learns cooperation and team play or individual development of skill, is encouraged to become self-aware, and learns, through plot elements and character development, the interplay of competition, fame, success, and the personal trade-off involved (Lipsyte's *The Brave*, Brooks' *Moves Make the Man*, Crutcher's *Staying Fat for Sarah Byrnes*). Sports stories speak to the all-American drive to be first and best but also examine the prices paid and the sometimes transitory nature of "glory days."

CORE AUTHORS AND SERIES BY GENRE

Romance

Authors: Cynthia Blair, Maureen Daly, Janice Harrell, Norma Klein, Linda Lewis, Norma Fox Mazer, Francine Pascal, Betty Smith, and Barbara Wersba.

Series: *Sweet Dreams, Love Stories, Cedar River Daydreams, Sunset, Voices Romance, Once Upon a Dream, Boyfriends/Girlfriends, Class of 2000, Video High, Wild Hearts, Caitlin, Sweet Valley High/University, Freshman Dorm, Heartsong, Springsong Books*.

Adventure

Authors: Will Hobbs, Scott O'Dell, Gary Paulsen, Chap Reaver, Theodore Taylor, Stephanie Tolan, Bill Wallace, G. Clifton Wisler.

Series: *Young Indiana Jones, Baywatch, Christa Chronicles, Survive!, Choose Your Own Adventure, Passport*.

Science Fiction

Authors: Orson Scott Card, Bruce Coville, Douglas Hill, H.M. Hoover, Monica Hughes, Gillian Rubinstein, Neal Shusterman, William Sleator.

Series: *Trio, Hitchhiker's Guide to the Galaxy, The X-Files, Time Tours, Tom Swift, Dr. Who, X-Men, Star Trek, Star Trek: The Next Generation, Star Trek: Voyager*.

Fantasy

Authors: Clare Bell, Susan Cooper, Diane Duane, Anne McCaffrey, Robin McKinley, Patricia McKillip, Meredith Pierce, Tamora Pierce, Terry Pratchett, Robert Silverberg, Rosemary Sutcliff, Laurence Yep, Jane Yolen, Ursula LeGuin, Madeleine L'Engle, Diane Wynne Jones.

Series: *Lone Wolf, Teen Angels, Forgotten Realms*.

Mystery/Suspense

Authors: Jay Bennett, Michael Cadnum, Richie Tankersley Cusick, Lois Duncan, Carol Gorman, Harry Mazer, Susan Beth Pfeffer, Joan Lowery Nixon, Christopher Pike, Joyce Sweeney, Chris Westwood, Robert Westall, Willo Davis Roberts.

Series: *Hardy Boys, Nancy Drew, Heart and Soul, Doris Fein, River Heights, Three Investigators, You-Solve-It Mystery, Jennie McGrady Mysteries, Samantha Crane, Undercover Cleo*.

Horror

Authors: V.C. Andrews, Caroline Cooney, Nicole Davidson, Diane Hoh, John Peel, Christopher Pike, Anne Rice, John Saul, L.J. Smith, R.L. Stine, Vivan Van DeVelde.

Series: *Horror High, Scream, Blood Moon, Midnight Place, Frankenstein's Children, Last Vampire, Bloodlust, Nightmare Inn.*

Humor

Authors: Paula Danziger, Matt Groening, Sheila Solomon Klass, Ron Koertge, Gordon Korman, Robert Lipsyte, Phyllis Reynolds Naylor, P.J. Peterson, Daniel Pinkwater, Julian Thompson, Paul Zindel.

Historical Fiction

Authors: Avi, James Collier, Irene Hunt, Mollie Hunter, Carol Matas, Philip Pullman, Ann Rinaldi.

Series: *Sunfire, Wild Rose Inn, Anne of Green Gables, Apple Valley, Southern Angels, American Dreams, Ellis Island, Brides of Wildat County,* Catherine Marshall's *Christy, American Diaries, Dear American.*

Realistic Fiction

Authors: Fran Arrick, Cynthia Voight, Francesca Lia Block, Ellen Emerson White, Judy Blume, Walter Dean Myers, Eve Bunting, Erika Tamar, Robert Cormier, Rosa Guy, Lynn Hall, Richard Peck, Ouida Sebestyen, Chris Lynch, Colby Rodowsky, Shelley Stoehr.

Series: *Reality 101, Real Life, Hot Line, One Last Wish, Nowhere High, Live from Brentwood High, Springsong, 18 Pine Street, DeGrassi Junior High.*

Sports

Authors: Chris Crutcher, Dean Hughes, R.R. Knudson, Chris Lynch, Robert Lipsyte, Will Weaver, Thomas Dygaard.

Series: *Hoops, Varisty Coach, Dojo Rats.*

CONCLUSION

The preceding lists may provide a starting point for a core collection of genre fiction for young adults. As librarians, it's our job to make titles available through selection; accessible through cataloging, shelving, signage, and booklists to identify genre collections; and appealing through eye-catching displays. Then stand back and enjoy the stampede.

NOTES

1. Betty Rosenberg and Diane Tixier Herald, *Genreflecting*, 3d ed. (Englewood, CO: Libraries Unlimited, 1991), xiii.
2. Francesca Lia Block, *Weetzie Bat* (New York: HarperCollins, 1989), 88.

    3. Linda A. Forrest, "Young Adult Fantasy and the Search for Gender-Fair Genres," *Journal of Youth Services* (Fall 1993): 38.
    4. Stephen King, *Danse Macabre* (New York: Berkley Publishing Group, 1983), 199.
    5. Michael Cart, *From Romance to Realism* (New York: HarperCollins, 1996), 64–65.

3

Trends in Young Adult Literature

Michael Cart

What was the first YA novel? Was it, as many claim, Maureen Daly's *Seventeenth Summer* (Dodd, Mead, 1942)? Or was it, as others assert, S.E. Hinton's *The Outsiders* (Viking, 1967)? The question is moot, of course, but not unimportant, since either choice made 1992 a signal year in the history of YA literature, for—if the debut honors go to Daly—it was the genre's golden anniversary. If, on the other hand, Hinton's was the seminal title, 1992 served as YA's silver anniversary. In either case it was an occasion for celebration that came, ironically, at a time when many doomsayers were predicting the imminent demise of a body of literature that, as author Robert Cormier wrote in a recent letter to me, has often been "neglected and misunderstood" and regarded as "a stepchild of children's literature."[1]

Academic critics agree. Caroline Hunt of the College of Charleston—citing Perry Nodelman's contention that "young adult fiction is merely a subgenre of children's literature"—notes that "not a single major theorist in the field deals with young adult literature as something separate from literature for younger children."[2]

Many of these attitudes are rooted, I think, in the relatively recent arrival of the concept of young adulthood as a separate state or stage of human development worthy of its own distinct body of literature. In my own book, *From Romance to Realism*, I point out that most observers date the emergence of the developmental phenomenon "young adult" to the World War II era. Even then and certainly since, it has been an amorphous concept. It wasn't until 1991 that the Board of the Young Adult Library Services Association officially defined young adults as "those individuals from twelve to eighteen years old."[3]

Yet, speaking again in developmental terms, this is a very broad-based definition that, if anything, has exacerbated the confusion over what kind of literature is appropriate for such an emotionally and intellectually diverse group.

Moreover, it suggests one reason for the doomsayers' dire predictions of the genre's demise at the dawn of the 1990s: one of the major trends that have defined this decade-in-progress has been the "youthening" of YA literature. In 1994, a panel of five editors debating the issue at a YALSA Preconference in Miami Beach agreed that, in editorial and marketing terms, YA now stops at age 14—that, in fact, YA literature has become middle-school literature. What is at risk, thus, is not young adult literature per se but a viable body of literature for older young adults of high school age. Many publishers seem to have abandoned those readers—the traditional YA audience—to the adult popular fiction shelf that houses the collected works of Stephen King, Tom Clancy, and John Grisham.

That this trend is continuing is evidenced by a review of the spring 1996 publisher announcement issues of *Publishers Weekly*, *Booklist*, and *School Library Journal*. It also reveals that the very phrase "young adult" is in danger of extinction. Consider that only three publishers—Holt, Farrar, Straus, and Knopf—actually used the term "young adult" in their *Publishers Weekly* ads. As for what age is presumed by the term, when it is used, consider that Farrar specified no age range at all for its two "young adult" titles; Holt listed one title for ages 13 to 18 and four others for either 11 and up or 12 and up, while Knopf listed one title for 12 to 17 and two other "young adult" titles for 8 to 12 and 6 to 12, respectively!

The most common designation applied to what used to be called "young adult" is now "12 and up," though the ads featured a flurry of "10 to 14" and "10 and up" designations, as well.

A significant difference between the ads in *Publishers Weekly*, a magazine aimed at the retail market, and those appearing in the institutionally oriented *Booklist* and *School Library Journal* is the emphasis in the former on original paperback series designated for readers "11- and 12-up," a trend we discuss in a moment.

Meanwhile, in its *School Library Journal* ad one other publisher, Bantam Doubleday Dell, did use "young adult," listing one title for "14-up," but its other five titles in this category were designated "12-up." Only one non-fiction publisher, Facts on File, invited readers to "check out our new young adult titles"; no age ranges were given for any of these, however, presumably because most had been published as adult titles.

To return to the year of dire predictions, 1992, we find a few other ironies: the American teen population increased that year for the first time since 1977 and began a growth spurt that will outpace that of the overall population until it peaks in the year 2010 at 30.8 million young people aged 13 to 19.[4] It was also in 1992 that Stephen Roxburgh, then head of books for youth at Farrar, Straus, told an interviewer that "publishing, in order to work, has to fit into boxes. One has to be clear on whether the publishing strategy for a title is adult or YA. A book's primary support, in terms of advertising and the review media, must be defined."[5]

He might as well have substituted "children" for "adult," since—as Anna Lawrence-Pietroni, another academic critic, cogently points out—"young adult and children's fiction defy easy categorization, and by their nature propose a more liberating view of genre as process rather than as circumspection and definition."[6]

In writing *From Romance to Realism* I quickly came to realize that the whole history of YA literature has been a process, a state of becoming rather than being, an exercise in evolution and that the evolution has, interestingly enough, seemed to proceed in decade-long spurts. This is wonderfully convenient for the literary historian and trend spotter alike. Thus the 1940s saw the emergence of romance literature for teenage girls, Daly being quickly joined in the literary lists by writers like Betty Cavanna, Rosamund DuJardin, Janet Lambert, Anne Emery, and others. The 1950s featured not only romance and proms but also a clutch of car stories (most by Henry Gregor Felsen), career novels, sports stories, adventure stories, and science fiction (Robert A. Heinlein's *Farmer in the Sky* was published in 1950). The 1960s saw the rise of realistic fiction in the work of Nat Hentoff, Frank Bonham, and the big three, S.E. Hinton (*The Outsiders*, 1967), Robert Lipsyte (*The Contender*, 1967), and Paul Zindel (*The Pigman*, 1968).

The realistic novel turned into the problem novel in the 1970s. The 1980s brought a reaction to too much hard-edged realism by spawning a return to the romance novel, though this time it appeared in original paperback series form. The 1990s, as previously noted, saw a youthening of YA and a powerful new trend in the rise of horror fiction, again in the form of paperback series, most of them "written" by R.L. Stine and Christopher Pike.

Any assessment of trends in YA literature must also include notice of socioeconomic and cultural change, since literature does not exist in a vacuum but, instead, reflects the realities of the society in which it is written. Consider that World War II brought teenagers into the workforce and gave them a disposable income and—perhaps most important—cars of their own. Rock and roll music came along in the 1950s and further defined a nation of teenagers (Gale Storm's "Teenage Prayer" was the first top-ten song to employ the word "teenage"). The 1960s brought us rebels without a cause, a distrust of anyone over 30, and an attendant focus on those under that notorious age. The 1970s' contribution was the shopping mall and a new kind of young adult, "the mall rat." The 1980s saw a decline in institutional funding for public and school libraries and a rise in chain bookstores located in the malls, which had become the home away from home for America's increasingly affluent young adults, the newest generation of archconsumers. Publishers, looking for a new market to replace the fading institutional one, turned to the kids themselves, hence the boom in original, affordable paperback series sold at the mall chains. The Sweet Valley empire with its countless spin-offs was spawned in this setting. Horrorland had its roots in the 1980s' work of the adult novelists Stephen King, Dean Koontz and Clive Barker and the slasher movies that began with Sean Cunningham's 1980 film *Friday the 13th* and Wes Craven's 1984 exercise in excess, *Nightmare on Elm Street*.

As the 1990s dawned, the small but ubiquitous chain bookstores began to be replaced by chain superstores, perhaps *the* trend that has most impacted YA literature as America shuffles off to the millennium. Although, as this is written in mid-1996, the superstores control only about 12 to 15 percent of the book market, they are growing at an exponential rate (one chain alone, Borders, opens approximately 40 new superstores annually, each boasting inventories of 100,000 titles or more), and because these chains purchase in such volume, they are in a position to define and redefine publishing. Certainly, the buyers for the superstores have dictated that "young adults" are now the 10–14-year-olds who populate the malls and, since they have observed that the paperback is the format of choice for this age group, the superstores rarely stock a hardcover YA book.

For a heady period in the 1980s, a trend that counterbalanced the appearance of the mall chain stores (which prefigured the superstores) was the appearance of the independent children's specialty bookstore, often started and staffed by librarians who had been "downsized" out of their professional jobs by library personnel cutbacks. These stores were never an ideal alternative to the public or school library as a source of YA titles, since they specialized in children's books as the children's room in a public library does. One constant of adolescence, one phenomenon that defies trends, is that teenagers would sooner die than be associated with anything that smacks of "children." Nevertheless, as the specialty stores became established, some of their young customers began growing up with the bookstore habit, and if the stores were careful to establish a separate area for YA fiction, these kid consumers would graduate to this area as they entered their teen years. Unfortunately, many of these stores are now being driven out of business by the superstores that are moving into their neighborhoods and, accordingly, another market—no matter how meager—for hardcover YA books is drying up.

Another trend that parallels the rise of the superstore is the conglomeration of publishing, the most recent example being the acquisition of the venerable Macmillan group of imprints by Simon & Schuster, which had already been acquired by the entertainment giant Viacom, which also owns Paramount Studios. At about the same time Farrar, Straus, one of the last independents, was acquired by the German conglomerate the Holtzbrinck Group, which had already acquired Holt and St. Martin's. A few years earlier Bantam Doubleday Dell had been purchased by another German communications empire, Bertelsmann; the venerable Harper & Row was acquired by Rupert Murdoch's News Corporation and merged with the British publisher Collins; and Viking, Dial, Cobblestone, and Dutton became part of the British-based Penguin organization. William Morrow and its imprints are owned by Hearst; Random House, Knopf, and Crown, by Advance Publications (which also owns the *New Yorker*, *Vanity Fair*, and the Condé Nast chain of magazines); Time Warner owns Little, Brown and Warner Books; Disney owns Hyperion; MCA owns Putnam/Philomel/Grosset; and so forth. Until Stephen Roxburgh left Farrar, Straus to form his own independent company, Front Street, Holiday House was left as the only independent publisher of books for young readers in America.

Andre Schiffrin, who calls this trend "the corporatization of publishing," points out its dangers: "Since the twenties," he writes, "the average profit for all publishing houses has been around four percent after taxes." However, the new owners—who have, typically, no background in publishing—are demanding that "the profitability of the book publishing arm should be similar to other subsidiaries like newspapers, cable television, and film. New profit targets have therefore been established in the range of twelve to fifteen percent."[7]

This has led to the rise of the so-called superstar syndrome in publishing; it started with the Grishams, Clancys, and Kings on the adult side of the publishing house, but it has recently begun infecting the books for the youth side, as well. It means the elimination of the traditional midlist titles, the serious, risk-taking books that command modest sales but justify calling YA and children's books "literature." It means that new, unproven talent is finding it almost impossible to break into publishing; it means that publishing has become synonymous with marketing and that editorial decisions are now made by committee, and, for the first time, representatives from the sales and marketing divisions of the publishing houses are influential members of these committees. It means, too, that unless a novel can be expected to command serious sales as a paperback reprint, it will not be published.

Even if there were no superstores or publishing conglomerates, there is no doubt that the paperback remains indisputably the format of choice for young adults, in part because of its portability and affordability but also in part because hardcovers are too reminiscent of textbooks and their aura of required reading. In a 1991 survey conducted by Cahners Research, 82.4 percent of public librarians and 50.6 percent of school librarians asserted that teenagers prefer paperbacks.

It would thus seem that one way to expand the body of literature beyond the prevailing "McPaperback" romance and horror series would be the publication of original paperback novels for the whole age range of YA readers, including the now neglected older teens. Unfortunately, publishers have resisted this for a number of reasons: the professional media are reluctant to review original paperbacks; libraries are reluctant to stock them because of their physical impermanence; and serious writers are reluctant to write them because of the smaller advances publishers pay for them and also because there remains a certain cachet to being published in hardcover. Given all this, a new trend that is emerging is the simultaneous publication of original YA fiction in rack-sized hardcover and paperback formats. Harcourt Brace pioneered this strategy in the early 1990s. More recently, HarperCollins has begun publishing small library editions of new fiction to capture reviews while simultaneously publishing mass market-size runs of the same titles in paperback; a recent example of this is Chris Lynch's *Blue-Eyed Son* trilogy.

The rising popularity of the paperback was further reflected by YALSA's establishment in 1995 of a new Popular Reading Committee to complement the work of its long-established Best Books for Young Adults Committee. This new committee's charge is to annually prepare one to five annotated list(s) of approximately 25 recommended paperback titles, selected from popular reading/ genre themes or topics. Its purpose is to establish a body of literature that can be read for pleasure as an alternative to the romance and horror series that have taken over the superstore shelves. In a partial effort to reclaim the now-overlooked older end of the YA demographic range, the guidelines clearly state that titles will be targeted at young adults as old as 18.

In the meantime, the new publishing house Front Street (mentioned earlier) represents another trend that is cautiously emerging as a counterbalance to the corporate giants that have taken over publishing: the emergence of the small trade house. According to the *New York Times*, the number of new small publishers has increased by 200 percent in the last decade, to a record 5,514 in 1995.[8]

Among these are a number of new niche publishers that are specializing in multicultural literature: Arte Publico of Houston, Children's Book Press in San Francisco, Lee & Low in New York, and Clear Light in Santa Fe, New Mexico. Many of these houses began appearing in response to another major trend of the 1980s: the arrival of new waves of immigration not from the traditional Northern European sources but from Latin America, Asia, and the Middle East. Recognizing that by 1991, some 2.3 million public school students spoke little or no English, a number of publishers began issuing bilingual editions of new and standard titles. Holt, for example, published *Cool Salsa*, a collection of bilingual poems for young adults on growing up Latin in the United States. The title was a volume in Holt's Edge series, which features both original work about the immigrant experience written in the United States and work imported from abroad (in translation, where necessary). The series' editor is Marc Aronson, one of the editors who participated in the Miami Beach panel who has written widely about current trends in YA literature (see, for example, his *School Library Journal* articles " 'The YA Novel Is Dead,' and Other Fairly Stupid Tales" and "The Betrayal of Teenagers," January 1995 and May 1996, respectively).

The title of the former article invites discussion of another trend of the 1990s, the publication of the crossover book. This trend started about 1989 with the publication of *The True Story of the Three Little Pigs* by that antic duo Jon Scieszka and Lane Smith. Their first collaboration was a picture book that, because of its wildly expressionist illustrations and ironic, fractured fairy tale text, developed a cult following among adults, particularly those of college age. Its publisher, Viking, became aware of this phenomenon when the two collaborated on another book, *The Stinky Cheese Man*, a title that was named not only a Caldecott Honor Book but also a Best Book for Young Adults.[9]

In addition to Scieszka and Smith, other "edgy" new talents that fit in this crossover category are Maira Kalman, Richard McGuire, William Wegman, Henrik Drescher, J. Otto Seibold, Istvan Banyai, Michael Bartalos, and William Joyce.

Closely related to this trend is the emergence of the graphic novel for young adults, which grew out of the action comic book phenomenon that started in the 1930s but also has roots in the true graphic novels for adults of Rockwell Kent that began appearing in that same decade. The quintessential current practitioner of this "new" art form is Art Spiegelman (*Maus*), but others, inspired by his success, include Howard Cruse (*Stuck Rubber Baby*) and Scott McCloud, whose *Understanding* comics is the definitive introduction to the whole new world of the visual novel. It's worth noting that YA novelist Avi, an inveterate experimenter, has also tried his hand at writing the text of a visual novel, *City of Light, City of Dark*, with art by Brian Floca.

It's much easier for the picture book to make the crossover leap than it is for the novel, but there is some evidence that this effort is also being made. The collaboration of adult novelist Mark Helprin and Caldecott Medalist Chris Van Allsburg on a new edition of *Swan Lake*, for example, was named a Best Book for Young Adults in 1990. The same duo has recently collaborated again, this time on an original illustrated novel, *A City in Winter*. Meanwhile, Knopf has given marketing treatment normally reserved for adult blockbusters to its fantasy title for all ages, *The Golden Compass* by the British YA novelist Philip Pullman. The book had a 100,000-copy first printing, Scholastic Productions bought its film rights and it was named an alternate of several divisions of the Book of the Month Club.[10] Despite the fact that it is listed in Knopf's catalog as being for ages "10 up," it was selected as a 1997 Best Book for Young Adults.

One reliable bellwether in assessing trends in YA literature has, in fact, been YALSA's annual Best Books for Young Adults list (for an excellent history of the lists see Betty Carter's *Best Books for Young Adults*).

Looking at three decades of these lists proves the validity of Lawrence-Pietroni's observation that YA literature is a process. The lists clearly demonstrate that the borders of the land of YA have always been ill defined and subject to negotiation, and many titles that have found their way onto the list have slipped across from the land of children's literature as well as from the world of books published for adults; in fact, three of the five titles to appear on all four of YALSA's periodic "best of the best" lists were published for adults: *The Bell Jar* by Sylvia Plath, *I Know Why the Caged Bird Sings* by Maya Angelou, and *Bless the Beasts and Children* by Glendon Swarthout. An examination of the 1996 list shows that 4 (of 47) fiction titles and 10 (of 34) nonfiction titles were published as adult books; in other words, 14 of 81 titles (or only 17 percent) were adult books. This is revealing, since only several years ago the lists were being criticized for having too many adult titles. On the other hand, 11 of the 81 were also listed on ALA's Notable Books for Children list, and five others were published as children's books.

Though one could not call it a trend, there is emerging support for creating two Best Books lists: one, focusing on books for the "12-up" group, would in reality be a Best Books for Middle School readers list; the second would target adult titles and books published for older young adults—if a market could be created for them. One way might be to create yet a third list, as Marc Aronson has suggested, of Best Young Adult Books for Adults.

This is not inconsistent with a proposal made by George Nicholson in the early 1990s, when he was vice president and publisher of Dell/Delacorte/Doubleday Books for Young Readers, to create a new kind of YA fiction with protagonists between the ages of 18 and 23.

All of this invites the question, "How Adult Is Young Adult?" which was the title of a program I moderated at ALA's annual conference in New York in July 1996. Appearing were Nicholson, now a literary agent; editor Marc Aronson; author Francesca Lia Block, whose YA novels have great appeal to readers in their 20s; and Carla Jenkins, then senior buyer for the Barnes and Noble chain of superbookstores.

The program's purpose was to explore the possibility of creating a viable body of literature for readers 16 to 24 years of age. This would refocus attention on the now-neglected older teens while expanding the definition of "young adult" to include 18- to 24-year-olds, members of the famous (or notorious, depending on your point of view) "Generation X." Such a literature, I proposed in my opening remarks, might be called "Gen-Y," a cross between Gen-X and YA.

This would require cooperation between the adult and young readers divisions of publishing houses, but that is not unprecedented. David Macaulay's 1988 book *The Way Things Work* was listed in both its publisher Houghton Mifflin's adult and children's catalogs, while the company's children's and adult publicity departments joined forces to bring this title to the attention of both markets. The result was Houghton Mifflin's fastest-selling title of the year; according to the December 26, 1988, issue of *Newsweek*, 100,000 copies were sold in six weeks (p. 67). A more recent example is Philip Pullman's *The Golden Compass*, discussed earlier.

What Andre Schiffrin, formerly head of Pantheon, had to say about his goal in founding, in 1990, the not-for-profit publishing house the New Press is relevant here: "We would need to show that audiences deemed unreachable by many publishers will respond to materials and formats designed to reach them. The search for new audiences is, of course, as essential to the future of the bookstores as it is to that of publishers" (and, I would add, libraries).

"We hope," Schiffrin continued, "to be increasingly successful at finding ways to reach those readers with meaningful, affordable books."[11]

Traditional ways may not work. Jennifer Joseph, publisher and editor of Manic D Press, notes that "unfortunately most members of the new generation feel more comfortable in record stores than in bookstores."[12]

Recognizing the validity of this observation, both Tower Records and Virgin have recently introduced book sections in their music stores. As for traditional bookstores, Joseph suggests establishing a new kind of section to be called "alternative culture" and stocking it with proven crossover titles by such cutting-edge talents as Douglas Coupland, Banana Yoshimoto, Mark Leyner, William Vollman, Kathy Acker, Sapphire, Art Spiegelman, and Francesca Lia Block. Also included would be graphic novels and "zines."

Joseph seems to echo Schiffrin when she says, that "maybe books that are actually relevant to the next generation need to be commonly available, promoted, and supported actively by the book trade industry."[13]

I made the same point at greater length in *From Romance to Realism*. For if, as Theresa Nelson, author of *Earthshine*, once told me "we read to know we are not alone," we as librarians, authors, editors, and publishers need to ensure that all members of the new generation are included in literature that deals realistically with the conditions of their difficult daily lives—lives that Russell Banks, in his extraordinary novel *Rule of the Bone*, memorably describes as being like "running through hell with a gasoline suit on."

A literature that stops at 14 cannot begin to deal with the hellish reality of the lives of gay and lesbian, homeless, sexually abused, impoverished, drug-addicted, and AIDS-infected young adults.

Some progress has been made in publishing mature non-fiction about such at-risk teens, but too many novels still seem to reflect the Ozzie and Harriet world of 1950s fiction. Non-fiction provides information for the mind, to be sure (and is deemed "safer" by publishers and, too often, by front-line librarians who must deal with the omnipresent censors), but fiction provides wisdom for the heart. It is a sad fact that since 1969 only about 70 novels dealing with homosexuality have been published to give faces to more than 2 million gay and lesbian teens. As for AIDS, since the plague first appeared like a demon out of the darkness in 1981, there have been no more than fifteen novels for YAs dealing with the issue.

Yet some progress continues to be made: the silence surrounding the issue of incest was shattered in 1992, when Ruth White's *Weeping Willow* was published; Cynthia Grant's *Uncle Vampire* appeared the following year; and in 1994 three novels dealing with this previously taboo issue were published: *The Hanged Man* by Francesca Lia Block, *When She Hollers* by Cynthia Voigt, and *I Hadn't Meant to Tell You This* by Jacqueline Woodson.

Who will publish books like these for the "Gen-Y" readers? I'm not sure that the publishing conglomerates with their new focus on author as celebrity and every-book-a-blockbuster syndromes are the best bet. But maybe the new literary imprints at a few of them—Metropolitan Books at Holt and Broadway Books at Bantam—might be. Or how about the new small presses like Front

Street, which are willing to take risks? As its publisher Stephen Roxburgh wrote me in a recent letter, "[U]nlike the adult book world, in our business controversy does not sell books; it often guarantees that they will not sell, and, more importantly, not reach the children they were intended to reach."[14] Nevertheless, in 1997 Front Street published Brock Cole's novel *The Facts Speak for Themselves*, an unsparing look at the causes and consequences of sexual activity during adolescence. Other small, risk-taking, cutting-edge presses include Riverhead, Milkweed, Counterpoint, Dalkey Archive, Delphinium, Serpent's Tail, 4 Walls, 8 Windows, Seven Stories, and others. It should also be mentioned that Andre Schiffrin's New Press, a not-for-profit, published *Growing up Gay/Growing up Lesbian* in 1994, arguably the first literary anthology geared specifically to homosexual youth.

How to market titles like these is a problem, though publishers are beginning to use the Internet as a means of communicating directly to potential teenage readers. Additionally, Joseph suggests advertising on MTV and in magazines such as *Spin*, since they are "the influential factors on this generation and are unequivocally national phenomena, reaching every nook and cranny in America."[15]

One example doesn't constitute a trend, but Penguin USA did advertise *The Stinky Cheese Man* on MTV, making it the first—but perhaps not the last—book for young readers ever to be advertised on national television.

If a viable new literature is to emerge for older readers, it will also require the joint support of the various professional organizations involved with young adults and their literature—not only the American Library Association's three youth-serving divisions (the Association for Library Sciences to Children [ALSC], YALSA, and the American Association of School Librarians [AASL]) but also such organizations as the Children's Book Council, the American Booksellers Association, the Association of Booksellers for Children, the Children's Literature Association, the Special Interest Group on Adolescent Literature of the International Reading Association, the Assembly on Adolescent Literature of the National Council of Teachers of English, and others. There has been too little cooperation among these organizations in the past; that must change. Not only literature but lives are at stake.

NOTES

1. Robert Cormier, letter to the author, April 13, 1996.

2. Caroline Hunt, "Young Adult Literature Evades the Theorists," *Children's Literature Association Quarterly* (Spring 1996): 5.

3. Betty Carter, *Best Books for Young Adults* (Chicago: American Library Association, 1994), 13.

4. Tom Kuntz, "Word for Word," *New York Times* (April 24, 1994), sec. E7.

5. Sally Lodge, "The Making of a Crossover," *Publishers Weekly* (November 23, 1992): 38.

6. Anna Lawrence-Pietroni, *"The Tricksters, The Changeover,* and the Fluidity of Adolescent Literature," *Children's Literature Association Quarterly* (Spring 1996): 34.

7. Andre Schiffrin, "The Corporatization of Publishing," *Nation* (June 3, 1996): 30.

8. Doreen Carvajal, "Do-It Yourselfers Carve Out a Piece of the Publishing Pie," *New York Times* (April 28, 1996), 1.

9. Michael Cart, "The Stinky Cheese Man Goes to College," *Booklist* (December 1995): 695.

10. Kit Alderdice, "How Random Created a YA Crossover," *Publishers Weekly* (April 1, 1996): 24.

11. Andre Schiffrin, "Between Us," *American Bookseller* (April 1995): 18.

12. Jennifer Joseph, "Bridging the Generation Gap," *American Bookseller* (July 1994): 59.

13. Ibid., 61.

14. Stephen Roxburgh, letter to the author, May 3, 1996.

15. Joseph, "Bridging the Generation Gap," 61.

4

Publishing for Young Adults

Audrey Eaglen

A HISTORICAL OVERVIEW

For most of this country's history, publishers have produced books for young readers, both children and young adults, but the nature of such books has changed drastically over the last two centuries. Before 1800, young people (who were considered nothing more or less than small adults) were expected to read only those books that would keep them on the straight and narrow path throughout their lives and thus guarantee their ultimate salvation. This meant, of course, that the books available to them were primarily Bibles, some religious novels (most intended for adults), and pietistic tracts that were produced by a plethora of religious groups of all persuasions. Always, the emphasis was on living on earth as a preparation for the real life that lay ahead once one's earthly journey was over.

The first half of the nineteenth century saw the beginning of a change both in attitudes toward young adults and in reading materials for them. A young United States was changing from a rigidly religious society to a more open-minded one; religion was still a powerful factor, but the societal changes fueled by such powerful movements as abolitionism and woman suffrage raised the social consciousness of Americans. At the same time, the Protestant work ethic became a powerful impetus to members of the growing society. It was believed that God's plan on earth could be advanced by working hard and achieving material success. No writer of the time spoke more strongly and convincingly in his books of the virtue of hard work and its ultimate rewards than Horatio Alger, and few writers have had such a profound influence on a generation of young readers as he did. By midcentury, as Alleen Nilsen and Ken Donelson write in their pioneering study of YA literature,

> More literature was written for young adults than ever before. An increasingly secularized society produced writers aware that love, adventure, work, and recreation existed in the real world of young people, and that these could provide useful themes in books. A new kind of novel began to appear aimed somewhat less at moralizing and instructing and more at interesting the young adult. If moral lessons were still there, they were less direct, less immediate, less heavenly. Getting ahead in life, possibly even enjoying some aspects of life became a central theme.[1]

Around the time of the Civil War, however, two new kinds of reading matter appeared that also had a strong impact on YA readers, material that proved incredibly successful even as it was roundly denounced by clerics and critics. Domestic novels were written by and for women, young and old, and were characterized by weepy melodrama, gothic thrills, and uniformly submissive (to men) female protagonists whose goals in life were happy marriage to a fine man (who most likely had not been fine at all until he was influenced by the novel's long-suffering heroine), a happy nuclear family, and, as in the past, the ultimate goal of exchanging one's earthly home for a home in Paradise. No matter how trite, how banal, and how stereotypic the domestic novel's plots and characters were, the books were a howling success with female readers of the era.

For boys there were dime novels. They were full of action and suspense, melodramatic, and written in the purplest of prose, with stock characters performing heroic acts of derring-do in vanquishing larger-than-life villains of the nastiest persuasions. Most took place in the Old West (or at least some hack writer's version of it), but a few, the dime detective and sports novels, were set in any place the authors wanted to put them. They were incredibly popular; just one publisher, Beadle and Adams, sold 4 million dime novels in 1865 alone—and the population was significantly smaller than it is now. But the novels were also roundly criticized for ruining young men's morals and setting them on the path toward mental illness and crime, as in the case of one young boy, "aged fourteen, who shot himself during a period of mental aberration caused by reading dime novels."[2] In spite of denunciations like this, the dime novels, while not of great (if any) literary significance, remained on the scene until about 1900, but they did break ground for young adult male readers in providing excitement and thrills through larger-than-life characters doing thrilling deeds in exotic and threatening settings. They also set precedents for being cheap and ubiquitous and introduced readers to series books—which have remained enormously popular with YAs ever since.

The demise of dime and domestic novels was not too traumatic for YA readers, however, because a man named Edward Stratemeyer and his legion of writers-for-hire (including his daughter, Harriet Adams) were waiting in the wings. Stratemeyer's Literary Syndicate employed hundreds of writers, each of whom was sent one or more plotlines sketched out by Stratemeyer or his daughter, which the writer would flesh out into a novel and return to the publisher for approval; if granted, the writer was paid a flat fee. Fast writers could earn a good living working for the syndicate, though the quality of the writing Stratemeyer published left a great deal to be desired. Nevertheless, such series as Tom Swift, the Hardy Boys, Nancy Drew, the Dana Girls, and others were wildly successful, selling millions of copies and creating a generation of fans who helped make the Literary Syndicate's owner a millionaire. But at the same time, the books were highly controversial among teachers and librarians. Those who decried the books, however, were as spectacularly unsuccessful in turning youthful readers away from Stratemeyer's books as they had been in protecting them from dime novels—and as they would be for the next half century in keeping YAs from reading pulp magazines, comic books, and, in our time, series paperback romances, horror, and "choose your own adventures."

CONTEMPORARY YA PUBLISHING

By the time most of Edward Stratemeyer's and others' series books had met their demise in the early 1940s, done in by both wartime paper shortages and increasing YA reader sophistication, a major change in the trade book publishing area had taken place. Trade publishing houses publish books for the general reader, as opposed to those that publish for specialized interests. Trade houses produce both fiction and non-fiction, hardcovers, and often paperbacks intended to be sold through bookstores and other outlets and to libraries. Before 1930 most trade houses published almost completely for the adult reader, but a few pioneering houses had the vision to realize that children needed books of their own and hired editors to set up children's book publishing operations under the houses' aegis. These editors were usually strong women who were dedicated to children and their literature and who quickly made children's book publishing not only a profitable venture for the parent houses but also a respected one. Most of the juvenile divisions flourished enough so that by 1941 juvenile literature was considered a big business within the trade publishing industry, having published some 15,000 titles over the previous two decades, including picture books, storybooks, and non-fiction intended for nonadult readers ranging in age from toddlers to teens.

The books for teenage readers turned out by these houses were a vast improvement over domestic and dime novels and the mass-produced series books turned out by Stratemeyer's and other syndicates, but they were still pretty innocuous. As Nilsen and Donelson put it so aptly:

Much young adult literature of the 1940s and 1950s celebrated those wonderful high school years. Books seemed at times to concentrate on concerns with dating, parties, class rings, working on the school newspaper, preparing for the school prom, senior year, the popular crowd (or how to avoid it), and teen romance devoid of realities like sex. That accounted for titles such as *Boy Trouble, Girl Trouble, Practically Fifteen, Going on Sixteen, Almost Seventeen, A Touchdown for Harold, A Horse for Sheila*. Books often sounded alike, looked alike, and read alike, but they were unquestionably popular.[3]

Controversy was nearly nonexistent in these early YA works. Unwritten but powerful taboos existed against even mentioning such things as sex, death, drugs, divorce, abuse, rape, and a host of other sticky topics. Profanity and obscenity were prohibited. As Nilsen and Donelson summarized, "YA books were generally innocuous and pervaded by a saccharine didacticism. They taught good, adult-determined attitudes [which] good boys and girls must accept . . . as good and just without question."[4] A few writers were able to approach forbidden territory in novels, however, even if only obliquely. John Tunis wrote sports stories, but their deeper themes were often such topics as racism and the nature of totalitarianism. Maureen Daly's *Seventeenth Summer* seems hopelessly romantic and innocent today, but its (muted) handling of such taboos as smoking, drinking, and even homosexuality was groundbreaking in 1942 and caused the book to be banned. Henry Felson's stories about teenagers and cars also dealt with death and grieving. These authors and a few more like them showed uncommon courage for their era and laid the groundwork for writers to come.

In 1967 a novel appeared that ushered in the birth of an entirely new realism in YA literature. S.E. Hinton's *The Outsiders* was a story about high school but a far cry from the high school books of the 1940s and 1950s. Hinton wrote not about proms and touchdowns and teachers but about the dark underbelly of high school life through the vicious clashes between two rival gangs, the Socs and the Greasers, in a Kansas school—and she pulled no punches. The book was an instant hit with YAs and has remained so ever since. It is still in print and still being read by new generations of kids who see the class struggle of the gang rivalry and its tragic effects as perfectly relevant to their lives today, 30 years after the book's publication date.

Hinton's having broken the ice, she was followed by a series of neorealist writers who followed her lead in ignoring long-standing taboos so that they could create works of power and honesty that spoke to the hopes, dreams, and concerns of contemporary young people in ways that earlier books for YAs simply had not. Judy Blume, Robert Cormier, Paul Zindel, M.E. Kerr, Norma Klein, Lois Duncan, Richard Peck, Cynthia Voigt, Alice Childress, Aidan Chambers, Norma Fox Mazer, Walter Dean Meyers, Chris Crutcher, Nancy Garden, Todd Strasser, Francesca Lia Block, Bruce Brooks, and dozens of other fine writers wrote fiction about real young people with real problems in real-life situations, without being Pollyannaish or didactic. It was a revolution in this body of literature that continues today and continues to draw new, excellent writers to the field, for which all YAs can be grateful.

YA readers do not live by fiction alone, however, so at the same time that

YA fiction was becoming a true body of literature on its own, non-fiction that would satisfy the informational needs of these readers was also growing and reaching new levels of honesty and maturity. How great a change this was can be seen in a brief excerpt from a book by Eleanor A. Hunter, published by the American Tract Society in 1890, entitled *Talks to Boys*. One of the "talks," dealing with "Out-of-Door Behavior," is about as close to a discussion of sex as the book comes:

The other evening Rob was lying on the sofa in the library and telling me about what he called a "little adventure" which he had had a day or two before. He had met a young girl on the ferry-boat whom he had never seen before, and, as he expressed it, "had had some fun with her."

"Why, Rob," said I, "you don't mean to say that you have been flirting, and with a young lady who was a total stranger to you beside!"

"Well," he answered, laughing a little, "she wasn't exactly a *young lady*, you know. But that is just what I did."

"I am sorry to hear it," said I.

"Where is the harm?" he answered. "She liked it. I would not have done it if she hadn't."

"That is just it," I responded, "and if you had not done it, certainly she could have not, for it always takes two to make a flirtation as well as a bargain."

"Seems to me," said Rob, sitting up and looking at me, "seems to me you are taking a little bit of nonsense very seriously."

"Yes," I answered, "I am serious, but it is because I do not think it is nonsense. See here, Rob, how would you like to have some one flirt with your sisters?"

"I'd like to see any fellow try it!" was the instant response. "I'd punch his head for him. But then no fellow ever would, you know, for my sisters are ladies."[5]

In contrast to *Talks to Boys*, the titles alone of a few books dealing with sexuality that were published over the last two decades give an indication as to how far YA non-fiction has come over that period. There are *Sex and Birth Control: A Guide for the Young*; *It Won't Happen to Me: Teenagers Talk about Pregnancy*; *The Facts of Love: Living, Loving, and Growing Up*; *Teens Parenting*; and *A Way of Love, A Way of Life: What It Means to Be Gay*, just for starters. In all these books, solid information that young people need to have in order to understand not only sex and sexuality but basic human relationships is presented in a nonjudgmental and nonthreatening manner, ignoring the taboos of the past as if they had never existed.

Informational books in other areas followed suit in presenting topics of concern to young adults. Health, careers, education, drugs, peer pressures, current issues, values, family life, abusive relationships, death and disease, money management, abortion, euthanasia, racism, sexism, ecology, God and religion, war, ethnic diversity and multiculturalism, sexually transmitted diseases (STDs), politics, gangs, computers, and cyberspace—just as there are no limits to the informational needs of young adults, neither is there a shortage of publishers who produce the materials to meet those needs (an overview of whom follows).

In addition to fiction and books to meet their informational needs, teenagers, like their adult counterparts, enjoy recreational reading in other areas and, more recently, in nonbook formats. Broadly speaking, these areas include biography and autobiography; poetry; drama; humor; sports; music; games and puzzles; hobbies; trivia; how-to-do-it; popular reference; for example, almanacs, Guinness record books; cartoons and cartoon series books; jokes; fantasy and role playing (Dungeons & Dragons, Mortal Kombat, Sega Genesis); MAD books; satire and parody; and much, much more. Again, there is no dearth of publishers willing to meet YA needs for recreational reading in these areas.

Some attention must be paid also to books in nontraditional formats, some of which are the product of today's new technologies. These include books on audiocassettes and compact discs, as well as on CD-ROM. Many of the audio books that young adults enjoy were intended for an adult audience but appeal to younger readers also; for example, books by Stephen King and Dean Koontz. Two companies, however, make a special effort to supply books for young adults on tape. They are Caedmon, which often has the books' own authors reading on the tapes, and Recorded Books, whose YA classics on tape are always unabridged. Books on CD-ROM are also available for YAs, some interactive and some not; outstanding among these are those published by Dorling Kindersley, with stunning graphics and sound. Then there are novels in cartoon form, perhaps the most prominent of which are Art Spiegelman's Holocaust tales, *Maus* and *Maus 2*. Although they have never caught on in the United States as they have in Europe and Latin America, fotonovelas, which are just what their name implies, novels in photo form, have a small but dedicated audience here. Finally, YA readers with visual problems can find certain YA books in both large print and braille formats.

TRADE PUBLISHING FOR YOUNG ADULTS

As was mentioned earlier, trade publishers publish books for the general reader as opposed to the scholarly, technical, or professional market. Most trade publishing is done for the adult audience, but many trade houses have young readers' divisions that produce books for children and young adults. Still other trade houses produce children's and YA books exclusively. Examples of the former are Farrar, Straus, & Giroux; HarperCollins; Harcourt; William Morrow; Harcourt Brace; and Random House. Examples of the latter are Scholastic, Holiday House, and Candlewick Press. Most hardcover YA fiction comes from these two kinds of trade publishers, but most of them publish good general non-fiction, too. If one examines the annual lists of Best Books for Young Adults produced by YALSA, it's easy to see that most of the books on the lists come from these trade houses; the best of these houses have a real commitment to publishing quality books for young readers, and this is brought out by the number of awards and honors they garner on a regular basis.

Many children's/YA sections of trade houses also produce an enormous number of paperbacks, some reprints of hardcover editions, and some original editions. Anyone who works with YAs is aware of the ubiquitous mass-market paperback series books, which readers seem unable to get enough of: Archway's *Fear Street*, Bantam's many *Sweet Valley* series and *Choose Your Own Adventure*—all sell in the hundreds of thousands of copies on a regular, often monthly basis. But trade houses also publish, to a lesser degree, paperback editions of hardcover YA books; many of the latter would go out of print within a year or so of publication date were it not for this. A good example of this occurred in 1982, when Farrar, Straus, & Giroux published a groundbreaking hardcover novel about two young women who fall in love with each other, Nancy Garden's *Annie on My Mind*. Although most reviewers and librarians praised it highly, its controversial subject matter kept many school and public librarians from buying it, so the publisher did not sell enough copies to pay the cost of keeping it in print as a hardcover—and it is a well-known fact that YAs rarely buy hardcover books, especially fiction. Several of the big paperback houses, Dell and Bantam among them, were offered paperback rights but refused them, presumably because of the book's subject matter. Finally, pressured by YALSA and hundreds of YA librarians, Farrar decided to do something the house had never done before. It published a mass-market paperback edition of *Annie . . .* , which is still in print and selling steadily a decade and a half later. In this case and probably others it is safe to say that without the commitment and courage of some YA and children's book editors at the major trade publishing houses such as Farrar, YA literature, especially fiction, would not exist as we know it today. Those people, who defied the taboos and pressures of those who would keep good books from their intended audience, deserve much of the credit for the respect accorded to YA literature today.

Not all trade publishers have juvenile or YA departments, but this is not to say that the books they publish for adults will not be read by young adults. Stephen King's first book, *Carrie*, did not do well as an adult hardcover at all. But when it was made into a movie, and the paperback version appeared as a movie tie-in, it became an instant YA hit and really launched King's prolific and profitable career. Andrews and McMeel is a trade house that publishes collections of comic strips such as ''The Far Side'' and ''Calvin and Hobbes,'' which are probably read (and reread) by more young adult than adult readers, and the same undoubtedly holds true for Ballantine's seemingly endless collections featuring Garfield the cat. Certainly, most science fiction and fantasy is published for adults, but its readership is predominantly young adult. Young adults read mysteries published for adults, as well as biography/autobiography, as well as general fiction, and non-fiction. Once again a look at YALSA's annual Best Books for Young Adults lists reveals that a good percentage of the titles appearing on them were intended for adult readers but are of significant interest and value to young adult readers as well.

NON-TRADE YA PUBLISHING

In addition to trade publishers, many independent nontrade publishers produce materials of interest to young adult readers. Some of these independents have as their primary target the YA audience, while others intend their materials primarily for adults and/or children. The common factor in both, however, is that the books they publish are important sources for meeting the informational needs of YAs. A detailed look at all these publishers in the space of a chapter is nearly impossible, but a broad overview of some of the more important houses follows.

One of the foremost publishers of YA informational books is the Rosen Publishing Group, which publishes a number of series books for YAs, among them titles in *The Coping Series*; *The Values Library*; *The Self-Esteem Library*; and a host of other series that cover such topics as careers, health, education, jobs, social problems, and contemporary issues. All Rosen books are frank, well written, accurate, balanced, and appropriately illustrated. Enslow Publishers is another producer of excellent series such as *The Drug Library* and series on women's issues, social issues, historical issues, and much more, all of which compare favorably with Rosen Publications.

Other publishers that aim all or most of their series and individual titles at YAs are Abdo and Daughter (*The Kids in Crisis Series* and others); Crestwood House; Lerner Publications (general non-fiction, biography, history); Oliver Press (general non-fiction and several series, e.g., *The Great Decisions Series*); Franklin Watts (general non-fiction, many series on just about every conceivable subject—all excellent); Greenhaven Press (issues series that present all sides of controversial issues, e.g., *The Opposing Viewpoints Series*); Marshall Cavendish (many series, e.g., *African Kingdoms of the Past*, excellent biography series); Free Spirit (self-help, self-understanding titles); Career Press (jobs, careers, and career preparation); Morning Glory Press (self-help, inspirational); and, finally, Arco, Contemporary Books, Peterson's Guides, the College Board, and Barrons, all of which produce excellent materials to help students and others of any age in passing entrance tests for college, obtaining scholarships, choosing colleges, passing civil services and vocational tests, and so on.

More publishers of excellent informational titles for young adults are Chelsea House, which produces many fine series for all ages (drugs series, biography series, health series, sports figures series, current issues series, literary series, including *The Young Adult Authors Series*); Facts on File (graphics/text non-fiction, many series, general reference non-fiction); Gale Research (excellent biography series, especially literary biography; general reference non-fiction; directories of black Americans, Hispanics, women, etc.); NTC Publishers (*Career Portrait Series*, skills series, *Business Portraits Series*, and a host of others);

Compcare (health reference titles); and Dorling Kindersley, whose magnificently illustrated reference titles and series on nearly every subject imaginable, from animals to sex, have set a new publishing industry standard for illustrated reference and general information books.

Dozens of other publishers produce materials of importance to YAs with more specialized interests. Some of these are TSR Inc., of Dungeons and Dragons fame; Sandwich Islands Publishing, with two extremely popular game book series, Mortal Kombat and Sega Genesis; Bethany House, which publishes Christian paperback series fiction for YA readers, meeting a need only recently recognized; and any number of computer book publishers, among them Microsoft Press, IDG (the wildly popular *Dummies* series), and many others.

This is only a representative sampling of specialized/independent publishing, but new publishers come along frequently to meet new YA informational needs, so no listing can be really comprehensive. The YA librarian or media specialist must look at the journals, both mainstream and not so, that review and advertise books and other materials for YAs on a regular basis to keep up with what's new, what's good, and where to get it all if they are to meet the enormous information needs of their YA patrons.

YA MAGAZINES

Many people, both adults and young adults, rarely if ever read a book but devour all kinds of magazines eagerly. Just as in book publishing, the magazine industry aims its products primarily at the adult market, but just as many adult books are read by young adults, so are adult magazines. Young adults are interested in current events, hobbies, sports, music, and so on, and if adult magazines cover these topics, they will be read by YAs. Some adult magazines that are of particular interest to these readers are *Bicycling, Inside Sports, Runner's World, Ski, Sport,* and *Sports Illustrated* for sports buffs; *Billboard, Musician, Rolling Stone,* and *Spin* for musicians and music aficionados; and *Hot Rod* and *Car and Driver* for auto lovers. Other titles that are read by many YAs are *Games* (games and puzzles of every kind); *Starlog: The Science Fiction Universe; Wired* (which may be the ultimate cyberspace journal); *Time* and *Newsweek*; several dozen computer magazines; and *Dance.*

A number of magazines are published specifically for the YA market, and they should be an integral part of any YA collection worth the name. Some are aimed at girls; these include *Teen* and *Seventeen*, both of which are for midteen readers and deal with their interests (e.g., clothes, health, careers, celebrities, popularity, school, parents, etc.), whereas *YM: Young & Modern* covers similar information for slightly older readers. Then there's *Teen Beat*, ostensibly for both male and female readers, but the teen heartthrobs that fill its pages are predominantly boys. For male teenagers there are *BMX Plus* (off-road and dirt biking), *Thrasher* (skateboarding), and *WWF: The Magazine of the World Wrestling Federation.* For kids interested in role-playing games there are *Dragon*

Magazine and *Dungeon Adventures*. Other titles of interest to YAs are *Calliope: World History for Young People* and *Cobblestone: History for Young People*; *Careers & Colleges*; *Choices: The Magazine for Personal Development & Practical Living Skills*; *Current Health*; *Dramatics* (new plays, college theater programs, etc.); *Faces: The Magazine about People* (multiculturalism); *MAD* (an old clinker that is the ultimate in sophomoric humor); *New Moon* (written and produced by girls for girls); *Odyssey* (science); *Science News*; and *3-2-1-CONTACT* (nature, science, and technology for young adults).

Finally, some mention must be made of one type of magazine that is extremely popular with many if not most young adults but that many adults, including librarians, do not think should be part of a library's collection. Comic books have been a subject of controversy for years, but regardless they are a part of young adults' reading matter and prove extremely popular when they are made available in the YA collection. The excuse is often given that they are difficult to obtain on a subscription basis, and this is probably true. But nearly every community has at least one comic book dealer or magazine distributor who will work with the library to ensure the receipt of comics on a regular basis as they become available.

In summary, magazines are available to meet almost every interest and need of YA library patrons, whether they are published specifically for YAs or for the adult market, and should be an integral part of every YA collection—including comics.

THE FUTURE OF YA PUBLISHING

Although publishing for young adults has been around for a long time, and YA literature has become a viable genre with its own body of criticism, it can still be described as an "endangered species." Only recently a number of juvenile book editors were quoted in *Publishers Weekly* as having to seriously consider cutting back on all publishing of nonadult titles, but especially of YA hardcover books. The reasons for this are purely economic and need to be understood so that YA librarians can do whatever is possible to keep publishing for young adults as a viable and at least minimally profitable area for those engaged in producing YA books. In the United States, for example, more than 80,000 new book titles appear each year. Of these, approximately 3,000 are juvenile titles, and of that number about 10 percent, or 300 titles, are YA books, which means for most publishing houses, especially trade publishers, YA books are a nearly insignificant part of their book output. Add to this the fact that the average first printing of a YA hardcover is around 1,000 to 1,500 copies per title (except in the case of such really big authors such as Robert Cormier or M.E. Kerr) and that YA titles are rarely reprinted in hardcover, and the picture is even worse. Why so few copies? The answer is simple. Young adults do not buy hardcover YA books, nor do their parents and doting grandparents; librarians do, and that number of copies is just about enough to meet the needs of the library market.

Unfortunately, the profit line for a few hundred copies of a new title is not enough to impress those who are concerned with a company's bottom line, so whenever cost-cutting measures are announced, the YA segment of a publisher's output is likely to be the first to face the ax. Perhaps it will be in fewer copies printed or fewer titles published each year, but the threat is always there. Only the dedication of a number of strongly committed editors in the various houses who believe in the value of books for the young adult reader has kept them alive in many publishing companies. Of course, there will always be the paperback edition of a new book to keep it alive—or will there be? Of the 300 or so YA trade books published each year, fewer than 100 of these will ever see the light as paperback editions; the case of Nancy Garden's *Annie on My Mind*, cited earlier in this chapter, is an example of what can happen, but rarely does, especially if a book is controversial in some way.

In short, librarians who care about YA literature must not only continue to buy new YA books but must do everything in their power to convince the publishing industry of their commitment to do just that. Through talking to publishing people at state, national, and regional conferences, to writing letters or e-mailing editors and publishers about books that are especially valuable or meet a need, those who produce YA books must be kept aware of the fact that materials for this age level are at least as important in the grand scheme of things as a new zillion-copy best-seller by Stephen King or Danielle Steel. If YA librarians are not willing to take this kind of stand, they will have no one to blame but themselves when this endangered species becomes an extinct species.

NOTES

1. Alleen Pace Nilsen and Kenneth L. Donelson, *Literature for Today's Young Adults*, 2d ed. (Glenview, IL: Scott, Foresman, 1985), 495.

2. Ibid., 507.

3. Ibid., 582.

4. Ibid.

5. Eleanor A. Hunter, *Talks to Boys* (New York: American Tract Society, 1890), 69–70.

5

Where Do I Begin? Developing a Core Collection for Young Adults

Catherine Ritchie

INTRODUCTION

In developing a core collection of materials for young adults, there is both good and bad news. The bad news is that there seems to be an overwhelming number of interesting titles published for that age group, and the good news is that there are many helpful sources available to help librarians wade through the abundance! It is no exaggeration to say that, after decades of little or no recognition, YA literature is now considered a genre worthy of praise and study. The boon in YA publishing has given birth to research, awards, and the literature's own group of specialists. No longer do teenagers or librarians need to settle for second-best when finding materials for school or leisure.

However, we still need to acknowledge that young adults can find themselves in a literary limbo of sorts, straddling the gap between adult and children's materials. While many teens choose to read adult books, they also need and want quality materials that are attuned to their unique life situations and concerns.

Therefore, as library professionals and staff members often burdened with small budgets and limited shelf space, we need to show respect for our teenage audience by having their books readily available, so that such a limbo need not be the norm.

FACTORS TO CONSIDER

As you purchase, you must evaluate the breadth, depth, and currency of your titles and weed as necessary. If your collection has been reasonably well maintained, it can provide a firm underpinning to your future collection development efforts.

However, if you are assigned to build a YA collection from scratch, there are unique factors to consider before plunging into reviews and catalogs. I characterize these as *internal factors*, which pertain to your library, and *external factors*, which relate to your community at large.

Begin by reviewing your library's policies, overall mission, financial situation, and space availability, then ask yourself these questions:

Internal Factors to Consider

1. Is service to young adults considered an important aspect of your library's role?
2. Will you have a separate area for YA materials in your library?
3. Will you have total autonomy in choosing materials, or is selection always done by committee?
4. Will the collection consist of fiction and paperbacks or a combination of non-fiction and fiction?
5. Will you need published reviews for everything you choose, or will your own expertise and suggestions from teen patrons help guide you?

External Factors to Consider

1. What is the general economic climate of your city?
2. What is the overall demographic/ethnic mix in your area?
3. What is included in the curricula taught in your local high schools? Are there honors classes, college preparatory courses, or technical/agricultural training?
4. Perhaps most importantly, are there any established links between the schools and your library? Do students use your facility for research more than the school libraries?

The most important single question to ask may well be, how much do your local students use the public library, and what do they *need* and want from you? Has your library done any kind of survey regarding teen usage? If so, keeping the answers—and your primary audience—in mind will help inspire your selection decisions through the long haul.

SELECTION BY GENRE

Due to factors of budget, space, staff, and so forth, YA collections may vary widely in their composition, but the ideal collection will likely contain both non-fiction for general reading and research and fiction for assigned book reports and recreational reading. While some selection principles and sources are common to both genres, there are also unique issues to be considered with each.

Non-fiction

To paraphrase a cliché, I firmly believe that "non-fiction is not just for term papers anymore"! While there will always be a need for quality research-oriented titles, non-fiction literature can also be a great source of enjoyment for the nonspecialist reader who's interested in gaining an overview of a topic without plunging into a minidissertation. A well-done piece of non-fiction can stimulate further reading on a subject or simply stand alone. As many teen readers enjoy exploring new topics in a leisurely, nonacademic setting, well-written non-fiction read at the person's own pace—be it biographies, sport stories, or "how-to"—can provide a painless and stimulating supplement to classroom lectures and textbooks.

As the YA non-fiction selector, ask yourself if your library has any sort of partnership with local schools in terms of supporting their curricula—is it within your library's official mandate to do so? Are you a prime materials resource for area YAs? Do you know about assigned term paper topics in advance? Your relationships with local schools may well affect your selection decisions.

Even if it is not possible to know precisely what topics are assigned, it is probably safe to assume some subjects are timeless and to plan accordingly. For example, the Holocaust, various social issues, and current events/people in the news never seem to lose their magic with teachers and students.

I think a worthy goal for non-fiction selection is to have basic volumes on many different subjects, with perhaps emphasis on the Dewey areas 300s and 600s. "Hot" topics that are always popular include rape, sexual harassment, addiction, domestic/family violence, teen pregnancy, AIDS, gangs, and ethnic conflict, among many others. In addition, career/college information is always a necessity for this age group, along with a healthy sampling of biographies and books on health, diet, and exercise.

But how does one decide which particular books to choose on various topics? I have found the best sources of YA reviews to be *Booklist*, *VOYA*, *Kliatt Paperback Guide*, and *School Library Journal*,[1] several of which also feature helpful bibliographic essays on various non-fiction topics. For retrospective purchasing, the ALA lists of *Outstanding Books for the College Bound*[2] are a good place to start. There are also booklets published annually by the New York City and Minneapolis public libraries that are wide-ranging and thorough.[3] The National Council of Teachers of English,[4] based in Urbana, Illinois, also publishes a large number of reader's/selector's advisory books for adults working with teenagers. Last, but certainly not least, the annual ALA/YALSA Best Books for Young Adults list can be a first stop in your efforts to build a quality collection.

Many individual authors produce superb writing and research. To name a few: Nathan Aaseng, Brent Ashabrenner, Eleanor Ayer, Janet Bode, Edward

Dolan, Kathlyn Gay, James Haskins, Elaine Landau, Albert Marrin, and perhaps the most highly respected YA non-fiction writer of them all, Milton Meltzer. You likely will never be disappointed by any of their efforts.

As for publishers of note, several are well known for their particular non-fiction specialities. For example, Rosen has a fine self-help series known as *Coping With . . .* , covering many issues.[5] For career material and college exploration aids, Peterson's, VGM, Macmillan, and the College Board are excellent.[6] For biographies, especially of women and so-called minority groups, Chelsea House is outstanding. Other quality non-fiction publishers include Watts, Enslow, Greenhaven, Facts on File, Henry Holt, HarperCollins, Lerner, and Millbrook.[7] Adding your name to their catalog mailing lists is a fine way to keep up with their new releases.

When actually assessing a non-fiction title as to its suitability for your collection, it is important to note copyright dates and, later on, watch for updates. Obviously, currentness is an all-important consideration in this area, but some topics prove to be more current than others. For example, when considering books on the Holocaust, a well-regarded title from 1994 probably will be acceptable, whereas a volume on the use of DNA testing in court cases needs to be as up-to-date as possible. Also, be on the lookout for good illustrations/photographs, readable overall design including typeface, and, especially, thorough footnoting, indexing, and lists of further resources.

Finally, I advise you to read widely in non-fiction as your own time permits so as to reinforce a sense of what seems especially useful and, above all, always keep in mind your ongoing goal—to provide a broad range of informative books that are bolstered by high-quality presentation of material. Your teenage patrons deserve nothing less.

Fiction

You will need to decide at the outset of your core collection building just how large a proportion fiction will fill in your YA area. I believe it is particularly incumbent upon the public library to maintain a vital fiction collection for this age group, not just to fulfill book report and English assignments but also to provide teenagers with all-important leisure reading materials, which may be lacking in their school libraries due to tight budgets and/or space constrictions. By doing so, you may well inspire a love of reading that will easily segue into lifelong reading as your patrons become adults.

Having made a case for recreational reading, I also must assert the need to include classic and contemporary fiction titles. I am referring to the adult books still read for school assignments and those time-honored examples of YA titles such as *To Kill a Mockingbird*, *Red Badge of Courage*, and *The Chocolate War*.[8] Just as adolescent reading preferences and abilities vary widely, so should a YA fiction collection.

As with a non-fiction collection, it is wise to assess the demographics of the community you serve. Once again, questions to ask would include: Do most graduating high school seniors in your city go on to college? What is the general ethnic/racial mix in your area? Is there a strong African/Asian/Hispanic, etc.–American presence where you reside? Fiction collections should ideally serve all segments of a population.

I believe that the best overall goal in YA fiction collection development is to include as many genres as possible, providing readers with the best of each category or the most representative authors. These genres should include mystery, horror, romance, social issues, historical, anthologies, and multi-cultural titles. Fortunately, thanks to a multitude of sources, determining which authors to include is not difficult, and since paperback reprints are now often issued within months of a book's initial publication, you can engender a good cross-section of materials in your library with a limited budget.

Now, a word about original YA paperback series, such as *Fear Street* by R.L. Stine, Pascal's *Sweet Valley High*, and so forth. While these titles may lack traditional literary qualities such as well-developed characters, true-to-life settings and situations, and engrossing plots, their enormous popularity with teenage readers cannot be disputed. Therefore, I firmly believe they should be included in any fiction collection purporting to serve that age group. Having them available is a guaranteed method of luring teens into the library; once there, they can find additional books of interest while stocking up on their favorites. Deny them those favorites altogether, and you may risk alienating your patrons for good. This is not to say, however, that you should allocate the lion's share of your money for series but that individual titles should be purchased as steadily as possible and replaced promptly if and when copies become damaged from overuse (and they will!). Above all, maintain a balance between those titles popular only until the next in the series is published and those that time and the experts say will be with us always.

Another selection issue regarding fiction involves potentially objectionable themes and language. Much of today's YA fiction is grounded in the reality of teenagers' lives, which often includes harsh situations couched in honest and, at times, graphic language.

Before beginning your selection, it is wise to review your library's philosophy regarding censorship and its mechanism whereby books challenged by patrons are evaluated. If your library has a firm policy in place—and in writing—you will feel more comfortable in your decisionmaking and will have institutional support to call upon if needed. All that said, it is still necessary to read YA fiction reviews carefully (although reviews often do not tell selectors everything they might need to know) and note any mentions of potentially controversial elements in a given book ahead of time. In cases of would-be censorship, forewarned is forearmed.

Fortunately, sources of YA fiction reviews are plentiful and closely dovetail those previously suggested for non-fiction. *Booklist*, *Publishers Weekly*, *School Library Journal*, *VOYA*, and *Kliatt* are vital and worth the subscription costs.[9]

I would also rate ALA's annual Best Books for Young Adults fiction citations (appearing in the March 15 issue of *Booklist*) as absolute musts for any YA librarian; they provide a novice selector with an excellent starting point for core collection building and, over time, lend perspective on the development of the YA genre, for example, which authors are cited most frequently.

In addition, ALA's Outstanding Books for the College Bound list for fiction is an excellent tool for retrospective purchasing of those so-called classics. A few of the standard magazines such as *Booklist* and *School Library Journal* frequently feature bibliographies by theme; several of the *Booklist* pieces plus many original ones appear in the book *Growing Up Is Hard to Do*[10] by Sally Estes.

Other books that may be helpful include *From Romance to Realism*[11] by Michael Cart, which is a general history of YA literature, and *What Do Young Adults Read Next?*[12] by Pam Spencer. As with non-fiction, annual lists published by the New York City and Minneapolis public libraries provide many titles by theme, along with brief annotations. *Senior High School Catalog*,[13] published by H.W. Wilson, may also be of use. Organizations such as the National Council of Teachers of English also provide lists, journals, and helpful selection tools.

I have learned from my own experience that publishers are all too eager to send catalogs to potential book buyers, so postcards mailed to a few major houses should result in a full mailbox in no time! In short, there is no lack of sources to help a novice or experienced YA fiction selector. The sheer volume of them all may be overwhelming at times, but so is the enormous satisfaction inherent in the task.

Finally, I share with you a partial (and admittedly selective) list of the YA fiction writers I believe to be "must-owns" for any library; if money and space are tight, paperback editions of titles by these authors will serve your clientele well.

Must-owns: Francesca Lia Block, Judy Blume, Sue Ellen Bridgers, Caroline Cooney, Robert Cormier, Chris Crutcher, Lois Duncan, S.E. Hinton, Carolyn Keene, M.E. Kerr, Stephen King, Norma Klein, Robert Lipsyte, Chris Lynch, Anne McCaffrey, Norma Fox Mazer, Walter Dean Myers, Joan Lowery Nixon, Francine Pascal, Gary Paulsen, Richard Peck, Christopher Pike, Ann Rinaldi, R.L. Stine, Cynthia Voigt, Jacqueline Woodson.

CONCLUSION

Librarians in charge of building a YA collection are embarking upon an exciting and worthy professional cause with the potential of enriching and possibly changing lives of teens approaching adulthood. Providing information to help guide adolescents toward their futures is a vital task. The goal of creating life-long readers, via a strong and varied collection chosen with care and conviction, is a calling significant enough to lift us above daily frustrations and to remind us of how influential we all can be in an information society.

NOTES

1. For subscription information, contact *Booklist*, published by the American Library Association (ALA), 50 East Huron Street, Chicago, IL 60611–2795, 1–800–545–2433; *VOYA* (Voice of Youth Advocates), published by Scarecrow Press, Inc., 52 Liberty Street, Metuchen, NJ 08840, 1–800–537–7107 or 908–548–8600; *Kliatt Paperback Guide*, 33 Bay State Road, Wellesley, MA, 02181, 617–237–7577; *School Library Journal*, P.O. Box 57559, Boulder, CO 80322–7559, 1–800–456–9409.

2. Outstanding Books for the College Bound lists include general fiction and non-fiction, plus individual subjects such as "theatre" and "fine arts." For ordering information, contact ALA Graphics, ALA, 50 East Huron Street, Chicago, IL 60611, 1-800–545–2433.

3. For purchasing information, contact New York Public Library, Fifth Avenue and 42d Street, New York, NY 10018, 212–930–0800; Minneapolis Public Library and Information Center, 300 Nicollet Mall, Minneapolis, MN 55401–1992, 612–372–6500.

4. Contact National Council of Teachers of English, 1111 West Kenyon Road, Urbana, IL 61801–1096, 217–328–3870.

5. For more information, contact Rosen Publishing Group, 29 East 21st Street, New York, NY 10010, 1–800–237–9932 or 212–777–3017.

6. For further information, contact Peterson's, P.O. Box 2123, Princeton, NJ 08543-2123, 1–800–338–3282 or 609–243–9111; VGM Publishing, 4255 West Touhy Avenue, Lincolnwood, IL 60646–1975, 1–800–323–4900 or 847–679–5500; Macmillan Publishing Company, Inc., 200 Old Tappan Road, Old Tappan, NJ 07675, 1–800–223–2336; College Board, 45 Columbus Avenue, New York, NY 10023–6992, 1–800–323–7155 or 212–713-8000.

7. For ordering information, contact Chelsea House Publishers, 1974 Sproul Road, Suite 400, Broomall, PA 19008, 1–800–848–2665 or 610–353–5166; Franklin Watts, Inc., Sherman Turnpike, Danbury, CT 06813, 1–800–621–1115 or 203–797–3500; Enslow Publishers, P.O. Box 699, Springfield, NJ 07081–0699, 1–800–398–2504 or 201–379–8890; Greenhaven Press, Inc., P.O. Box 289009, San Diego, CA 92198–9009, 1–800–231–5163 or 619–485–7424; Facts on File, Inc., 11 Penn Plaza, New York, NY 10001, 1–800–322–8755 or 212–967–8800; Henry Holt and Company, Inc., 115 West 18th Street, New York, NY 10022–5299, 1–800–331–3761 or 212–207–7000; Lerner Group, 241 First Avenue North, Minneapolis, MN 55401, 1–800–328–4929 or 612–332–3344; Millbrook Press, 2 Old Milford Road, Brookfield, CT 06804, 1–800–462–4703 or 203–740–2220.

8. The following books are available in various editions: Harper Lee, *To Kill a Mockingbird*; Stephen Crane, *The Red Badge of Courage*; Robert Cormier, *The Chocolate War*.

9. To subscribe to *Publishers Weekly*, write to 245 West 17th Street, New York, NY 10011 or call 1–800–278–2991 or 212–463–6758.

10. Sally Estes, ed., *Growing Up Is Hard to Do: A Collection of Booklist Columns* (Chicago: ALA, 1994).

11. Michael Cart, *From Romance to Realism: 50 Years of Growth and Change in Young Adult Literature* (New York: HarperCollins Children's Books, 1996).

12. Pamela G. Spencer, *What Do Young Adults Read Next?* (New York: Gale, 1994).

13. *Senior High School Catalog* (New York: H.W. Wilson). Published annually.

6

Where Do I Go Next?
How to Select
Materials for Teens

Jeri Baker

Who is buying books and other materials for teenagers at your public library? Is there a plan for building a collection, or is it the neither-fish-nor-fowl method? The reasoning goes that if it isn't a children's book, and it isn't an adult book, then it must be classified as YA. The youth services librarians complain that the children's book budget isn't large enough to cover YA, and the adult librarians hate to waste the book dollars on a YA title that might sit on the shelf when they could be getting another copy of a best-seller. When this happens, YA books fall through the cracks, and nobody ends up taking the responsibility for making selection decisions about YA.

WHAT MAKES A YA SERVICE PROVIDER?

In planning customer services for young adults, the most crucial selection decision is to identify the staff member who will undertake building a YA collection. This is especially true for the vast majority of public libraries that operate without a YA librarian. While administrative patterns for collection development differ widely from library to library, as Mary K. Chelton has argued, "No system is perfect or foolproof, and all have an inherent capability to ignore YA."[1]

Therefore, identifying this staff member may not, at first, seem easy. Observe staff, particularly during peak hours of service to teenagers. The person most likely to succeed has what Patrick Jones has described as a "YAttitude," the passion and enthusiasm to serve teens.[2] This individual must possess a sense of humor, a sense of perspective, and courage. After all, making selection decisions about YA materials requires stamina and a willingness to take risks. Selection decisions to be confronted include: (1) How do you make a collection policy and plan work for YA? (2) Who is the target audience? (3) What is in the collection and what selection criteria work best? and (4) How is the collection promoted and maintained?

WHAT IS A YA COLLECTION POLICY?

To clearly delineate the goals and objectives of the collection is the purpose of the policy statement. It describes the constituencies to be served and specifies the methods whereby wise and responsible evaluation may be achieved. In writing the goals and objectives, begin with the general mission statement of your library and adapt this statement to what is known about the YA clientele. Research has indicated that teens use libraries for homework-related research and personal interest materials. To reach the goal of responding to the informational needs of teenagers, the objectives for the collection development policy will state that titles from assigned reading lists, coping skills materials, and college and career information will be acquired.

Patrick Jones has outlined some of the issues to be resolved in writing a collection policy:

1. Library's total collection development philosophy
2. Quality and quantity of school library collections
3. Budget, staff, and space available
4. Reading interests of YAs in your community
5. Your own personal values
6. What needs your collection should meet
7. Your goals for the collection
8. Roles the library has chosen for itself[3]

Budget constraints usually dictate the limitations of the collection. However, the collection policy should place parameters. YA collections in public libraries may offer a variety of formats from leisure reading to self-help books, from career videos to popular music. Unlike the school media center, the collection does not have curriculum support as its primary goal. Of course, it's nice to have it all, but tough decisions must be made to give the collection focus. If the collection is not going to have textbooks, then this should be stated in the collection policy.

Most general collection statements address the integrity of the collection, with the inclusion of procedures for maintenance, duplication, and reconsideration.

The American Library Association Library Bill of Rights and the Free Access to Libraries for Minors Interpretation provide the professional ethics for the YA collection policy. Materials in YA collections tend to arouse controversy, so it is best that all staff are well prepared to respond to any challenge.

The distinguishing characteristic of a policy statement for YA collections is that the emphasis is upon the user. Carolyn Caywood has discussed the frequently asked question, Who is a teen?[4] She explains why most collections tend to focus upon the 12- to 15-year age group, while at the same time provides a strong argument for service to the young adult, ages 16 to 18:

Budding adolescents seek library programs and services that meet their new interests and abilities. The growing awareness of sexuality means that teens want a safe environment to explore their changing relationships with peers. Their interests diversify as teens become more aware of their own uniqueness. They want to participate in the planning of programs and services not just to be passive recipients.

Once teenagers have their own driver's licenses their library needs seem to become less obvious. Outside of career and college information and specialized self help books, they are using adult materials. Work and other activities leave less time for involvement with the library. They are also somewhat more secure in their identities and require less of the library's staff attention. Still these are changes in degree, not kind. Older adolescents should not be neglected just because they seem better able to use the library on their own.[5]

WHAT'S IN A YA COLLECTION?

As you consider the focus, target audience, and parameters of the collection, a framework begins to take shape. The challenge now is to select the very best materials that will fulfill the promised potential of your collection policy. The majority of decisions, for most selectors, will be book-related. In a YA popular reading collection, the fiction may outweigh the non-fiction by as much as a 3:1 ratio, according to Evie Wilson-Lingbloom. In her outstanding text, *Hangin' Out at Rocky Creek*, Wilson-Lingbloom offers the following formula for reading categories in a YA collection:

1. 33 percent—YA literature genre
2. 28 percent—adult books that are recommended for young adults
3. 22 percent—classics or adult books that contain subjects of interest to young adults
4. 16 percent—authors whose books bridge the step from children's literature[6]

WHAT CRITERIA WORK BEST?

Several very fine professional educators from the academic field have outlined criteria to help selectors. Foremost in the area are Alleen Pace Nilsen and Kenneth Donelson. Their textbook, *Literature for Today's Young Adult*, is widely used in both education and library science courses. Among the most recent works in this field is *Teaching Young Adult Literature* by Jean E. Brown and Elaine C. Stephens. These educators write:

Although it is easy for most of us to think about and identify the really good books we have read over the years, it is not always easy to explain why a specific book is good. It may be easier to identify bad books we have read or attempted to read and describe those qualities that detract from the book's quality. The reasons an individual likes a book are complex and often not entirely expressed at a conscious level.[7]

Brown and Stephens suggest the following criteria:

Indicators of quality:
1. Believable characters—carefully crafted characters that are multifaceted
2. People who are neither stereotyped nor prototyped
3. Coherent, but not predictable, plot
4. Reasonable conflict
5. Satisfying resolution of conflict
6. Meaningful interaction among characters
7. Significant themes
8. Appropriate settings[8]

Additionally, how a book is written influences selection decisions. These indicators of quality pertain to style:

1. Authentic dialogue
2. Clarity of language
3. Vivid images
4. Rich, but not effusive, descriptions[9]

The third area examines the questions of the integrity of the work. At the most fundamental level, readers have the right to expect to be treated as intelligent participants in the literary experience. Readers should never be exploited, and they have the right to expect the following:

1. Language that is appropriate to the character
2. Timeless themes that speak to timely issues
3. Responsible presentation of controversial ideas[10]

HOW DO YOU USE SELECTION TOOLS?

Familiarity with retrospective and current selection sources helps the selector to become more knowledgeable about working within the framework of an existing collection or selecting new materials. Usage of standard sources and recommended periodicals effectively balanced by suggestions from teens, visits to bookstores, and selection from nontraditional sources helps to weigh the scales of popularity and quality.

Retrospective sources are used in:

1. *Evaluating an existing collection*—Using these sources will assist you in noting areas that need to be updated and areas in which more materials are needed.

2. *Reader's advisory work*—Using the sources appropriately will help you to give the right book to the right reader at the right time. Remember that the more experience you have with reader's advisory work, the better you will become. However, there will always be areas with which you are less familiar. When presented with a request, it's always best to be ready with one or two suggestions. A good retrospective source will either help to jog your memory or expand your base of suggestions.

3. *Preparing special reading lists*—Requests are frequently made by teachers, parents, community organizations, and, yes, even teens.

4. *Providing authority and credibility*—Retrospective sources give credibility to your collection, especially when you encounter a challenge.

5. *Promoting an existing collection*—Retrospective sources are helpful in creating book displays and promoting programs and services.

6. *Staff development*—Retrospective sources will assist other staff members in serving young adults when you are not available. An ongoing component of staff development or department training and staff meetings should be the introduction of any new reference source.

7. *Basic collection development*—Retrospective sources are used to create core or opening-day collections.

Like other reference materials, YA retrospective sources should be evaluated to determine how useful the sources will be to you. In either using a source or determining to purchase a source, you should consider:

1. *Authority of the title*—Who compiled or edited the source? Who published the source? Is it a standard source that has gone through a variety of editions? If you purchase a new edition, do not automatically withdraw the older edition. Be aware of any changes, additions or features added or dropped.

2. *Scope of the work*—How did the editors actually go about selecting the listed titles? What information does each entry provide?

3. How much does it cost, and is the information found in other sources?

4. How will the source be used? What is the intended audience?

In evaluating a retrospective source to be used specifically in building a YA collection, be sure to consider:

1. *Timeliness*—Are the titles in print? Will the source really help you to select those titles that teens will read?
2. Is the emphasis on popular or more academic titles?
3. Does the source reflect the developmental tasks of adolescence?
4. What is the focus? Does it offer a really good selection of YA titles, or is YA just "stuck on," to boost sales?

HOW CAN REVIEW SOURCES HELP?

There are five standard review periodicals for YA materials: *Booklist, Book Report, Kliatt, School Library Journal*, and *Voice of Youth Advocates*. The savvy YA selector keeps an eye out for any review columns that may be published, even on a sporadic basis, in teen magazines such as *Seventeen*. Whether it appears in a standard source or in a nontraditional source, professional reviewers suggest these guidelines:

1. Authority? Where is review published?
2. Features or elements that would attract a reader.
3. Is review signed?
4. Does reviewer offer other titles for comparison or recommendation?[11]

As you read the review, ask yourself the following questions:

1. Would the inclusion of this item fit in with your overall plan for development of the YA collection?
2. Will this item appeal to both male and female readers?
3. What is the authority of the author or creator in relation to the subject matter?
4. How does this item compare with others of its type?
5. What is the degree of difficulty both in vocabulary and in concepts in relation to the primary audience of your collection?
6. If the item is a book, is it worth paying the hardcover price?
7. If the item is another piece of media, what will you have to give up, if anything, in order to make this purchase?[12]

Basically, the reviewer should cover the author's scope and purpose and indicate any omissions as well as inclusions. If possible, the reviewer should state the reliability of the information or the credibility of the author. The reviewer should describe the clarity of style. Is the book accessible to the student reading on, or slightly above, grade level, or is it intended for the special reader? There should be some indicators, where applicable, of illustrative material, indexes, and/or glossaries. Each review of a fiction title should include, but not be dominated by, a plot summary. A comparison of the work in hand with other materials is helpful. A statement of recommendation should be given.

Reviews of YA materials should note:

1. Does the reviewer indicate any warning signals about the item? Does the reviewer alert the selector to any possibly controversial issue in the book, be it strong language, explicit sex, or violence?

2. Does the review describe the cover art? While we might feel that no one should judge a book by its cover, the truth is that everyone does. It doesn't matter how popular the content will be with young adults if the cover design keeps them from picking it up off the shelf. Be alert to reviews that say "cover certain to grab readers" or "dull cover may make for shelf sitter."

3. Does the reviewer indicate other audiences which might use this item? For example, would the title be of interest to adolescent care providers, health educators, social workers, or counselors? Is this a title which parents could use? What is the value as a title to support the curriculum?

4. Finally, a really good review offers an element of literary style. An outstanding review tells us more than whether we ought to buy the material in the first place. For example, spelling out the multiple and potential uses for a title is a way of helping us to know which of the many otherwise acceptable titles are worth our money when we can't afford to buy them all.[13]

Literary critic Betsy Hearne has characterized the review process as being "relate, rate, and be done with it."[14] Too often that is true of reviewers in the library media. A good review is no more or less than an honest personal reaction to a book. It can be as imaginative, as incisive, as intelligent as the person who writes it. Award-winning author Walter Dean Myers has argued that every review should contain a clear-cut statement as to whether or not the item is recommended. Myers has written, "I always suspect that if the reviewer merely gives the story line of something I've written, it's because he or she didn't care for the book and was too lazy to write the more difficult panning or negative review."[15] Young adult book reviewer Patty Campbell sums it up best when she writes: "I want to know if the book has magic for YAs. What is there about it that is going to click with kids right now?"[16]

HOW DO YOU UPDATE A COLLECTION?

Annual selection lists are another source for finding titles that are hot right now and will click with kids. For over 68 years, *Books for the Teen Age*, published by the Office of Young Adult Services of the New York Public Library, has combined the very best attributes of a retrospective source and an annual list. This selection tool, which is annually reassessed and revised, is outstanding for both reader's advisory and collection development. Every year, numerous other lists are compiled to reflect the best in YA literature. Using these lists and comparing the lists to find titles that make more than one list are a convenient process for keeping up with trends. Obviously, any selector, when handed a new list, will want to check holdings first. The next step is deciding whether to duplicate popular titles or initiate orders for titles that might have been overlooked. Finally, lists may be used to create displays, promote reading interests, and share with colleagues at staff meetings.

It is the rare entry in a paperback series that is going to make any annual list. It has happened, but the very formulaic nature of series writing inhibits the quality. Yet reading surveys have found that most teens enjoy reading horror, mystery, and romance titles. Much has been written about the very toughest of selection decisions—quality versus demand. In resolving this selection issue, keep in mind the following. First, research has proved that series paperbacks do offer a similar portrayal of adolescent developmental tasks as that offered by the more frequently recommended realistic fiction.[17] Second, paperback collections do not have to be limited to just series titles. Building a paperback collection offers the opportunity to take risks at very low costs. Third, the paperback titles, especially in the fiction genres, offer teens a certain comfort zone. Ilene Cooper, writing in the *New York Times*, offers an explanation for the popularity of series paperbacks:

In speaking to a group of inner city children who were big fans of Sweet Valley Twins she inquired what they liked about the stories. Was it the idyllic setting of suburbia so different from their own neighborhood? No, it was that Elizabeth was so nice and Jessica was so conniving. The series offered a predictability that made these readers feel safe. In an uncertain world, there is security in knowing that somewhere nice kids win out, the others get their comeuppance, and the story will end with expectations met.[18]

Many adults, argues Cooper, ask the same of their genre fiction.

HOW DO YOU MAINTAIN A COLLECTION?

The fourth area for decision making concerns the credibility of the selections. How do you know when your collection is working? How do you maintain the collection to make it viable and current? How do you promote the collection so young adults will become more aware of the library? Obviously, you do so when all the titles on display are checked out, or when the titles showcased in a book-related program or during a school visit are eagerly sought.

The more you interact with the teens in your library, the better you will be able to judge their needs. Teens like to choose their materials by browsing and are often reluctant to ask for help. To help promote the collection, a variety of techniques may be used. These may be inexpensive and made in-house. A free-standing flip chart that invites teens to jot down their favorite title provides a way of communicating while still maintaining anonymity. Remember the basic axiom: reader's advisory is a learned art—the more you do it, the better you will become. Janet Dickey and Patrick Jones have offered some quick tips that even a novice may use to learn a collection. Using a 3" x 5" card to start a reader's advisory file is a great help. On the card you list the books that you could suggest for the real or imagined reader. Creating an in-house best-seller list or posting peer reviews will also help teens to make choices.

A *VOYA* quiz featured a YA area needs-assessment test.[19] The respondent could earn points for correctly offering certain activities in the YA area. On weeding, the statement was, "If it's been so long you can't remember, then lose 25 points." A browsing collection must be weeded frequently. Teens are not patient enough to hunt through a lot of deadwood to find the good stuff.

Wilson-Lingbloom suggests that weeding be done when:

1. Materials have not circulated for a long time.
2. Misinformation is given.
3. Unless in great demand, keeping more than one copy of a catalogued item takes up too much shelf space.
4. Materials are in poor condition.[20]

Belinda Boon, in a manual developed for the Texas State Library, recommends that in a YA collection, weeding should be done when cover art has become dated, reading levels change, or interest in subject lags.[21]

WHAT IS YOUR VISION?

The wise selector of YA materials has a vision of how the decisions made today about materials will provide a groundwork for decisions to be made in the future. Just as adolescence pushes the limits, YA literature tests the waters. This often means taking risks and being unafraid to try something new, no matter how controversial it might be considered. When Patty Campbell began a column for *Horn Book* on controversial YA books, she explained that she planned to do some "heavy breathing." Her column, which is an inspiration for helping selectors to make tough decisions with courage and tenacity, is titled "The Sand in the Oyster." Campbell says she got the title from the inimitable Christy Tyson, who had told her, "We should cherish the opportunity to be uncomfortable with certain books, because it is the speck of grit in the oyster that produces not only irritation but, eventually, a pearl."[22] Michael Cart, in his history of YA literature, challenges YA authors to "risk taking the gloves off and tackling dangerous subjects and to deal with them unflinchingly and honestly."[23] Selection decisions in YA literature will always be tough, but selectors have the unequaled opportunity of making a difference in the lives of young adults.

NOTES

Appreciation is expressed to Janice Fisher-Giles and Katherine Stone for their assistance with this chapter.

1. Mary K. Chelton and James Rosinia, *Bare Bones: Young Adult Services: Tips for Public Library Generalists* (Chicago: American Library Association, 1993).

2. Patrick Jones, *Connecting Young Adults and Libraries: A How-to-Do-It Manual* (New York: Neal-Schuman, 1992), 13.

3. Ibid., 33.

4. Carolyn Caywood, "What's a Teen?" *School Library Journal* 39 (February 1993): 42.

5. Ibid.

6. Evie Wilson-Lingbloom, *Hangin' Out at Rocky Creek* (Metuchen, NJ: Scarecrow Press, 1994). (*Note*: figures do not total 100 percent due to rounding.)

7. Jean E. Brown and Elaine C. Stephens, *Teaching Young Adult Literature: Sharing the Connection* (Empire, KY: International Thomson, 1995).

8. Ibid.

9. Ibid.

10. Ibid.

11. "What Makes a Good Review? Ten Experts Speak," *Top of the News* 35 (Winter 1979): 146–52.

12. Ibid.

13. Ibid.

14. Ibid.

15. Ibid.

16. Ibid.

17. A. Hubbard, "On Analysis of the Incidence of Havighurst's Developmental Tasks in the Adolescent Horror Novels of R.L. Stine and Christopher Pike" (master's thesis, School of Library and Information Science, University of North Carolina at Chapel Hill, 1994).

18. Ilene Cooper, "Sweet Are the Uses of Predictability," *New York Times Book Review* 97 (November 8, 1992), 52.

19. "It's Not Totally Dreamland," *Voice of Youth Advocates*, August 18, 1995, 150.

20. Wilson-Lingbloom, *Hangin' Out at Rocky Creek.*

21. Belinda Boon, *The CREW Method: Expanded Guidelines for Collection Evaluation and Weeding for Small and Medium-Sized Public Libraries*, revised and updated (Austin: Texas State Library, 1995).

22. Patty Campbell, "The Sand in the Oyster," *Horn Book Magazine* 69 (September–October 1993): 568–72.

23. Michael Cart, *From Romance to Realism: Fifty Years of Growth and Change in Young Adult Literature* (New York: HarperCollins, 1996).

7

R.L. Stine Meets Horatio Alger: Quality versus Popularity in the Young Adult Collection

Ann Sparanese

pop•u•lar•i•ty–the state of being liked by the people in general; well-liked; ease of comprehension; suitability to the majority of the people.
qual•i•ty–the level of excellence of something; superiority.

"THE QUESTION OF QUALITY VS. POPULARITY IS AS OLD AS THE PUBLIC LIBRARY MOVEMENT ITSELF"[1]

As long as librarians have been selecting materials for library collections, they have confronted choices about whether to emphasize popular materials that address the expressed needs of the population they serve or to emphasize the merit of the materials, even though they will never make the best-seller list or even achieve a high circulation figure. With circulation one of the most easily measured library outputs and most often relied upon to demonstrate library effectiveness (although this is changing), this statistic takes on a special immediacy, akin to the earnings report of corporations. A library's stock may go up or down with its funding sources based on circulation figures. Beyond this, a school of thought defines a best library collection by its ability to fulfill the public's demand for the most popular items. Thus there are entire library systems built on the principle that public libraries should "give 'em what they want,"[2] relegating issues of merit, values, breadth (i.e., quality) to the lower berth.

In the case of the YA collection, the debate comes into even sharper relief due to several factors specific to the young adult or teenage "public": (1) Budgets are often extremely constricted, because library management believes most of the needs of this age group are fulfilled by the children's or adult collections or both. (2) The teenage clientele is categorized as students whose primary library need is for curriculum support, further reducing budgets for the recreational reading needs of middle and high school kids. (3) Many teenagers are in that period of their lives where they are less apt to accept what adults tell them they "should" be reading or adult views about what is "good" for them. (4) The tribal behavior of many teens puts emphasis on what is hot, up-to-the-minute, cool, or acceptable to their peers. (5) It is a time when "good books" with hardcovers may take a back seat to preferences for music, magazines, fanzines, series paperbacks, and other less literary-oriented and more portable materials.

For these reasons, the dichotomy between building a quality versus a popular collection is never completely resolved by librarians, especially YA librarians. But the dichotomy is less that than a continuum, and most librarians would probably find a collection situated squarely on either end to be severely lacking. Compromise solutions may vary widely from library to library and may look more different in the YA collection than in any other department in public libraries. What is a stock part of the YA department in one library (e.g., graphic novels) may be totally absent in another. Some of the issues surrounding selection and YA librarians' varying responses are explored in this chapter.

"YA BOOKS" VERSUS THE LITERARY COLLECTION

As most of us may have experienced, courses in YA materials, services, and programming are not numerous in the library school curriculum. There will usually be a course dealing with "adolescent literature" and its context in the "developmental tasks of the age." Perhaps there will be a course dealing with programming for children and young adults. But as Patrick Jones points out in his excellent how-to-book *Connecting Young Adults and Libraries*:

The few library school courses with "young adult" in the title almost exclusively concern young adult literature [defined as "well-written novels in hardback format"]. There might be a session on booktalking and some discussion of popular trends, but most of the time is spent on discussing classic YA literature. Such courses are not especially helpful in selecting, promoting and managing YA collections. Collection use by YAs is not synonymous with YA literature. . . . YA literature is studied in library school and put on the Best Books for Young Adults list, but it is not primarily what YAs read. YA books— defined as the mass market paperbacks that glut bookstores and libraries—are more popular.[3]

Jones also discusses what he terms "YA products," which are "brand-name" series, and the nonbook items (recordings and magazines, for instance), which may be the most popular of all but whose role in the YA collection is not given much emphasis in our formal educational preparation as YA specialists.

One goal often stated in collection development policies for adult and children's collections is to build a "lasting collection." To this end, librarians rely heavily upon published reviews of hardback books, replacement of classics, and award winners and usually have as a selection criterion "literary merit." But in the YA section of the collection development policy of one large county library system, "literary merit" is entirely omitted as a criterion for the YA collection, while it is on the list for both children and adults. Another missing criterion for YAs is "multicultural" emphasis. Specific criteria for the YA fiction collection are "reputation and popularity of author among young adults" and even "usefulness of the material for homework assignments."

In developing the YA collection, we struggle with whether we should be striving to build a "timeless" collection or a collection very much grounded in the here and now, with lots of weeding and lots of changes. True, the classics will always have a place, especially in paperback editions and primarily because of the academic life of teenage students. But YA clientele, more than either children or adults, are madly journeying between two phases of life. At the same time, they are living passionately in the here and now. They appear to be more stylish, influenced by popular culture, more involved in what is "hot" or "cool" with the peer group. They are, as Richard Peck describes them in his book *Love and Death at the Mall*, "tribal." Their sensibilities relate less to timelessness than to relevance and timeliness. Books themselves may take a back seat to magazines, magazines to the latest CDs, and most certainly, hardbacks to paperbacks. These realities pose particular challenges to the YA librarians who view themselves as readers' advisers, the conduit of good and challenging reads for teens, and not simply bookstore "buyers" of surefire hits of the lowest common denominator.

Paperbacks, especially the series variety, are rarely reviewed in most of our selection journals, but they are certainly what teens are buying from the bookstores, as well as what they are scarfing off library shelves when they are available. Even a brief perusal of the small but growing YA shelves in the book superstores will demonstrate that only hardbacks by well-known authors will be stocked, usually inter-shelved with the latest popular genres and paperback reprints of award-winning or quality YA titles. If one wanted to follow the bookstore model, buying mostly genre titles in multiple copies will surely result in a higher YA circulation and get closer to the mission of "givin' 'em what they want." But, "The mission of public libraries never was and does not have to be the same as that of mass market merchandisers . . . for ours is an educational institution, basically—and our service is to individuals."[4]

Much of the debate involving quality or popularity in the area of book selection concerns the library's relation to the YA series fiction, which has become increasingly in demand over the last decade. At this writing, it is the horror series pioneered by R.L. Stine and Christopher Pike; but in the 1980s, concern centered on the proliferation of the romance series like *Sweet Valley High*, *Sweet Dreams*, and a host of others. Of course, series fiction has been popular for ages: Nancy Drew and the Hardy Boys have made the transition to modernity and are still appealing to the teenage audience. Recently the e-mail was flying over PUBYAC, a popular listserv for YA and children's librarians, concerning a rumor that a West Coast urban library center was going to drop the Nancy Drew series (the New York Public Library did not even stock the Nancy Drew series until the 1970s). Protests arose from librarians, sparking another debate over the "value" of series, especially in regard to their ability to help create lifelong readers by making reading accessible, delightful, and easy.

Mary Leonhardt's engaging book *Parents Who Love Reading, Kids Who Don't* has as its thesis that if we as adults (parents or librarians) want to help young people find a lifelong joy in reading, then kids have to be able to read what they enjoy—*whatever* they enjoy. Only by finding pleasure and joy in reading of any sort will young people develop a reading habit and grow to become lifelong readers. She argues that series fiction, magazines of all varieties, and comic books all have important roles to play in developing a young person's joy in reading and therefore should be stocked in great quantities by libraries, as well as purchased by the armful by parents. Leonhardt cites an informal survey she did as a teacher with ninth graders who scored above the 90th percentile in reading on standardized tests.

What did they read as kids, we asked them. Did they do a lot of reading? Every student but one reported reading some kind of serial or category fiction. The holdout was a black inner city student, who tested in the ninety-fifth percentile. No, she didn't read Nancy Drew. She didn't read the *Little House* books, she didn't like romances, or fantasy or mysteries. . . . How did she score so high? I didn't find out until a couple of weeks later, when another teacher came to me to complain because he had caught her reading comic books in his class. "Aha! I said to her. "That's what you read—comic books." She laughed and admitted it. "My brother and I have hundreds," she told me. "We collect them. I've read them for years."[5]

Although she is writing primarily for parents in her book, Leonhardt makes a powerful argument to librarians to include lots of what is popularly called "junk" or "trash" in our collections, exhorting us not to be literary snobs and not to choose materials on the basis of what would appeal to us, lest we miss the boat entirely and leave kids thinking that reading is boring and joyless. Her viewpoint parallels a long-held but sometimes overlooked belief of librarians and teachers that as long as kids read, that is positive. *What* they are reading is less important.

When Margaret Edwards wrote *The Fair Garden and the Swarm of Beasts*, the center of the debate was the place of "teenage novels" in the YA collection.

Edwards defended their inclusion against those who would have the youthful readers tackle only the classics of literature.

At the appearance of teenage novels the literary critics went into tailspins and vied with each other in expressing their scorn. Some librarians agreed with them, while others who have read and circulated these books and listened to the reactions of young readers have come to believe that the public library can make good use of teenage novels to teach the apathetic the love of reading ... and to lead him to adult reading. . . . Unless the adolescent can be convinced that reading is fun and that he must make time for it in his busy life, he will never become a reader.[6]

It is hard today to envision the same controversy swirling around the problem novel as has embraced *Sweet Valley High* and *Fear Street*, but arguments in favor of including the popular against those who would exclude it go back to this quote from a *Literary Journal* article of more than 100 years ago: "[W]hat is trash to some, is, if not nutrient, at least stimulus, to others. Readers improve; if it were not so, reading would not be a particularly useful practice."[7]

The ability of "trash" and "junk" to provide an impetus to the development of reading tastes is upheld by those who advocate its inclusion, on more than a token basis, in our collections.

I buy fiction series on a regular basis ... if I can get them in for the series books, I hope to get them to discover the other books we have. (YA librarian, Kansas)[8]

Popular magazines that can be circulated and a good selection of paperback books (including those series romances that are the despair of literary critics but the delight of teenage girls) should take their place among the hardbound copies of so-called adolescent literature that often collects dust on the shelf. And, if we place the *New Yorker* alongside *Seventeen* and *Sports Illustrated* or slip some good young adult authors (in paperback of course) in among the series romances, who's the wiser?[9]

If your goal is to build readers it is essential that they get to read what they want to read, usually what is considered trash. I firmly believe that first we need to develop readers, then make the better quality stuff available when they are ready for it. (YA librarian, Colorado)[10]

Another frequent topic in listserv cyberspace has concerned the value of "graphic novels" in YA collections. The inclusion of these graphic novels and their close relatives, the comic books, has been attacked by would-be censors in some communities and is defended by YA librarians much along the lines described earlier, eloquently and with extensive bibliographies to back up the passionately held opinions. One librarian wrote:

With their big bold colors, comics are a great draw to the reluctant reader raised in a visual world. A truly skilled comic book writer can get many sophisticated, creative and innovative ideas across through a few pages of printed medium. I've come across many comics that make me sit back and think, many that make me laugh and cry and many that contain a number of valuable morals imparted through the story. They're also great vocabulary builders, fast reading or slow reading, and a great introduction to the "better" literature, should a kid be so inclined to seek it out. Isn't anything that brings kids and reluctant readers into a library considered a benefit? (YA librarian, New York)[11]

Many of us would agree, and this is why the best YA librarians try to keep abreast of trends, fads in genre reading, and popular musical groups and strive to keep an open mind on "products" that may not find a place on library shelves, were it not for us. In our own literature, we will find many exhortations not to fall into the role of standard-bearer for literary values in our selection process. "YA collections sometimes look like sermons, reflecting what the librarian feels should be read by adolescents. Such 'sermon selecting' is avoided at all costs by librarians whose credibility with kids themselves remains strong."[12]

However, simple dependence on the formulaic "give 'em what they want" does not translate well into real-life youth librarianship. It reduces our role to a quarterly visit to the local book superstore to see what's hot, in order to "select" our recreational reading materials. Such a visit is probably not a bad idea, since much of what teens are buying we will never read about in our professional journals. But this coin has another side, as most serious issues do. That other side is our professional role as librarians, our mission to serve youth as a group and as individuals broadly and well; our presumed knowledge and education as reading advisers; and our role, after all is said and done, as adults working with the young.

Lillian Shapiro in her article "Quality or Popularity: Selective Criteria for YAs" makes a very powerful case for quality selecting. It is based on consideration of the professional imperatives of librarians as well as an assessment of the many factors that contribute to what teenagers (and actually all readers) "want." Although her article was written in 1978, her points are even more valid today:

Today, those inchoate desires are even more visibly translated into popular demand by advertising and promotion, and powerfully boosted by television commercials. The public can be manipulated to demand anything and everything. Shouldn't there be, for young people in so formative and vulnerable a stage as adolescence, some influences that temper those demands? The human condition does not have to resemble that of lemmings.[13]

Why do we call what we do "selecting" rather than simply "ordering?" Why do we steep ourselves in reading, pore daily over reviews (often on our own time), and care about good reading for kids, if not to do a better job at bringing kids and books together and helping young people actualize joy in reading?

If the measuring stick . . . is simply "what they want," let us remember that under those conditions there is no need for a trained cadre of reading advisers. . . . Response to popular demand [then] turns libraries into what one librarian calls a drugstore collection. I would think the drugstore and the library serve different purposes. If this is not so, why have professional personnel in one and not in the other?[14]

It is also our responsibility to serve youth as individuals as well as part of a defined group, whose tastes and interests may well be generalized for the purposes of discussion but who in the end are as individual and far-reaching as any other group of people in our society. "It is no secret that among our youthful patrons there are many young people whose mathematical, scientific, artistic and literary capabilities are so special that they are left without materials in YA collections."[15]

Finally, the concept of "sermon selecting," to which most of us would be opposed in principle, can also be seen as an easy pejorative for an idea that is not so easily dismissed.

Don't the books they read, the films they see, and the television programs they view have an effect on our youth? . . . there is an aura of unreality that adults, including teachers and librarians, should not impose their values on others. Those who adopt this seemingly . . . neutral position, pride themselves on being above the battle. Yet the decision not to choose any values is also a choice. The questions is: "which choices are the wisest . . . for future generations?"[16]

The role of librarians as professional selectors who care about quality materials for young people and purchase them is heavily relied upon by editors who seek and publish YA literature, especially in traditional hardcover editions. Despite the tendency of teenagers themselves to favor paperbacks and despite the popularity of boilerplate series fiction among them and the publishing profits this trend represents, some editors remain utterly committed to publishing the best new and highest-quality writing that comes onto the scene. One prominent editor in the field trusts that "if we do something right, it will find its way to the right readers." His goal is to publish "books that kids will treasure." He agrees with Leonhardt's concept of developing readers but is "happy to have other houses producing the easier fare." He believes there is, indeed, room and an audience for quality work—the new literary voices who are writing for young adults. If we think that there is not, then "we really underestimate kids."[17]

In publishing houses as well as in libraries, a dialectic between quality and mass appeal is generated and played out, and librarians are an intricate part of it. YA hardcover publishers rely greatly on the library market (some, 100 percent), so that starred, featured, and positive reviews are essential for the financial success of a book, both in initial sales and for paperback rights. YA hardcover publishing can be extremely rewarding, economically and professionally, to the editor who publishes a highly acclaimed book. Is this threatened by what seems like an increasing tendency of YA librarians to buy many more paperbacks than hardcover? Apparently not, because the sales do not need to be as numerically high as in paperback sales to generate a healthy profit. In contrast, although we librarians seem to purchase so many paperbacks, the primary outlet for paperback reprints and series fiction is actually the bookstore, not the library, and the market is direct sales to teenagers. Therefore, a starred review and/or an inclusion on a "bests" list will usually generate sufficient demand to make a hardcover book not only a financial success but a successful debut for a new and potentially important voice on the YA scene.

YALSA's Best Books for Young Adults (BBYA) list is a microcosm of the quality/popularity continuum on which we all seek a comfortable niche. Since its inception, this committee has confronted and weighed the issues in its nominations and at the meetings where the books are discussed and voted upon. Potential or demonstrated appeal is one of the criteria for inclusion, but so is literary merit.

In her comments on "best" lists, Leonhardt takes one side on this issue. She deplores the fact that "best" lists for young people virtually never have popular series books on them or comic books or horror books by R.L. Stine or *Star Trek* books. In fact, she says, "all of the really 'bread and butter' reading books are omitted." She continues:

The sad thing is that these award givers and critics really do mean well. But they haven't seen what I've seen in the last twenty years: thousands and thousands of high school kids who hate reading. I think many of these kids would have been literate, enthusiastic readers if they had been encouraged to read the series books and comics they can easily love.[18]

While this point of view is persuasive, what would be the state of YA publishing if literary merit played no role in our selection? Where would this put the YA reader who is ready to enjoy more sophisticated fare, if what we did as librarians, reviewers, and award givers was to simply endorse mass appeal and follow the whims of popularity?

Michael Cart, a past member of the committee, a YA author, and a 1997–1998 president of YALSA, wrote:

The part that such popularity should play in evaluating the merits of a book for young adults has occasioned much lively debate over the years, particularly among members of the Best Books committees, as I discovered when I served in 1989. The committee guidelines then—as now—in force were silent on this particular point though the committee members were certainly not! For my part, I think that if popularity is to be a major consideration, then we might as well declare R.L. Stine and Francine Pascal to be the greatest young adult authors of the century and be done with it![19]

The dilemma that Best Books committee members face is the same one we face in our own everyday selection process. How much emphasis to place where? Two *Booklist* advisers to the BBYA comment:

When I was doing a study [for the "Still Alive in '75" ALA Preconference] it was fascinating to me to see the number of "best" books from twenty-five years ago that kids were still reading twenty-five, thirty years after they had been on the list. I thought, "Well, there are some that really lasted and didn't go out of date." They were still popular, still in collections, still on the New York Public Library's recommended Books for the Teen Age. That leads straight to the '$64 question.' For the purpose of this business, "best" should not just be popular. It seems to me you always start out with quality and then go to appeal. Quality should take priority. It's why you're doing this, for heaven's sake. (Barbara Duree)

Any librarian on the floor is trying to make readers out of kids. We may start them off with something really simple, but we're trying to move them up into more sophisticated reading. And this is what this kind of list should do. We have to have a wide range because we have our reluctant readers who are reading *Headman* and we have the more sophisticated ones who are reading *Handmaids' Tale*. What we're trying to choose for this list are the books that have quality and something to offer. They're not just light fluff. They have, I don't want to say "a message," but they have a certain significance or value. There are so many fantasies, so many science books, so many of every kind of book. What we're looking for is the best. There are so many whodunits that you read like you eat popcorn, that don't belong on the list. But then there is Mary Higgins Clark's best. That's where we want to move young adults to from Nancy Drew.[20] (Sally Estes)

But this does not, of course, negate the value of having Nancy Drew herself. Many librarians, even those who say they buy mostly paperbacks and lean heavily in the direction of popularity, use the BBYA list every year to aid them in selection. But they still understand the role of "rubbish," as YA author Peter Dickinson affectionately calls it, in library collections for young people.

If they did not have this diet they would not be reading at all, and in a verbal culture I think it is better that the child should read something than read nothing. And perhaps . . . the habit of reading—even the habit of reading rubbish—may somehow evoke a tendency to read things that are not rubbish. I know two or three of my contemporaries who were . . . total philistines in their boyhood; but they used to read a considerable amount of rubbish and have now, from the habit of reading, become considerably more literate than I.[21]

Having been on both the adult and children's selection committees, I think that both tend to buy anything that is popular and then enough quality so we can sleep at night. (YA librarian, Alaska)[22]

Adjectives like cheap, frivolous, and homogenized abound when series fiction for teenagers is the topic for discussion . . . [but] teens should have the same freedom of choice as their elders to read *Moby Dick* one day and *Sweet Valley High* the next. [23]

And they do. My own informal surveys with teens in the library show that even the "good" readers—maybe especially the good readers—all report reading series fiction at least some of the time. Among the reasons: in a series, the characters and setting are familiar, and it's like coming home. Some other comments:

Question: Do you believe that the librarian should buy books that are challenging or serious reading even if they are not "popular" with everyone? Answers: "Yes, because people can like a book and everyone else may not agree." "There are young adults who just don't read 'teen' books, and who enjoy the type of books they read in school, and the library should cater to everyone." "No, because if people don't take it out, it's a waste of time and library money."[24]

I polled them directly about the criteria librarians should consider when choosing books for the YA collection; the choices were "mostly popularity," "mostly quality," or "equal consideration of both." The third choice won. Maybe teens are more open-minded than we give them credit for!

HARDBACK BOOKS VERSUS PAPERBACK BOOKS: HERE FOR TOMORROW OR TODAY?

So how do librarians resolve the question of paperback versus hardcover collections? Again, the solutions are extremely varied, depending on the particular librarian, the role of administration, budgetary considerations, and how much is devoted to other sorts of materials.

I have been purchasing far fewer copies of hardback fiction than has been done in the past. Basically because they don't circulate very well and I get tired of pitching boxes of pristine books. Requests for new YA fiction . . . primarily come from YA librarians, not their clientele." (YA librarian, Washington)[25]

So, teens prefer the paperback format. Yet, with a few exceptions, the reviewing journals focus on hardback books. Any librarian with a commitment to the purchase of new paperbacks must either pay frequent visits to the local book superstores, get subscriptions to *VOYA* and *Kliatt Paperback Book Review*, make sure to read all the advertisements and publishers' catalogs and not just reviews, or a combination of these.

In recent years, some publishers, in a recognition of the role of the paperback in the teenage reader's life, have published simultaneously in hardcover and paperback. This change was welcomed by YA librarians, especially those who regularly "wait for paper" for all but the most highly reviewed and/or proven YA writers.

Published reviews play a big part in buying decisions, especially for hardcovers. I do wish that new books came out in paperback. There is no contest between the circulation of hardcovers and paperbacks. I'll often wait to buy a paperback of a slightly less well-reviewed book. I assume that in four or five years I'll be discarding the hardcover. Some of our YA librarians question ever buying hardcover for their libraries. I would estimate that I buy paperback to hardcover fiction about four to one. (YA librarian, Ohio) [26]

From a former YA librarian who utilized a lot of teen input throughout her selection process:

They want the series stuff, *Fear Street*, *SVH* etc., but there were also teens who wanted stuff like Rinaldi and Francesca Block. I tried to buy hardcovers of authors or books I thought would be important mostly as encouragement to the publishers to continue publishing great stuff. I did probably buy about fifty paperbacks for every hardcover. I bought more duplicates especially for middle schoolers as friends like to read the same thing at the same time.[27]

I do think that YA librarians are preoccupied by quality vs. popularity in a way that adult librarians aren't. . . . What adults want is by definition OK. I buy some paperback series, not too many because it irritates me to spend too much on all the imitation series that pop up. But it seems OK with my patrons. I also make sure I have new paperback copies of classics in the rack. I would estimate that I buy paperback to hardcover fiction about 4 to 1.[28]

My entire YA fiction collection is all paperback. This decision is very hard every time I see great material only come out in hardback. My parameters are budget and library popular materials policy. Published reviews do greatly influence what I buy. I use *Hotpicks* and *Kliatt*, but supplement heavily with *VOYA* and *SLJ*. (YA librarian, California)[29]

In his analysis of why YA librarians continue to buy hardcover books, while teens clearly prefer paperbacks, Patrick Jones lists ''inertia'' at the top of the list. But some teens, like adults, like the feel of a new book in their hands, and others are smart enough to know that if you wanted to read the latest in YA fiction, you'd better be ready to read a hardcover! How many of those teens are part of your reading public?

BOOKS VERSUS "OTHER" : NARROW OR BROAD COLLECTIONS

The issue of quality versus popularity also has its ramifications in the choice of the types of materials in the collection. Some YA collections still consist of only print materials: hardcover books, paperback books, and some magazines. It may be assumed that purchasing comic books or graphic novels involves a quality decision, or these materials may be seen as a ''waste'' of the taxpayers' money because they are so easily destroyed or stolen. Any reading of Leonhardt's or Jones' books will encourage the inclusion of comics or graphic novels for the value they have in attracting young people to reading.

CDs, which are popular with teens and which may vary widely depending on the ethnic mix of the served population, are often not purchased by the YA department because they are faddish or rapidly "walk." But the presence of popular CDs in the YA area may create a link with kids who might otherwise view the section as a highbrow collection or a place where they will never find anything interesting. Books on tape may also be an important part of a popular YA collection when so many teens' encounters with books may be limited, their literacy may be weak, or their romance with the Walkman may be strong.

YA librarians need to employ maximum powers of observation and their people skills with teenagers to determine which items, outside the traditional materials, might have appeal and should be stocked in their department. Informal polls, written surveys, and good rapport with teens will help librarians, and popularity may be the main criterion in building this segment of the collection.

CURRICULUM SUPPORT VERSUS RECREATIONAL READING: TEEN AS STUDENT VERSUS THE WHOLE TEENAGER

Librarians report that much of their YA collection is curriculum-driven. That is, since many, if not most, teens come most often to the library in connection with class assignments, materials to help with this aspect of their lives is a focus of collecting. Non-fiction books on a YA and adult level and literary classics therefore claim their place as budgetary giant, especially where school media centers are weak or underfunded. In many libraries the non-fiction materials are interfiled with the adult collection to give the teens the maximum spread to suit their variable abilities. The percentage of materials purchased in this area varies widely with library and philosophy but could come to more than 50 percent of the budget. Other non-fiction items will also be included in the collection because of the popularity or timeliness of the issue; books on self-help, teen pregnancy, and coping skills of all varieties are among these items.

Finding a balance here is a key job for the YA librarian, because, unlike school libraries, our role is to serve the whole teenager, not just the student. We also strive to address the recreational and spiritual needs of our clientele. Sometimes public YA specialists become so enmeshed in their relationship with schools, teachers, and assignments that we lose sight of our mission as public librarians—to serve the needs of the individual teenager in all his or her facets.

Therefore, while relations with teachers and school librarians are important— especially so we can receive that all-important assignment alert before the deluge!—our emphasis must be on serving the whole teenager. Non-fiction balance also falls on that continuum of quality and popularity. We are only partly members of the educational hierarchy; our root connection must be to the teens themselves.

CULTURAL DIVERSITY IN THE YA COLLECTION: POPULAR WITH WHOM?

Building a "popular collection" does not mean the same thing in every library. "Know your community," a principle in library service, is no less important in the YA collection. It may be even more important because identities are being formed, and teens' seeing themselves in what they read plays a role in self-knowledge and self-acceptance. Further, what is immensely popular with a majority of teens in one town may be absolutely nowhere with their counterparts in the next town.

Many towns and cities have large immigrant populations, and many of these immigrants are teens or preteens. Who these immigrant teens are and what their interests and needs might be are also crucial in building both a quality and a popular collection for YAs in your particular locale. Therefore, a continuing awareness of community change is as crucial to YA librarians as to their director.

Is quality vs. popularity an issue? Always. I try to serve a 50% Latino population in the school. Popularity becomes more important when it means my kids will read more English and identify with it more. Yet quality is never too far away. (YA librarian, California)[30]

Although the idea that young people should find *themselves* reflected in the books they read may be generally accepted, the idea that teens also need to *see others* reflected in the books they read is not always given the same lip service or budgetary support. In places where there are few African-American teens, for example, I hear librarians express that, except for the best-known authors, books about black kids are "shelf-sitters" and therefore can't be purchased. The rationale is that teenagers do not want to read about people and places so far from themselves. In her book-length bibliography, *Against Borders*, Hazel Rochman addresses this assumption:

We're too quick to say, "kids won't read this." We each live in a small world and talk to people like ourselves and reinforce each other and we think everyone agrees with us. If you choose good stories and *if you promote them*, it's not true that books in translation or about foreign cultures are only for the "gifted," that young people won't read books with a strong sense of a foreign place.[31] (emphasis added)

While continuing to consider the issue of popularity—what kids will select on their own—we need to balance this again with our expertise as reader advisers, as adults knowledgeable and excited about a good story. Kids might not pick it up on their own, but if they are persuaded to do so, they might enjoy it immensely and may come to see it as "a real find."

It's obvious that for mainstream young people, books about "other" cultures are not as easy to pick up as *YM* magazine, or as easy to watch as *Beverly Hills 90210*, and, in fact, they shouldn't be. We don't want a homogenized culture. If you're a kid in New York, then reading about a refugee in North Korea, or a teenager in the bush in Africa, or a Mormon in Utah, involves some effort, some imagination, some opening up of who you are. In talking about books with kids, I always start with a story set where they are, here and now. Then, once they're listening, I move to other cultures, in this country and across the world and back again.[32]

In our role as book promoters, not merely book buyers, we can influence what becomes popular and what is appreciated by our teen readers. An example is a 1995 title, *Damned Strong Love*.[33] It is a Holocaust story with a twist: a non-Jewish Polish teenager falls in love with an occupying German soldier, which leads to catastrophe because the teenager is a young gay man. Described in the first person, this book—hardly one to be chosen by teens without pushing—proved to be one of the most memorable books read by my teen group that year. It was a love story, a war story, a story of innocence, error, ambiguity, and regret. It was based on true events. It brought them someplace they had never been and never expected to go. It gave them a view of the Holocaust they had never considered. (One teen even gave it to her mother to read, with the same results.) It changed their views, and what's more, they really enjoyed reading it. We can never underestimate our readers, because we do them a great disservice. As Hazel Rochman says:

A good book can help to break down . . . barriers. Books can make a difference in dispelling prejudice and building community: not with role models and literal recipes, not with noble messages about the human family, but with enthralling stories that make us imagine the lives of others. A good story lets you know people as individuals in all their particularity and conflict; and once you see someone as a person—flawed, complex, striving—then you've reached beyond stereotype. Stories, writing them, telling them, sharing them, transforming them, enrich us and connect us and help us know each other.[34]

THE BOTTOM LINE: SELECTION WITH KNOWLEDGE, INTELLIGENCE, EMPATHY, AND RESPECT

Perhaps the whole quality/popularity puzzle is another way of saying that we need to employ all of our professional skills as librarians and human experience as adults in building collections for young adults. We need to take into account the whole range of their needs as developing adults and, hopefully, lifelong readers. As Richard Peck says:

We can get caught up in the surface tastes of the young for science fiction, romance, horse stories, sports sagas, fantasy and the grotesque. We do better to realize that they read, as all fictions readers do, for the human relationships they have or want. [35]

NOTES

1. "Library Journal Classics," *Library Journal* 121, no. 11 (June 15, 1996): S1.

2. Nora Rawlinson's article by this title in the November 15, 1981, issue of *Library Journal* fostered a debate within the library world that centered around the Baltimore County Public Library's focus on circulation figures to judge a book's value in the library.

3. Patrick Jones, *Connecting Young Adults and Libraries: A How-to-Do-It Manual* (New York: Neal-Schuman, 1992), 29.

4. Murray L. Bob, "The Case for Quality Book Selection" (partial reprint of an article first published in 1982), *Library Journal* 121, no. 11 (June 15, 1996): S2.

5. Mary Leonhardt, *Parents Who Love Reading, Kids Who Don't* (New York: Crown, 1993), 28.

6. Margaret A. Edwards, *The Fair Garden and the Swarm of Beasts* (1969; reprint, with a foreword by Patty Campbell, Chicago: American Library Association, 1994), 58.

7. George Watson Cole, "Fiction in Libraries: A Plea for the Masses" (partial reprint of an article first published in 1894), *Library Journal* 121, no. 11 (June 15, 1996): S8.

8. E-mail correspondence facilitated by the PUBYAC listserv, July 1996.

9. Constance Mellon, "Teenagers Do Read: What Rural Youth Say about Leisure Reading," *School Library Journal* 33, no. 6 (February 1987): 30.

10. E-mail correspondence facilitated through PUBYAC listserv, July 1996.

11. Dennis Kininger, PUBYAC posting, 8/27/95.

12. Evie Wilson-Lingbloom, *Hangin' Out at Rocky Creek* (Metuchen, NJ: Scarecrow Press, 1994), 106.

13. Lillian Shapiro, "Quality or Popularity: Selective Criteria for YAs," *School Library Journal* 24, no. 9 (May 1978): 24.

14. Ibid., 27.

15. Ibid., 26.

16. Ibid., 24.

17. Author's personal interview with Marc Aronson, Senior Editor at Henry Holt, July 24, 1996, notes.

18. Leonhardt, *Parents Who Love Reading, Kids Who Don't*, 31.

19. Michael Cart, *From Romance to Realism* (New York: HarperCollins, 1996), 85–86.

20. Betty Carter, *Best Books for Young Adults* (Chicago: American Library Association, 1994), 32.

21. Peter Dickinson, "In Defence of Rubbish," *Children's Literature in Education* 3 (November 1970): 10.

22. E-mail correspondence.

23. Cart, *From Romance to Realism*, 102.

24. From author's informal surveys of teen reading preferences, June 1996.

25. Author's correspondence, July 1996.

26. E-mail correspondence.

27. Ibid.

28. Ibid.

29. Ibid.

30. Ibid.

31. Hazel Rochman, *Against Borders* (Chicago: American Library Association, 1993), 25.

32. Ibid., 28.

33. Lutz Van Dijk, *Damned Strong Love* (New York: Henry Holt, 1995).

34. Rochman, *Against Borders*, 19.

35. Richard Peck, *Love and Death at the Mall* (New York: Delacorte Press, 1994), 72.

8

Young Adult Non-fiction: Not Just for Homework Anymore

Rick Kerper

In 1976 non-fiction author Milton Meltzer posed the question "Where Do All the Prizes Go?" in his classic article bearing this title. He levied an indictment against the literary community, charging them with bias against non-fiction. Meltzer pointed out the numerous literary prizes awarded to fiction year after year, with almost no recognition of the excellence produced by writers of non-fiction.[1]

During the past 20 years the literary community's outlook on non-fiction has changed slowly. As Meltzer stated in 1994:

Nonfiction writers have struggled long and hard to break down the stereotype that plagues our work. The books we write are still, in many places, by many people, dismissed as "fact" books. But are they merely "informational"? Not if they are any good. To their creation the same quality of imagination is as essential as it is in the writing of fiction. For history has to be imagined before it can be written. Yes, the historian relies first of all on documents and other sources. But the events and personalities have to be reconstructed by the imagination.[2]

In some quarters non-fiction now is recognized as literature—as art. It is no less creative than Paul Janeczko's poetry, Cynthia Voigt's realism, Robin McKinley's fantasy, or David Macaulay's picture books. Like these talented authors and illustrators, creators of non-fiction for young adults render their subjects with the "skill and care of art." They write the *literature of fact*.

Today, non-fiction books are strong contenders for, and winners of, major literary prizes.[3] This revised outlook is directly attributable to the skillful writing and meticulous production of non-fiction. In this chapter I discuss some of the outstanding contributions made in this genre during the mid-1990s. I focus on books in three areas: the humanities and social sciences, the sciences, and biography. Outstanding writers and works of non-fiction are presented, as well as some of the characteristics that make them exceptional. I deal with content and craft as I discuss non-fiction as the literary and sometimes visual art that it is, for as Milton Meltzer states:

Literary art has ... two related aspects: its *subject* [italics in original], what a book is about, and the *means* [italics in original] the writer uses to convey that material, the *craft*. The craft is the making, shaping, forming, selecting. And what the reader gets from the exercise of the writer's craft upon a subject is an experience. If the subject is significant, and the artist is up to it, then the book can enlarge, it can deepen, it can intensify the reader's experience of life. Imagination, invention, selection, language, form ... these are just as important to the making of a good book of biography, history, or science as to the making of a piece of fiction.[4]

THE HUMANITIES AND SOCIAL SCIENCES

As a middle school and high school teacher, I found that students heightened my awareness of the power that visual images had upon them. It was apparent that some of the most dominant messages in our society were conveyed to them through visual forms. Whether through television, cinema, or magazines, images hooked their attention, and ideas embedded within remained with them for long periods. Books, however, did not have the same effect. The almost exclusive use of print, except for brief folios placed in the center of the book, failed to capitalize on the visual nature of the audience. Straight text did not speak to these teen readers. Visuals drew responses.

Recently, one of the most dramatic changes in non-fiction has occurred in the visual displays. More than ever before, illustrations and other graphics have been incorporated throughout the pages of non-fiction books. The inclusion of carefully selected, archival photographs, of color photography, and of lavish illustrations speaks to a society in which technology has increased young adults' visual orientation.[5] Close-ups and unusual perspectives are central to meanings constructed from the books. In some cases, photographs have assumed a dominant position, "with the words forming a backdrop to the pictures much like a voice-over on television."[6]

Russell Freedman's *Kids at Work: Lewis Hine and the Crusade against Child Labor* is an exemplar within the fields of art and history. This book visually documents the abuse of children in early twentieth-century factories, fields, mines, mills, and streets. The investigative photographs taken by Lewis Hine speak loudly of this exploitative activity. Freedman's text emphasizes the need for social reform within early industrialized American society. Integrated with this social history, Freedman presents a partial biography of a photographer who raised the country's social consciousness and helped to bring about a change in child labor. Connecting the past to the present, Freedman ends with a brief commentary on current conditions:

Compared to conditions in 1904, when the National Child Labor Committee was founded, gratifying progress has been made. Still, child labor has not vanished from America. It exists today among the children of recent immigrants who toil next to their mothers behind the closed doors of sweatshops; among a half-million poverty-wracked children of migrant farm workers; among hundreds of thousands of youngsters who hold jobs prohibited by law, or who work excessive hours while attending school.[7]

Kids at Work presents a crusader for social reform as well as a glimpse at social history. However, as an art book *Kids at Work* is also highly notable. With a box camera Hine captured a perspective of youth that gives a viewer pause and beckons action. Freedman's well-crafted text sews Hine's black-and-white photographs into a compelling American quilt. Each panel presents the face of America at an earlier time in this century. Although connected to the whole, each photograph can stand on its own and communicate in rich detail.

The Middle Passage by Tom Feelings relies on historical narrative and illustrations to communicate the emotions as well as the facts of the African diaspora. Feelings consciously chose to expound through images alone on the middle leg of the slave trade triangle that brought human cargo to America:

Callous indifference or outright brutal characterizations of Africans are embedded in the language of the Western World. It is a language so infused with direct and indirect racism that it would be difficult, if not impossible, using this language in my book, to project anything black as positive. This gave me a final reason for attempting to tell the story through art alone. I believed strongly that with a picture book any African in this world could pick up and see and feel what happened to us on those ships.[8]

Through an explanation of Dr. Feelings' process for creating the book and historical background to African slave trade by Dr. John Henrik Clarke, Feelings uses words as an introduction to his narrative pictures. The images, however, carry the burden for informing the reader about people's inhumanity to people. They simultaneously communicate the nonlinear dimensions of knowledge such as feelings and relationships much better than the linear sign system of words. This uncommon union of print and pictures creates an outstanding work of art and history.

In addition to the visual transformations in non-fiction, a change in tone has occurred in some books. Non-fiction, the once-serious genre of fact, has expanded to include humorous treatments that are no less informational. Bruce Brooks tackles the issue of masculinity in a collection of twelve essays titled *Boys Will Be*. While many books on teen girls and their bodies, feelings, and relationships exist, Brooks' essays fill a void for teen boys. He focuses on many choices that face boys as they travel the road to manhood and explores them with feeling, with humor, and with wit. In "Chitchat" Brooks explores why boys taunt one another with what appear to be hateful and contemptful remarks. "It would simply never occur to a boy to walk up to a box turtle sunning itself on a rock in the woods and say, 'Yo, Buttface! Did you know your eyes are crossed and your nostrils look like a two-car garage?' Yet this is precisely the sort of comment"[9] that boys hurl at one another continually.

In "Real Boys Read Books" Brooks challenges the oft-heard contention of librarians and educators, "Boys don't like to read!" Chiding the adults and societal norms that perpetuate such antiquated thinking, Brooks persuades young adults that the independent nature of reading prepares boys for their adult lives:

Boys want to avoid anything that casts doubt upon their masculinity. They want to dissociate themselves from girls (who, as we have seen, have pretty much claimed libraries as their turf).

But—boys also want to read. They *love* [italics in original] to read. . . . And funnily enough, the main reason boys like to read is that they gravitate naturally toward activities that develop the strengths that will make them good men. Reading is an act of independence: you do it alone, and you are in charge. It is an act of liberty . . . it is true that reading can be subversive—that is, it can allow boys to discover things men would rather hide from them, or encourage boys to think in ways men would prefer they didn't. But this relentless pursuit of discovery—finding things out for yourself, new things, your *own* [italics in original] things—is a big part of preparing for manhood.[10]

Each of these books speaks to the interests of young adults. They address important societal and personal issues with which teenagers grapple. Topics such as child labor and the African diaspora are common subjects for school reports. They represent the injustices in society that teens ponder beyond the classroom. Similarly, the topics addressed in *Boys Will Be* provide young adults with an opportunity to consider coming-of-age issues. Thus teenagers recreationally read and view these books to deal with issues arising in their attempt to define their places in the world and to visualize experiences removed from their lives. As the primary audience for *Kids at Work*, *The Middle Passage*, and *Boys Will Be*, these books belong in the YA collection rather than the juvenile collection, a place teenagers hate to be seen, or the adult collection, a place teenagers will head if they need information for reports. (See Table 8.1 for notable humanities and social science titles.)

THE SCIENCES

Non-fiction literature in the sciences is extremely important to teenagers' studies in our schools. Yet, it is a literature from which many teens shy away, fearing

Table 8.1
Notable Non-fiction in the Humanities and Social Sciences

Author	Title
Ashabranner, Brent	*Still a Nation of Immigrants*
Bode, Janet	*Death Is Hard to Live With: Teenagers and How They Cope with Loss*
Colman, Penny	*Rosie the Riveter: Women Working on the Home Front in World War II*
Denenberg, Barry	*Voices from Vietnam*
Lawrence, Jacob	*The Great Migration: An American Story*
McKissack, Patricia and Frederick	*Red-Tail Angels: The Story of the Tuskegee Airmen of World War II*
Murphy, Jim	*Across America on an Emigrant Train*
	The Great Fire
	A Young Patriot: The American Revolution as Experienced by One Boy

an inability to understand. At a time when the advancement of scientific understanding is a major goal of our educational system, science trade books play an important role. The best non-fiction simplifies and synthesizes highly complex concepts, making them understandable to young adults. The skilled writer of science books achieves this end without sacrificing accuracy. The creation of tightly organized exposition rests upon the logical exploration of a guiding statement.[11]

Donna Jackson's *The Bone Detectives: How Forensic Anthropologists Solve Crimes and Uncover Mysteries of the Dead*, with photographs by Charlie Fellenbaum, asserts that "all [bones] tell their secrets to the few who speak their language."[12] The alluring title and provocative lead limit the focus of the book. Through the use of a chronological structure and headings, Jackson organizes her information and makes the reader an insider to forensic anthropologists' application of their science to human bones and the solving of a murder. She concludes by discussing briefly how forensic anthropologists have applied their science to mysteries involving human remains from the dawn of humankind to the Old West.

In presenting how the forensic anthropologist identifies a human victim, Jackson uses clear, simple sentences: "Luckily everyone's skeletal frame is unique. Sometimes heredity carves out distinctive markers. Other times, important events such as injuries, illnesses, and childbearing etch their imprint. To the bone detective, each inscription is another clue to identifying the unknown."[13] This writing style makes a complex subject more comprehensible. It invites the uninitiated reader into the technical world of the scientist. Asides and pages of simply presented, related technical information titled "Forensic File[s]" also help the reader to construct a broader knowledge of the topic.

In addition to a clear text, Fellenbaum's sharp color photography enables the viewer to create a mental picture of the recovered skeletal remains, facial restoration, and the computerized skull-photograph superimposition. Carefully sequenced and crisply captioned images illuminate the running discourse.

Bruce Brooks' *Making Sense: Animal Perception and Communication* uses varying camera perspectives to show in full color the sensory organs of some of the animals discussed. He explores the twofold question, How do animals perceive the things that they do and know the things that they know? Brooks uses the individual senses to organize a consideration of these questions. Each sense-oriented chapter layers example upon example of animals' using their senses to interact within their environment. For example, Brooks discusses how honeybees depend on sight within their communities:

When different scouts found different spots, they met and danced to describe the qualities of their sites to each other and a small, select group from the hive—sort of an architectural review board. When this "conference" reached a consensus, the hive would swarm out and occupy the chosen site.

Now, *that's* [italics in original] visual communication—in fact, it's practically sign language. Still, quite a few skeptics claim they are unconvinced that it is "real" communication.[14]

The result of this rich detail is an awareness of the complexity in sensing and knowing within nature. As this example also demonstrates, Brooks presents a coherent viewpoint but notes challenges to his ideas.

In the end, Brooks moves this exploration of an "animal's physical and mental readiness to understand the messages of the environment"[15] to a more encompassing level—the level of communicative intelligence. He raises a critical question:

When we add up all the input of the senses, do we have the whole story of an animal's moment-to-moment life? A crackle in the underbrush, a scent on the shifting breeze, a flicker of white feathers through the leaves, the feel of the dry earth underfoot, and the metallic aftertaste of food that was too little and too long ago—does this sum really give us the sense of what it is to be a hungry fox waiting to pounce on a towhee in the late afternoon of a cloudy fall day? No. Something is missing, something that flows between the smelling and the hearing and the feeling, and so on, something that translates their input into knowledge, memory, foresight, strategy, and action. Something that doesn't just receive sensory data but, rather, makes sense out of them.[16]

Like the scientist, Brooks carefully observes the natural world and considers the implications of the evidence surrounding him. From the evidence he hypothesizes about the "wholeness" of the sensory systems and animals' ability to "make sense."

Bob Friedhoffer also has observed the natural world. From the time he was a child Friedhoffer wondered about what made toys work. In *Toying around with Science: The Physics behind Toys and Gags*, he offers young people with the same curiosity an opportunity to explore the scientific principles behind toys. He breaks the book into eight types of inexpensive toys: air and water pressure, magnetic, friction, flywheel, vibration, lever, spring-powered, and windup. As a final chapter, Friedhoffer briefly reviews scientific principles related to matter and energy, mass and weight, simple machines, and pressure. Line drawings, a glossary, and an index enhance the clarity and accessibility of the material in the book. Friedhoffer also offers suggestions for further reading to the inquisitive mind whose appetite for science in the real world has increased from this exploration.

Many of the teenagers whom I have known have left behind the curiosity about the physical world that was so natural when they were preschoolers and elementary school students. Books like those described invite young adults to become inquirers once again. Through photographs offering unique and intriguing perspectives, text using figurative language to create clear mental images, and subjects relating to students' lives, much scientific non-fiction draws readers into books and makes them wonder, question, and hypothesize. The grisly topic of murder and photographs of the application of forensic anthropological science make Jackson's book a perfect selection for a book talk. Superior writing and bookmaking on many topics, leading to presentations that are interesting and understandable to teens, make scientific trade books important choices for YA collections. These books can lead to clearly focused and intriguing reports and ongoing reading about topics of personal interest. (See Table 8.2 for notable science titles.)

BIOGRAPHY

Over the years I have observed the frequency with which teenagers read biographies and autobiographies. Clearly, the more personal and more human the account is, the more interest it generates among teen readers. At a time when young adults are experimenting with various life choices, opportunities to delve into the choices that others have made is fascinating. These narratives remove some of the mysteries from life decisions and connect the teenager with the competing emotions and ideas of the famous and infamous alike.

Quoting the *Times Saturday Review* critic Dennis Potter, Margery Fisher states:

To explore that "tangle of contradictory motives, warring emotions, habit ridden responses, fearful apprehensions and improbable longings" beneath a man's [*sic*] "outer front" . . . the biographer needs the imagination of a novelist; even when he uses imag-

Table 8.2
Notable Non-fiction in the Sciences

Author	Title
Bortz, Fred	*Catastrophe*
Brandenburg, Jim	*An American Safari: Adventures on the North American Prairie*
	Sand and Fog: Adventures in Southern Africa
Fradin, Dennis Brindell	*"We Have Conquered Pain": The Discovery of Anesthesia*
Freidhoffer, Bob	*Magic and Perception: The Art and Science of Fooling the Senses*
Giblin, James Cross	*When Plague Strikes: The Black Death, Smallpox, AIDS*
Pringle, Laurence	*Coral Reefs: Earth's Undersea Treasures*
Quinlan, Susan	*The Case of the Mummified Pigs and Other Mysteries in Nature*
Scott, Michael	*The Young Oxford Book of Ecology*
Skurzynski, Gloria	*Get the Message: Telecommunications in Your High-Tech World*

ination to go behind fact and interpret character, he is faced in the end, with mystery.
. . . Myth and reality are constantly at war in the biographer's enterprise.[17]

Winston Churchill, a former British prime minister, has become a mythic figure of the twentieth century. In *Winston Churchill: Soldier, Statesman, Artist*, John B. Severance imbues this notable statesman with humanity, enabling the teenage reader to sit down and to participate in this life story. Recognized for his leadership, military mind, and writing, Churchill was less well known as a warmhearted family man who reveled in success and wallowed in depression. Severance explores the complexity of this man known in later years as Sir Winston. Highlighting the impact of parental inattention, the unsuccessful Dardanelles campaign in World War I, the attack of appendicitis during an election campaign, and the unpopularity of his support for his friend's, King Edward VIII, marriage intentions as well as his numerous political and military triumphs, Severance gets beneath Churchill's "outer front." He reveals a man in turmoil between warmth and gruffness, conservatism and liberalism, happiness and despair. Citing the essay "Consistency in Politics," in which Churchill quotes writer and philosopher Ralph Waldo Emerson, Severance exposes an individual who is not doggedly devoted to consistency of thought. "A foolish consistency is the hobgoblin of little minds. . . . Speak what you think now in hard words and tomorrow speak what tomorrow thinks in hard words again, though it contradict everything you said today."[18]

These words frame the picture of Sir Winston that Severance paints—a man who remained true to his own beliefs, a man who "knew how to use words as an artist uses colors."[19]

Russell Freedman's writing in *The Life and Death of Crazy Horse* reveals the clash of myth and reality. Crazy Horse is a mythic Teton Sioux (Oglala) figure remembered for his wild and daring deeds in battle. However, as Freedman discloses, Crazy Horse was a much more complex individual. He was a quiet and sensitive man who provided for the needs of the less fortunate within his tribe. Freedman's finely wrought and engaging narrative captures this complexity in his personality:

As a war leader, he was forceful and inspiring. But at home in his village, he remained a quiet loner who spent much time by himself. Though a shirt-wearer [honorary protector of the people], he seldom attended leadership councils. And when he did attend, he rarely spoke. "In his own tipi he would joke, and when he was on the warpath with a small party, he would joke to make his warriors feel good . . . but around the village he hardly noticed anybody, except little children."[20]

The child's body lay on top of the scaffold, wrapped in a red blanket. Tied to the blanket was a deerskin doll. And on the scaffold's posts hung some of the playthings that They-Are-Afraid-of-Her had loved—a rattle of antelope hooves strung on rawhide, a bouncing bladder with little stones inside, a painted willow hoop. When Crazy Horse saw all this, he could not contain his grief. He mounted the scaffold, lay facedown beside the body of his daughter, and with wracking sobs let his sorrow sweep over him.[21]

In addition to Freedman's humanizing text, the black-and-white photographs of Sioux pictographs capture notable tribal events. They complement the text and provide access to a Sioux perspective—a reality constructed within the society. As a historian pointed out, "The picture is the rope that ties memory solidly to the stake of truth."[22] These images anchor a mythic Oglala chief within the real world.

The collector of diaries also seeks to get beneath subjects' outer fronts. The interpreting of an original diary requires the collector to search beneath the facts and to seek connections. In *Keeping Secrets: The Girlhood Diaries of Seven Women Writers*, Mary E. Lyons demonstrates how writing for an audience of one helped famous and lesser-known female writers to discover themselves. One chapter in this collective biography is titled "Genteel Poet." It explores the diaries of Alice Dunbar-Nelson, the first African-American woman to publish a book of short stories, and reveals a woman discovering herself. Through her diary writing Dunbar-Nelson, a mulatto, comes to grips with her racial identification in a racist society, her gender in a sexist era, and her sexuality in a homophobic culture. Lyons uses this effusive writing to grapple with the mystery of Alice Dunbar-Nelson's identity. In the end she constructs a character from the life fragments represented in the writing and reveals a woman finding a voice of her own.

Table 8.3
Notable Biographical Non-fiction

Author	Title
Bober, Natalie	*Abigail Adams: Witness to a Revolution*
Cleary, Beverly	*My Own Two Feet: A Memoir*
Denenberg, Barry	*An American Hero: The True Story of Charles A. Lindbergh*
Duggleby, John	*Artist in Overalls: The Life of Grant Wood*
Fleischman, Sid	*The Abracadabra Kid: A Writer's Life*
Freedman, Russell	*Eleanor Roosevelt: A Life of Discovery*
Greenberg, Jan & Jordan, Sandra	*American Eye: Eleven Artists of the Twentieth Century*
Marrin, Albert	*Unconditional Surrender: U.S. Grant and the Civil War* *Virginia's General: Robert E. Lee and the Civil War*
Meltzer, Milton	*Frederick Douglass: In His Own Words*
Reef, Catherine	*John Steinbeck* *Walt Whitman*

Lyons also captures the self-discovery of folk artist Minnie Evans in a limited biography, titled *Painting Dreams: Minnie Evans, Visionary Artist.* At the age of 43, this descendant of African slaves responded to the visions that she had been seeing day and night from the time she was a child. Only as an adult did she begin to render the images that she had collected in her mind. Only after many years of work were her creations recognized within the art community in the United States and abroad. The brightly colored drawings included in the book illuminate the text and the artistic life of Minnie Evans.

Like the books presented, outstanding biography reveals the person within. YA librarians should recommend these books to teenagers in search of the persons beneath their "outer fronts." The riveting stories told within their pages make biographies and autobiographies excellent choices for reading aloud to teens. The life struggles and decisions of others are sure to draw responses from young adults. (See Table 8.3 for notable biographical titles.)

CONCLUSION

As the books discussed in this chapter demonstrate, non-fiction for young adults has changed. The once visually limited and textually dry genre has blossomed. Some of the best writers of fiction are also writing non-fiction today. They have transferred techniques used in writing novels to the creation of non-fiction. Their books do more than present information. Authors of these works "arrange factual materials into artful, literary"[23] presentations, evoking aesthetic responses. Similarly, publishers are taking greater care in the overall design of non-fiction books. The careful attention given to picture books is now being given to non-fiction. The result is more artistically interesting and visually communicative books.

The literary and artistic nature of today's non-fiction is a significant change for YA readers and library collections. No longer is non-fiction a genre that is picked up only when a report is due. It has become a genre that commands the teenage reader's leisure-time attention just as well-written fiction does. These books should hold a place of prominence equal to that of fiction. YA non-fiction has come of age.

NOTES

1. Milton Meltzer, "Where Do All the Prizes Go? The Case for Nonfiction," *The Horn Book Magazine* 52, no. 1 (1976): 17–23.

2. Milton Meltzer, "Where Have All the Prizes Gone?" in *Nonfiction for the Classroom: Milton Meltzer on Writing, History, and Social Responsibility* (New York: Teachers College, Columbia University, 1994), 24. Meltzer has been a long-standing advocate of non-fiction. He has railed against what he perceives as inequitable treatment by award committees and reviewers. See a protest against reviewing in the November/December 1996 issue of *The Horn Book Magazine* (p. 660) and Roger Sutton's reply (pp. 664–65).

3. See award lists for the Orbis Pictus Award for Outstanding Nonfiction for Children, available from the National Council of Teachers of English, and for the John Newbery Medal, available from the American Library Association. The lists are also provided in *Children's Books: Awards and Prizes*, published by the Children's Book Council and updated periodically.

4. Meltzer, "Where Have All the Prizes Gone?" 25.

5. James Cross Giblin, "A Publisher's Perspective," *The Horn Book Magazine* 63, no. 1 (1987): 104–7. Giblin is an outstanding writer recognized for his non-fiction books. He is the recipient of the 1996 Washington Post/Children's Book Guild Award for Nonfiction. This award is given for the body of work produced by an author or an illustrator of non-fiction.

6. Barbara Elleman, "Illustration in Nonfiction," *The Bulletin* 13, no. 3 (1987): 10.

7. Russell Freedman, *Kids at Work: Lewis Hine and the Crusade against Child Labor* (New York: Clarion Books, 1994), 97. Hine quit his job as a New York City teacher to become an investigative photographer for the National Child Labor Committee. He fought for children's right to be children by photographing their use as industrial workers. He believed that pictures tell powerful stories and could raise society's social consciousness. They continue to tell powerful stories today.

8. Tom Feelings, *The Middle Passage* (New York: Dial Books, 1995), unpaged. This book was awarded the Coretta Scott King Award for Illustration. It is given annually to an outstanding African-American illustrator.

9. Bruce Brooks, *Boys Will Be* (New York: Henry Holt, 1993), 10. Brooks writes non-fiction and fiction. He has received an Orbis Pictus Honor Award for his non-fiction and two Newbery Honor Awards for his fiction.

10. Ibid., 70–71.

11. Jo Carr, "Clarity in Science Writing," in *Beyond Fact: Nonfiction for Children and Young People* (Chicago: American Library Association, 1982), 43–53. This book is a significant work in the critical analysis of non-fiction literature.

12. Donna Jackson, *The Bone Detectives: How Forensic Anthropologists Solve Crimes and Uncover Mysteries of the Dead* (Boston: Little, Brown, 1996), 7. Jackson and Charlie Fellenbaum, a photojournalist, followed Dr. Michael Charney, a forensic anthropologist at the Forensic Science Laboratory in Fort Collins, Colorado, through the investigation reported, which required bone-reading to identify skulls and skeletons.

13. Ibid., 24.

14. Bruce Brooks, *Making Sense: Animal Perception and Communication* (New York: Farrar, Straus, Giroux, 1993), 25–26. Brooks received an Orbis Pictus Honor Award for this book.

15. Ibid., 65.

16. Ibid., 65–66.

17. Margery Fisher, "Biography," in *Beyond Fact: Nonfiction for Children and Young People* (Chicago: American Library Association, 1982), 130. Fisher is the author of an important work on non-fiction literature titled *Matters of Fact: Aspects of Nonfiction for Children*, published by Crowell in 1972. Today, this book provides a historical perspective on non-fiction literature.

18. John B. Severance, *Winston Churchill: Soldier, Statesman, Artist* (New York: Clarion Books, 1996), 68.

19. Ibid., 127.

20. Russell Freedman, *The Life and Death of Crazy Horse* (New York: Holiday House, 1996), 72–73. The pictographs used to illustrate this book were produced by Amos Bad Heart Bull, Crazy Horse's cousin. Thirteen years after Crazy Horse's death, Amos purchased a ledger book and began a detailed pictorial history of the Oglala Sioux, which eventually included 400 drawings. These drawings provide an insider's cultural perspective of the tribe's past and traditions.

21. Ibid., 96–97.

22. Ibid., 153.

23. Jack Roundy, "Crafting Fact: Formal Devices in the Prose of John McPhee," in *Literary Nonfiction: Theory, Criticism, Pedagogy* (Carbondale: Southern Illinois University Press, 1989), 71.

9

Pump Up the Volume: Selecting and Developing Recording Collections for Young Adults

James Cook

The connection between young adults and popular music is as strong today — if not stronger—as it has ever been. Most librarians, particularly YA librarians, seek to respond to this interest, struggling with issues of selection and censorship, in an attempt to provide young adults with materials that meet their informational and recreational needs. How to do this is an important aspect of YA librarianship.

THE IMPORTANCE OF MUSIC FOR YOUNG ADULTS

The importance of music in the lives of young adults can arguably be traced back to the advent of the rock and roll of Elvis Presley, solidified with the invasion of British musical groups like the Beatles and the disintegration of racial musical barriers accomplished by the Motown sound of the Supremes. Jones says that "music has been a channel for teen rebellion for years."[1]

A recent poll (see Table 9.1) sponsored by the National Association of Secondary School Principals (NASSP) revealed that 87.4 percent of teenagers identified music as the number one nonschool activity they engage in, with 67.5 percent identifying music as a hobby (and 88.1 percent saying this hobby is a very important part of their lives).[2] Indeed, to today's young adult, music has become a "continuous background of sound."[3] It permeates many of the other

Table 9.1
Nonschool Activities

Activities	% Total	% Males	% Females
1. Listening to music	87.4	83.2	91.6
2. Spending time with friends	82.2	78.8	85.7
3. Watching television/videos	81.9	84.0	79.8
4. Hobbies	57.9	62.4	53.6
5. Playing video games	48.9	68.3	30.3
6. Going to movies	45.4	40.7	50.0
7. Shopping	44.7	23.9	64.7
8. Sports/fitness activities	43.2	52.1	34.9
9. Using personal computers	40.6	46.4	35.3
10. Reading for enjoyment	40.3	26.0	54.0
11. Working	39.0	43.1	35.1
12. Participating in church/religious group	33.2	27.4	38.7
13. Watching sports activities in person	30.9	35.4	26.7
14. Playing a musical instrument	22.6	21.9	23.5
15. Exploring the Internet/on-line services	14.1	15.5	12.8
16. Participating in clubs	12.5	14.4	10.7
17. Volunteering	11.9	7.7	16.0

Source: The Mood of American Youth 1996 (Reston, VA: National Association of Secondary Principals, 1996), 30.

activities young adults engage in, from sports and driving, to doing homework and dating. Even much of television watching (with the popularity of MTV) and going to movies (as seen by the sales of sound-track albums) involves the enjoyment of music.

About this attraction to music, Deane believes that "to the confoundment of many professionals, it is a seeming life-source to many adolescents—and to some, the *most* important life-source." He attributes this turning to pop culture to the combined factors of the decline of formal religious observance and the breakdown of families and institutions. Pop culture "provides more of the necessary bonding and common experience [young adults] require."[4] Jones agrees that music, particularly rock and roll in all its guises, contributes to the young adult's search for identity, excitement, acceptance, and independence.[5]

From a different perspective, Haise advises Christian bookstore managers on ways to attract more young adults and, presumably, teens' disposable incomes to their stores, saying that music is an "integral part of youth culture, and it's likely to be what first attracts most teens to your store."[6]

LIBRARIES, POPULAR MUSIC, AND YOUNG ADULTS

Given this primacy of music for young adults, Setterington says that "the library must acknowledge that music is a part of the life of today's teen,"[7] while

Jones sees it as "a perfect opportunity for libraries to make connections with YAs."[8] Wilson-Lingbloom believes that CDs and cassettes are "certainly valid components of YA collections, where budgets allow,"[9] but a strong argument can be made that it is important to make sure budgets accommodate musical recordings. The justification for this is that YA interest in popular music recordings exists and that "this interest has some legitimacy."[10]

It would serve YA librarians well to heed the advice Haise gives Christian bookstore managers in how to create a teen-friendly atmosphere. First, he says, "you must take steps to make them feel comfortable." His suggestions for doing this rely heavily on music, including offering a wide selection of music, stocking music magazines, and installing a monitor for showing music videos. Perhaps most important, he says to "create a special youth section *near* the music department" (emphasis added).[11] How many libraries have their YA sections in close proximity to their audiovisual collections?

As a way to make libraries more musically appealing to young adults, Setterington advises that "equipment for music listening is an asset in any room for teens."[12] YALSA's *Directions for Library Services to Young Adults* goes even further, saying that "a separate but visible area where music and conversation will not disturb other patrons is highly desirable."[13]

MUSICAL TASTES OF YOUNG ADULTS

What exactly do young adults want to listen to? The NASSP poll identifies the musical forms that are currently popular, showing some differences between males and females (see Table 9.2). Two important points have to be made.

First, musical taste among young adults is not monolithic but rather spans the spectrum. Jones makes only a throwaway mention of country music when defining the various forms teens enjoy, yet the NASSP poll shows it to be the choice of 31.2 percent of teens. This popularity might be due to country music's new social awareness, with recent songs touching on spousal abuse, sexual harassment, and even tolerance of different lifestyles.

Second, musical taste is fluid, changing from generation to generation of young adults. The previous NASSP poll in 1983 didn't even have rap on its list of musical preferences, yet the current poll shows rap the choice of 44.3 percent. New Age music was the second most popular type of music in 1983 but ranks eleventh in the current poll, enjoyed by 15.8 percent of the respondents. Similarly, within the musical genres, groups come and go rather quickly. In 1992, Jones identified several groups or artists as examples of various genres, most of which had faded from the scene by 1996.[14]

Another trend to notice is the rise and popularity of contemporary Christian music, often referred to as CCM. Seeming, at one point, to be a poor imitation of popular music forms, it now can boast a myriad of artists of quality creating music that runs the gamut of style and often performing in secular venues. Frequently charting high on *Billboard*'s chart of the 200 best-selling albums,

Table 9.2
Types of Music

Music	% Total	% Males	% Females
1. Alternative rock	58.2	55.4	61.1
2. Rock	49.3	51.2	47.5
3. Rap	44.3	42.9	45.6
4. Pop	41.0	30.9	50.8
5. Oldies	33.7	26.5	40.3
6. Country and western	31.2	29.1	32.6
7. Classic rock	28.3	29.3	26.9
8. R & B/blues	26.3	22.1	30.3
9. Heavy metal	23.9	28.4	19.5
10. Classical	17.6	15.5	19.5
11. New age	15.8	13.1	18.3
12. Soul	15.8	13.1	18.3
13. Jazz	10.6	11.2	9.7
14. Folk	2.6	2.4	2.5

Source: The Mood of American Youth 1996 (Reston, VA: National Association of Secondary Principals, 1996), 31.

independent Christian music labels have almost all been absorbed by large recording firms.

In deciding what recordings to select, YA librarians should first admit that they are probably out of the loop when trying to identify which artists or groups are going to be popular, since their own preferences were likely formed during their own teen years. Conger and Galambos say that the adolescent years are so important that "the friendships we formed in those years, our first loves, the music we enjoyed, and the activities we participated in all have a certain permanence in our minds."[15] A YA collection filled with recordings by the Beatles, the Bee Gees, and the Village People will probably not appeal to today's teens, even though some librarians may still see these groups as leaders of rock and roll. Curiously, though, some groups have maintained popularity with new generations of listeners, such as Led Zeppelin, the Doors, Aerosmith, and Jimi Hendrix. Still, Deane maintains that young adults take pleasure "in listening to music most professionals won't listen to."[16]

MATERIAL SELECTION POLICY

Before discussing the ways of selecting musical recordings, it is necessary to explore selection policy. Not only should every library have a materials selection policy, but that policy should include a section on recordings that spells out the guidelines to be used in selection. Ideally, guidelines for recordings should mirror the guidelines for print collections. If the policy is to buy only books of high quality, then the policy may limit recording selections to those that are very well reviewed. More likely, the policy in most libraries will be to have a book collection of both "good" books and "popular" books. How, then, can there be any justification to select only "good" recordings, at the expense of what many teens find popular? Again, your recordings collection will most likely include both quality and popular recordings. (Of course, the ideal with both print and nonprint materials is to find those that have both good quality and popularity, but this seems to happen too rarely.)

SELECTING POPULAR RECORDINGS FOR YOUNG ADULTS

When deciding which recordings to select to appeal to young adults, the best way is to ask young adults themselves. Ideally, there is already a YA advisory group in the library that can identify those recordings. If not, a special YA recordings selection group could be formed. Or, does the library employ teen workers? They could be another source of advice. Ideas could be solicited during class or school visits (which would also help promote the recordings collection). A survey might be developed and given to young adults who patronize the library, or the librarian could engage young adults in casual conversation about their favorite groups. There is no single appropriate method for obtaining the needed information, as long as it generates input from real, live young adults.

The YA librarian has a role in selection that goes beyond merely soliciting input. As was mentioned before, it is necessary to ensure that the collection contain a wide variety of musical genres. Haise also points out that it is "important to identify local and regional variations in musical tastes."[17] Just as books of quality are introduced into the collection in hopes of expanding readers' tastes, so too can recordings of merit be added to help expand listeners' tastes (unless the selection policy allows only for popularity when selecting recordings).

Probably the single most helpful publication for selection is *Billboard*, which identifies itself as "the international newsweekly of music, video and home entertainment." This periodical includes industry news, some reviews, and several charts. It is useful for gauging popularity and finding information about new recordings. At the same time, it has to be remembered that the charts reflect national sales, and a particular recording may have little popularity in the library's service area. The charts also don't allow for age preferences, and there is the danger of simply ordering by chart position, negating the whole concept of selection.

Unfortunately, there is no single source of reviews of recordings that can be used for selection. Two of the more helpful ones are *Rolling Stone* and *Spin*. Both offer about a dozen or so serious reviews of albums that they believe will appeal to their readers. Regretfully, the target audience for both magazines is older than young adults. Still, these reviews can be used for selecting "quality" recordings and could be helpful in responding to challenges made against the recordings that have been selected.

Other review sources of lesser help include the *Village Voice*, *Stereo Review*, *Musician*, and *High Fidelity*, among others. New music magazines are released constantly, and the YA librarian would be well served to regularly peruse that section of the local newsstand. Fan magazines such as *Black Beat* and *Hit Parader* will offer limited reviews. *CBA Marketplace*, a journal for Christian bookstores, contains about ten reviews each month, including a chart of album best-sellers compiled only from reports of Christian bookstores.

Making friends with the owner of your local record store can be extremely helpful. Not only can the owners share with you what the popular sellers are at their store, but you might even be able to arrange a discount to purchase your selections there. Record store managers keep close watch on their inventory and are probably a more reliable source of popularity than any chart.

The newest source of information about recordings is the Internet. Mega-Net stores such as CDNow have information about recordings, often including ratings and reviews and even biographical sketches of artists and groups. Record labels, as well as individual groups and artists, are more likely than not to have home pages, easily located through the use of Internet search engines. Many groups or artists will also have pages created and maintained by fans and probably will be quite unofficial.

The YA librarian should not use these various methods of selection as a substitute for becoming personally acquainted with recordings popular with teens. Just as YA librarians constantly read new works by authors in order to keep up with the field and to aid in reader's advisory, so too should they regularly dip into MTV and listen to recordings that seem to be popular at their library. The goal here is not to become a fan of the music (though this may be a surprising benefit) but simply to become and remain familiar with an important part of youth culture.

PARENTAL ADVISORY STICKERS AND CENSORSHIP

No examination of the selection of musical recordings can be complete without looking at the "Explicit Lyrics—Parental Advisory" stickers and their role in selection. In 1985, after well-publicized hearings and to appease the Parents Music Resource Center (PMRC), the Recording Industry Association of America (RIAA) agreed to the voluntary labeling of albums that contained lyrics some might find objectionable. Each business was free to set its own guidelines and to design its own labels. Many found this labeling inadequate, and by 1990 legislation was introduced in several state legislatures to codify labeling. In reaction, the RIAA developed a uniform label to be used by all its members. This label is to be used on albums that have explicit lyrics dealing with sex, violence, suicide, drug use, bigotry, and satanism.

Unlike movie ratings, which are given by a committee, record labels are free to determine which albums will be labeled and what their criteria will be. The discrepancy between labels is great.[18] Contrary to popular belief, an album may contain no "dirty words" and still bear this label. At the same time, absence of the label does not guarantee the absence of profanity on the album.

This labeling is insufficient as a criterion for selection. The label in and of itself gives no real information about the contents of the album. Indeed, the label may appear solely because the ideas expressed will be offensive to some listeners. This raises the issue of censorship, with Eaglen saying that "labeling records is censorship."[19] Intellectual freedom is not limited to print materials but covers all forms of media. Refraining from selecting a recording only because it may cause potential problems is precensorship. Unfortunately, musical genres that are likely to have these labels—alternative rock, rap, heavy metal—are some of the more popular among YA listeners.

What should be the response to challenges to these recordings once they have been added to the collection? Ideally, the library will already have a policy on how to handle all challenges, with those against recordings treated just as those against books. This policy should include a formal request for review and a method to accomplish that review. The reconsideration should take into account such items as printed reviews, popularity of the album since it was added to the collection, and an examination of how it meets the criteria set forth in the material selection policy. All reconsideration requests should be dealt with in a serious manner yet should not cave in to demands for censorship.

CONCLUSION

Serving young adults well in the public library leads to responding to their interest in popular music. By developing tools of selection that include both the input of young adults themselves and standard professional methods, the library can offer a collection of popular music that will meet the needs of the YA patron and also serve as an enticement for the young adult to patronize the library. The YA librarian can play an important role in this process by remaining acquainted with the medium and by serving as an advocate for recording collections that young adults want.

NOTES

1. Patrick Jones, *Connecting Young Adults and Libraries: A How-to-Do-It Manual* (New York: Neal-Schuman, 1992), 19.

2. *The Mood of American Youth 1996* (Reston, VA: National Association of Secondary School Principals, 1996).

3. Kenneth Setterington, "The Physical Layout and Set-Up of the Young Adult Area," in *Meeting the Challenge: Library Service to Young Adults*, ed. Andre Gagnon and Ann Gagnon (Ottawa, Ontario: Canadian Library Association, 1985), 81.

4. Gary Deane, "Young Adults and Non-Print Services: A Popular Culture Perspective," in *Meeting the Challenge*, 124–25.

5. Jones, *Connecting Young Adults and Libraries*, 62.

6. Larry Haise, "Grab Your Slice of the Youth Market," *Bookstore Journal* 26, no. 5 (May 1993): 31.

7. Setterington, "The Physical Layout and Set-Up of the Young Adult Area," 81.

8. Jones, *Connecting Young Adults and Libraries*, 62.

9. Evie Wilson-Lingbloom, *Hangin' Out at Rocky Creek* (Metuchen, NJ: Scarecrow Press, 1994), 113.

10. Deane, "Young Adults and Non-Print Services," 127.

11. Haise, "Grab Your Slice of the Youth Market," 28–29.

12. Setterington, "The Physical Layout and Set-Up of the Young Adult Area," 81.

13. *Directions for Library Services to Young Adults*, 2d ed. (Chicago: American Library Association, 1993), 16–17.

14. Jones, *Connecting Young Adults and Libraries*, 64–65.

15. John Janeway Conger and Nancy L. Galambos, *Adolescence and Youth: Psychological Development in a Changing World*, 5th ed. (New York: Longman, 1997), 3.

16. Deane, "Young Adults and Non-Print Services," 123.

17. Haise, "Grab Your Slice of the Youth Market," 31.

18. Jeffrey Ressner, "To Sticker or Not to Sticker . . . ," *Rolling Stone* (February 7, 1991): 17.

19. Audrey Eaglen, "Strictly off the Records," *School Library Journal* (July 1990): 33.

10

Sex, Thugs, and Rock 'n' Roll: Magazines for Young Adults

Patrick Jones

One of the more ironic facts about materials for young adults, especially in public libraries, is that some of the most popular items—paperback series, music compact discs/cassettes, and magazines—are rarely reviewed in the library professional media. Instead, review sources concentrate on school report-oriented non-fiction and just about every YA hardback novel. Librarians know a lot more about the most recent offering of a respected YA author like Cynthia Voigt than about exciting new magazines for their YA patrons. Librarians, of course, know about standard magazines like *Time* or YA magazines with a school focus like *Scholastic Update*, but information about popular recreational periodicals is not readily available. These types of magazines are for the browsing collection, not the reference collection. They are disposable materials with little research value but lots of immediate importance, as they hit YAs where they live, focusing on sex (the teen girl magazines), thugs (sports and comic books), and rock and roll (as well as rap and other music genres). Magazines provide YAs with information they crave about things that are hot, vital information about lifestyle concerns, and special interests they are developing. Magazines speak to teenagers' passions and help them deal with developmental tasks like independence, identity, and acceptance. Magazines give YAs both what they want and what they need.

YA magazines can do the same double duty for libraries: giving them what many want (higher circulation) but also what they need. Magazines fulfill the mission of most public libraries—to provide materials for educational, recreational, cultural, and informational purposes. YA magazines like *YM* are filled with answers to questions about YA problems, fan magazines (fanzines) like *Bop* and music magazines like *Vibe* report and are part of teen pop culture, sports magazines like *Slam* or comic books like *The Uncanny X-Men* fulfill the recreational mission, and many titles aimed at adults but popular among teens like *People* or *Rolling Stone* often help fulfill the educational role. For many YAs, magazines provide information for homework, recreational reading, and, in the advice columns/articles of *Seventeen*, important information for life work. Magazines also offer the most bang for a library's buck: lots of use for (normally) very little money.

In addition to fulfilling the primary roles of a public library, magazines for YAs have fringe benefits. A shelf of them can be a good method for creating an identity for a YA area or department. A face-out display featuring *Teen* announces to patrons that a particular area belongs to YAs. Magazines are a merchandising tactic to generate interest and pull YAs into the "tent," where perhaps they will find other materials. Magazines are also a great public relations tool. Librarians visiting schools (or classes visiting libraries) can use magazines as a promotional gambit to demonstrate that libraries are not just encyclopedias and homework books. Magazines can also be a crowd control strategy for libraries facing groups of YAs doing nothing but "hanging out." If there is a need to occupy the time of these YAs, providing magazines is at least one option to help maintain order and keep the YAs busy and interested. Finally, magazines provide reluctant readers—always a difficult group to serve—with materials they can and will read. While there are many reasons that YAs are reluctant readers,[1] two of them are that they can't find materials of interest and that they find reading difficult because they lack skills. Magazines, by definition, aim for high interest, and many contain low vocabulary.

The primary benefit to a public library of a YA magazine collection is circulation. For the cost of one hardback book, a magazine subscription can be purchased. That one hardback book could, in the best possible world, circulate perhaps 26 times in a year with a two-week check-out period. The same money spent on a magazine subscription would net many more circulations—12 issues × 26 checkouts. That is a conservative estimate as often magazines, especially comic books, come back before their due date. One primary tool to build support for services for YAs is demonstrating their impact. This increase in circulation might bring about an increase in a YA librarian's visibility and credibility in the library and the teen community. All of this creates a level of excitement: YAs are excited about materials coming into the library, and the library can find the energy and interest of young adults to be contagious.

It is hard to imagine a library serving YAs without a popular magazine collection. Magazines are favorites among young adults, as documented by reading interest surveys and casual observation. This is not surprising, as magazines are visual, which is a huge drawing card for the stereotypical members of the "MTV generation." Magazines appeal to the short attention spans and busy schedules of many young adults—they read quickly in short bursts of time and energy. Magazines are considered socially acceptable reading material. Sometimes a YA who reads a book is made fun of by peers; the same teen packing a magazine is asked to pass it around. Often when librarians say that YAs don't like to read, they must mean books, because YAs do like to read magazines. YAs are rarely assigned to read magazines in school. Since there is no adult or school pressure or negative connotation to read magazines, that alone makes them appealing. As YAs grow older, they begin to develop a personal culture and special interests.

Providing information about a special interest is the function of a magazine— for almost any YA area of interest, there are magazines available to answer that need. One interest that is not special but is normal is the need for information on the important stuff of YA life such as sex, love, and health. Magazines, especially ones like *YM*, can provide some of the best, most up-to-date, and most reader-friendly information on these issues. Other magazines provide information and glossy photos of teen celebs/heartthrobs. While certainly not at the same level, information on fads and celebrities can be fascinating stuff. Vital information is of no use if the reader cannot read it. For that reason, most magazines for YAs have a fairly low reading level and augment text with lots of graphics and photos. For all of these reasons, it is obvious why YAs like magazines and therefore why libraries should like them as reading material.

Many libraries purchase comic books from the same subscription agent as magazines. They are published monthly and handled/processed like other periodicals. On the other hand, many public libraries do not carry comic books. Reasons for this often include the violent nature of comic books and a desire not to waste tax dollars purchasing, processing, or circulating comics. Bluntly stated: libraries don't carry them because librarians don't like them. The sad thing about this decision not to carry comics is that it flies directly in the face of overwhelming evidence about the value of comics. Since the big scare in the 1950s about comics' causing juvenile delinquency, research about comics has actually been quite favorable.[2] Myths that comics retard reading skills, cause violent or antisocial behavior, and are a menace have been dismissed. A few years back an article in *School Library Journal*[3] argued that libraries did a poor job of choosing materials for preteen boys. While the reasons behind this argument were dubious, the thesis was not without merit. Comics are an answer to a 12-year-old boy's question, "What's here for me?" Comics provide libraries with a format that is hugely popular, inexpensive, attractive to hard-to-attract library users, and easy to shelve, weed, and process, and generally has high circulation. There are a few review sources for comics in the library profession, but a great deal of information is also available from local comic stores, periodicals like the *Comics Journal*, and sites on the Internet. The real question shouldn't be: "Do we carry comics?" It should be "Which ones should we carry?" (hint: buy the *X-Men* and all its mutations).

The same selection quandary holds true for all magazines for YAs. Like any library collection, the exact mix of materials depends a great deal on the library's size and budget and mainly on the community that it serves in terms of both demographics and values. What is acceptable in San Francisco or New York might not fly in rural Tennessee or medium-size midwestern burgs like Fort Wayne, Indiana. Even within a large public library system, two different branches could have radically different magazine collections for YAs. Similarly, school libraries, for good reason, tend to focus on materials to supplement the curriculum; thus many YA titles are not housed unless the school also tries to play a role in recreational reading. YA magazines, like many YA materials, present librarians with lightning rods to challenges: magazines often contain frank, even graphic language and can display artwork or photography that some could call obscene, and the ads might be for products that are not legal for young adults to purchase or are of a suspicious nature. The first steps in developing a collection of magazines for YAs are to make sure that these materials are covered under the library's collection development policy, that they can and will be defended by library administration, and that they are indeed library-appropriate.

Reviews, normally the backbone of defending against intellectual freedom challenges, are often absent in regard to these magazines. While occasional titles might show up in *Library Journal*'s column on magazines, most do not. None of the major review sources for young adults review magazines on a regular basis, and only a few articles surveying the teen magazine field have been published over the past decade.[4] A book like *Magazines for Young Adults*[5] has some value, but in addition to being outdated, the focus is on educational or informational titles, while even the list prepared by YALSA's Media Selection and Usage Committee[6] was more of an objective bibliography than a subjective list of recommendations. The best source for a list of magazines is teenagers themselves—either through formal or informal surveys, most teenagers know what they want.

The following titles are suggestions based on experience, popularity among YAs, YA input, and appearance in library collections. Magazine titles, like all media products, tend to change locations, prices, and owners with great frequency; thus those interested in obtaining more information about any of these titles should check with the library magazine subscription agency (e.g., Ebsco) or with a current directory of magazines. Magazines also, sometimes without warning, change their focus: *Seventeen* and *Thrasher* are prime examples of magazines that have expanded their audience from teenagers to 20-year-olds.

General Interest

Fanzines (about teen celebrities)

   Bop, Sixteen, Superteen, Teen Beat, Tiger Beat

Fashion/advice and such

   Seventeen, Teen, YM

Religious

Breakaway, Brio, Youth (Catholic)

Sports

NBA Inside Stuff (basketball), *Sports Illustrated, Sports Illustrated for Kids, Slam* (basketball)

Action Sports

Warp, Transworld Skateboarding, BMX Plus, Thrasher

Other Sports-Related

Beckett Baseball Card, WWF Magazine

Music

Rolling Stone, Spin, Vibe, Right On, Circus, Word Up, The Source, Option, Fresh, Rap Pages, Nerve

Humor

Mad, Nickelodeon, Cracked

Computers

GamePro, Electronic Gaming Monthly, Nintendo Power, Game Players

Literary

Meryln's Pen, Voices, Writes of Passage

Science Fiction/Fantasy/Horror

Starlog, Analog, Wizard, Dragon, Hero Illustrated (comics), *Fangoria*

ADULT TITLES OF INTEREST TO YOUNG ADULTS

Auto-Related

Hot Rod, Motor Trend, Car and Driver

Fashion

Cosmopolitan, Vogue, Elle

Sports

Field and Stream, Outdoor Sports, Sport

Mass Media

People, Premiere, Entertainment Weekly

Other

USA Today, Weekly World News

This is just a sampling. Depending on a library's community, the selection of magazines will vary. Many of these titles, like *Sports Illustrated*, are already in collections. If possible, the YA magazine collection should be physically separate. For many of the adult titles, the questions are whether or not they should be housed in a YA area and/or whether or not a second copy is needed.

There are several magazines not listed here; in 1994 three new teen titles were announced: *Quake, Tell,* and *Mouth2Mouth.*[7] Despite hype and big media pushes (and media tie-ins) and riding on articles about the increased number of young adults and their increased buying power, none of the titles survived. Similarly, *Sassy* magazine had been for years attempting to launch a boys' version called *Dirt.* Despite great amounts of marketing, test issues, and cross-promoting (some came via shrink wrap with selected Marvel comics) *Dirt* failed to sink in. While magazines are popular, there does seem to be a limit to how many the market can handle, primarily due to a limited number of advertisers willing to use the written word to promote products, in particular to hype them to boys. A magazine like the now-defunct *YSB*, while outstanding in quality, had a difficult time not in finding an audience but in finding advertisers who wanted to sell to both teenage boys and girls. *YSB* became aimed more at young adults in the more traditional sense of the word: 18- to 25-year-olds—but it didn't help.

Magazines aimed primarily at girls are also problematic. In addition to values and morals issues presented by these magazines and their effect upon self-esteem,[8] the magazines are fiercely competitive. While *Seventeen* remains the leader among advertisers, it has changed both its layout and its focusing, marketing itself to the older, rather than younger, young adults.[9] The younger teenage girls are the biggest buyers of teen fanzines like *Bop.* The popularity of fan magazines is directly related to the popularity of any current teen idol—when someone is hot, like New Kids on the Block in the 1980s, the sales for *Bop* and other fanzines soared but dropped once the group cooled off.[10]

One method magazine publishers have used to combat the boom or bust of teen magazines is spin-offs.[11] Some of the first spin-offs, like *Zillions*, a child of *Consumer Reports*, were just junior versions of adult titles. While most of these titles, like *Field and Stream Jr.* or *Sports Illustrated for Kids*, are aimed at younger (fourth through sixth grade) YAs, they are important because they get kids hooked early on certain titles. Most of the interesting new youth magazines in the past few years are preteens titles like *Girl's Life* and *New Moon.*[12]

Titles like these are also considered a safe bet for youth magazine collections. The materials in them are neither controversial nor the stuff of challenges. The same could not be said of many of the other magazines for young adults. Many of the music magazines, in addition to the ads for 900 sex lines, sex toys, and term papers, report on rap and alternative music. Both of these musical genres are based on many things, but the desire to shock the system is among them; thus magazines about music like *Spin* will often contain obscenities in describing the music, in reviews and interviews, or if song lyrics are reprinted.

A magazine like *Thrasher* presents several challenges. The readership of the magazine is huge, as the skate community ranges from 10- to 30-year-olds, and there are certainly a skate culture and attitude. Much of this attitude is very punk, very raw, and, to many, offensive. *Thrasher* is about skateboarding, but it is also an alternative culture magazine that is very popular among teen boys. Magazines on tattooing, body art, and piercing have great appeal yet often do not end up in public libraries. Many newsstands house these magazines with the pornography or require a buyer to be 18 to purchase. Finally, magazines like *Fangoria* consist primary of color photos taken from R-rated slasher/horror films. It is of great YA interest yet is often not selected to be in library collections due to its graphic content, controversial nature, and potential for challenges. Magazines spin librarians around the "is it censorship, or is it selection?" issue repeatedly.

Another challenge to magazines comes from library staff frustrated by the high loss rate of teen magazines. Due to the nature of the magazines and the readership, teen magazines, perhaps more than other formats, are often mutilated. Many boast lots of glossy color photos; few are returned with all photos intact. Libraries with or without security systems report high loss rates, as well as a tendency for even ones that are not stolen to be so creatively reshelved that they are rarely found. There are some solutions. Giving users a feeling of ownership over the collection and attempting to get them to apply peer pressure against destroying or stealing the magazine can help. If necessary, current issues can be held at desks for limited use, or all copies of some titles may require an extra level of security. Libraries have a responsibility to spend tax money wisely and should not passively allow magazines to be stolen and defaced yet at the same time must face the realities of the nature of the audience coupled with the high interest rate of the material. *Value Line*, Sunday newspaper want ads, and *Sports Illustrated* swimsuit issues also disappear from libraries, and they are not taken by 15-year-olds.

Print magazine readers, however, might be disappearing as more magazines move onto the Internet (cybermags) or are being created specially for the Web (e-zines).[13] Both styles of magazines should attract YAs to virtual newsstands, where they can browse the latest copy of *GamePro* magazine or download the new issue of an Internet-only e-zine like *Virtually Re-act*. As the Web changes daily, a complete list of magazines of interest to young adults is both impossible and out-of-date as of this writing, yet what follows are (as of March 1998) some of the best choices:

Drive-Thru<http://www.primenet.com/~joelmot/drive/index.html>

FishNet<http://www.jayi.com/sbi/Open.html>

GamePro <http://www.gamepro.com>

Lift <http://www.lifted.com>

MidLink Magazine<http://longwood.cs.ucf.edu/~MidLink>

TeenNet Magazine<http://www.mbnet.mb.ca/~strauss>

Virtually Re-act<http://www.react.com>

YO (Youth Outlook) <http://www.pacificnews.org/yo>

For more information on teen e-zines, a search of "Yahoo (http://www. yahoo.com)" in either the category "Entertainment: Magazines: Children" or "Society and Culture: Age: Teen" should bring up more and new titles, as will looking at the magazine section of the "Young Adult Librarian's Help/ Homepage (http://www.kcpl.lib.mo.us/ya)."

Certainly, the Internet is changing how young adults get information and spend their recreational time. While once libraries were the only free source for magazines, now the Internet stands in direct competition. Yet just as radio, then television didn't destroy the magazine industry but changed it, the proliferation of the Internet should create similar havoc and improvement and opportunities. In fact, the Internet might just increase YA interest in information, heighten their interest in their own favorite pastimes, and create chances for them to communicate. Libraries can help young adults find the best magazines on the Web, help them create their own e-zines, or simply provide them with more print magazines about the Internet.

Magazines for YAs present libraries with tremendous opportunities to improve YA services. Magazines increase circulation and visibility. They provide nonreaders with materials, and even the most reluctant reader should be able to find a magazine of interest. That YAs should flock to magazines is no surprise; they have so much in common. Magazines are about short attention span, graphics, energy, and motion. While not every teen and every teen magazine is about sex, thugs, and rock and roll, teen magazine publishers, perhaps better than the book publishers, have the pulse of YA life and are the lifeblood feeding, growing, and changing YA popular culture. Popular culture is what public libraries do best: from providing paperbacks, to best-sellers, to videos, public libraries give people what they want. For many YAs, a magazine is exactly what they want, and maybe even what they need.

NOTES

1. Arthea Reed, *Comics to Classics: A Parent's Guide to Books for Teens and Preteens* (Newark, DE: International Reading Association, 1988); G. Kylene Beers, "No Time, No Interest, No Way! The Three Voices of Aliteracy; Part One," *School Library Journal* (February 1996): 30–35; G. Kylene Beers, "No Time, No Interest, No Way! The Three Voices of Aliteracy; Part Two," *School Library Journal* (March 1996): 110–15.

2. Stephen Krashen, *The Power of Reading: Insights from the Research* (Englewood, CO: Libraries Unlimited, 1993).

3. Ray Nicolle, "Boys and the Five-Year Void," *School Library Journal* (March 1989): 130.

4. Patrick Jones, "A to Z and In-Between: New Magazines for Young Adults," *Voice of Youth Advocates* (February 1994): 352–56; Patrick Jones, "Spy! The Source and Son of Sassy: New YA Magazines," *Voice of Youth Advocates* (October 1992): 219–22; Patrick Jones, "Wrestling with Young Adult Magazines," *Voice of Youth Advocates*

(April 1989): 10–12; Judy Massey, "Girl Talk Magazines," *School Library Journal* (October 1992): 54; Jana Fine, "Teen Zines," *School Library Journal* (November 1996): 34–37.

5. Selma Richardson, *Magazines for Young Adults: Selections for School and Public Libraries* (Chicago: American Library Association, 1984).

6. "Magazines for Young Adults," *Journal of Youth Services in Libraries* (Fall 1993): 97–100.

7. Deirdre Camody, "Teen-Age Magazines Are Facing a Shake-Out," *New York Times*, October 1994, sec. C, p. 5.

8. Anastasia Higginbotham, "Teen Mags: How to Get a Guy, Drop 20 Pounds, and Lose Your Self-Esteem," *Ms* (March–April 1996): 84–89.

9. Mary Huhn, "At Seventeen, Teens Look a Little Older," *Mediaweek* (June 15, 1992): 4.

10. Tony Silber, "Teen Titles Take Tumble in Circulation Game," *Folio* (October 1, 1991): 17–18.

11. Ellen Turin, "New Mags on the Block," *Folio* (November 1, 1990): 83–84; Lorne Manley, "Spin-Offs for Kids Aren't All Child's Play," *Folio* (January 1, 1993): 17+.

12. Barbara Findlen, "A Magazine for the Girl's Movement," *Ms* (September–October 1993): 79.

13. Serena Herr, "The Changing Face of Zines: The Underground Press Embraces Electronic Publishing," *Publish* (June 1996): 70–76.

11

Connecting with the Young Adult Reader: A Reader's Advisory Strategy

Tom Reynolds

Reader's advisory service is fast becoming a lost art in our nation's libraries.

Evie Wilson-Lingbloom[1]

Over the last 20-plus years, conventional wisdom about the importance and proper role of reader's advisory to young adults in public libraries has changed markedly.

In 1969, Margaret A. Edwards, head of the Enoch Pratt Free Library's Young People's Department, wrote *The Fair Garden and the Swarm of Beasts*. The book's examination of the problems and challenges of working with young adults and its great enthusiasm for YA librarianship made *The Fair Garden* the most influential work on the subject of its time.

Edwards placed reader's advisory at the center of library service to young adults. As part of her training at the Enoch Pratt Free Library, Edwards required new assistant librarians to read at least 300 of the approximately 2,000 titles in the New York Public Library's *Books for the Teen Age*.[2]

As a hapless new assistant finished each ten new books, he or she would have a conference with Edwards, who used these discussions "to teach the assistant to evaluate books" and to discuss ways of interesting readers in particular titles. The assistant graduated from Edwards' tutorial by reading 300 new books from the list. However, it was expected that the new librarian would continue to read and keep current on new titles appearing in *Books for the Teen Age*.[3]

In Edwards' view, the librarian served YAs as their primary guide to the world of books. This world was essentially one of classics and adult age-appropriate novels;[4] and both teenage reading interests and information retrieval (reference work) were to be subordinate to the function of making YA readers into "citizens of the world."[5]

Then, as studies revealed that school-related information retrieval was the primary focus of YA activity in the public library and that teenagers often did not seek help from librarians when looking for new books, "opinion shifted dramatically."[6]

Today the central role of reader's advisory in library service to young adults has been replaced by the primacy of the information retrieval function. Reader's advisory is now viewed as a secondary role, even for YA specialists.

This new reality is expressed most clearly in the writing of Patrick Jones. In Jones' world young adults seldom ask librarians for reading advice. There are so few YA specialists, and they have so little opportunity to interact with YA patrons that only a patron-centered, self-service reading promotion system can or will work.[7]

Librarians should acknowledge that "our advice is rarely called upon," says Jones, and that "our role has changed from reader's advisor to presenter of materials."[8]

Since browsing is the primary mechanism used by YAs to find what they read, the new dominant opinion emphasizes merchandising over booklists, book-talks, and reader's advisory for promoting YA reading.

"We should select the most popular items and plenty of them. Then we should shelve them in a way that increases access and makes the collection 'user-friendly' for the browser."[9]

Contrast this with Margaret A. Edwards' view that most adolescents looking for recreational reading "do not know what they want" and that, because of this, a competently trained (well-read) librarian could become a valued guide in helping young adults discover the world of books.[10]

Today few librarians would argue with Patrick Jones' assertion that to serve YAs public libraries must respect their interests and opinions. Beginning with the advent of the YA novel in the 1960s, publishers have increasingly targeted and marketed directly to young adults. As a result, teens have become more sophisticated and demanding about what books they choose to read.

For the public library, addressing the needs of YA readers clearly means buying high-demand materials (popular YA series and graphic novels), stocking formats that YAs like (paperbacks and magazines), and making YA collection areas comfortable and user-friendly places for teenagers to hang out.

All this said, as a YA specialist I do find myself advising YAs about books to meet their reading needs, and this work is among the most challenging I perform. The truth is that between the two views of Margaret A. Edwards and Patrick Jones most librarians—YA specialist and generalist alike—work both to help YAs find the books and materials they want and also to nurture and encourage teens' reading interests. Reader's advisory service for young adults is alive, if not completely well, in our public libraries.

TEENS AREN'T IN THE LIBRARY TO READ, ARE THEY?

Conventional wisdom holds that patrons approach finding material in the library from one of two perspectives, reading-interested or reading-resistant.

A number of recent studies have examined reading resistance behavior among YAs. This complex, often paradoxical behavior can range from the simple tentativeness of not making time to read,[11] to the "unmotivated" attitude of teens who don't identify themselves as readers and feel negatively about reading itself.[12] What is categorized as reading resistance in teens is often a shifting mixture of values learned in childhood, past experiences with libraries and library staff, and the simple inability to make time for reading in their fast-paced, school-focused lives.

Because school is the major occupation of most YAs, it is a common assumption among librarians that many YAs are in the library only because they need to be.[13] This view of YA library use further devalues the importance of reader's assistance to teens. But is this view too negative or at least too simplistic?

Studies of adolescent reading behavior reveal a complex picture. While leisure reading appears to decline after 15,[14] age and sex differences in reading interest and behavior are significant.[15] In fact, research indicates that young adults, particularly middle school-aged teens, do read for pleasure—over 70 percent in some surveys.[16] Depending on their sex, teens also read both fiction and nonfiction.[17]

It appears that reading for pleasure does drop off as teens move into high school. For many older YAs, as their lives become busier and more school-centered, reading for enjoyment is replaced by reading for utilitarian purposes. Yet even high school students who reported valuing reading primarily for its contribution to their success in school exhibited positive attitudes toward reading for personal growth and enjoyment.[18]

Indeed, students who are motivated by the utilitarian value of doing well in school are more likely to be interested in finding reading material—whether a classic or a title from a school reading list—they can enjoy as well as read to complete an assignment.

Having advised a YA reading group at the Edmonds Public Library, I can attest to the fact that many teens, despite their busy lives, are avid readers. This doesn't mean that they aren't uncritical in their selection or that they may not appear reading-resistant at first glance. How many librarians have worked with a young adult, suggesting titles and authors, only to have the teen reject most of the suggestions? It happens a lot, yet not all of these teens are truly reading-resistant. In fact, many are avid, albeit very critical or selective readers.

Still, many teens don't get pleasure from reading, and they tell us that all the time. Ironically, for these young adults a thoughtful reader's advisory can be of greatest importance. Just helping such teens find the least painful way to complete a school assignment will help them to return to the library with less trepidation and possibly even a more positive attitude toward reading.

Young adults, like their adult counterparts, have many reasons for coming to the library, and they bring to reading many different attitudes and patterns of behavior. The salient fact is that YAs are in the library and that most are reading—either because they want to or because they are required to read. Given this, librarians will continue to be asked to provide them reader's assistance.

Unfortunately, because little formal training is provided that is specific to working with young adults, many YA librarians have been required to develop their reader's advisory skills on the job.

Faced with the need to perform YA reader's assistance and the lack of formal training in either YA literature or YA reading habits, developing a flexible personal strategy for connecting with YA readers is a prerequisite for librarians working with teens in public libraries.

REASONS YOUNG ADULTS ASK FOR READING ASSISTANCE

In developing strategies to assist young adult readers, it is important to understand the most common types of reader's assistance questions they ask and to be prepared to address these in the reader's advisory interview.

The basic types of reader's assistance requests made by young adults in public libraries break down into three broad categories: pleasure reading, school-related assignment reading, and bibliotherapy. Related to these is a fourth type of request made for a teenager but by someone else, usually a parent, and to which librarians must be prepared to respond.

Pleasure Reading

Just as with adults, requests for pleasure reading by young adults may involve a request for a specific title or series, for the works of a particular author, or for titles in a specific genre. These include books with a music, movie, or television connection. On the other hand, such a request can be as nonspecific as, "I'm just browsing, but can you suggest any good books?"

School-Related Assignment Reading

This is the book report question in all its many variations. The librarian may be asked to recommend a "classic," a title or titles from a reading list, or a novel set in a specific time period or by a specific type of author.

Bibliotherapy

This is when a young adult explicitly or implicitly asks for a book about "someone just like me."

Request by a Parent, Friend, or Someone Else for a Young Adult

Because the YA may not be present when the request is made or may find it difficult to participate in the book selection process, this type of question can prove a particular challenge to the YA reader's adviser.

While librarians hear many variations and combinations of these basic questions, most YA reader's assistance questions fall into one or more of these descriptive categories. Developing and refining a competency in answering all four categories of question are essential to providing successful reader's assistance to young adults.

DEVELOPING A READER'S ADVISORY STRATEGY: PREPARING TO WORK WITH YOUNG ADULTS

As Mary K. Chelton and James Rosinia point out, "The best [reading] promotion system combines both personal and impersonal approaches."[19] Using good merchandising techniques to catch the YA reader's eye is essential. But in this section I want to concentrate on identifying the key elements of successful librarian-centered reader's advisory work. This type of "floor work" is direct and personal and makes a strong connection between the YA reader and the library.[20]

The first two of these key elements involves preparation.

Learning about Young Adults

Learning about young adults, which really means learning something about adolescent psychology, is the first step in developing a strong reader's advisory competency. Adolescence is a time of great change, and the developmental needs of young adults primarily determine their interests and activities during this period.

Librarians, teachers, and other YA service providers know that working with teenagers can sometimes be frustrating. But as Patrick Jones points out, "All the behaviors that drive us crazy about YAs stem from the developmental tasks essential to adolescence: emotional, social, sexual, intellectual, and psychological changes."[21]

Alleen Pace Nilsen and Kenneth Donelson in their text, *Literature for Today's Young Adults*, provide a list of recommended reading on adolescent psychology.[22] This list provides a good starting point for the librarian who wants to learn more about this subject.

Understanding young adult psychology should help librarians address the problem of negative stereotypes, which, Evie Wilson-Lingbloom points out, keep "many adults from developing understanding, empathy, and good communication with YAs."[23] Such stereotypes are too prevalent among librarians and often color the initial interaction they have with teenagers.

Reading about what makes teenagers tick is only the first step for the librarian who wants to develop skills as a reader's adviser for young adults. The successful reader's adviser takes an interest in young adults and takes the time to learn about them from popular culture and other sources. There are many ways to stay aware of young adult interests. These include reading YA magazines and listening to popular music, as well as watching television programs and movies targeted at young adults.

This said, the most valuable approach is also the most direct—ask young adults. Talk to your young adult patrons, to the YAs who work in your library as pages and volunteers, and to the teenagers you know outside the library.

The more a librarian understands about adolescent psychology, the more easily that person can talk to young adults and learn about their interests and needs. Identifying these is of key importance to providing successful reader's assistance.

Finally, an understanding of adolescent psychology will lead to a broader appreciation of the role of young adult literature in addressing the needs of this age group.

Prepare by Reading

1. As you start talking with YAs and learning about their developmental needs, begin to follow Margaret A. Edwards' dictum to start reading and continue reading. Read across the spectrum of YA-appropriate literature, including popular YA series titles and books by "hot" authors (e.g., Cusick and Stine), titles from *Books for the Teenage* and the YALSA Best Books lists,[24] and titles by high-demand adult genre authors like Stephen King, John Saul, and Anne Rice. If you are not sure where to start, ask some YAs what they are reading or check the return carts or circulation records and read those titles that have circulated most recently. If possible, read the paperback edition of books.

2. Develop a repertoire of short "jacket talks" to use in your conversations with YAs. "Booktalking to YAs in schools and community organizations has long been one of the most popular methods of promoting reading among adolescents."[25] Many resources exist to help the librarian develop skills in the preparation and presentation of such booktalks. Joni Bodart and Patrick Jones provide two of the best.[26]

But the "jacket talks" librarians use in floor reader's advisory work are shorter and more informal and are often tied to one single dramatic feature of the book, for example, the title or paperback cover art.[27] Chelton and Rosinia describe these "spiels" as "thirty seconds of verbal promotion for a particular title."[28]

You don't have to be an accomplished booktalker or even be comfortable presenting formal booktalks to a group to be successful doing jacket spiels to one or two YAs at a time in the library. But you do need to have a mental core collection of titles you can draw from when working the floor with a YA reader. As you finish reading a book, make a list of its three or four key themes. Highlight those you know teenagers will find interesting. Then practice various ways of talking about the book using these key themes. Finally, write the best of these short jacket talks on a card. Remember these need be only a couple sentences long. Keep the card until you feel comfortable talking about the book without review.

Here's a sample jacket talk using Annette Curtis Klause's *The Silver Kiss*:

Zoe's mother is dying of cancer, she can't talk to her father, and her best friend is moving away. So she turns to someone who seems to understand her conflicted feelings about death, the strange and attractive Simon. Then Zoe learns his secret. Simon is a vampire!

Ideas for, and examples of, such short booktalks can be found in Gale Sherman's *Rip-Roaring Reads for Reluctant Teen Readers*.

The process of reading, outlining, and updating book spiels is an ongoing one. But once you're comfortable talking from a modest mental list of titles, you can begin trying your hand at assisting YA readers.

BUILDING YOUR READER'S ADVISER COMPETENCY: TECHNIQUES FOR WORKING WITH YA READERS

The best way to test and refine your reader's advisory skills is to start providing reader's assistance and see what works and what doesn't when interacting with young adults. At the same time, several basic techniques should be part of any reader's advisory strategy. Knowing these basic techniques provides a second set of key elements in developing a strong YA reader's advisory competency.

When a young adult comes to the reference desk or stops the librarian in the young adult area to ask for reading assistance, the request may be as general, as, "I'm looking for something to read." Even questions that seem specific (those, for example, requesting a particular title or the books of a hot author) may come to the librarian fairly unfocused or containing incorrect information.

A good example of this are the frequent requests librarians get from middle school teens for titles in "that horror series" by R.L. Stine. It is a good bet these YAs are looking for books from the *Fear Street* series and that they won't be pleased if you send them to the children's paperback collection for *Goose-*

bumps titles. But the only way you will know for sure is if you begin the reader's advisory interview by asking questions.

Ask Questions and Listen to the Answers

"Ask questions. . . . Then, ask more questions," says Patrick Jones.[29] While you are using open-ended questions to clarify the YA reader's request, remember to practice the other basic skills of a good reference interviewer, particularly "active listening."[30]

Mary K. Chelton in a 1993 article on performing reader's advisory lists a number of specific questions librarians can ask to pinpoint reader preferences.[31] With a little revising, most of these can be used in interviewing a young adult who has requested something to read. An active reader's adviser often falls back on a few key questions to get patrons to articulate what they want. With YAs I often find myself asking either or both of the following questions: "What was the last book (or author) you read that you really enjoyed? Have you heard of any good books (or authors) from friends that you think you would like to read?"

Then, as you clarify what the YA reader wants, try identifying the question using the basic descriptive classification outlined earlier in this chapter.

Use the Books to Promote Themselves

If the question is specific enough, you may need to show the patron only how to check the electronic catalog to find where a particular title is located. But if the request is more general, or you have difficulty getting solid clues about what your YA patron wants, you should move the interaction to the YA area and use the books, particularly paperbacks, to help promote themselves. As soon as it becomes obvious that a YA patron wants advice or general assistance rather than just a specific title, I take the patron to the paperback collection in the YA area. Once there I start pulling out titles to show the young adult while I begin talking about the books.

"A successful book must sell itself on the shelf."[32] Teenagers often do judge a book by its cover. Smart publishers know this, and the librarian can use the cover art and promotional information on paperback editions of YA, classic, and genre titles to hook YA readers.

This basic strategy remains the same even when I am working with an obviously reluctant YA reader. However, I may vary my jacket talks, choosing books that seem sure hits or have eye-catching cover art and promotional text that might hook the reader.

Keep the Interaction Low-Key

Stay away from the hard sell and hyperbole in your conversations with YAs. Guard against seeming judgmental about YA reading interests or putting down popular YA series.[33] To make the reader's advisory process work, YAs must feel comfortable in rejecting a librarian's suggestions, and the librarian must appear comfortable in moving on to another book when this happens. One technique I use with YAs who don't respond to any of my book suggestions is to leave a selection of books with them and allow them to make the choice. Some teenagers won't make a selection while the librarian is with them, so once you've made your suggestions, sometimes it's best to step back and see what happens.

Oh, and maintain a sense of humor. It is normal for teenagers to hang out in groups in the library. This often increases the possibility that someone will tell a joke or make a crack, sometimes at the librarian's expense. Laugh and play along with the joke. As long as it doesn't disrupt the reader's advisory interview, appearing relaxed during your conversations with teens helps build rapport with your YA patrons.

A good rule of thumb when working with YAs is "Don't sweat the small stuff." It doesn't matter what they're wearing, or if they're talking while you're giving your book spiels. As long as they are looking at the books, passing them around, and reacting (positively or negatively), they are getting something from the process.

ADVISING YA READERS: A TOUGH COLLABORATION

At its best, reader's advisory is a collaborative effort. The goal should be, says Patrick Jones, "to find the right book for the right YA at the right time for the right reason."[34] But assisting YA readers is often a tough collaboration.

Paradoxically, I find that teens who really don't want to be in the library and have no interest in reading but need a novel or classic for a report are more likely to accept the first book in which they have even the slightest interest or that catches their eye.

The more demanding (and exciting) challenge is to work with a YA who has at least some interest in reading but who also has strong opinions about what he or she does and doesn't like. Such a YA reader may have read extensively in a specific genre or have read all of a particular author's work, and the librarian will need to use all of his or her accumulated knowledge and book promotion skills to find a new title or author the teenager will accept.

A case in point was Roger, a 13- or 14-year-old who asked me for help about a year after I started working full-time as a young adult librarian at the Edmonds Library. I could tell from the moment we started to talk that Roger was going to be tough. First, he was a guy, and he had that "I'm not really excited about anything" kind of attitude. Second, he knew what he wanted and what he didn't want. "No fantasy! No love stories or girl books! Something exciting!"

As we talked, it became clear that Roger had read a lot. Having graduated from the Hardy Boys and classics authors like Jack London, he was now struggling to find books he liked that were at his age and reading level. He read sports and photography magazines and volunteered that he was a swimmer. After about 20 minutes of looking through YA paperbacks, Roger grudgingly took three books—based as much on the covers as on anything I said. Sometime later I ran into Roger again looking through paperbacks in the YA area. I asked him if he'd read the books he had picked out earlier, and he was quick to tell me that, according to him, most of the books were boring. But then he added matter-of-factly, "That book about the swimmers was cool." Pleased and not a little surprised, I shared with him that *Stotan!* was one of my favorite YA novels. Then I pulled off a couple of other books from the YA paperback rack for him to look at.

The point of this story is that Roger and I were involved in a tough but successful collaboration to get him "the right book" for that moment. Roger was not reading-resistant or even a classically reluctant reader. He was rather a typical teenage boy with a low tolerance for things he didn't find interesting.

All of the tools and techniques of a successful reader's advisory strategy are aimed at getting the collaboration of your YA patrons. Unlike many adults, such collaboration by young adults may involve a shrug, a single word or phrase indicative of interest, or just picking up a book for further inspection.

A SPECIAL CASE: THE PARENT REQUEST SCENARIO

Often a teenager and his or her parent will show up together at the reference desk looking for a book for the YA to read. Sometimes this is a collaborative effort, but too often the YA has been dragged to the library for some specific reason. Either the parent doesn't like what the teen has been reading, or the teen hasn't been reading at all, and the parent feels this needs to change. The common strategy to follow in such a situation is to separate the parent and teenager. Suggest that the parent look through some of the common YA reader's advisory reference sources for ideas and titles while the librarian takes the YA to the young adult collections to see what's on the shelf. My experience is that this strategy is most successful when the parent is there to give a shy or nonverbal teen encouragement and is happy when the YA takes the initiative in finding a book.

If the parent is insistent on setting the direction of the reader's advisory interview, then the librarian must find subtle ways to encourage the YA to get involved. Even though the parent may be dominating the conversation, address your response to the YA as much as possible. While talking with the parent, hand the teen a copy of a YA paperback you think he or she might like and gauge the teen's reaction. Often parents have a very restrictive view of what their teen should be reading. You can't disregard these views, but you can try to get parents to broaden them to include modern classics or YA genre novels that might be more interesting to the YA.

Stock paperback copies of Christian YA series and some older classics. Talk about these in conjunction with titles in similar popular YA series, and see if you can get parent and teen to agree on something they both like.

Whenever you notice the teenager's reacting positively to a suggestion, steer your recommendations in that direction.

ADDITIONAL TECHNIQUES FOR PROMOTING YA READING

Use the YA area to promote books and to make yourself more accessible to the YAs in your library.

"Spend time looking busy in the YA collection at periods of high YA use," advises Evie Wilson-Lingbloom.[35] If you are a YA librarian or have YA responsibilities, you should regularly spend time each week in the YA collections, straightening books, weeding, putting up displays, or putting out handouts. Once teens see you regularly in the YA area, they will approach you more often. Almost half of the YA reader's assistance requests I have received at the Edmonds Public Library have come while I was "looking busy" in the YA area.

If your library doesn't have a YA area, work on getting one. It should include comfortable seating and all the library's YA book and periodical collections. (This may be impossible, particularly with non-fiction, but move as far in this direction as you can.) Remember, "it is next to impossible to merchandise YA collections if they are not all in one area."[36]

Most teens who regularly hang out around the YA collections do so to browse or read. Work on developing a nonintrusive style for talking to YA browsers. For example, if you see a teenager is having trouble finding material in the cataloged collection, suggest trying the YA paperbacks. Or ask a teen who is looking at the YA new book display or the bulletin board for ideas for displays. Some won't respond, but some will, and you will get some interesting ideas.

Encourage Word-of-Mouth Advertising among YAs

Many YAs come to the library looking specifically for books they have seen their friends reading or heard them talking about. Peer recommendation is clearly the most important factor affecting the book selection habits of younger YAs (followed by librarian booktalks).[37] Any way you can get teens talking to other teens about books or magazines encourages reading.

Karen Hultz and Lisa Wemett have suggested a dozen specific activities librarians can try to get YAs talking about books and excited about reading.[38] Sally Kintner of the Whatcom County Library System asks for recommendations from YAs when she booktalks at schools.[39] This is a perfect way to start word-of-mouth advertising about popular titles. Two ways I have used to disseminate young adult opinions on books are a critics corner posting short YA reviews and a YA newsletter.

Try putting some card-size review forms in books in the YA collection. Ask readers to indicate whether or not they liked the book (thumbs up or thumbs down) and then to say why. Have a spot near the YA collections where teens can post their reviews. Then watch and see if the books that get reviewed increase in circulation.

In the past the Edmonds Public Library had a young adult review group that met and discussed books group members had read. This group wrote reviews for books they liked, and we published them in a newsletter called *Check-It-Out*. Such a young adult-authored newsletter can be a very effective way to promote YA reading, particularly if it can be published regularly and distributed outside your individual library. (Two such outside locations are local recreation centers where teenagers congregate and secondary school libraries.)

Booklists and Electronic Reader's Advisory Services

Placing booklists of YA material in the library, especially near the YA collections, is a good self-help promotional tool for encouraging YA reading. Short subject or genre lists in bookmark or hip pocket (small, folded) format are best. These are easy to display. Teens are more likely to take them because they can easily be stuck in a book or pocket, which means they are more likely to be used. Another use for these short booklists is as a handout to encourage further reading when you do booktalking. I have used our system's "hip pocket" genre reading lists as such a hook, giving them out at the end of my class booktalking visits.

The newest tools for providing reader's assistance in the library are the electronic reader's advisory services, Kids Catalog and Novelist being the most notable examples. In their infancy, these services offer readers guidance to genre and juvenile fiction but have notable limitations.

The wonderful and mysterious world of the Internet will undoubtedly have an impact on how young adults get information about books, magazines, and other sources of entertainment. Those libraries with the Internet already have access via the World Wide Web to a number of young adult-created home pages that give comments and reviews by teenagers on books, movies, and music. Most of these have been linked together under a Web site called the Young Adult Librarian's Help/Homepage (http://www.kcpl.lib.mo.us/ya/). Originally created by Patrick Jones at the Allen County Public Library, the YA Librarian's Help/Homepage is now based at the Kansas City (Missouri) Public Library.

TAKING UP THE CHALLENGE

Yes, young adults are in the library. They are reading, either because they want to or because they have to; and this means that librarians, both YA specialist and generalist, will be providing them with reading assistance. While libraries that have a YA specialist are fortunate, much of the time reference desk generalists will find themselves providing reader's advisory assistance to young adults. For these generalists, a preparation in adolescent psychology and an ongoing program of reading popular YA fiction are essential.

Reader's advisory is a collaborative process. Because adolescence is a time of great changes, many of them "invisible or perplexing to outsiders [like adults], but dramatic and disconcerting to the [young adults] experiencing them,''[40] teens can sometimes be tough collaborators. All the tools and techniques of the reader's advisory strategy discussed in this chapter are aimed at getting their help in this process of finding them the right book(s) at the right time for the right reasons. The process of successful reader's assistance to young adult patrons is conducted every day in libraries around the country. The key is to have librarians who treat teenagers with the same respect and concern as other patrons, have prepared by studying something about adolescent psychology, and have worked to develop reader's advisory skills specific to working with young adults. For those who want to take up this challenge, the outcome can be very satisfying.

NOTES

1. Evie Wilson-Lingbloom, *Hangin' Out at Rocky Creek: A Melodrama in Basic Young Adult Services in Public Libraries* (Metuchen, NJ: Scarecrow Press, 1994), 97.

2. Margaret A. Edwards, *The Fair Garden and the Swarm of Beasts* (1969; reprint, with a foreword by Patty Campbell, Chicago: American Library Association, 1994), 17.

3. Ibid., 18.

4. Patty Campbell, "Reconsidering Margaret Edwards: The Relevance of The Fair Garden for the Nineties," *Wilson Library Bulletin* (June 1994): 35–36. Patty Campbell's "Foreword" to the 1994 reprinted edition of *The Fair Garden* provides a clear, concise examination of the career and influence of Margaret A. Edwards.

5. Edwards, *The Fair Garden and the Swarm of Beasts*, 16. Classics and adult titles appropriate for teenagers—books for the college-bound type material—are what Edwards uses as examples in *The Fair Garden*. The works of S.E. Hinton, Barbara Wersba, and Paul Zindel, pioneers in developing the young adult novel in the late 1960s, are not mentioned in the text of the 1974 revised edition, although she does include their titles in one of her reading lists in Appendix A (pp. 134–35).

6. Campbell, "Reconsidering Margaret Edwards," 36. Patty Campbell mentions the 1963 survey by Lowell Martin at Enoch Pratt, which highlighted the "proportional importance of the information function in working with teens." Patrick Jones, *Connecting Young Adults and Libraries* (New York: Neal-Schuman, 1992), 35. In *Connecting Young Adults and Libraries*, Jones lists the results of a number of YA reading surveys, including those reviewed in an influential article by Donald Gallo in *American Libraries*, November 1985. Jones uses Gallo's conclusion that "browsing" and "friend's suggestion" are the major ways teens find pleasure reading to support his argument that YA reading promotion should emphasize merchandising. The Gallo surveys are also referenced by Evie Wilson-Lingbloom in *Hangin' Out at Rocky Creek*, 97.

7. Jones, *Connecting Young Adults and Libraries*, 80, 88, 196.

8. Ibid., 198.

9. Ibid.

10. Edwards, *The Fair Garden and the Swarm of Beasts*, 18–19.

11. Margaret MacKey, "The Many Faces of Resistant Reading," *English Journal* (September 1993): 71–72.

12. G. Kylene Beers, "No Time, No Interest, No Way! The Three Voices of Aliteracy; Part One," *School Library Journal* (February 1996): 32.

13. Jones, *Connecting Young Adults and Libraries*, 13.

14. Elizabeth Rhae Fair, "What Young Adults Like to Read: A Comparison of Iowa Books for Young Adults Data from 1982–1989 with Other Reading Interest Studies" (Ph.D. diss., University of Iowa, 1990), 65.

15. Fair, "What Young Adults Like to Read," 63–64, 66; Terry L. Mitchell and Terry C. Levy, "The Reading Attitudes and Behaviors of High School Students," *Reading Psychology: An International Quarterly* (1996): 79–80.

16. Constance A. Mellon, "Leisure Reading Choices of Rural Teens," *School Library Media Quarterly* (Summer 1990): 224.

17. Betty Carter and Richard F. Abrahamson, *Nonfiction for Young Adults from Delight to Wisdom* (Phoenix, AZ: Oryx Press, 1990), 3–5.

18. Mitchell and Levy, "The Reading Attitudes and Behaviors of High School Students," 65, 82.

19. Mary K. Chelton and James M. Rosinia, *Bare Bones: Young Adult Service Tips for Public Library Generalists* (Chicago: American Library Association, 1993), 14.

20. Ibid.

21. Jones, *Connecting Young Adults and Libraries*, 19.

22. Alleen Pace Nilsen and Kenneth L. Donelson, *Literature for Today's Young Adults*, 4th ed. (New York: HarperCollins, 1993), 35–36. A clear, brief discussion of the issues in adolescent psychology important to libraries is presented by Chelton and Rosinia in *Bare Bones*, 7–8.

23. Wilson-Lingbloom, *Hangin' Out at Rocky Creek*, 10. Wilson-Lingbloom discusses the various items to consider when "building a profile of the adolescent" (pp. 11–16).

24. YALSA's "Best Books" and "Reluctant Reader/Quick Picks" lists are published each year in either the March 15 or April 1 issue of *Booklist*.

25. Wilson-Lingbloom, *Hangin' Out at Rocky Creek*, 100.

26. Joni Bodart, "Booktalks Do Work!" *Illinois Libraries* (June 1986): 378–81; Jones, *Connecting Young Adults and Libraries*, 112–33; Carter and Abrahamson examine how to booktalk non-fiction books in *Nonfiction for Young Adults from Delight to Wisdom*, 189–93.

27. Chelton and Rosinia, *Bare Bones*, 15.

28. Ibid.

29. Jones, *Connecting Young Adults and Libraries*, 81.

30. Wilson-Lingbloom, *Hangin' Out at Rocky Creek*, 91.

31. Mary K. Chelton, "Read Any Good Books Lately? Helping Patrons Find What They Want," *Library Journal* (May 1, 1993): 34.

32. Carolyn Caywood, "Judge a Book by Its Cover," *School Library Journal* (August 1993): 58.

33. Wilson-Lingbloom, *Hangin' Out at Rocky Creek*, 99.

34. Jones, *Connecting Young Adults and Libraries*, 81.

35. Wilson-Lingbloom, *Hangin' Out at Rocky Creek*, 99.

36. Jones, *Connecting Young Adults and Libraries*, 189–90. Jones provides the outline

of a YA area design plan (Figure 7.1), which lists the key factors to consider in designing a YA area.

37. Mary Elizabeth Lomax, "To Choose or Not to Choose: The Effects of Varied Influences on the Selection of Library Books by Junior High School Students" (Ph.D. diss., University of Nebraska, 1993), 60–61.

38. Karen Hultz and Lisa C. Wemett, "A Dozen Ways to Reach Young Adults When You Are Short on Space, Staff, and Time," *VOYA* (December 1994): 298.

39. Sally Kintner, "Written Comments on Chapter Draft," personal communication, October 1996.

40. Chelton and Rosina, *Bare Bones*, 7.

12

Young Adult Reader's Advisory: Recommending the Right Reads

Barbara Auerbach

While it's true that many young adults come to the library to do their homework or research for a school project, others browse the shelves looking for a good read, and even the most independent need our help from time to time in choosing a book. Many will never ask for help; a few courageous or particularly outgoing ones will approach the desk, but it is up to the young adult librarian to offer help and guidance to even the most reluctant who find themselves in the library. How can we best offer our services without patronizing or intimidating? In the article "Breaking the Ice with YAs," Avis D. Matthews cautions that reader's advisory can be tricky because young adult patrons are wary of the librarians' "rehearsed approach." They are also hesitant to admit that they need help due to shyness or the desire to be independent as well as reluctance to open up to a stranger. Further, they may actually be embarrassed to admit that they read for pleasure at all, especially in front of other YAs. Taking these barriers into account, Matthews advocates "floor work" as an essential method of promoting books to YAs.[1]

Interestingly, I have found that most opportunities for reader's advisory in Main Youth Services, the Young Adult Division at the Central Library of the Brooklyn Public Library, occur when I am shelving mass-market paperbacks on the floor. Young patrons seem to find me far more approachable as I kneel among the Fear Street and Sweet Valley displays than when I am seated behind the reference desk. When I asked a coworker what she thought was different about doing reader's advisory with young adults, she suggested that due to schoolwork and social and familial responsibilities, most young adults have less time for leisure reading during the school year than do children. Also, young adults are less likely to be adventurous and try new authors than children are. "They want what they want." This particular coworker happens to be very friendly and engaging with the young adult patrons and, as a result, is privy to what is "hot" and which new authors to stock the shelves. "Take tips from them, and be a good listener" is the advice she gives to the novice reader's adviser. In addition to this basic credo, this chapter introduces many other innovative and exciting ways for the young adult librarian to share an enthusiasm and love of books with middle and high school patrons.

BOOKTALKING AS A READER'S ADVISORY SOURCE

Although young adults are sometimes hesitant to ask for recommendations for leisure reading, there are many ways librarians can help them to make satisfying choices. Class visits and after-school programs are excellent opportunities for presenting short booktalks plugging the latest fiction and non-fiction for YAs. Brief, enticing descriptions, provocative quotes, or entertaining character sketches can all be used to effectively "sell" a book.

What follows is a [sampling from an] alphabet of hooks. Each one represents a different spin or angle that can make a booktalk unique, intriguing, and therefore memorable.

Audience participation: Get the audience to repeat the title or a key phrase from the book like a refrain. The repetition alone will help sell the book; giving the audience a part to play is even better. . . .

Cliffhanger: The classic hook. Bring the audience to the edge, then stop.

Dialogue: Copy dialogue from the book and read it with the audience. Talking with, not at, the audience will increase the energy level in the room.

Empathy: Ask questions to put the audience in the shoes of the character. If the theme of the book is loneliness, then build a booktalk using a series of rhetorical "How does it feel?" questions. For most teens, reading is as much an emotional experience as an intellectual one, and an invitation to share feelings can be a powerful hook.

First sentence: Read only the first line . . . for a short but effective book-hook.

Gross-out: Read or describe the goriest, grossest scene in the book.

Headlines: Refer to an article in the news, then link it to a book (good for contemporary biographies; also for crime or survival stories). . . .

Linking: Link the book to a popular movie with a similar theme or setting. . . .

Props: Use an object to lead in to a scene, or to help act it out.

Questions: Ask a series of these to set a mood or to pique curiosity. . . .

Themes: Talk about several books that share the same theme (one of the titles should be well-known). . . .

You: Relate events in the book to events in the listeners' lives.

Zonk: Save one "can't fail" talk in case all the others do. But if you've got your hooks into the audience, they won't![2]

Young adult librarians have an invaluable resource in the booktalk books by Joni Richards Bodart. This series of books provide prewritten booktalks on selected young adult titles.

The following sample booktalk is just one of many from *Booktalk! 4*:

The Face on the Milk Carton   Grades 7–12
By Caroline B. Cooney

How would you feel if you were having lunch with your friends in the school cafeteria and suddenly saw a picture of yourself on the back of a milk carton? Yourself as a kid— the caption says you were stolen from a shopping center in New Jersey twelve years ago, when you were only three years old. Everyone at the table thinks that you're joking, but you're not—you can remember that dress, and then later you realize you can remember the shopping center, and walking with someone who was going to buy you an ice cream soda . . . maybe she should just keep quiet and pretend it never happened. But what can she do about all those memories that keep coming back, stronger and stronger, memories of another life and of another family? She *has* to do something—but what?[3]

BOOKLISTS

When school is out, summer reading lists also provide librarians with a perfect chance to guide students in their choices. So often students are presented with a lengthy list of titles with no annotations, and they haven't a clue what the books are about or which ones they'd actually enjoy. They are usually quite open to suggestions at this point and grateful to be able to make an attractive choice. Of course, teens should choose whatever they want, but if the pickings are slim, or they're just plain undecided, a recommendation, informal booktalk, or YA booklist can make the choice easier. Speaking of booklists, staff-generated booklists and bookmarks with popular YA authors and titles, especially if done in an appealing format, are another way to guide young adult patrons to books. The American Library Association publishes "The Best of the Best Books for Young Adults: Top 100 Countdown" in a brochure that looks like a CD brochure at Sam Goody. YALSA recently developed a reproducible bookmark of "Best Books" for 12- to 18-year-olds listing ten popular new titles with annotations written by teens.

MERCHANDISING

Thematic displays and merchandising are yet other means of promoting books to YAs. As librarians, we often forget how intimidating the library can be. Many patrons are overwhelmed by the sheer number of books to choose from and don't know how to begin to narrow their selection. In the fall of 1987, Sylvia Mitchell and Karen Chun asked approximately 400 eighth and tenth graders "what would the teens' 'fantasy' library be like?" One response was, "Have a special section where the best books are."[4] An alternative to the "New Books" section, which many libraries already have (though not necessarily for young adults!) would be a "recommended" or "choice picks" area, which could include new and older titles and be rotated and updated regularly. Displays should not be limited to new books, however. Be aware of topics in the news and media events. If a big election is coming up, a serial killer is on the loose, or a favorite star gets married, be creative and display fiction as well as non-fiction that tie-in with the subject. A few eye-catching photos or clippings will help teens make the connection.

Fred Schlipf, executive director of the Urbana Free Library in Illinois, suggests separating fiction by genre, subject, or interest. "Arranging fiction alphabetically suggests that if you like Kipling, you'll love King."[5] This may seem radical to some, but merchandising, attractive, easy-to-read signage, and face-out book displays all make the library a friendlier place to YAs. Although my division shelves fiction alphabetically, we do employ a series of colored tape and dots on the spine of many books indicating fantasy, historical fiction, mystery, science fiction, and so forth, with the most popular and prevalent being the neon orange dot for African-American interest. Other divisions in the Central Library offer a separate black heritage section. Other possible sections could include multicultural literature or, more specifically, sections like Jewish interest, Native American interest, Hispanic interest, Asian interest, gay and lesbian literature, and sports stories. However, one advantage of the traditional alphabetical shelving of fiction (aside from easy retrieval) is that patrons may be drawn to individual titles they would have missed had they been shelved in a section of no interest to them. For instance, the cover and blurb of a book like *The Watsons Go to Birmingham, 1963* might appeal to a young adult anticipating a family car trip or one who enjoys funny family stories who would never have thought to look in the African-American interest section.

Of course, a major prerequisite to any reader's advisory service is that the librarian must be familiar with young adult literature. Aside from reading *School Library Journal, VOYA, Booklist,* and other review sources, reading the books themselves is invaluable in order to make genuine recommendations. A young woman once came to me explaining that she really liked Terry McMillan, but could I recommend other books she might like, as she'd read every McMillan she could get her hands on. At first I showed her Connie Briscoe and Bebe Moore Campbell, but when I saw I had her confidence, I took more liberty, recommending *Coffee Will Make You Black* by April Sinclair, *Browngirl Brownstones* by Paule Marshall, *Betsey Brown* by Ntozake Shange, a few Jacqueline Woodson titles, and any other favorites I could think of. She left with a pile of good reads and a big smile. I, too, had a big smile on my face all afternoon. I have to admit, though, that as I browsed the shelves with this young woman, I felt regret at the great number of books I was not familiar with and the disservice to these books as well as to patrons that this implied. Of course, no one can read everything, but the more familiar you are with your fiction collection, the better reader's adviser you will be. It is possible, however, to use our shortcomings to our advantage on occasion. Recommend a book you haven't yet read and ask the young adult to read it and tell you how her or she liked it. This not only flatters the patron and says that you care about and respect his or her opinion but also encourages the young adult to read the whole book and come back to the library.

READING LOGS

One way staff members in my division become familiar with new fiction is through the "fiction file." All new YA fiction is scrutinized to determine its suitability for the file, which includes popular YA authors, subjects that might be requested or be of interest (our subject headings fill up six typed pages!), award winners, and titles that appear on best book lists for that year. Mass-market titles and books that are "too young" or that we just don't like circulate immediately; fiction file titles are placed on a shelf for staff to peruse. Each month we try to read three or four new books and write them up for the fiction file. This involves assigning the book one or multiple subject headings, writing a brief summary, and sharing our annotations at a staff fiction file meeting. In this way staff become familiar with many new books each month, not just the ones that each librarian has read for the meeting. The annotations are typed on blank index cards and filed by subject in file boxes at the reference desk. Patrons requesting historical fiction about the Civil War, Holocaust fiction, fiction about teen pregnancy or eating disorders, and so on can take the fiction file cards for a particular subject to the shelves and search for titles that sound interesting.

STAFF INVOLVEMENT

Another way to encourage staff to read and get a well-rounded familiarity with the collection is to have genre meetings focusing on a different genre each month. One month everybody reads two science fiction titles of his or her choice; the next, maybe two romances or sports titles or horror novels. I have to confess that my partiality to coming-of-age fiction usually shapes my fiction file selections; the science fiction collection may as well be on another planet, as far as my tastes go. These meetings give everyone exposure to all parts of the collection, as well as introduce everyone to the titles that the other staff members have read. It also creates instant booktalks.

At the Brooklyn Public Library, all new librarians are required to take part in a series of monthly book discussions to expose them to classics, both new and old, as well as other important titles for children, young adults, and adults. In addition, many regions sponsor book discussions based on a theme or exploring a particular author or series, to keep librarians reading and talking about reading.

All of these activities encourage us to read new YA fiction and make it accessible to the young adults who approach the desk for help. Yet, as mentioned earlier, many YAs don't approach the desk. How can they be reached? Libraries might consider creating a "browsing associate" position, as the Rocky River (Ohio) Public Library did. "Recommending titles and authors, conducting reader's advisory interviews to discover a reader's preferences, merchandising books, holding publicity events such as book and author luncheons and author book signings and appearances, and participating in collection development (specifically for fiction and genre fiction)" are all part of the browsing associate's job.[6] In addition, the library features a browsing room with face-forward displays. While this position is not YA-specific, it could be. Unfortunately, many libraries cannot afford to create a new staff line devoted entirely to reader's advisory, but they might want to consider investing in a database for YA patrons who need help finding a book but prefer to search independently or who just enjoy interacting with computers. There are a number of choices available.

READER'S ADVISORY DATABASES

The Rocky River Public Library has over 1,200 titles on its "Good Reads" browsing database, which includes both adult and young adult titles and utilizes the database management software Panorama II. Still another, highly successful interactive program exclusively for YAs is "Computer Pix." In 1980 the Wayne Oakland Library Federation (WOLF) Young Adult Services Committee (YASC) first came up with this innovative program. "Computer Pix" started as a computerized summer reading program for young adults and is likened to a computer dating service, "matching teens with books." The program features 1,200 titles with graphics, updated all year long as librarians read new fiction.

YASC can allow the reading trends of the teenagers themselves to guide the inclusion of new books on particular subjects. During the 1980s for instance, books on Romance and Teen Problems were the hottest ticket. During the 1990s, escapist literature such as Adventure, Mystery/Crime and Supernatural/Horror have risen to the top, dropping Romance and Teen Problems down to the middle of the pack. Guided by the rising statistics in these subject areas over the past few years, the YASC was able to search for and add titles in time to meet these new demands. They continually analyze current statistics, hoping to predict what the next reading craze might be.[7]

Another possibility is "Book Brain" for seventh through ninth graders, which is available from the Oryx Press and SIRS, Inc. as a multimedia CD-ROM. SIRS now also offers additional subject modules in "Science and Technology" as well as "Spanish." They already offer a "Sports" module, which complements the 1996 New York State Summer Reading Program "Read to Win." Books can be accessed by subject or title or by solving a reading mystery game. "Book Brain will help librarians 'sell' books and reading by getting kids to look at the shelf and find a book they like. It's a great way for them to extend themselves and will definitely make their work easier."[8]

READER'S ADVISORY SOURCES

The appeal of the computer, along with the independence and anonymity this option allows, will attract many young adults who might otherwise never ask a librarian for help in choosing a good book. For the less technologically (or economically) endowed, a book such as *What Do Young Adults Read Next?* is an excellent resource. Each listing includes the subject(s), major character(s), time period, plot summary, and more, as well as other titles by the same author and even other books young adults might like if they like this one! An array of indexes from "character description" to "subject" is also quite helpful. Other sources for YA recommendations include *Best Books for Junior High Readers* and *Best Books for Senior High Readers*, both of which include brief annotations of books that received at least two positive reviews. Non-fiction is arranged by subject, fiction by genre. Betty Carter's *Best Books for Young Adults: The Selections, the History, the Romance* includes the annual "Best Books for YA" lists selected by YALSA from 1966 to 1993. Finally, H.W. Wilson's *Middle and Junior High School Library Catalog* and *Senior High School Library Catalog* include short, descriptive annotations with grade level and excerpts from published reviews. The initial hardcover catalogs cover more than 4,000 titles each, and four paperbound annual supplements include approximately 600 titles apiece. Both include author, title, and subject indexes as well as a directory of publishers and distributors. In addition to these sources, reading the monthly library literature and review sources is also invaluable for librarians doing reader's advisory.

TEEN INVOLVEMENT

More influential than any computer or even a friendly librarian are other young adults. Any psychologist will affirm that teens look to their peers to affirm "what's cool." On that note, teen newsletters, advisory boards, and reviews are excellent vehicles for recommending books to young adults. One easy method is to

form an informal teen reviewers' club by creating a simple book review form that will fit in the back of a book. Invite young readers to record their thoughts on this form after they read the book. Their comments will then be available to the next patron browsing through the books, trying to decide what to read.[9]

Another success story is YARC, the Young Adult Reading Club at the Bryans Road Library, part of the Charles County Public Library, in southern Maryland. In addition to doing YA book reviews that are published in *The New YARC Times* (pun intended!) monthly, the club encourages writing and creating games based on popular YA books. Another favorite club activity is going on field trips to author readings such as by Richard Peck and Paula Danziger.[10] The St.

Louis County Library publishes YA book reviews in "Books Reviewed by Teens for Teens." Natalie Oleshchok, who started the reviews to "promote a love of reading among teens," maintains that

"Books Reviewed" shows our young patrons what great books are out there, just waiting to be taken off the shelf and enjoyed. The teens who read and review the books gain a better understanding of why they like a particular book. I hope this process has made avid readers of them all.[11]

Staff-generated newsletters that include teen reviews as well as summer book discussion groups are also ways for young adults to share their reading tastes with their peers. Last summer, one branch of the Brooklyn Public Library offered "Fear Street Fridays," a book discussion featuring the works of the ever-popular R.L. Stine.

As important as peers are at this age, librarians still need to be aware of what young adults like to read as well as be familiar with young adult authors and new titles. One obvious way to find out what young adults like to read is to ask them.

Just as the reference interview is vital for satisfying patrons' informational needs, the reader's advisory interview helps match the patron with the right books satisfying their recreational needs. Questions like "Who are your favorite authors?" "Do you enjoy a particular genre such as horror, romance, science fiction, or problem novels?" or "Do you prefer short, quick reads or longer, more leisurely ones?" help to shape recommendations. Another simple technique for calling readers' attention to books is to customarily suggest another title in addition to the one they request,[12] for example, "If you like R.L. Stine, you'll probably enjoy Christopher Pike and Caroline Cooney."

MISCELLANEOUS

As professionals, we all read the monthly journals and YA periodicals we subscribe to at work. In my division, each librarian reads and initials *School Library Journal*, *VOYA*, and *Booklist* regularly as part of the ordering process. But recently, I became aware of another important source of book reviews: popular YA magazines! Examples would be the "Pass the Word" column in *Word Up! Magazine*, "Book Bag" in *Black Beat Magazine*, "Bookmarks and Essence Bestsellers" in *Essence Magazine*, and the Book Review page in *Source Magazine*. These are among the most popular magazines at the Central Library in Brooklyn. While it's true that some of these sources review adult books, most of our teens read either series titles or popular adult titles. Often, the traditional YA fiction collection is checked out for school or summer reading lists. Recently, dozens of teens have repeatedly requested *How Stella Got Her Groove Back*, a Terry McMillan title. If we want to attract teen users, we are going to have to give them what they want. The "popular materials center" role advocated by the American Library Association is particularly apt for young adults. We have found that our teens do, indeed, read book reviews in the aforementioned magazines, in addition to being aware of books that are being promoted in the media. Authors appearing on television talk shows as well as movie tie-ins are definitely "in." "Oprah's Book Club" resulted in a huge demand for Toni Morrison titles; when a few teenagers asked for Jane Hamilton's *The Book of Ruth*, there was no denying the power and influence of the media. Other, less literary but nonetheless "hot" media-inspired titles have included *The X-Files* and *Clueless* series. As disgusted as some of us may be with popular series titles such as these,

If these books are so popular with teenagers, then it should behoove us as professionals, to familiarize ourselves with them, analyze why they are so popular, and use this knowledge to our advantage in dealing with YAs. Make lifetime library users of these teens now by supplying what they want.[13]

CONCLUSION

Although I've repeatedly stressed how important it is to be aware of what young adults want, what their influences are, and what books are being heavily promoted in the media, as well as in teen zines, another aspect needs to be mentioned. Upon reflecting on a few recent reader's advisory experiences of my own, it occurred to me that what some teen patrons are really interested in knowing is what *I* like to read. The young woman who approached me for books like Terry McMillan's trusted me and felt enough of a kindred spirit to embrace whatever I recommended. She happily added title after title to her stack of books, way after I had exhausted the McMillan style. Again I was struck with all the titles I was still unfamiliar with and how limited my suggestions were. Knowing your collection—not just reading blurbs or reviews but actually reading both new books as they arrive as well as older titles you've missed— is an invaluable tool in reader's advisory. Nothing can be as effective as your honest enthusiasm for a good book. Which credo should you follow, "give them what they want" or "give them what you like?" My advice is, both. Some YAs look to adults for guidance; others are just plain gregarious. These types will certainly appreciate knowing what books you've enjoyed personally. But many will either not ask or will feel that anyone older than 20 couldn't possibly know what they'd like. This group necessitates outreach and marketing via booktalks, displays, posted reviews from YA magazines, programs, and other services. Both groups deserve our attention and efforts; both are readers waiting to be awakened to the wonderful world of books and reading.

NOTES

1. Avis D. Matthews, "Breaking the Ice with YAs," in *The VOYA Reader*, ed. Dorothy Broderick (Metuchen, NJ: Scarecrow Press, 1990), 175.

2. Patrick Jones, "Don't Tell, Sell: Putting Hooks in Your Booktalks," in *Booktalk! 4*, ed. Joni Richards Bodart (New York: H.W. Wilson, 1992), 7–8.

3. Joni Richards Bodart, ed., *Booktalk! 4: Selections from the Booktalker for All Ages and Audiences* (New York: H.W. Wilson, 1992), 78.

4. Sylvia Mitchell and Karen Chun, "Out of the Mouth of Babes," in *The VOYA Reader*, 78.

5. Barbara Hoffert, "Getting People to Read: A Talk with Librarians, Booksellers, and Publishers," *Library Journal* (February 15, 1991): 162.

6. Patricia Belcastro, "A Matchmaking Tool for Readers," *Wilson Library Bulletin* (June 1995): 34–37.

7. Silvia A. Makowski et al., "Computer Pix: A Computerized Summer Reading Program for YAs," *VOYA* (August 1994): 132–36.

8. Dale Buboltz, Book Brain Promotional Brochure, 1996.

9. Karen Hultz, and Lisa C. Wemett, "A Dozen Ways to Reach Young Adults When You Are Short on Space, Staff, and Time," *VOYA* (December 1991): 298.

10. Joanne Petrik and Janice Hummel, "Teens Join YARC," in *The VOYA Reader*, 181.

11. Natalie Oleshchok, "Teens Review Books," *Public Libraries* (March/April 1996): 110.

12. Mary K. Chelton, "Read Any Good Books Lately?" *Library Journal* (May 1993): 33.

13. Silvia K. Makowski, "Serious about Series: Selection Criteria for a Neglected Genre," *VOYA* (February 1994): 349–51.

13

teens.on.the.net @yourlibrary.com

Susan Weaver

THE INTERNET PHENOMENON

There are over 40 million places to visit in cyberspace, or so says *PC Novice*.[1] The magazine cites another report that found 17 percent of the on-line respondents spending 40 hours a week on the Net, with the average amount of weekly on-line time being 21 hours. If there is any question as to how anyone could spend so much time cruising on the "information highway," consider this statement from Alta Vista: "The Web is immense. If you only spent a minute per page and devoted ten hours a day to it, it would take four and a half years to explore a million web pages, a lifetime to explore just this index."[2]

The Internet, in the simplest of terms, is a network of computer networks. It was created in 1969 by the U.S. Department of Defense as an experimental network called ARPAnet (Advanced Research Project Agency). The idea was that military communications could be maintained even in the event of a nuclear war. Later that same year, four American universities were added to the network. Academics soon saw the value in the network and employed it to share research.

Today approximately half of the Internet networks are commercial and one third are associated with educational and research institutions. There are about 40,000 registered computer networks containing over five million host computers and an estimated twenty to thirty-five million users worldwide.[3]

It is used by all ages and by all types of people. There are Web sites for the under-5 crowd such as Dr. Seuss' "My Many Colored Days" and the "Winnie the Pooh and Friends Expotition [*sic*]." At the other end of the age spectrum, the over-50 crowd can surf "Senior Site" to find "unique, informative, interesting, and entertaining" on-line opportunities.[4] It is difficult to say how many young adults are Internet users, but the number of Web sites designed especially for teens is large and growing. It is safe to predict YA use will only increase as access becomes more affordable and more widely available in schools and libraries.

So how do YAs use the Internet? What is it that they find interesting or useful? Research offers few answers for these questions. However, a review of Internet features might reveal those options that have special appeal for young adults as well as those that are targeted to YAs. The following information serves as an entry-level guide for teachers, librarians, and parents or anyone who has an interest in young adult use of the Internet.

THE KILLER APP

The Internet burst out of the academic world and into suburbia with the advent of the killer application, the World Wide Web (WWW). Since the Internet's inception in the 1960s, the network has generally been thought of as being "unfriendly" and a resource reserved for techies. Then in the 1990s, the Web, combining many Internet processes such as FTP, Gopher, and Telnet, was created. A heaping dollop of multimedia and a generous amount of hypertext were added, and the result was a deliciously fun new resource for all levels of computer expertise.

Originally developed by physicists at the European Laboratory for High Energy Physics (CERN), the WWW was designed to present research, not only with the usual text but with graphics, sound, and video. Full-color images, animation, hypertext links, and audio features have now come together to transform the silent page into an action-packed, interactive, recreational learning tool. Is there any doubt that this glossy-paged, live version of a magazine is sure to appeal to young adults?

Graphical interface "browsers" such as Netscape Navigator and Microsoft Internet Explorer are clients that allow access to the Web's resources. The resources are like those in any library. There are sources that are fun and entertaining, and others that are educational or scholarly. There are even sites that are poor in quality and content. Each of these resources is found by typing a uniform resource locator (URL), and then the site with that address is retrieved (URLs are often called addresses). Usually, each site will have links to related resources. Links appear on the screen as highlighted text or graphics, and the user may click the mouse on that area to move to the next link. This is the hypertext part of the Web.

Search engines, such as Yahoo, Alta Vista, Webcrawler, or Lycos, are tools

for finding specific information on the Web. Search terms are entered onto a
form, and the URLs of sites that contain those search terms are retrieved. The
user then has a list of sites to peruse. Some search mechanisms, such as
Magellan Internet Guide (http://www.mckinley.com/) and NetGuide Live
(http://www.netguide.com/) rate the sites and note when they have content that
is considered inappropriate for children. Other search machines have been designed especially with children in mind and retrieve only information that has
been evaluated and determined safe. For example, Yahooligans (http://
www.yahooligans.com) is the child-safe version of the well-known search engine Yahoo. Other search devices that supervise the searches and assist in evaluating content are:

- a2z-Just for Kids: http://a2z.lycos.com/Just_For_Kids
- Magellan's KidZone: http://www.mckinley.com/browse_bd.cgi?KidZone

LET'S TALK

Chat Rooms

Chat rooms may be the Internet's biggest attraction for young adults. Chat
rooms, Internet Relay Chats (IRCs), or chat lines are actually virtual living
rooms on the Web. This is interactive e-mail, where the messages of the participants are posted on screen, and everyone has an opportunity to join in. It is
easy to see how this cyberhangout might attract young adults, who can converse
with their peers without the pressure of being physically correct or having to be
spontaneous with the charming comeback or clever quip.

Chat rooms are real-time, multiuser, multichannel networks. Each IRC user
has a nickname or is identified by the channel that he or she is using. Like
"live" conversation, the chat may be limited to a topic of interest, such as
sports or politics, or just small talk on any topic. Sports enthusiasts might like
"Baseball Chat" (http://www.4-lane.com/sportschat/pages/bb_index.html) or
"Hockey Chat" (http://www.4-lane.com/sportschat/pages/hk_index.html). Prime-
time viewers can discuss the latest episodes in chat lines such as "Friends and
ER Fan Chat Club Rooms" (http://tvchat.ultimatetv.com/TVChat/friends_er.
html) or just check into http://tvchat.ultimatetv.com/TVChat/ to select the show
of choice.

Chat rooms also provide a forum for people with special needs. For example,
the URL http://www.castleweb.com/diabetes/ will access a site with chat rooms
for people with diabetes, including a room for teens with diabetes. "Marty's
HIV/AIDS Support Group and Mailing List" (http://www.smartlink.net/~mar-
tinjh/chatnews.htm) is open only to those who are HIV positive or have AIDS.

There are adult chat rooms as well as chat rooms specifically designed for
children and young adults. The ZIA Young Adult Chat Room (http://sara.zia.

com/ziachat/zia16/zia16.htm) states that it is for YAs between the age of 16 and marriage. Other electronic hangouts for teens are:

- Webchat: http://pages.wbs.net/webchat3
- Teen's Mall: http://ont.net/Chat/chat.cgi
- Rock Online Chat: http://www.rockonline.com/rol.html

Chat room guides help users to select the chamber of their choice and also give some tips on appropriate behavior while visiting. These sites list many rooms on a variety of topics:

- Chat-O-Rama: http://www.solscape.com/chat/chat_a-m.html
- Chat Lines: http://members.tripod.com/~jjulian/chatlines.html
- World of Chats: http://pcwww.uibk.ac.at/subz/c40334/abc.sht

A new and, depending on your point of view, possibly improved version of the chat line is the "chat world." These animated, 3-D worlds allow the user to assume a fictitious persona, known as an avatar, and then converse with friends face-to-face. "Worlds Chat" (http://www.worlds.net/wc/) was recently rated by the Computer Network (CNET-http://www.cnet.com) as the best of the avatar chat worlds. "Palace" (http://www.thepalace.com/) and "Microsoft Network V-Chat" were also rated high and were described as "fun and interesting."[5] "Worlds Away" (http://www.worldsaway.com/) is another one of these make-believe worlds where participants talk and laugh, smile, frown, and wave.

A noteworthy chat world, called "Starbright World" (http://www.starbright.org/projects/world/html), links terminally ill children, including teens, from their hospital beds into a fully navigable interactive community. Their home page states:

Starbright World, a 3-dimensional, multi-user environment is a virtual reality playspace in which children can play, explore, and verbally and visually communicate with each other through the use of an on-screen character or avatar. This project is not only a tool for hospitalized children to play and collaboration [sic], but one in which they are able to be a part of the community of their peers. Through ProShare teleconferencing technology, the kids, as avatars, can speak to each other via microphones; or by clicking on the camera icon, see each other and speak face-to-face.

"Addictive," even "seriously addictive" are words often used to describe chat lines. The use of chat rooms may possibly be the chief cause for workstation monopoly in public libraries and labs. It is not uncommon for a young adult to get hooked and spend hours chatting.

E-Mail

Whereas chat rooms are like being at a virtual party, e-mail is equivalent to writing a note to a friend. "E-mail" is short for "electronic mail." The user types a message, enters an e-mail address in the appropriate section of the on-line form, and then sends that message to another computer, where it is read by the friend or colleague. Generally, an e-mail message can be printed or saved to a disk. It is also possible to send an attachment, such as a word-processing document, along with the message.

The user must have an account on a computer network in order to send or receive mail. Home users must subscribe to a national network service provider (NSP) or a local Internet service provider (ISP) in order to use e-mail and access other Internet services. The users connect to the service providers via a modem.

Usenet News and Listservers

Other methods of conversing on the Net include Usenet News and listservers. Usenet News is a system where messages about any subject can be posted, and other people on the Internet can respond to them. Accessing Usenet requires a piece of software called a news reader. The "reader" takes the huge database of information and presents it in a manageable format.

Newsgroups of interest to young adults might include "alt.teens" or a pen pal forum called "alt.kids-talk.penpals." College-bound teens will find "soc.college.financial-aid" a good source of information. Information about newsgroups (Frequently Asked Questions [FAQs] how to access, what's out there) may be found at the Useful Information Center Launch Pad (http://sun-site.unc.edu/usenet-i/).

Listservs are programs that maintain one or more mailing lists where people with common interests share information. There are thousands of interest groups that may be joined by sending an e-mail message indicating the wish to subscribe. It differs from the newsgroups in that the "conversation" of the group shows up in the subscriber's e-mail box. In other words, the listserv automatically distributes a message from one member of the list to all the members on that list. Some members just follow the discussion, called lurking, while other members take a more active role and respond frequently.

Many listservs are academic or professional. A good source for identifying these mailing lists is the "Directory of Scholarly and Professional E-Conferences," which is available at http://www.N2h2.com/KOVACS/. A search of this directory, using the term "young adult," results in eighteen lists. Of this group several will be of interest to YA librarians. YALSA-L (listproc@ala1.ala.org) is ALA's list for young adult services. PUBYAC (listserv @nysernet.org) is for public librarians who serve children and young adults. The University of British Columbia's School of Library, Archival, and Information Studies is another guide to listserv resources.

Of course, there are lists for hobbyists as well as for academic or professional concerns. For example, YAWRITE (listerv@psuvm.sps.edu) is a mailing list of writing by young adults. Enthusiasts of the game Doom can get together at "dooml" (majordomo@grinch.cs.buffalo.edu) while "Humor-L" (listproc @cornell.edu) provides comic relief with "humorous, witty, and amusing information."

The library at Malaspina University, British Columbia, has compiled a page called "Newsgroups, FTP, Internet Discussion Groups: Listservs and E-Conferences," which is a superguide to finding mailing lists and learning how to use them (http://www.mala.bc.ca/www/discover/library/resource/internet).

Many libraries and universities that issue e-mail accounts forbid users to subscribe to listservs. The reason for this obvious: if a user does not regularly read the mail, the volume of messages may become a burden to the system.

THE GLORY OF THE WEB

Reading, Writing, and Virtual Reality

The educational value of the Web cannot be underestimated. As a resource for teachers, librarians, parents who are interested in education and educational sites, and students who need homework help, it is downright awesome. "AskERIC" (http://ericir.syr.edu/) not only includes over 700 lesson plans for teachers but has a virtual library and a service that allows students to post questions and receive answers within 48 hours. "Classroom Connect" (http://www.classroom.net/) is another source for teachers but can be used by students as well. The sites are divided into subject categories and graded. A+ sites are especially informative.

"Homework Help" (http://www.startribune.com/stonline/html/special/homework) provides a general discussion on academic topics, displays past questions and answers, and also allows for questions to be posted. Teachers from the Twin Cities monitor the forum and reply with answers or Internet sites where the answers might be found.

Help can also be obtained from the New Jersey NIE (Networking Infrastructure in Education) at http://njnie.dl.stevens-tech.edu/curriculum/aska.html. Experts in the fields of science, medicine, technology, marketing, and economics provide assistance.

Science-minded students can find loads of scientific information on the Web. "The Why Files" (http://whyfiles.news.wisc.edu/) is supported by the National Institute for Science Education. It uses current events and explains the "science" behind the news. The "Super Science Site" (http://www.super-science.com/home.html) provides creative ideas for science fair projects and other easy-to-perform science experiments.

Of course, YAs can place their information requests with any number of search engines. Whether they are searching for subject material for school or pursuing an interest of their own, search engines scan the Web and retrieve lists of sites on the chosen topic. A drawback with any search directory for kids is that it is not as comprehensive as the search machines that do not evaluate or screen. They may also be too elementary for many young adult needs. For example, the search engine Yahooligans is intended for 8- to 14-year-olds. For more complex teen needs, Alta Vista (http://altavista.digital.com/), Webcrawler (http://www.webcrawler.com/), or Lycos (http://www.lycos.com/) might be consulted.

Cyberspace Hangouts

The Web is fun! Besides lurking in chat rooms, young adults can find many ways to interact and have fun on the Web. Here are some suggestions for finding entertainment on the WWW.

Check out the many Web sites that have been created for kids. These pages will lead to the thousands of fun-filled nooks and crannies of the Web. Young adults can use these pages to access chat rooms, read zines, explore hobbies, play games, join fan clubs, visit virtual cafés, and find the latest information on books, movies, television shows, sports, humor, and rock and roll. Created by organizations, librarians, or the teens themselves, these pages generally contain user-safe or preevaluated links. Here are some good places to explore:

- Teenage Lounge: http://yourtown.com/teen/lounge/index.html
- OH! Kids: Webteens: http://www.oplin.lib.oh.us/EDUCATE/WEBTEENS/
- Teen Home Page: http://www.1starnet.com/teen
- Teens Only: http://education.indiana.edu/cas/adol/teen.html

The Web is a great place to turn for reading guidance. Visit ''Book Awards'' (http://www.acs.ucalgary.ca/~dkbrown/awards.html) to check out award-winning books from all over the world. Or check out the ''Young Adult Literature Page'' (http://www.ct.net/%7Epatem/yalit/) created by library science students. Some others to try include:

- YA-Zine: http://www.harperchildrens.com
- Fiction Recommended for Young Adults: http://www.econoclad.com/whatsnew/fiction.html
- Young Adult Reading (http://www.spruceridge.com/reading)

A zine is an on-line magazine and, like its paper counterpart, many are created for the YA reader. ''Fishnet'' (http://www.jayi.com/jayi) is a visually attractive zine. Filled with articles on a range of topics, it is geared toward academically gifted teens and their parents. Often the teens themselves are the authors of zines, as in the case of ''Bits & Pieces'' (http://www.ryzone.com/toc.htm). Here students present a thoughtful magazine of art, essays, and short stories. Teens also publish "TeenNet Magazine" (www.teens-online.com/page2.html), which is full of entertainment stories, sports, and other teen issues. Other zines to check out include:

- Virtually React: http://www.react.com/
- Empowered Young Females: http://www.eyf.com/
- YO (Youth Outlook): http://www.pacificnews.org/yo/
- Cameo: http://www.canuck.com/Cameo/index.html
- Spank: http://www.spankmag.com/col/ted/index.html
- Shadow: the Fiction Magazine for Teens: http//www.santarosa.edu/~tmurphy/shadow.html

FTP, TELNET, AND GOPHER

Yes, there was cyberlife before the Web. FTP, Telnet, and Gopher are Internet services that debuted long before the Web and are still valuable today. FTP, standing for file transfer protocol, is a tool that allows a user at one computer to get files from another computer. Business and research institutions often use FTP to retrieve documents or software. Young adults will find many games and other software programs available through the FTP process.

To initiate the process and connect to a remote computer, the address must be known and the user must have an ID and password. Many computers, however, allow for "anonymous FTP." In this situation the user ID is the word "anonymous," and the password is the user's e-mail address (for more information about FTP, see the FTP Frequently Asked Questions [FAQ] at http:// hoohoo.ncsa.uiuc.edu/ftp/faq.html).

Telnet is another method of logging onto a computer to look at the files it contains. For example, Telnet was often used to log into a library's on-line catalog. The Telnet FAQ (http://www.redrock.net/redrock/faq/telnet.html) alludes to the overshadowing of Telnet by the Web:

Telnet has been around for a long time and represents one of the oldest resources available in the Internet. With Telnet you can connect as a dumb terminal to another computer supporting Telnet. . . . Many of these computers are set-up specifically for some applications, for example, you can access university card catalogs and the like using Telnet. Often, Telnet is used to play MUDs (Multiple User Dungeons) which is a text adventure game where you can explore and fight the scenery and each other. . . . It is important to note that most users will never use Telnet. It is generally a tool for pointy-headed computer guys.[6]

Gopher, developed at the University of Michigan, was the first Internet service to be considered user-friendly. It is a client/server system that uses a simple menu-driven system to locate information. The word itself is a play on the words "go for." Once a menu item is selected, Gopher goes off into computerland, grabs the information, and brings it to the screen. Like Telnet and FTP, the preferred method of using Gopher is now often via the WWW.

THE ROLE OF THE MENTOR

Parents, teachers, and librarians must do more than provide the Internet connection. The Internet must be "embraced," and the mentor should prepare to guide and educate the young adult user. What greater opportunity is there to appear "cool" in the eyes of the young adult than to be an expert in using the grand Web? But here's the catch: the young adult is often the one who possesses computer expertise and perhaps is even Internet-savvy. Some of those who hope to do the mentoring may have a lot of catching up to do. In general, librarians may have more opportunities than parents to learn about the Internet and are a logical source for the parents to turn to for help. Consider Cynthia N. James-Catalano's statement in *Internet World*:

After buying computers and getting an Internet connection, many parents expect their trip to the library to be a thing of the past. Then they get online and discover they don't know where anything is! Where are all those great resources the media keeps writing about?"[7]

This situation may be seen as an opportunity for librarians to promote the services of the library and to educate parents about the positive uses of the Internet.

Internet advocates will find support and information in a Web site of the same name. "The Internet Advocate" (http://www.monroe.lib.in.us/~lchampel/netadv.html) not only provides examples of positive use of the Internet by young adults but offers guidance on how to respond to inaccurate perceptions of pornography on the Internet. Here can be found links to resource guides for librarians, examples of Acceptable Use Policies (AUP), guidelines for creating policies, information about blocking software, and lists of other organizations that are committed to electronic freedom.

The American Library Association (http://www.ala.org) is another excellent source for policies and guidance. "The Library Bill of Rights" and "Access to Electronic Information, Services, and Networking: An Interpretation of the Library Bill of Rights" are two important documents located on this Web site. Another choice is the Internet Public Library's "Services to Librarians and Information Professionals Home Page" (http://www.ipl.org/svcs). They state their mission as striving to:

• supply resources and materials to support the professional development of librarians

• provide a virtual meeting place for colleagues in the profession to connect and communicate with one another

- train and inform about the use of the Internet in library and information settings
- increase the value of the Internet for librarians and information professionals[8]

Adequately armed with information and Internet skills, the mentor might consider the "home page" as a means of guiding and educating. A home page is the site that is retrieved every time the Web is accessed. It can serve as a springboard to the Web. A home page for a specialized audience, such as young adults, could provide links to appropriate entertainment, information, and instructional material. The instructional materials would include the policies of the institution such as the Acceptable Use Policy. In addition to providing links to valuable content, a home page can organize that vast amount of information and present it to the teen in a manageable format.

A simple home page can be created with very minimal training on HTML. HTML, or "hyper text mark-up language," is the name of the programming used to create Web pages. Still, the task should not be underestimated. Finding the links, verifying URLs, and organizing the material are a very time-consuming process. A site called "WWW Lifesavers" (http://interactiveads.com/interact/tips.html) lives up to its name in that it provides access to sites that instruct in every aspect of creating home pages and Web use. Another useful resource is "The Young Adult Librarian's Help/Homepage" (http://www.kcpl.lib.mo.us/ya/), which is "designed to gather resources on and off the Web to help librarians serving teens." LION, or the Librarian's Information Online Network, (http://www.libertynet.org/lion/lion.html), is a resource for K-12 school librarians.

The creation of a home page should include input from the young adults. YAs will enjoy being Web sleuths who seek and evaluate sites. They can play an important role in the on-line collection development process without any additional cost to the library or school.

CYBERPORN, ACCESS, AND THE AUP

The now-notorious *Time* magazine article of July 3, 1995, reported the existence of porn on the Internet and initiated a chain of overreaction. The article was based on a Carnegie Mellon University report that has since been scrutinized and criticized by many scholars. Still, the bottom line is that it brought the cyberporn issue to the front page of national newspapers and into the laps of American parents.

There is no denying that there are pornography and the potential for crime on the Internet. A brochure titled *Child Safety on the Information Highway* and developed by the National Center for Missing & Exploited Children gives the topic some perspective with this viewpoint:

Although there have been some highly publicized cases of abuse involving computers, reported cases are relatively infrequent. . . . The fact that crimes are being committed online, however, is not a reason to avoid using these services. To tell children to stop using these services would be like telling them to forgo attending college because students are sometimes victimized on campus. A better strategy would be for children to learn how to be "street smart" in order to better safeguard themselves in any potentially dangerous situation.

It continues by saying that teenagers are particularly at risk because they are often unsupervised and more likely to engage in on-line discussions regarding companionship, relationships, or sexual activity. The brochure, which is available on-line and in print, helps parents to understand the true nature of the Internet and advises on setting guidelines.[9]

Robert Sanchez in "Students on the Internet: Can You Ensure Appropriate Access?" (http://www.aasa.org/FrontBurner/Technology) provides additional thoughts:

Educators nationwide tend to agree on several points. First, the potential educational value of the Internet is immense. Second, the ready availability of pornography on the Internet only mirrors other aspects of American society, especially other forms of mass media. Finally, if one does not look for pornography on the Internet, one's chances of stumbling on it are slim.

As mentioned, the Internet Advocate and the American Library Association are Web sources that educate and attempt to correct the misperceptions regarding the extent of cyperporn. "Safe Surf" is another organization interested in safety on the Internet. Safe Surf is working to create an Internet Rating Standard so that Web users will be able to detect the content of a site before accessing it. Cyber Angels (http://www.cyberangels.org), an all-volunteer Internet patrol, is part of the "International Alliance of Guardian Angels." Their mission is to be a cyberspace "neighborhood watch" and to make young people "cyber street-smart."

Librarians must be prepared to discuss the issues and lead parents to Web sources that give guidance. They must also take on the task of instilling street smarts and creating good Net citizens of young adults. Policies have often been used to protect libraries and to establish desirable behavior patterns for patrons. The Acceptable Use Policy has emerged as a means of guiding patron use of the Internet. An AUP should:

1. Educate students, patrons, and their parents about the kinds of tools they will use on the Internet and what they might expect from these tools.
2. Define boundaries of behavior and specify the consequence of violating those boundaries.
3. Specify the actions that might be taken in order to maintain or police the network.[10]

For suggestions on creating a policy see "AASA Front Burner Issues" (http://www.aasa.org/FrontBurner) and Classroom Connect (http://www.classroom.net).

Many schools, colleges, and libraries that have AUPs have made them available on the Net. Sample policies may be at these sites: gopher://ericir.syr.edu/11/ Guides and http://chico.rice.edu/armadillo/Rice/Resources/acceptable.html.

Although the policy should be unique to the institution, each should include a core body of information. Expectations for Internet use should be clear. The philosophy of library Internet use, such as "for educational and entertainment purposes," must be stated. There should be a disclaimer for Net content and accuracy. The policy should explain who can use the system and what type of support will be provided.

Expected behaviors should also be made clear. These would include Internet courtesy (Netiquette), security, time limits for use, and printing limits or costs. If certain features are forbidden or limited, for example, chat rooms or newsgroups, the reason for the restriction should be stated. The policy should be posted, and copies made available in the library. Some libraries require that the user, perhaps even the parent, sign the document before access is allowed.

Other types of agreements may also be issued and signed in order to keep children safe on the Net. For example, the Safe Surf Parent/Child Agreement (http://www.safesurf.com/lifegard.htm) is a good guide and one that parents might post by home computers. It states:

1. I will tell my parents right away if I come across any information that makes me feel uncomfortable.

2. I will not give out my address, telephone number, or the name and location of my school without my parent's permission.

3. I will never agree to get together with someone I "meet" online without first checking with my parents. If my parents agree to the meeting, I will be sure that it is in a public place and bring my mother or father along.

4. If I get a message that is mean, or makes me feel uncomfortable, I will not respond. It is not my fault if I get a message like that, and I will tell my parents if I do.

5. I will work with my parents so that we can set up rules for going online. We will decide upon the time of day that I can be online, the length of time that I can be online, and areas that I am allowed to visit. I will not access other areas or break these rules without their permission.

The AUP and on-line agreements are the least restrictive methods of monitoring young adult use of the Net. Perhaps the most restrictive is the use of filters or blocking software. This software filters out sites with objectionable language or allows access only to sites that have been evaluated and are proven to be "child-friendly." Net Nanny, SurfWatch, Internet in a Box for Kids, Cybersitter, and Cyber Patrol are just a few of the many products to choose from.

The world's largest information resource has much to offers to today's young adult. Like the real world, it has places of learning, amusement parks, and even dark alleys. With guidance and education, the teen on-line can experience the cyberworld of communication, discovery, and fun.

NOTES

Editors' Note: The WWW sites mentioned in this chapter were verified prior to publication.

1. "The Survey Says," *PC Novice* (August 1996): 9.

2. Alta Vista Technology Inc., http://altavista.digitial.com/av/content/help_simple. htm.

3. Stephen Pastan, "Evolution of the Net," *The Lancet: Guide to the Internet (supplement to The Lancet)* (1996): 4.

4. Seniors Site. http://seniors-site.com.

5. "CNET Recommends," http://www.cnet.com/Content/Reviews/Compare/Chat/ ss01.html

6. Telnet FAQ, http://www.redrock.net/redrock/faq/telnet.html.

7. Cynthia James-Catalano, "Inquiring Minds," *Internet World* (October 1996): 32.

8. Internet Public Library: Services to Librarians and Information Professional Home Page, http://www.ipl.org/svcs.

9. National Center for Missing and Exploited Children, "Child Safety on the Information Highway," http://www.missingkids.org/.

10. "What You Need to Know about Acceptable Use Policies," http://www. covis.nwu.edu/AUP-archive/CoVis_AUP.html.

14

Targeting Teens: Marketing and Merchandising Young Adult Services

Mary Anne Nichols

Over a decade ago, large companies such as McDonald's, Coca-Cola, Columbia Pictures, and Revlon had not really realized they had a primary target in teens. Over the years, these companies, along with libraries, eventually came to the same conclusion: teens are a marketing segment opportunity too powerful to ignore. Why is this? Of importance to businesses, teens have real spending power, are able to influence household spending, and will be future spenders. Relevant to libraries, teens constitute approximately 25 percent of a public library's patrons and will be future voters who can help pass levies and continue to support its services.[1] They are also a growing market. In 1995, there were 29 million people aged 12 to 19 in the United States. The teen population will continue to expand until the year 2010, as baby boomers' children reach this age.[2]

In response to this marketing push, libraries are changing the definition of what they do. Before, emphasis was placed on products (collections and services), whereas the shift now is to become customer-oriented. A true marketing approach determines the needs and wants of its target markets and uses resources available to deliver the desired products and services. A library today must be willing to adapt collections and services to satisfy the customer. This adaptation may or may not reflect the way things have always been done. An example of this is a young adult librarian who is reluctant to provide comic books or paperbacks because of short shelf life and budget constraints, but who does so because these are what young adults prefer to read. If a library is to be successful with its marketing efforts, it needs to be aware of the following points: who its customers are (library patrons are referred to as customers because there is an exchange of services), who or what its competition is, and verbalizing what the customer will get only from the library.[3]

Why should YA librarians concern themselves with marketing? Too often librarians feel that a library markets its services just by the goodwill feeling it projects to the public. Librarians are enthusiastic about their profession and at times project this enthusiasm into an image of what their library is like. However, this image is not realistic as to what the library really has to offer. Preschoolers (even infants and toddlers) and school-aged children enthusiastically attend programs and use library services, but I have observed that library usage tends to lessen as teenagers come of age. Good marketing efforts can keep YAs interested and active in the library by understanding their developmental needs and promoting services to meet those needs to make them lifelong library advocates.

Before beginning a marketing plan, one should remember that marketing is not solely for the purpose of providing customers with new services but also to reinforce and improve existing services. Staff must be active—not passive—in responding to the needs of its customers.[4] Be prepared to capitalize on, and expand, strengths and remedy weaknesses. Like businesses, libraries should realize that future growth will not depend on current customers but on potential ones.[5] To begin, analyze the current situation of the young adult services. Refine your product or service. Look at your competition. Can something be learned from what they have to offer? Direct competition can stem from activities at local bookstores where it is "cool" to hang out and be seen, latchkey programs, or church youth groups. Indirect competition can come from the fact that some YAs may not be able to obtain a ride to your library.

It will be easier to predict and influence your YA customer behavior by employing market segmentation. Market segmentation divides customers into groups with unique characteristics and needs. Your market is already segmented by age—12- to 18-year-olds—and many of your "best" customers are those avid library users you see day-to-day or week-to-week. Other user groups or market segments can be distinguished by the following ways: geography, reading interests, social status, amount of library use, gender, income, and education level. Your YA segment can further be broken down into the following: grade, age, type of school attending (public versus private), readers versus nonreaders, cardholders versus noncardholders, those going to college versus those not going to college. As you can see, the list is endless. Knowing your segment will allow you to plan services and collections accordingly. Planning a program on choosing a four-year college or having a large collection of college planning guides may not be appropriate in an area where your market segment attends trade or vocational two-year colleges.

Now that you know who your target markets are, how do you know what they need and want? Determining what services your customers require and how you plan to provide them can be the most critical elements of marketing. One way to determine needs is through user surveys. Survey techniques can include interviews, telephone surveys, written surveys, and focus groups. Probably, the technique with the lowest cost and the easiest to perform is the written survey. The results of any survey can be tabulated into finding the average age of YA users, why they use your service, what they like most or least like about your collection and services, how much they use the library, and so on. Using these results, you can match your services to their needs.

Another way of determining wants and needs is evaluating and analyzing users and usage. *Output Measures and More: Planning and Evaluating Public Library Services for Young Adults* by Virginia Walter is an invaluable tool for young adult librarians. Using this manual will enable you to provide effective YA service and even integrate these services into your library's overall strategic plan. Lastly, direct observation of customers, by yourself and other staff, can also be a means of determining needs and wants. For example, observing after-school behavior or noticing how YAs use current services can provide information without a formal means of gathering data.

THE MARKETING MIX

By looking at what we have learned so far, you now understand that marketing does not stem from a single idea but is a complex collection of activities. The application of these activities as the marketing mix is also essential in the development of a marketing plan. Every marketing professor using any basic marketing text has for years referred to the marketing mix as the four Ps—product, price, place, and promotion.

Product

The products in a young adult department are what services you offer. These can include programs, activities, your collection, staff, and special services such as reader's advisory, reference, keeping a notebook with school assignments, homework centers, computers and Internet training, Infotrac, and so on. As you can see, the list is endless. Young adult librarians need to concern themselves with product design in that they arrange their products and services in a way that will attract YAs to the library.

Price

The price element of marketing can be simply defined as what it will cost you to offer the desired services, not what your customer pays for them. Programs can be costed out and evaluated to see how resources are being used. Obvious costs you can include are moneys spent on refreshments, collection development, shelving, furniture for your YA area, and any costs for special services provided. Don't forget to consider the cost of staff time involved in the preparation of programs and services. Another cost is the opportunity cost of both the staff and the library user.

The opportunity cost of staff members can be considered as the time spent on developing or maintaining a service or product. Is it cost-efficient for you to be doing this? Are you spending an inordinate amount of time planning programs that are not well attended? In other words, does it meet the needs of your market segment, or could your time be spent on something else that does? The opportunity cost of the YA users is the activity given up in order to come to the library. Remember, the customer is interested in the benefit of the proposed product, not necessarily its value. Is your product or service able to compete with this?

Other ideas to consider within the pricing element are ways to save money and staff time. For example, belonging to a standing order plan for series paperbacks can save time when ordering for your collection. Teen volunteers and/ or young adult advisory councils can develop programming and aid in collection development. Developing a good relationship with Friends of the Library groups that can provide you with money for your collection and services is essential. Memberships in regional library systems and using the resources of the state library can help with program development, professional resources, and networking. Tools such as a good desktop publishing program or an Ellison machine can provide low-cost ways to create displays. Another way to cut promotion costs can be advertising services in community papers or Parent-Teacher Association (PTA) newsletters for free.

Place

Place is where you offer your young adult services. This includes the arrangement and location of the young adult area. Is it next to or included in the children's area, or is it close to the adult materials? Hopefully, the latter. Is the space allotted to young adults equipped with comfortable furniture and a place to do homework? Does the collection fill the shelves and overflow the book dumps, or can things be easily located? Is an OPAC or Internet station where students can do research nearby? Most important, is it appealing to the YA user? Place can also be outside the library. This can include displays in schools or taking your show on the road to schools or the institutionalized.

Promotion

The last "P," promotion, is the one element that most people easily associate with marketing. Promotion can occur both inside and outside the library. Promotion inside the library encompasses programming to promote your services, presenting library tours and bibliographic instruction during class visits, and displaying local school artwork in the YA area to draw students (and their friends and families) to the library. Make sure that staff are aware of programs or special events that are offered for YAs. A teen approaching the circulation desk with a question regarding a program or service deserves a straight answer. An uninformed staff member can give the appearance that the library does not care about teens or that nothing is offered especially for them. Other ways to promote your collection are displays. Materials should be displayed with covers facing out. Borrow from the world of retailing by displaying items on end aisles or at the circulation desk (point of purchase). These are successful in spurring impulse buying or borrowing, in a library's case.

Promotion outside the library can occur at schools, for example, scheduling your time booktalking to classes. Promotion of the library also occurs at schools through the services offered to teachers. Developing a good relationship with the school media specialist and attending media center staff meetings can go a long way in helping you to establish rapport with teachers and staff. Do you offer teacher's loan and/or assignment planning and preparation? Also consider having a display table or giving a presentation during a school open house or parent–teacher conference nights.

Networking within the library's community can also help with promotion. Do you have displays or participate in local events? Examples of this can be having a booth at a community celebration or fair or decorating a float for a local parade. Or you can offer to give presentations to groups such as Junior Achievement or local church youth groups. Plan a program in conjunction with the local parks and recreation department—anything to gain exposure. Place exhibits or flyers in local teen hangouts, storefronts, or community gathering places.

Promotion includes paid advertising plus all aspects of public relations. Public relations involves any relationship with the media, community organizations, patrons, politicians. Using a simple calendar, develop a publicity plan that indicates what events you will publicize and to whom you will send publicity materials. Include in your plan any arrangement for speakers or intended displays or exhibits. Indicate on your calendar when steps leading up to an exhibit or presentation need to be accomplished. Become familiar with and read the newspapers in your local community. Make appointments to meet editors and reporters of local newspapers, cable news networks, and local radio stations. Ask when their deadlines are and the date on which the newspaper is distributed to the community. Verify the name of the person to whom you should send information. Newspapers and radio/television are interested in newsworthy items of general interest that affect and involve the local community. Events that occur within your young adult service are natural for this type of publicity. Make sure you allow yourself enough time to write a press release and send it to a newspaper in sufficient time for it to be used. News releases should answer these fundamental questions: *Who* is the organization involved? *What* will happen? *When* will it happen? *Where* will it happen? *Why* is it happening? and *How* did this all come about? Be sure to use everyday language that will conjure up a picture in the reader's mind.

All of these ideas for promotion accomplish the same goal: gaining attention of customers, giving them a positive feeling, and influencing them to use the product or service.

Using all that has been discussed about marketing thus far, you are now able to develop and implement a marketing plan for the different segments within your area of YA service. Obviously, to reach every segment will take time and cannot be done all at once. Appendix 14.1 uses general terms and can be used as a guide to help you develop your individual marketing plan. Appendix 14.2 is provided so you can see what your finished plan could look like. It is an example of targeting a specific market segment and planning for it.

MERCHANDISING

Merchandising is related to marketing—especially the promotion aspect of it—but is basically concerned with distribution or placement of items and taking specific actions to get your product sold. In libraries, this means having your books circulated or enticing YAs to come to your programs. Most YAs find the books they read through browsing and rarely ask or follow up on a teacher or librarian's suggestion. Therefore, merchandising efforts should not solely rely on theme-related displays, such as sports books on a table with sports equipment every year in time for the Super Bowl or the World Series. Merchandising involves displaying your collection in eye-catching ways that encourage customers to use it. The following highlights successful ways to merchandise YA services.

The best places for displays are near the entrance to the YA area, at the end of cross aisles in heavily traveled areas, or near the circulation or other service desk. Never display any material that cannot be immediately checked out. Try to keep displays at eye level and make sure that lighting is adequate and signage is professionally done and readable. Merchandising encourages library users to pick up materials just as they pick up items at the grocery store while waiting for checkout.[6] This employs point-of-purchase displays, where YA browsers select something beyond what they originally set out to find.

Unlike bookstores, libraries like to use the old-fashioned shelving methods that show the materials spine-out. The concept of display shelving is becoming more popular in libraries throughout the country. Special display shelving units can be purchased that have shelves that enable face-out display. Even having limited budgets, by thinking creatively, existing shelving can be transformed for this type of display. The space required for this type of shelving is greater than traditional library shelving, but the ability to display materials face-out increases turnover rates so that more items are in circulation at a given time.[7] The old adage "you can't judge a book by its cover" does not ring true in young adult literature. YAs are attracted to flashy covers, and publishers spend large sums of money on the visual impact of book jackets.[8] Display shelving takes advantage of this.

In order for it to be successful, proper maintenance of display shelving must be done every day. Straighten the collection daily. Make sure the books displayed are eye-catching, clean, and in good repair. Weed any book in disrepair and buy replacement copies. Purchase multiple copies of items, especially paperbacks. Vary the display and avoid repetitious displays in the same shelving display unit. Train your staff in the art of displays and inform them that they need to restock and straighten the shelves on a regular basis. Make shelvers aware that they can display titles face-out at the end and top of shelves and place titles with multiple copies alternately spine-out and face-out. Buy and display multiple copies of materials that are the most popular and currently trendy, including the ones with short shelf life, like magazines, comic books, and paperbacks.

What are some elements of a successful, exciting display? Color is one. Libraries make the mistake of thinking that they don't need to compete with consumer-oriented businesses. YAs are bombarded with and attracted to the color, noise, enthusiasm, and excitement of television and advertisements for the brand names they love to buy. Use bright, bold colors and simple details. Avoid arranging items in a straight line. Using humor and doing the unexpected can be attention grabbers.[9]

Booklists are relatively inexpensive and easy to compile as ways to merchandise YA collections. You can take advantage of award-winning lists from ALA or professional journals or compile your own. Circulation staff can force-feed or put a copy into items borrowed by YAs at the checkout desk. Bibliographies of award-winning titles can be sent with letters to teachers. Staff can also distribute booklists to those who ask relevant reference or reader's advisory questions. Booklists can contain print and nonprint materials. Make sure to include titles for which you have multiple copies and authors who have written several works. The library's name, location, and hours of service should also be included.

CONCLUSION

Successful marketing and merchandising require active staff involvement and a solid commitment to the process. Young adult librarians cannot afford to make the mistake of thinking they don't need to compete with the consumer-oriented and product-driven world of teenagers today. A solid young adult services marketing and merchandising plan will enable the library to reap the immediate benefit of teen use and allow it to compete with the normally busier adult and children's section of the library.

APPENDIX 14.1: MARKETING PLAN FOR YA SERVICES

I. Analyze current situation

    A. Determine strengths and weaknesses

    B. Study competition

    C. Analyze opportunities and set objectives

II. Define market segments in YA services

III. Choose one segment of YA services

    A. Define characteristics

    B. Determine needs

IV. Implement marketing mix

    A. Product strategy

    B. Price strategy

    C. Place strategy

    D. Promotion strategy

V. Evaluation

    A. Internal considerations

        1. Was staff time used efficiently to complete strategies?

        2. Was cost worth the effort?

    B. Formal

        1. Analyze usage/program attendance

        2. Circulation

    C. Informal

        1. Observation

        2. Comments from users

APPENDIX 14.2: MARKETING PLAN FOR A SPECIFIC YA SEGMENT—HIGH SCHOOL SENIORS

I. Analyze current situation

    A. Determine strengths and weaknesses

    B. Study competition

    C. Analyze opportunities and set objectives

II. Define market segments

III. Choose one segment—high school seniors

    A. Characteristics

    B. Determine needs

        1. Term paper help

    2. Career opportunities

    3. Transition to college

    4. Choosing a college/major

    5. Bibliographic instruction

IV. Implement marketing mix

  A. Product strategy

    1. Collection

      a. Videos of college campuses

      b. College undergraduate catalogs

      c. Barron's and Peterson's Guides

      d. SAT practice guides

      e. Career manuals

      f. Classic literature

      g. Turabian or MLA manuals

    2. Services

      a. Computer/OPAC training

      b. Internet training

      c. Circulation of preceding products

      d. Programming:

        (1) Choosing a college

        (2) College life—how to survive

        (3) Career nights

        (4) Job fairs

  B. Price strategy

    1. Cost of materials

    2. Staff time

    3. Opportunity cost of staff and high school seniors

  C. Place strategy

    1. Inside the library

      a. OPAC in YA area

      b. Internet site in YA area

      c. CD-ROM

      d. Homework center

      e. Comfortable area to do homework/group projects

    2. In the community

      a. Work with guidance counselors

      b. Contacts at local colleges for programming

    D. Promotion strategy

        1. Inside the building

           a. Homework centers

           b. Be available for after-school crowd

        2. In the community

           a. School visits

           b. Flyers to schools

           c. Press releases to local newspapers/PTA newsletter

           d. Attend media center staff meetings

V. Evaluation

    A. Internal considerations

        1. Was staff time used efficiently to complete strategies?

        2. Was cost worth the effort?

    B. Formal

        1. Analyze usage/program attendance

        2. Circulation

    C. Informal

        1. Observation

        2. Comments from users

NOTES

1. Department of Education, National Center for Education Statistics Survey Report, *Services and Resources for Young Adults in Public Libraries* (Washington, DC: Government Printing Office, 1988).

2. Peter Zollo, "Talking to Teens," *American Demographics* (November 1995): 22–25.

3. State Library of Ohio, *Marketing and Libraries Do Mix: A Handbook for Libraries and Information Centers* (Columbus, 1993), 1.

4. Ibid., 3–4.

5. Ibid., 12–14.

6. Cosette Kies, *Marketing and Public Relations for Libraries* (Metuchen, NJ: Scarecrow Press, 1987), 169.

7. Baltimore County Public Library's Blue Ribbon Committee, *Give 'Em What They Want!* (Chicago: American Library Association, 1992), 126.

8. Karen Litt, "Visual Merchandising of Books," *The Unabashed Librarian*, no. 60 (1986): 3.

9. Ibid., 3–4.

15

Techno Teens: The Use of Technology by Young Adults

Lesley Farmer

What fascinates youth about technology? Is it the bells and whistles? Is it the movement? Is it the sense of control? Is it just plain familiarity? Probably each of those factors plays into the picture of technology-using young adults.

Quite frankly, technology-friendly YAs have been on the scene for a long time. Think about the record and, more recently, CD and videotape collections. Teens like being surrounded by the stimuli that technology provides.

Likewise, the public library has involved young adults in those technologies. Teen councils or advisory boards often provide input in the selection of music-based technology. In the Radnor Township Memorial Library (Pennsylvania), for instance, the librarian had the local halfway-house teens accompany her to the local music store and select the records for the YA collection. Not surprisingly, they were the first ones to check out the albums and tell their friends about the new acquisitions.

The downside of technology is equally obvious in library history. It has taken money from an already slim budget, it has required staff time and training, it has attracted "exploratory" teens, it has raised issues of censorship and copyright, and it has duplicated products available in stores and other commercial enterprises. Haven't librarians dealt with enough problems as it is?

What keeps libraries technology-accessible has been librarian belief that information should not be limited to book format, belief in bridging the gap between the haves and the have-nots, and belief in preparing users who will become taxpayers. Librarians need to plan thoroughly and get substantial support from the community so libraries can provide the best information most effectively to teens as well as to other constituents. What is involved is a basic issue of access, not only to technology but also to decision making.

VIDEO

Recently, video has come into play as a library technology format. Video has been used by young adults as a means for education, for recreation, and for self-expression. Community colleges have provided videotaped lectures and correspondence courses via videotape for over a decade. As young adults have taken college courses in high school, they have made use of these videotapes. In some cases, public libraries have circulated these course tapes so users could view them at their own convenience. Particularly with more teens seeking alternatives to traditional high school education, videotaped courses have become more attractive to this audience.

Videotapes also serve as a cheap recreational option. Teens may borrow a tape and escape the crowd to view it alone—or bring them in to watch en masse. In some cases, a teacher may check out a tape for class viewing. The most important factor in serving this population is to match the users' interests and needs.

Especially if it has a YA advisory council or interest group, the library may provide video production options. Students may tape library programs or even take their show on the road to tape community events and have the library archive them. Bibliographic instructional sessions may be taped, and new users can view those tapes in the library at their convenience.

IN-HOUSE ACCESS BY COMPUTER

Generally, when libraries discuss technology these days, they're talking about computer technology, and the greatest library use of computers by young adults is research, either for school or for personal issues. Particularly when half of the public library users are teens during many afternoons and evenings, it behooves librarians to keep up on computer advances and provide adequate service to that population.

The basic use of technology in most libraries, by all types of users as well as by the library staff, is the computerized catalog/circulation program. YA indicators should be included in the cataloging record, either in the call number or notes so teens can find items of particular interest to them, especially in those cases where no separate YA section exists. If such a section is available, an Online Public Access Catalog (OPAC) should be installed nearby to facilitate teen efforts to bridge the YA collection with the rest of the library's holdings. To aid access to the catalog's information, simple, self-explanatory signs should be placed by the computer stations.

Unfortunately, some computer-savvy teens like to push the envelope of the

OPAC system, and have been known to exit the catalog system and get into other applications. Occasionally, they even make changes to the catalog or circulation records. Other less computer-literate users sometimes get out of the program by accident. Therefore, the library needs to make its computer system robust and secure.

The basic technology access tool to local periodicals is a magazine index, now usually in microfiche or CD-ROM format. Since teens often consider magazines to be their reading material of choice, the magazine index should be available near the periodicals section. Librarians should make sure that the index chosen includes YA titles. The index should also mark those titles held by the library, or a sign by the index should note available magazines; teens become frustrated when they get a useful list of potential articles and assume that the library subscribes to all of them only to find that the library owns just a couple of those magazines. Libraries should also try to provide a print option with their index since teens appreciate being able to instantly print out relevant citations. Pushing the magic button can have its drawbacks, though, as some teens lack the experience to develop a sophisticated and well-constructed search strategy and end up printing out 30 pages on Bill Clinton. Librarians can take two preventive measures: help teens learn how to search efficiently (through clear guide sheets and personal attention) and establish search/print options within the administrative portion of the magazine index. These steps can help avoid setting fees for printing, which could pose a financial constraint for some teens. While fee-service libraries can assert that they are still providing access because their users can take notes from the screen, they are sending an unfriendly message to teens. Free printing services are a wise investment in our youth.

SURFING THE NET

Nowadays, with teens using computers at home, especially in conjunction with the Internet, some libraries further extend their service by providing access points to their OPAC and magazines via the World Wide Web. The San Francisco Public Library goes the extra mile by providing free full-text articles via the Net to library card-carrying teens. Imagine the power that such YAs have and the regard with which they bestow such libraries!

For many teens, however, no such home access to computers or the Internet in particular exists. Thus, libraries provide the main information access safety net for them. Because our society is facing an information have/have-not class system, because YAs are the immediate future's hope, and because teens often face covert disfranchisement because of their lack of political power, libraries have an incredible opportunity to make a social difference. On that basis alone, libraries should avoid charging teens any fees for accessing telecommunications services. If budgets are a constraining issue, then librarians should seek community financial backing rather than cut teens out of the information loop. In any circumstance, any fees charged should be consistently applied to all constituents regardless of age.

Beyond giving information about in-house resources, libraries that provide free and public access to the Internet open the world of information to their users. What information do YAs access through the Internet via library services? The research mainstays are remote databases: to scientists, to government sources, to educational institutions, and to commercial ventures. These days, teens can experience Internet information through text, graphics, sound, and even motion. Teens can access other libraries, each of which offers links to other valuable sources. Teens can also surf the Net for sites that interest them personally, be it sex, drugs, or rock and roll. As much as possible, libraries should try to provide teens free public Internet access, preferably at the graphical WWW level.

As YAs explore the Net world, some people become anxious that teens will haunt subversive or destructive sites. Crass and inaccurate materials do exist. Teens do write negative letters on the Net (one student threatened to bomb the White House, which brought the Federal Bureau of Investigation (FBI) on the scene immediately). Adult Netters have molested underage e-mailers and chatters who have given out their home addresses and phone numbers.

School sites can be held legally accountable for minors' accessing pornographic sites or writing inflammatory messages, so many institutions have established usage "contracts" in order to avoid suits and other allegations of neglect or conspiracy (or be kicked off a local Internet service provider). A few have acquired constricting programs that filter out Internet sources with "provocative" terms such as "sex" (which can result in a student's not being able to get information about sextants); such practices constitute a type of censorship. Public libraries do not have that type of responsibility, usually, so can more easily provide unfettered access to electronic information, services, and networks; librarians can normally lay access restriction burdens on the shoulders of parents and legal guardians. According to the 1996 American Library Association discussion about electronic access to information, "reasonable restrictions placed on the time, place, and manner of library access should be used only when necessary to achieve substantial library objectives and should be applied in the least restrictive manner possible."

The healthiest way to approach problematic Internet issues is to educate YAs, explaining possible legal ramifications of certain behaviors on the Net. For instance, teens should know that they may be held responsible for typing bomb threats or slandering someone in "public." Giving youth the facts to make reasoned decisions about Internet use goes along with existing library objectives.

In actuality, the critical problem is that some teens are not able to find the information they want or need. As with other access tools, YAs may not have intellectual access because they have not been instructed in Internet search strategies. In some cases, teens don't know how to navigate through the Net to find information; in other cases, teens can locate sources but can't tell the relative use and relevance of those sources. While some circles cry the demise of libraries and the need for librarians, in reality, librarians play a more critical role than ever. In the past, libraries constituted a balanced collection of resources preselected critically by professionals. Sources on the Internet are not subject to such across-the-board evaluative scrutiny. The Internet accessor becomes the critic. Unless librarians intend to conduct all Internet searches themselves, which would result in overtaxed staff and codependent users, they need to help their users learn those evaluation/selection skills. Every librarian must assume a proactive educator role, empowering teens to make decisions more wisely.

One creative way to model Internet use and provide guidance in locating useful sites is to develop a library Web page—or better yet, have YAs design one for the library. The main body of the home page can show the variety of library services and resources. The easiest approach is to develop a short list of linked options that the user can access. These links can refer to embedded pages or to external files. Some topics to consider for inclusion are library orientation (resources and services); what's new in the library; announcements about upcoming events, programs, contests, activities; in-house databases (such as hot lines and community contacts); reader's advisory; Internet sites of the week; or, Web-based bibliographies or "pathfinders."

Finding good URLs (Uniform Resource Locators, or Internet addresses) calls forth professional evaluation and selection skills. If teens do this task, librarians should check their results for accuracy and value. Teens can be recognized for good work by "signing" their pathfinders. In addition, any library pages need to be updated on a weekly basis since sites and addresses change so frequently. While significant time is needed to develop and maintain high-quality Web pages, the impact of such intellectual effort is considerable because of its great access potential; it visibly demonstrates the critical and highly developed skills that librarianship offers and passes on to YAs.

RESOURCES HANDED ON A SILVER PLATTER

CD-ROMs have become a way of life for teens in many libraries. They provide full-text magazine articles and expanded index access, store mega-amounts of data such as library catalogs and encyclopedias, enrich topics with animated graphics, and offer video clips of historical events.

CD-ROMs benefit both teens and librarians. They can even be inexpensive—and, in some cases, may replace hard copy. The durability of CD-ROMs outlasts newsprint, both in terms of the medium as well as in terms of vandalism. CD-ROMs take up much less storage space than their print counterparts. In terms of information access, CD-ROM technology facilitates the use of a search engine so teens can combine key words using Boolean logic to find a specific article or text quickly.

YAs love them. Teens have been known to stand in line for a half hour in order to access *Grolier's Encyclopedia*, while a newer print encyclopedia dejectedly rests on the shelf (at least, in the librarian's eyes). There's something enticing about seeing the Hindenberg crash on the monitor screen via video clip or "witnessing" Martin Luther King's "I have a dream" speech on CD-ROM. The added interactive features of CD-ROMs—a combination of text, graphics, sound, and video—offer more ways to accommodate different learning styles of youth; chances are, teens will become more engaged and ingest more information.

Typically, CD-ROMS acquired for libraries serving YAs fall into these categories:

- encyclopedias, especially multimedia titles such as Grolier's, World Book's InfoFinder, Compton's, and Encarta
- indexes to magazines (e.g., InfoTrac, ProQuest, Wilson Disc, Magazine Article Summaries), literary criticism, poetry
- newspapers and other full-text periodicals, such as the *New York Times*
- timetables and almanacs, either general or topical (two favorites are the *Time Almanac* and the *Sports Illustrated Almanac*)
- atlases and other geographic titles, such as 3-D "tours" or travel itinerary makers
- subject-specific reference titles, such as art collections, scientific topics, and "transformed" pictorial books

A few CD-ROM reference titles, such as Microsoft's Bookshelf, link sources. This product, for example, incorporates a dictionary, thesaurus, concise encyclopedia, atlas, and quotations so teens can explore and compare the differences between topics.

Because the CD-ROM market and product line have increased so dramatically in the past few years, librarians can insist on high-quality CD-ROMs that meet existing selection policy standards. As with other YA materials, collection development should take into account active teen suggestions and basic considerations of teen tastes and needs.

TECHNOLOGY TOOLS

Technology is used by teens for generating information as much as for information access. School libraries regularly provide word-processing programs; desktop publishing (DTP) has become commonplace for YAs who create sophisticated products. Libraries support this activity to varying degrees, from providing basic writing programs to offering scanners, CD-ROM drives, clip art collections, OCR (optical character reader) programs, and high-end illustration programs.

One fallout of DTP applications is higher expectations of the library by teens. Teens sometimes spend more time on getting just the right look than on the content or research process and demand high-quality programs. The good news is that these same teens import text and graphics from other library resources, thus making effective use of technology in the library (and saving paper). The bad news is that DTP requires more library staff time, both to learn it as well as to teach others.

When approached creatively, though, DTP motivates teens to help in the library. With guidance, YA library aids produce creative library signs, flyers, and newsletters. Especially when those teens show off their work to peers, the library benefits from the free public relations (PR). Teens can also train others in DTP skills, thereby freeing up professional librarian time and empowering young people to serve as resident experts.

A related production tool that libraries are starting to provide is presentation software. As libraries acquire more CD-ROM and laser discs, YAs are beginning to create multimedia presentations that link various resources using authoring programs such as HyperCard, HyperStudio, and LinkWay. Simpler programs that allow teens to link "screens" of text, graphics, and motion include PowerPoint, ClarisWorks, SlideShow, and the like. Because sound and motion require so much computer space, libraries run into problems of file storage; much of the work generated cannot be stored on the usual floppy disk. Libraries have to decide whether to invest in high-storage devices such as ZipDrives or CD creation equipment. At this point, few teens have access to such peripherals at home or other places.

A few libraries also make programming language software available. The usual languages that teens use include BASIC, Pascal, and C++. Because programming is typically introduced and taught in schools, public libraries are less likely to offer these programs. In addition, because programming languages often provide a back door that clever teens occasionally use to modify other computer applications or the systems themselves, most libraries are reluctant to tempt YA hackers by putting those languages on public workstations.

One interesting use of expert programmers has been made by rare YA librarians: they have teens create programs for other teens to use or help design programs for library administrative use. Teens create screen savers that publicize library YA services; programmers discourage their peers from copying software because they realize how many hours it takes to develop a program.

Regardless of the type of software, certain YA-related issues arise. One is acquisitions. Librarians would do well to purchase only widely known, standard programs that are easy to use. Otherwise, either staff will be called upon all too often to train and troubleshoot, or expensive programs will lie neglected on the shelf. One cost-effective idea is to purchase basic integrated programs that both staff and teens can use. Sample titles include Claris or MS Works and MS Office. A second issue is use. Popular software may be subjected to hard use. If at all possible, programs should be installed on computer hard drives to prevent the disk from wearing out. The system should also prevent users from downloading those programs so teens are not tempted to violate copyright laws.

Alternatively, just as most libraries post copyright signs on photocopiers so users will keep to legal practices, so can that same approach be used for technology.

INSTRUCTION

For teens to use technology effectively, they need adequate instruction. Traditionally, school courses have assumed that responsibility. However, with the introduction of so many media and specific products, all librarians need to spend time teaching teens how to make good use of these resources. Fortunately, YAs can help in this process as cotrainers and technology tutors.

Content for instruction on technology poses many possibilities. The most popular training these days focuses on the Internet and other telecommunications. DTP attracts teens, especially as they create their own graphical publications. Another attractive area remains videotaping, particularly, computer-based editing. Librarians also see a need for instructing YA users in CD-ROM and other technological reference tools—even the OPAC. These applications, however, don't have the same glamour as the other technological applications.

Instruction can be accomplished using several approaches: clearly written posted instructions, handy videotaped instruction, tutorial sessions by either volunteers (especially YAs) or library staff, and formal workshops. The first two methods allow teens to self-pace their learning progress. The last two, while attractive to teens because of the interpersonal contact, usually require scheduling and preparation time.

Signs and fact sheets often constitute a library's main instructional effort; they require some front-end development time but are often cost-effective in the long run. The following guidelines can help librarians develop written material that will actually be used by teens:

- Instructions should be clear and legible.
- Sequential information should be numbered or somehow marked to be followed step by step.
- Critical features should be accentuated: by arrows, type differential, or color.
- Instructions should be pilot-tested, preferably by teens, before they are used publicly.

Ideally, teens could write instructions. Librarians should tap these natural resources as much as possible!

Workshops can be effective because several people can be trained simultaneously. However, workshops should be carefully designed. In most cases, technology workshops should be interactive and hands-on; yet most public libraries do not have the luxury of owning a lab's worth of computers. Workshops are typically considered in the same league as other YA programming and so need adequate publicity and registration procedures. Additionally, because teens usually have so many competing activity options, any workshops should be done on a one-shot basis. If teens conduct the workshops, they should give a dry run before a librarian audience in order to polish their delivery. Unless the library is truly committed to large-group instruction, the workshop approach is seldom worth the effort, particularly since schools and other computer-related agencies offer the same kind of instruction.

Regardless of the format, YAs can be great instructors, and librarians need to exercise professional judgment in recruiting, assessing, and using these budding teachers. Teens may be recruited from school (e.g., library aides and computer classes), community organizations (e.g., youth groups, computer clubs), or the library itself (e.g., YA advisory councils or steady users). An application form is a useful practice because it shows that the job merits serious consideration. It can be as easy as this: name and address, availability, skills, interests, reason for volunteering, references. An interview with the prospective teen can concretize expectations and facilitate assessment. The candidate can also demonstrate skills firsthand at that time. Librarians should look for teens who are honest and dependable and exhibit good interpersonal skills as much as they should check technical abilities. At first, the librarian should observe student teachers in action; after helping them refine their techniques, the librarian can feel more comfortable allowing YAs autonomy in instructing others.

ACCESS ISSUES

Several issues about equitable access to technology have already been raised: printing, fees, censorship, and copyright. Another major point is physical use of technology. Where limited equipment is coupled with high demands, then scheduling and prioritization come into play. Any policy should be aligned with the library's mission and objectives. All efforts should be made to ensure that everyone has a fair chance to use the technology. In some cases, that may entail limiting the amount of time that any one person can access a particular technological tool to 30 minutes or an hour. Because teens are usually in school during the day, librarians may consider encouraging other patrons to use those technologies during school hours and giving higher priority to students after school. Librarians may also feel a need to prioritize the use of computers or access to the Internet, such that research needs would get a go-ahead before recreational uses. However, such value judgments can be tricky and possibly discriminating, for no other reason than they may violate the user's right to privacy and confidentiality. Likewise, some portions of the youth population may more aggressively demand access to technology; traditionally, boys have used these kinds of resources more than girls. While librarians may want to act as advocates for female users, they need to make sure that they are not behaving in a prejudicial manner. The need for thoughtful decision making is crucial—and often a complex matter.

Security is another significant factor. Keeping systems secure from computer break-ins has been discussed in terms of downloading and programming. Other obvious measures can be taken to prevent common security breaches: installing an antivirus program to scan user disks for possible corrupting routines and using a desktop controller program, such as FoolProof or At Ease, to limit transfers of files onto the computer.

Security issues also relate to physical security. Backup or archival copies should be made in case of software theft. Software, including CD-ROMs, should be stored in areas not accessible to typical library users. Sometimes the equipment itself has to be bolted down or wired to prevent loss. Certainly, all technology should be registered, and all equipment "tagged" with a serial number. The best preventive measure, though, is conscious supervision and a trusting relationship between librarian and user. Teens, especially, respond positively when shown that the librarian trusts and respects them. With such a personal foundation established, active YA library users almost automatically take responsibility for making sure that peers do not abuse or steal library resources.

As for destruction, most stems from ignorance, such as accidentally erasing a hard drive when the user meant to erase his or her own disk's contents or shoving a disk into some strange position. Here is where the adage "a little knowledge is a dangerous thing" rings true. Again, the best action is wise supervision. It is usually the same person who seems to get into trouble time after time—or tries to make trouble, rather like the inveterate late book returner. Keeping a close eye on such individuals is probably the wisest course of action.

THE BOTTOM LINE

Technology is here to stay, although its forms and applications regularly change, and teen fascination with technology also remains a constant. Since libraries are in the information business and the service business, it makes sense that they would keep abreast of technological breakthroughs and try to provide teens with the most effective access possible to information through technology. One exciting prospect is that YAs will probably be eager to help librarians carry out that mission. Welcome that teenage enthusiasm and expertise!

16

Youth Participation: Involving Young Adults in Library Services

Lynn Cockett

Youth participation in public libraries is, conceptually, something that almost everyone agrees upon as a good thing. Why, then, is it so difficult? This chapter examines youth participation as a phenomenon, from both a philosophical perspective and a practical one. It should be noted that my perspective is gained from practice, and many of my insights and suggestions will make sense to others only when they are tried in one's own unique setting. First, however, we should examine youth involvement in library services as a concept. What is it?

THE CONCEPT OF YOUTH PARTICIPATION

Libraries need a way of assessing how participation pays off and why it might be beneficial. On the outset, it appears that although involving young people in the decision making at a library will produce more "customer adaptive" practices and programs, it will clearly be extremely time-consuming for the librarian. How often we have wished we could just make a decision ourselves, instead of sitting in a staff meeting for 45 minutes to decide how to shelve the compact disc collection.

Similarly, seeking out young adults for input into planning and decision making will be, at first, frustrating and time-consuming. However, there are enormous payoffs. This chapter examines some of the potential benefits and principles of youth participation and focuses on the specific efforts of this author in creating a participative environment for young adults at a small public library.

The practice of participation recognizes that the old system of YA services doesn't work. There are two levels at which participation can work in a library. First, on a more basic level, the participative environment has a strong commitment to customer focus. During the late 1980s and early 1990s it became common practice to use the word "customer" in place of "patron" in the library literature. While I believe that "customer" is perhaps an incorrect term for what we seek to encourage in those who use our libraries, the same conclusion can be drawn regardless of what we call those who use libraries: customers, patrons, learners, students, and so on. If the library values the learner, then the learner's perspective will always come, if not first, at least near the top in our modes of decision making and planning.

There is a second way in which participation can work. If we think of our library users as "stakeholders" in the process of doing library work, they become part of the team, and they become heavily involved in making things happen at the library.

WHAT IS YOUTH PARTICIPATION?

The primary focus of youth participation is the practice of involving young people in decision making, program planning, collection development, outreach, and the myriad things that contribute to the total plan of service at the library. This involvement is deliberate on the part of the young adult librarian. In creating environments where YAs are encouraged to contribute to these processes, all of the preceding principles can be met. In these environments, there is no one authority or decision maker (power is shared; there is no clear line between the "idea person" and the "grunt worker"); thinking and doing are clearly linked; many ideas are expressed, appreciated, and considered; diversity is valued; and the sharing of ideas, combined with carrying them to fruition, provides enormous opportunities for learning.

Normally, involving young adults should be seen as an opportunity to build relationships with young people. When young adults are involved in the decision-making process in any organization and at any level, the outcome is that they are significant members of your community, and they feel needed and important. Essentially, the ideas and needs of young adults become the focal point, and the message is that the librarian needs to hear from them.

From a philosophical perspective, this might not appear on the outside as radical, but it is. The librarian who says, "I need you to tell me" rather than, "I am here to tell you" what your needs are, takes the perspective of the novice, letting the YAs know that they are the experts. This turning of the table creates a sense of power for young people. It allows them to work together with the librarian to develop a program of service that truly meets their needs. Further, if the goal of the public library is (and I believe that it is) to create and sustain in citizens a desire to become lifelong, independent learners, the deliberate attempt to make young people part of a decision-making process is perhaps the first step in the direction of realizing this goal. Aside from the opportunity to choose a few elective courses in schools, young people are rarely given room to determine just what it is they need and want.

It is necessary in schools to create parameters for curricular and behavioral choice. The library, on the other hand, does not have a set of curricular objectives. So in this setting young adults may be given the opportunity to begin making these decisions for themselves, in order to create a lively and progressive community of independent learners.

WHY OFFER YOUTH PARTICIPATION OPPORTUNITIES?

"Youth participation gives young adults role rehearsal experiences, uses their intense developmental need for social experiences with peers, offers opportunities to employ their fledgling hypothetical thinking abilities, and channels their enormous emotional and physical energies."[1] In addition to the enormous benefits for the young people involved, creating a dynamic program of youth participation is beneficial to the library and the librarian. Usually, a program in which students are heavily involved receives attention from the community and the media. Even if it is by a small local newspaper, libraries benefit from coverage that promotes their good services. From a practical standpoint, it behooves a librarian to have a hardworking group of young people who will help to make realistic decisions and to volunteer their efforts. Finally (but certainly not exhaustively), making connections with those we serve is perhaps the greatest sense of satisfaction that a librarian can feel. When strong relationships are formed, the hard work of librarianship pays off.

A TIMELINE: MAKING YOUTH PARTICIPATION WORK

When I first took my position as a young adult librarian in a small New Jersey public library, I came to it from a history of work with children. This information is important only insofar as one considers the examples given and the degree to which they can be generalized to others in different settings. In many small, independent community libraries, public demand requires that there be a children's librarian. Because of this, one person is hired to do collection development, cataloging, reference, reader's advisory, outreach, publicity, and programming for all children, from birth to grade twelve. Clearly, regardless of the size of the community, this is an enormous task. Preschool story time is synonymous with the public library, and it has never been my experience that if children's librarians have to make a choice, they are able to choose to concentrate their efforts on young adults. Invariably, there is too much work to do, and the young people who receive the most attention are the *youngest* people.

While it is necessary to make decisions like this, it is also, sadly, the case that young adults are often left with a gap in service.

This was, at least in my experience, the case. Children up through grade five were usually well served in the libraries where I was children's librarian, and after that, well, good luck to them. So, whether a librarian has been hired to work specifically with young adults or is a children's librarian hoping to create some services for young adults, a major priority should be to work with young people grade six and older. Having cut my professional teeth in a library system where the coordinator of children's services had as his motto "if they know me, they know the library," I took it as my own and decided that the primary focus of a brand-new plan of service for the small library that I'd be serving would be just that. I would do outreach.

Create objectives that state an exact percentage of time you will spend outside the library. Visit schools, churches, synagogues. Eat lunch every day along the main street in town, where the high school students go for their lunch period. Attend school sporting and drama events. The young adults of your community will know you if you do this. Clearly, in larger towns or cities, there is no single active strip where all the young people spend their time, but there are always places where young adults congregate and where you will not feel as if you are elbowing your way in.

For me, "if they know me, they know the library" was a good plan. Everywhere I went, I saw kids I knew. Students with whom I'd shared lunch would ring up my groceries at the supermarket. My next door neighbors' young adult children would ring my doorbell at night to borrow books from my own collection. I would go in town for a bagel, and the teenagers would talk to me, recognizing that I was the library woman who came to their school to talk to the media specialist and who was at the reference desk when they needed something. I went to the middle school and told the students that for the first time, the library had hired someone whose job was simply to serve them, and I asked for their help. I played my part as concerned, knowledgable, and a bit confused.

I was unaware that I had just taken the first major step in creating a youth participation program. What follows is the two year timeline I followed and that you can adapt for your own use. Notice that many steps in this process do not seem to be completely oriented toward youth participation. Major projects in collection development and programming are highlighted to underscore the importance of the total plan of services for the community of young adults. Further, many of the projects I implemented flowed from something done the month before. My timeline starts in August, but if you read through these months, you'll find things that can be lifted out and planned at other times of the year. Remember, however, that if your library does not already have excellent reference services to support homework and assignments or exciting collections to support leisure reading and listening or a plan to implement them, it is unwise to invite participation from the young adults you serve.

Why invite participation if the collections and services are already excellent?

Because of the enormous benefits of participation for the young adults and because of the changes that we can implement to better serve young people with their help.

Month 1: Know Your Position in the Library Where You Work

In August, I accepted my position and started working at the library. Starting in the middle of the month meant having to get ready immediately for the coming school year. The high school librarian came in, and we got acquainted, and for two weeks, I generally wandered the library, talked to staff, and looked at the collections of materials for young adults, both in the YA area and in the reference department. It often felt during these two weeks that I was not really working. As it turned out, I could probably have spent more time wandering before making any major changes. Regardless, it is good for anyone to take time to observe the culture of the library at the initial stages.

Months 2, 3, and 4: Know Your Collections; Know Your Young Adults

"If they know me, they know the library" became my mantra during these first few months. This was the first opportunity to meet and talk with young adults in the community, and so I seized it. In doing so, I spent a lot of time around town during lunch hour and eventually started to see faces I recognized at the pizza shops and deli.

I also decided to completely overhaul the collection of materials during these months. Every college undergraduate who takes a management class learns the wise adage that "if you fail to plan, you should plan to fail." In response to this, it was extremely important to plan for what would happen when (if) a positive response to my outreach measures began to take place. The first priority was the collection. Prior to my employment, the adult services librarian had ordered young adult books. In a dilemma similar to what many children's librarians face, this particular staff member would have liked to spend more time with young adult materials but found that the demands on her time in maintaining the entire adult fiction and non-fiction collections took precedence. While she ordered excellent books and maintained a decent collection, it was clear that young adult needs and concerns could not be this librarian's priority.

The collection was chock-full of hardcover books—many of them old—and few of them were ever checked out. All of Lois Duncan's books had, since their purchase, been reissued with paper covers that rival many of the popular young adult horror series, so they were replaced immediately. Other paperbacks were ordered to replace classic young adult titles that were owned only in hardcover.

The next step involved cataloging all the new paperbacks as they arrived. Previously, young adult paperbacks were never cataloged, but this left horror books, like R.L. Stine's *Fear Street* series, virtually unable to be located. Cataloging these books was a positive signal to the young adults that their tastes were no longer going to be neglected.

It was good to spend a majority of my time with my paper copy of *Books in Print*—working on the tables in the YA area of the library—while I reviewed the collection. This gave me the opportunity to talk to the few young people who did come to the library after school to do their homework and meet with friends.

Many librarians are nervous and scared about talking to young adults. Many young adults are unaware of this and perceive librarians' noncommunicative style as disdain. As the young adult librarian, however, regardless of my fear of their response, I talked to every young person who walked by. I asked any question I could think of to get them to tell me about themselves. In doing so, I learned a great deal about what the young adults in my town did and thought, and, based on the suggestion of a few, I created a voting ballot so that those kids who used the library could tell me what magazines they would like to see in the collection. I left the ballots in the YA area at the library, and as a result, four months after I began working in the library, we ordered about eight new magazine titles and moved a few of the old ones into the larger reading room, usually used by adults only.

Month 5: Know Your School District

In January, I created my first young adult newsletter. I called it *Bookin' Good* (an admittedly horrible name) and wrote only about changes to the collection of materials for young adults. The newsletter was created on an old 286 processor PC and photocopied on plain white copy paper in the library. It was single-sided and of little interest. I put copies of it at the circulation desk and on the tables in the YA area. With my makeshift newsletter and a decent collection to boast about, I thought I was ready to face the kids on a large scale. Late in the month, I called the middle school and asked the principal and school librarian if I could come to the school and introduce myself to the students.

I sent a copy of my newsletter to the board of education office and to the middle school for their approval for distribution. This gave the district the opportunity to suggest changes and to know that I was well intentioned about the process in which I was about to engage.

Month 6: The First Vestiges of Youth Participation: Visit Your Schools

After receiving a warm invitation from the school and approval from the board of education, I visited every seventh and eighth grade study hall to say, "Please help me rename this horrible newsletter." I told the kids about the new magazines added to the collection, which previously contained only a few old standards like *Seventeen, YM*, and *Rolling Stone*. As a result of the earlier poll, I had added *Fangoria, WWF,* and *Thrasher*, among others. These magazines represented specific interests of young adults. They spoke specifically to hobbies like horror movies, professional wrestling, and skateboarding.

Because I invited the students to help rename the newsletter, I again created a ballot box. I left it in the YA area and created a large banner above the new magazines. Young adults came in to check out the magazines, and a few actually left me some suggestions for my newsletter. We immediately experienced an enormous number of stolen magazines, which, for me, was a sign that I had done an excellent job of selection but which, for others on the library staff and administration, was a sign that the library was starting to get out of control. The next month was the beginning of a series of behavioral changes at the library that took a great deal of time to handle.

Month 7: Using Your Community Connections

As a result of my school visit, the library observed a major influx of young adults, which, of course, went hand in hand with noise and business for which no one was prepared. It is important at times like these that librarians realize that the ''problem'' of behavior is not their own. Certainly, for those who understand adolescent development and the need for kids to spend time with their peers, it should be expected that if the library invites young adults to come in, there will be more business at the reference desk and more noise at the study areas after school. This is particularly true in small communities where the schools and library are close together, and where there are not a lot of options where kids can spend their free time.

The perceived ''problems'' in library behavior are also the result of library architecture. Most public libraries are designed with special rooms, away from quiet areas, for young children. However, the rest of the building is often a shrine to the quiet reader of the newspaper. Adolescents simply do not function this way. It is of paramount importance that the staff understand that these changes will take place and that the library is prepared for a busier, louder few hours in the afternoon.

What to do if there is a serious problem? Involve others in the community who care about kids and who know them well. Certainly, parents are an option. But it is often difficult to contact parents. In our case, a number of seventh grade boys decided that with my invitation to attend the library came the opportunity to wrestle and play football on the floor of the library. It cannot be stressed enough that your greatest ally in a situation like this is your local principal. One phone call, with a positive remark like ''The kids are really enjoying the library,'' followed by an example or two of the inappropriate behaviors, completely stopped the negative behavior.

Do not be afraid to involve the whole community. Hanging out at the library and the potential raucous behaviors that come with it are not your problem alone.

They result from a community that often doesn't have anything for young people to do. If you recognize this and do not let others in your community know, young adults will never have appropriate places to be and things to do. The more vocal you are about how important it is for young adults to have positive ways to spend their time, the more likely the community will be to start recognizing them as important and viable citizens.

The last thing I did in the seventh month was to create flyers and announce the beginning of a youth advisory board.

Month 8: Meet with Your Core Group of Young Adults

In April, aside from planning the summer reading program for young adults and making plans to visit all the elementary schools' sixth grade classes, we held our first Youth Advisory Board meeting. The meeting room of the library was packed with mostly seventh and eighth grade girls and also a few high school students whom I had spoken to nearly every day. These high school students were extremely important members of the group whom I looked to for maturity and leadership. They attended at first at my request. Telling them that I needed them to handle important issues and carry the meeting along if the young students were uncreative, the older students came to act as my liaisons to the younger ones. Again, my relationship with the school was important in that the middle school media specialist was able to promote the advisory board to her active library users.

The publicity for this event was excellent. Reporters from both of our small town's local newspapers came as a result of my sending press releases; and photos of the YAs made the front page on both of them the next week. At the meeting we started small. The best bet at your first Youth Advisory Board meeting is to start with something simple and exciting. At mine, we talked about the newsletter, and kids told me what we should call it. I took their advice and didn't care if I thought it was not perfect. We talked about each of the young people's special interests and abilities and came up with a production schedule, a graphics crew, a book review committee, and a title that reflected the multicultural community in which we lived.

Our only other piece of business was to discuss the library's music collection. By staff attrition, I was granted permission to take over collection development for music. While this added countless hours of cataloging compact discs (CDs), it provided me with another very popular medium to promote. The Youth Advisory Board came up with a list of essential artists and titles to start the newly revamped CD collection, ranging from Bob Dylan to Nine Inch Nails.

Month 9: Do Something Tangible with Your Youth Advisory Board

This month, the most important thing to be done, aside from finalizing the summer reading program and getting ready to promote it, was to create tangible evidence that the hardworking young adults who were giving their time to the library had really helped me. So, we made our first collaborative newsletter. The Youth Advisory Board decided to call it *Hello*, and on the masthead, our language experts in the group came up with about 25 different languages' words for "hello."

The Advisory Board decided that the ugly white copy paper was clearly not eye-catching, so I went to the local office supply store and purchased neon-colored paper. They designed it by hand, wrote book, music, and magazine reviews, and wrote a promotional piece about the summer reading program. My job was simply to act as editor and typist. Within the month, the newsletter was out at every school in the town.

Month 10: Show the Youth Advisory Board You Value Their Contribution by Actually Taking Their Advice for Program Planning

During June, I visited every elementary school in town to invite sixth graders to join the summer reading program. Because the library had previously never offered a summer program for young adults, the most logical thing to do was to invite those who were accustomed to children's programs to attend the YA programs. As anyone who works with young adults knows, programming in general is difficult to do. Young people have enormous demands on their time. This, coupled with the fact that the library is not generally considered the coolest place in town to spend one's time, makes generating attendance difficult.

In order to create some interest, I brought applications for adult library cards (some libraries really do still have two library cards!) and promised each student a graduation gift as soon as school was over. Our Youth Advisory Board chose neon-colored pencils with the summer reading program logo on them and also chose prizes to give out to any individual who registered for any program hosted by the young adult department. They scoured catalogs from Oriental Trading Company until they arrived at the conclusion that since we were financially unable to give anything that was substantial, the gift should be as goofy as possible.

The Youth Advisory Board, whose numbers had dwindled a bit because initial response is often much larger than actual participation, was glad that many people signed up for the program. They advised me on ways to continue promoting it and to make it a program that did not require attendance. Essentially, individuals who came to the weekly evening programs got a chance to win a prize—these were good prizes like magazine subscriptions—and got extra points for their final "contest" score. Attending the programs each week was a bonus but not required. Anyone who missed a program was allowed to come in any-time during the week to record his or her score with me. The young adults on my Advisory Board could not have been more wise to advise me to make this part of the program. As a result, only about half of the participants came each week, but we had about 12 percent of the seventh grade population actually complete the program.

Month 11: Continue Moving Forward and Give Your YAs Credit for Their Work

During July, the summer reading program continued to run. In addition, we started a reading club, comprising only those who would ''apply'' to attend. Of course, everyone who applied participated, but the application process gave the young adults the notion that this was important. The Youth Advisory Board was given the right of first refusal for this program, and many of them applied. The promise was that at the end of the summer, I would write a paper about our experience that would be published as a book chapter for other young adult librarians to use as a model for their own work. The reading group focused for the entire summer on humorous books for young adults, reading titles from the YALSA genre committee and from various *Booklist* columns and reader's advisory tools recommending funny books for young adults.[2]

Month 12: Take a Break from All Your Hard Work; Work on Your Collection

By this time, if your summer reading program is a success, you'll probably need to weed your collection and replace all the paperback books that have spent one too many days at the beach. August was a chance for me to spend some time getting ready for the coming school year by ordering materials we knew the library could not provide for homework support during the previous school year.

Year 2, Month 1: Give Your Youth Advisory Board Some Power

After a full year in the position and with a bit of wisdom regarding what a normal school year was like, I was able to really plan for the second year. The most important thing I did in September was to bring the Youth Advisory Board back together and get them involved in a big and exciting project. By this time a core number of students were committed to the Youth Advisory Board and were taking ownership of what was happening for young adults at the library. Their first order of business was to rename themselves from the standard ''Youth Advisory Board'' to the Young Adult Reading Organization (YARO). The newsletter, on its way into volume 2, would be called *YARO News and Book Reviews,* and every member of YARO had favorite genres for review, as well as definite strengths and weaknesses in the governing and planning of YARO. Two strong young women acted as leaders, giving directions, planning meetings, and always bringing the group back to the discussion at hand. There were four fiction readers, all with different tastes. We had a film expert, a photographer, and a lover of non-fiction. The group was solid.

Aside from renaming themselves, which I believe gave the students an idea that what they were doing was their own, they planned what they would do to participate in the library's daylong 80th anniversary celebration to be held the next month.

Year 2, Month 2: Hold a Big Event

October was perhaps the defining month for the young adults of YARO. For the library's anniversary carnival, they set up their own informational table, complete with press releases from the past year's local papers with their pictures in them, copies of previous newsletters, self-designed bookmarks with titles of their favorites from the past year's reviews, an annotated bibliography of the books that the humor reading group had discussed, and a mailing list sign-up for others who might be interested in learning about YARO events.

In addition, the young adults recruited junior high school musicians to play chamber music in the lobby and high school drama club members who dressed in popular children's book character costumes for free photographs with little children. They also ran a daylong free raffle, for anyone to join, giving away copies of autographed young adult titles.

The response was tremendous. The young adults generated a list of about 50 people for mailing purposes, ranging from ten-year-olds to senior citizens, and gave out balloons and photographs all day long. Their yearlong commitment to the library paid off, and they (and I) were really excited about our huge success.

Year 2, Months 3, 4, and 5: Keep the Momentum Going

From November through January, YARO continued to meet, read, and write. The newsletter was now a regular monthly "publication of the Young Adult Reading Organization," and the young people involved loved seeing their names in print each month. They also spent some time with me planning an art show and reception. The director of the art department at the middle school had contacted me to ask if the library would like to display her students' art, and YARO thought it was a great idea.

Year 2, Month 6: Hold a Program Involving the Students' Work

February brought "art stars," a monthlong display of artwork by middle school students, culminating with a punch and cookies reception. Again, YARO was involved, helping to design artful-looking invitations and spending countless hours hanging the artwork and addressing envelopes. The program drew about

40 artists from the middle school, as well as the principal, art teachers, and members of the board of education, library board of directors, and parents. There were over 150 people in attendance. Again, YARO recruited students from their school to play classical music on strings and flute and volunteered their time for setting up, serving, and cleaning up after the program.

Year 2, Month 7: Involve the Young Adult Leaders in Solving Problems

As is often the case, inviting young people to a library that is architecturally not prepared to handle normal adolescent behavior can have some negative consequences. Staff members from the library were unprepared for what it meant to hire a young adult librarian and ask young adults to use the library heavily. Clearly, this lack of preparation on the part of the staff was, to a large degree, my own fault. In my zealous anticipation of creating a great young adult program of services, I forgot what it would mean for the day-to-day activities of the rest of the staff. Staff and administration were very unhappy about the noise in the library, and frankly, I was, too. Having spent over a year now with a wonderful Youth Advisory Board, I was unaware of the tremendous resource of help that was right under my nose. It was time for the Youth Advisory Board to function as problem solvers.

Eight students from both the high school and the middle school (some were members of YARO; some, just library users) came together with me for a period of six weeks and drafted a new policy for rules. Their plan was to ask the library board of directors to ratify the policy document and use it to complement the one that was already posted throughout the library. The young adults' rules were more target-oriented, in that they spoke directly to young adults, and they were positive instead of negative. The group listed what to do at the library from A to Z on the front of the page, and on the back, they explained three specific rules and why the library had to have them. It was a lot of work, but in the end, they and I were pleased with the result. The advisory group signed the document and asked me to take it to the library board.

We all thought that this would be the step we needed to begin mending fences and making peace between young adults and library staff. The young people involved in creating this code of conduct were sure that their leadership would provide a good example for others using the library and would indicate to the library staff, administration, and board that they were serious about using the library. In effect, although there was little support from the administration, and the document never made it to the library board, the staff was aware of the efforts on the part of this group of young adults and appreciated the gesture.

When spring came, the weather eased up, and the enormous amount of traffic and noise in the library began to wane. This whole time period provided a lesson to me that planning for programs and services is clearly not enough. If a young adult librarian in a small library is her or his own department, she or he needs to be extremely explicit with the staff about what the planning process entails and what to expect from it. Additionally, other library staff members from other departments ought to be included in young adult activities. Inviting a member of the circulation staff to YARO meetings allows that person to see the hard work that the majority of young adults do and gives the young adults a new forum in which to meet library staff.

Year 2, Months 8, 9, and 10: Plan and Promote a Summer Reading Program

Much like the previous year, this year was full of school visits and young adult participation in the planning of the summer reading program. In the previous year, YARO had helped think of ideas for encouraging large numbers of young adults to register for the program. This year, they were heavily involved in the planning of the programs and the promotion of the library. YARO chose laser-printer brochure paper and helped design flyers to give to all the sixth graders in town again and helped plan a calendar for the summer, knowing that is when people were most likely to attend programs.

Year 2, Months 11 and 12: Create Big Goals with the Advisory Board

Because we lived near New York City, my YARO (and many other young adults) invariably wanted to plan activities that would allow me to take them to the city. Having a healthy dose of fear about driving any number of young people into the city alone, I always resisted, but finally I found a way to do it that would please the young adults and be approved by their parents. I promised to take the participants in this summer's reading group to New York to participate in YALSA's Best Books for Young Adults (BBYA) committee.

I ordered every book that had been selected for the previous year's Best Books for Young Adults list and created a reading and discussion group. A small but committed number of young adults joined the group and met each week to discuss the books they'd read from the list. Giving the books P and Q ratings, in the style of reviews from *VOYA*, and using the standards that the real Best Books committee uses, the students started a summer-long project in which they analyzed the list. I promised them that if we got through a significant portion of the list, I would take them to New York to talk to the committee in order to make recommendations.

Aside from the huge success of this program, as far as library statistics are concerned, students had practice in reading critically, thinking about their reading needs, discussing the likes and dislikes of others, and working together as a group. At the last meeting, they ranked the books they had read and made a number of suggestions for the BBYA committee.

Because I decided to leave this position at the end of August, it was clear that it would be impossible to keep all of the ties that I had made with these wonderful young adults, and the prospect of going to New York began to dim. However, I wanted to keep my promise to them in at least some significant way, even if it meant that I could not take them to an ALA meeting. Instead, I contacted Dorothy Broderick at *VOYA* and told her to watch her mail for an article about these kids. Four months after leaving my position an article about the students and their recommendations for the BBYA list appeared in *VOYA*.[3]

Interestingly, another article about the BBYA list appeared in that issue of *VOYA*. Patrick Jones had analyzed the list using a rigorous method of comparison vis-à-vis the reviews of each of the books.[4] Jones' conclusions regarding the very best books were similar to those of the students who participated in the summer reading group at my library. It makes one wonder, then, what the purpose is of a YALSA committee or a group of students to analyze the committee's work. The answer, of course, is clear. While Jones' method makes an important contribution to the field, showing us that there are ways to "validate" both the committee's work and the synergy of the many reviews we read every year, the students engaged in a communicative act. They needed to find ways to gain one another's compliance, to speak convincingly, to defend their personal tastes and sensibilities. They did just that. They worked closely with an adult (myself) as their intermediary as they made meanings together and singly; and they did this respectfully, along with a great deal of enthusiasm. Finally, but certainly not exhaustively, they read an average of four books per week each during their summer vacation, with the knowledge that they might make an impact on a group of adults (the BBYA committee) who make decisions and selections for them and their peers.

Although I resigned from this position before the article was published, *VOYA* was extremely gracious and sent all of the participants a copy of the magazine with a letter of congratulations for the good hard work that they had done. They were commended for having truly made an impact on the field of young adult librarianship, and letters were sent to the library board of trustees and the young adults' parents.

OUR ORIGINAL QUESTION—WHAT IS YOUTH PARTICIPATION?

The programs described in this chapter vary in the degree to which young adults participated in their planning and design. Of course, the best books reading group seems, on the surface, to have simply been a reading club, and many would not define it as participation, except to the extent that the students participated in the program itself. It is, however, perhaps the most significant participation experience these young adults had. While enjoying themselves and feeling as though they were not wasting away their summer vacation simply reading books, these young adults helped to make an impact far beyond their small town or its library. They were empowered through their suggestions and decisions to make an impact on the larger community; they used critical thinking and reading skills in order to make recommendations; they argued and discussed a variety of points of view; and they learned a great deal while, at the same time, they taught others about what is best for young people.

Of course, they also did a variety of things, small and large, to help their own community, including the planning of the anniversary celebration; the creation of a supplement to the library code of conduct; the advice they gave regarding programs; and the many other things described. The creation of a participative environment for these young adults fostered values, such as shared power, thinking and doing, diversity of ideas, and learning. Further, it transformed the library, at least for a handful of young people, into a democratic environment where the truly meaningful aspects of participative governance took precedence over the individualistic or hierarchical structures that are reinforced so often. Kids made their library better for themselves and others through action.

Youth participation is worth doing. It gives young adults not only the opportunity to use their energies in constructive ways but also a different perspective on what it means to be a part of a community—whether that community be their school, their town library, or their peers all over the country.

APPENDIX 16.1
A CHECKLIST: THE ESSENTIALS FOR YOUTH PARTICIPATION PROGRAMS THAT WORK

Doing youth participation in your library *is* possible. A good idea to help get you started is to work your way through the following checklist, asking the following questions or doing the tasks. Or make your own checklist that suits your library and your position better.

- *Know the library's mission statement.* Does your library have a mission statement? Does it have a formal set of annual goals and objectives? If so, commit them to memory. If not, write them. Be sure that what you want to do will fit into the library's overall plan and goals of service.

- *Provide yourself a list of goals for youth participation.* What would you like to see happen? Is it possible in the library where you work? Would you like young adults to participate at an administrative level? Do you want them to help you plan your programs? Think through these kinds of questions, because each participatory action requires different work.

- *Talk through your plans with your director.* No matter what the support level is from above, your successful programs cannot sustain themselves unless you have an administration that is informed and philosophically convinced that your plans are sound.

- *Educate the library staff.* If you have the money, approach your director and pay for a half-day training seminar on adolescent development. The library staff is clearly more willing to believe an expert (even though you are one, it often behooves you to have an outsider tell people what they ought to know).

- *Be sure you have the time to do this.* In the position you hold, do you ever have time away from the reference desk or from cataloging books? Know that youth participation, while good for both you and the young adults you serve, is time-consuming. It is a much easier task to sit down with a music catalog and spend your budget in an afternoon than it is to invite young people to come to the library to advise you on which CDs to purchase.

- *Invite other staff members to participate in your programs.* Now that the library staff is educated about young adults, invite them, one or two at a time, to attend functions with your young adults. This gives both the staff and the YAs a chance to see each other away from their normal roles, usually those in which staff are powerful, and YAs have very little power. Bringing the staff in on a program in which young adults are making decisions provides the young adults with an opportunity to show that when asked, they can make good decisions.

- *Make sure your collections and services can support the work you want to do.* It is silly to think that young adults will participate in a library where essential services and collections are inadequate. Make your young adult collections attractive.

- *Have a separate area for young adults.* As mentioned before, young adults are different from the rest of the people who use libraries. Do your best to provide YAs with space that is their own. Be sure it is away from the quiet study areas of the library and be there yourself.

NOTES

1. Mary Kay Chelton, *Excellence in Library Service to Young Adults* (Chicago: American Library Association, 1994), xii.

2. The reading that these young people did all summer long was summarized by Janet Kleinberg and me and published as "Why Angels Fly: Humor in Literature for Young Adults," in K.E. Vandergrift, *Mosaics of Meaning: Enhancing the Intellectual Lives of Young Adults through Story* (Lanham, MD: Scarecrow Press, 1996), 283–314.

3. Lynn Cockett, "Best Books for Young Adults: Real Young Adult Opinions of the List, the Process, and the 1995 Selections," *Voice of Youth Advocates* 18, no. 5 (1995): 284–88.

4. Patrick Jones, "The Best Book for Young Adults in 1994," *Voice of Youth Advocates* 18, no. 5 (1995).

17

Homework Assistance Programs in Public Libraries: Helping Johnny Read

Cindy Mediavilla

INTRODUCTION

In late 1991 the Library Research Center of the University of Illinois Graduate School of Library and Information Science conducted a nationwide public opinion poll on library services. The results were overwhelming: "[T]he American people believe strongly in the educational roles of public libraries."[1] A year later, these findings were validated by a national Gallup study that confirmed that "the public considers the library's role of supporting the educational aspirations of the community to be its most important role."[2]

Considering that at least one out of every two individuals entering a public library is under the age of 18, this educational role takes on an even greater significance, as students of all ages use their local library to research school assignments. As one librarian noted several years ago, "Public libraries are . . . an educational agency providing the way and the means to a better informed citizenry, enlarging the life of the individual, the wisdom of the nation."[3] It is no wonder, then, that many public libraries have assumed the role of formal education support centers and offer, as part of this role, after-school homework assistance for children and teenagers alike.

EVOLUTION OF HOMEWORK ASSISTANCE IN PUBLIC LIBRARIES

Though the phrase "homework center" is a relatively recent addition to the library lexicon, the idea of public librarians' helping students with their school assignments is, of course, not new at all. Actually, in the early years of the library profession, school and public libraries were often administered as part of the same jurisdiction. Where this arrangement did not exist, forward-looking public librarians, such as Mabel Williams of New York Public Library, began visiting classrooms. As she noted, "No young people's librarian can fail to realize the importance of cooperation with schools . . . [for t]here sit in even rows her entire clientele."[4]

With the introduction of industrialization in the early twentieth century, more and more teenagers began returning to school. As a result, librarians soon realized a need for YA services. At the Cleveland Public Library, for instance, the Stevenson Room was established specifically for teen use. Although its initial purpose was to improve the reading tastes of its adolescent patrons, librarians quickly found themselves scrambling for school-related materials. Elsewhere, "teen rooms" were developed in Milwaukee, Muncie, and Sacramento. In New York City, an entire facility—the Nathan Straus Branch—created for the sole use of children and young people became a model for librarians and educators throughout the country.

So widespread did YA services become that by 1948 the American Library Association (ALA) issued *The Public Library Plans for the Teen Age*—a handbook of suggested standards for serving youth. According to this document, schools and public libraries were obligated to work together "toward a common goal—the development of individuals equipped to function effectively in a democratic society."[5] Furthermore, ALA recognized that, though the primary function of school libraries is to provide academic support, "[w]hen school days are over the public library is an indispensable source for self-education . . . information, reading, study and research."[6]

Heavy dependence on public libraries for researching homework assignments continued through the 1950s. In fact, the situation became so critical at the New York Public Library that drastic measures were enforced:

[S]pecial committees on school reference work [were] set up . . . to select materials to meet the increasingly sophisticated school needs, and attempts [were made] at the main library at 42nd Street to divert the flood of high school students. In 1952, a young people's librarian was stationed in the lobby at 42nd Street to steer young people to the Circulation Department, register them, and send them to Bronx Reference or to the Saint Agnes or 96th Street branch to look for their materials.[7]

With the launching of Sputnik and the new national emphasis on education, public library use reached an all-time high by 1960. At the Enoch Pratt Library, over half the patrons were high school students working on school-related assignments.[8] In Los Angeles, according to city librarian Harold Hamill:

Heavy student use of the public library is on the verge of turning it into an extension of school libraries. . . . In recent years . . . we have seen students flocking to local libraries in greater numbers than ever before. This is a result of recent efforts to strengthen the educational program, an endeavor I wholeheartedly endorse. The problem is that our public libraries are not equipped to handle this increasing student trend.[9]

Suddenly, teenagers, who had been the darlings of YA librarians everywhere just a decade before, were now considered the *student problem*. In an attempt to control the situation, librarians began restricting student use of the library: borrowing privileges were limited; reference service was curtailed or denied altogether; permits were required from teachers and/or parents; teenagers had to sign in and were limited to certain hours and/or areas of the library; and boys and girls could not use the library on the same evenings.[10] Not surprisingly, as research presented at the 1967 ALA conference disclosed, while adults were rarely critical of library staff, 25 percent of student patrons complained about how poorly they were treated. The study went on to say, "One of the greatest blocks to the total use of public libraries has been the attitude of generations of public librarians towards students."[11] Unfortunately, as Holly Willett has pointed out, though "[h]istorians have not yet studied the impact of this period on present library services . . . [a] lingering residuum is the occasional limitation on student use at some public libraries, such as refusing telephone reference service for homework assignments."[12]

PUBLIC LIBRARIES AND THE YOUNG ADULT STUDENT TODAY

Though some administrators still think that "[i]t would be a grave mistake to assign an additional mission to the public library, specifically one in education,"[13] many librarians have come to understand just how intertwined school and public library services are. Not only are library management experts advocating the creation of policies stating that it is the responsibility of all staff to help students with their school assignments, but many public libraries have begun setting aside specific areas where children and teenagers can receive free homework assistance. As defined by Virginia Walter in her handbook on evaluating YA services, these "homework centers" "may be an elaborately equipped special room in the library or just a table in a corner with a computer and some special reference tools and study aids. [Their] purpose is to help students find and use materials for their homework assignments."[14]

Examples of notably successful homework centers include PASS! (Oakland, California), Student Express Services at the Enoch Pratt Public Library (Baltimore), Homework Helpers (Montclair, New Jersey), VICTORY (Austin, Texas), and the After-School Study Center (Long Beach, California). Despite their seemingly disparate circumstances, these and other homework assistance programs are driven by the desire to help students succeed by becoming educated adults. As Rosellen Brewer of the Monterey County Free Libraries (California) observed, "If the existence of the Seaside Homework Center keeps only one student from dropping out of school, then the money for the center is well spent."[15]

ELEMENTS OF SUCCESSFUL HOMEWORK CENTERS

Assessing the Need

The need for a homework center may be dictated by events either within or outside the public library. Both the Homework Helpers program in Montclair and the Seaside Homework Center in Monterey County were born out of internal problems with latchkey children. On the other hand, homework assistance centers in Riverside, California, were established as a preventive measure against behavior exhibited in the 1992 Los Angeles riots. The Homework Assistance Center of the Oakland Public Library was instituted because of findings indicating that school dropouts and below-grade literacy levels were among the most serious problems faced by teenagers in the city of Oakland. The VICTORY (Volunteers in Communities Tutoring Our Responsible Youth) Program of Austin Public Library was organized to help address the fact that 25 percent of local area high school students had dropped out in 1992–1993.

According to youth services officer Nancy Messineo,[16] the foundation of any homework assistance program is a needs assessment. For example, staff of the Long Beach Public Library discovered through surveys that teachers were unable to assign certain kinds of homework because school supplies were not available in many homes. Also, through interviews they learned that language barriers often prevent students from getting the homework assistance they need from their immigrant parents. In a barrio not too far from Long Beach, a study of residents served by the Orange Public Library revealed the need for a youth-oriented facility where teens could receive homework tutoring in a positive, structured environment. The Friendly Stop homework center was created to meet these particular needs. At a branch in Bloomington, Indiana, the Math Homework Help program was started in response to a questionnaire asking young patrons, "If the library could provide help with homework, what subject should it be?"[17] Whether it takes the shape of formal surveys or one-on-one interviews, an assessment is necessary to determine exactly where the community's needs lie and how the public library can address them.

Partnerships and Funding

While not all homework assistance programs require huge sums of money to get started, all of them do require a commitment from the community they serve. Once the library successfully creates partnerships with local organizations and/or businesses, gifts of equipment, grants, or volunteer services often soon follow. For instance, in Dallas, the Bank of America Foundation and Bank of America Texas contributed $35,000 to the Lancaster-Kiest Branch homework center because, as bank president David Berry explained, "Bank of America's commitment to education is based on our belief that a well-educated person will make a better citizen, a better employee, and a better customer."[18]

In another example of strong library/community cooperation, the Los Angeles Public Library received hundreds of thousands of dollars from the CBS Foundation, Unocal, and other groups to buy computer equipment and software for all of its branch homework centers.[19] Monroe County Public Library's Math Homework Help is supported financially by the local teachers' union and McDonald's, which even holds tutoring sessions in one of its restaurants. Kraft Foods contributed $3,500 to Austin Public Library's VICTORY Program,[20] while a shopping mall in Riverside, California, gave $5,000 to its local public library's homework assistance center.[21] In Orange, California, the Young Women's Christian Association (YWCA) provided $12,000 in United Way-targeted money for after-school tutors.[22] Finally, in Contra Costa County (California), a library patron and his employer, Chevron Corp., recently donated enough funds to expand one branch's hours during final exam week. As the adult services librarian pointed out, "Spending this donation to benefit teens in this way affirms the important connection between academic achievement and the use of public libraries."[23]

Homework Tutors and Mentors

Though some homework centers may consist of only computer equipment and shelves of materials, the most effective programs incorporate one-on-one after-school tutoring. According to the Carnegie Council on Adolescent Development, "With a trained tutor, ninety-eight percent of students do better in school than they otherwise would."[24] This is corroborated by librarians such as Riverside's Jean Baird, who noted, "The increased self-esteem in middle school students receiv[ing] assistance with their homework has been apparent."[25]

Fortunately, homework assistance programs are so universally popular that, once word spreads of their existence, recruiting volunteers to provide the service is often relatively easy. Enoch Pratt's Student Express Service (Maryland) is staffed by college students and volunteers from Baltimore Gas and Electric, while Monroe County's Math Homework Help utilizes engineers from the NSWC Crane School Partnership Program. High school students serve as *junior tutors* to younger children at Newark (New Jersey) Public Library's Club Success. At the Orange (California) Public Library, the Friendly Stop supervisor recruited tutors from local colleges and the Student Teachers Association. Meanwhile, librarians in Montclair, New Jersey, and Austin, Texas, got help from the Literacy Volunteers of America and the federal VISTA program.

As Stan Weisner explains, relying on volunteer homework assistance can be challenging, however, because "[u]nless the library can assure students that there will be an adequate supply of tutors and vice versa, enthusiasm for the program may wane."[26] For this reason, many libraries offer their tutors incentives, such as extensive training or a small salary. One of the earliest after-school tutoring programs, "Project My Turn" in National City, California, paid high school students minimum wage to work with junior high pupils. In a similar program, PASS! hires high school students through the Youth Employment Partnership, a local agency working exclusively with young people. Remuneration includes agency-run workshops on resumé writing, job interviewing, and drugs and AIDS prevention. Not only do these young mentors provide a worthwhile service to their community, but they, in turn, develop valuable skills while learning how to become responsible adults. As the Carnegie Council on Adolescent Development contends, like peer counseling, "there is considerable evidence that tutoring benefits the young tutors."[27]

Homework Center Collections

The assumption that homework centers should be located within public libraries seems only natural. After all, the collection is readily available for doing research, and many libraries now offer public access to the Internet, as well as other on-line sources. Yet not all libraries have space to allocate as a separate homework area. A notable exception is Enoch Pratt's Student Express Service. Located one floor above the YA fiction stacks, this special room, decorated with a neon sign and bright posters, gives teens a place to start their research in an otherwise dauntingly large central library. Staff has pulled all relevant books—for example, science fair projects, literary criticism, and career information—from other library departments and gathered them together in one manageable collection. In addition, students can tap into "A Whole New World," the library's networked access to the Web, e-mail, and grade-appropriate reference sources.

Though some programs, such as the Homework Center at Rolling Meadows Library, Illinois, and Project My Turn in National City, California, stock text-books, for the most part public libraries provide mainly supplemental curricular materials. Part of the success of Long Beach Public Library's After-School Study Center was its magazine collection and free photocopies of reference materials needed for homework assignments. Participants in Project My Turn also found pamphlets an invaluable resource. As Mary K. Chelton and James M. Rosinia advise, "[W]hile the public library does not take the place of a school library media center, it has a responsibility to support the work of students, young and old, by developing collections to support their work."[28]

Hours of Operation

According to the Carnegie Council on Adolescent Development, "Unsupervised after-school hours represent a period of significant risk; it is a time when adolescents may engage in dangerous and even illegal activities. . . . Unsupervised teenagers are also more likely to be subject to negative peer pressure."[29]

After-school library programs help divert students from negative influences. For this reason, most homework centers are staffed weekdays, 3–6 P.M. Math Homework Help is also available Monday evenings, 7–9 P.M. Though some libraries provide homework assistance on weekends, the Friendly Stop, PASS!, and the Seaside Homework Center discontinued Saturday hours because of low attendance. Because homework is apparently more of a priority the day it is assigned, it is important that librarians be prepared to provide appropriate assistance as soon as school lets out.

Media and Public Relations

When the Oakland Public Library opened its after-school tutoring center in 1991, it not only distributed the usual flyers, press releases, and advertisements but held a press conference featuring the California state librarian and a well-known young adult author. The center received local cable television coverage, and a special rap-style public service announcement was aired on teen-oriented radio stations.

Once a homework assistance program is established, librarians must aggressively *advertise* its existence by whatever creative means possible. For instance, to win the trust and interest of its ethnic community, Long Beach's After-School Study Center sponsored a booth at a Cambodian New Year celebration, displaying brochures and materials in the Khmer language. The response was overwhelming and helped give the center credibility in the community. Likewise, the Orange Public Library brought attention to its Friendly Stop by holding a daylong "Día de la Familia" festival on the front lawn of its homework outlet. Over 400 local residents enjoyed mariachis, a traditional Mexican fashion show, ballet folklorico, a juggler, a rapper, an art exhibit and an *ofrenda* (offering) honoring Latin American artist Frida Kahlo. The next day, people who had never used a library before checked out their first library books. As a wise librarian from Indiana once said, "The best propaganda available . . . is the educating of the public library's community, and certainly this includes the high school student."[30]

Evaluating Service

Rosellen Brewer realized early on that if the Seaside Homework Center was "going to get more funding, we needed to have a way to evaluate how well the center was actually helping students. We knew the center was helping students, because they told us it was. But funders need hard data."[31] However, until recently, measuring the effectiveness of homework centers was difficult at best.

Today, librarians have access to *Output Measures and More*, Virginia Walter's handbook for evaluating YA services. In it, she outlines several ways of determining the success of homework centers, including "homework fill rate" (the proportion of successful searches for information needed to complete assignments), homework center "visits" (the number of teens using the center), and user interviews (young adult motivation for using and their opinions about the services offered by the homework center). To get an even more comprehensive idea of their program's effectiveness, staff of the Oakland Public Library's nine PASS! centers also survey not only the students but the teachers, parents, homework mentors, and branch personnel as well. Based on this input, program goals and objectives for the following year are developed.

CONCLUSION

In its landmark study of the after-school activities of youth-at-risk, the Carnegie Council on Adolescent Development calls on community organizations of all kinds to promote the positive growth of young people by participating in the "process through which adolescents actively seek, and are assisted, to meet their basic needs and build their individual assets or competencies. Parents, teachers, school administrators, peers, siblings, religious leaders, coaches, *librarians*, and youth group leaders can all serve as agents in this process" (emphasis added).[32]

Though providing homework assistance can be difficult and frustrating at times, this service is imperative for the public library that has traditionally supported the educational and informational requisites of its community. Not only does providing this service meet the needs of the public, but in so doing, the library ensures its own future. As Harold Hamill admonishes, "Not only would the public library be socially unjustified in erecting barriers against students, but it should actually welcome the opportunity to encourage students to become life-long customers of its wares."[33]

NOTES

1. L. Estabrook and C. Horak, "Public vs. Professional Opinion on Libraries: The Great Divide?" *Library Journal* 117, no. 6 (1992): 53.

2. G. D'Elia and E.J. Rodger, "Public Opinion About the Roles of the Public Library in the Community: The Results of a Recent Gallup Poll," *Public Libraries* 33 (1994): 25.

3. E. Bishop, "Students and the Public Library," *California Librarian* 20 (1959): 178.

4. M. Braverman, *Youth, Society, and the Public Library* (Chicago: American Library Association, 1979), 19.

5. American Library Association, *The Public Library Plans for the Teen Age* (Chicago: American Library Association, 1948), 9.

6. Ibid.

7. Braverman, *Youth, Society, and the Public Library*, 95.

8. H.G. Willett, *Public Library Youth Services: A Public Policy Approach* (Norwood, NJ: Ablex, 1995).

9. E. Moore, "Serving Students in Time of Crisis," *California Librarian* 22 (1961): 220.

10. Willett, *Public Library Youth Services*; American Library Association, *Student Use of Libraries: An Inquiry Into the Needs of Students, Libraries, and the Educational Process* (Chicago: American Library Association, 1964).

11. Margaret A. Edwards, *The Fair Garden and the Swarm of Beasts* (1969; reprint, with a foreword by Patty Campbell, Chicago: American Library Association, 1994), 74.

12. Willett, *Public Library Youth Services*, 94.

13. D. Sager, "The Best of Intentions: The Role of the Public Library in the Improvement of Public Education," *Public Libraries* 31 (1992): 15.

14. Virginia A. Walter, *Output Measures and More: Planning and Evaluating Public Library Services for Young Adults* (Chicago: American Library Association, 1995), 51.

15. R. Brewer, "Help Youth at Risk: A Case for Starting a Public Library Homework Center," *Public Libraries* 31 (1992): 212.

16. N. Messineo, " 'ASSC' and You Shall Receive: Community Partnerships in California," *School Library Journal* 37, no. 7 (1991): 19–22.

17. Mary K. Chelton, *Excellence in Library Services to Young Adults* (Chicago: American Library Association, 1994).

18. "Dallas, Newark Homework Plans Expanded with Gifts and Grants," *Library Hotline* 24, no. 8 (1995): 7.

19. "New, Revitalized Branches for NY, LA, and Spokane," *Library Hotline* 25, no. 25 (1996): 6.

20. Chelton, *Excellence in Library Services to Young Adults*.

21. J. Baird and J. Plessner, "Homework Assistance Centers," *California Libraries* 3, no. 9 (1993): 13.

22. Cindy Mediavilla, "Final Summary Report: California State Library Services and Construction Act; Project Title: Friendly Stop," State Library, Sacramento, CA, 1992; photocopy.

23. "Contra Costa Patron's Donation Extends Exam Week PL hours," *Library Hotline* 25, no. 23 (1996): 2.

24. Carnegie Council on Adolescent Development, *Great Transitions: Preparing Adolescents for a New Century* (New York: Carnegie Corporation, 1995), 54.

25. Baird and Plessner, "Homework Assistance Centers," 13.

26. S. Weisner, *Information Is Empowering: Developing Public Library Services for Youth at Risk* (Oakland, CA: Bay Area Library and Information System, 1992), 9.

27. Carnegie Council on Adolescent Development, *Great Transitions*, 54.

28. Mary K. Chelton and James M. Rosinia, *Bare Bones: Young Adult Services Tips for Public Library Generalists* (Chicago: American Library Association, 1993), 18.

29. Carnegie Council on Adolescent Development, *A Matter of Time: Risk and Opportunity in the Nonschool Hours* (New York: Carnegie Corporation, 1992), 33.

30. American Library Association, *Student Use of Libraries*, 68.

31. Brewer, "Help Youth at Risk," 212.

32. Carnegie Council on Adolescent Development, *A Matter of Time*, 37–38.

33. Moore, "Serving Students in Time of Crisis," 222.

18

Programming for Young Adults: No Holds Barred

Elaine McGuire

THE WHY

Why even offer programs specifically targeted for teenagers? The answer is simple: public libraries must do programming for young adults because they are a part of the public. (Duh! As a teen, herself, might say.) The difficulty of YA programming doesn't result from the actual *programming* but from the age group. For some reason, planning a Thanksgiving story time/craft hour featuring *Little Bear's Thanksgiving* and the creation of paper plate turkeys is vastly easier than planning a murder mystery for teens. Why do we suppose that is? The idea of YA services certainly isn't new. Although the majority of her book focuses on getting the right books into the hands of adolescents, Margaret A. Edwards' *The Fair Garden and the Swarm of Beasts* strongly advocates equal services to these important patrons. "Public libraries consider young people an interruption to business, yet they *are* the business, more so than the middle-aged adults the librarians are waiting for."[1]

The unfortunate truth is that teenagers are a perpetual challenge because they are so unlike children and yet youthful, and they are so like adults and yet not completely mature. It's practically a given that a great majority of children will enjoy the heck out of a story time featuring *Corduroy* because he's a lovable teddy bear in a well-told story. You cannot count on teens to uniformly enjoy any one thing.

What YA programmers need, then, is a vital connection to the YA age group as defined by your library system (generally, ages 12 to 18). Ideally, you are a full-time young adult librarian with a mission to serve. More likely you are a half-time reference/half-time YA, youth services head, idealistic library student, or library staff member motivated (or assigned) to serve YAs along with your other 1,007 duties. The connection can be made by all of you. Successful programs for young adults will be made, executed, and enjoyed. How often and what kinds of programs are up to you and the YAs you serve.

Carolyn Caywood's article "To Linger in Good Company" in *School Library Journal* has some important messages about teens in public libraries. She asserts the need for hanging out and recommends that "loitering must be condoned and even preferred to structured activities."[2] I agree with this statement and do not propose YA programming as a means to control or entertain an out-of-control after-school crowd.

Back to the original question. One should provide YA programs for the same reasons one offers any public library programs—to bring the public into the library, to make them aware of educational and entertaining library materials, and to give them positive library experiences.

The excellent *VOYA* editorial, "We Don't Want You—We Want Your [Dumb] Friends" includes some brilliant insights on exactly whom we should be targeting with programs. The gist of the article is that we should best serve our existing audience. If a rollerblading program brings in some 15-year-old boys who have never before darkened the doors of the library (but frequent only the parking lot), that's wonderful. But don't have a program just to reach out to these invisible patrons. Spend too much time on this mission and you'll lose the kids who stuff your suggestion box with requests for a science fiction reading club. In the best of all worlds, we will serve all, but that's just not reality, not in YA, children's, or adult services. We cannot feel guilty about not planning the program that turns the at-risk, drug-addicted juvenile delinquent around.[3]

I'll say it again: to begin or to continue young adult programming is not really an option. If your library has programs, you must include YA programs. It seems that everybody who believes in YA services spends much time apologizing or making excuses for "our" kids. For Pete's sake, let them in, they are part of the public we serve.

THE HOW

This chapter is divided into the five crucial parts of programming: getting ideas, planning, promoting, executing, and evaluating.

Ideas

When everyone is agreed that a YA program is in order, the next step is deciding what to do. There are basically three ways of getting program ideas.

1. Do what you already do.

2. Do what they ask for.

3. Do what somebody else did.

1. *What you already do.* Young adults can be served with existing "children's" or "adult" programs with teenage twists. A popular children's program might be an *American Girls* tea. Using that same theory (what do they like to read?), create an equivalent young adult program—a horror reader's Halloween party. A successful adult program is a how-to-invest seminar. Using that same idea (how to do something that's important to me, but I don't have time to pursue in depth on my own), create an inviting YA program—a college admissions or car-buying workshop.

2. *What they ask for.* Jane Pratt, founder of the original *Sassy* magazine, is asked frequently by adults, "What's your secret to communicating with teenagers?" Her advice is clear and on target: "The only key, I think, is listening to them. Teenagers get talked at so often. . . . It's so rare for someone to actually take the time to listen to them with respect, taking what they're saying seriously, and not judging them first."[4] She recommends ultimately treating them "the way you like to be treated, not as you treat children or convicts."[5]

Listen to the teens and then use their ideas. Establish rapport. Create a forum for young voices to be heard and get administrative support to really listen to them. Whether it's a young adult advisory council, teenage library workers, or a suggestion box in the young adult area (preferably, all three), solicit their program ideas and, whenever possible, execute them. Not only will the teens be able to tell you what will be a workable topic, but they will also tell you good and bad times for scheduling.

Be open-minded. Anything can be related to the library, even if library materials are not central to the original idea. "Plastic eyeball putt-putt golf" sounds like a weird suggestion, but do it and you'll gain new library users. Consider the young people's ideas no matter how goofy they sound. A suggestion might be in-line skating races through the library lobby. The librarian might suggest the more reasonable rollerblading demo in the library parking lot. The kids could propose a food fight as the perfect thing to draw a major crowd. Through gentle guidance the teens and library staff can compromise on a program involving sucking Jell-O through crazy straws or eating M&Ms with thumbs and pinkie fingers. These ideas are generated by YAs but molded into something more doable and administration-friendly with the expertise and perspective of library staff.

One of the best ways to achieve good communication with local teens is to create and maintain a young adult advisory council. There is an entire chapter on the topic of youth participation in this book, but groups such as this will be mentioned here as a vital part of program-planning success. If you don't have a group of your own, you must be creative in finding other ways to chat with teens. One captive audience is most likely in your library every day—your student workers, pages, or whatever your library calls the 16- to 18-year-olds working in your book stacks. They are a great resource for program, scheduling, and any teen water-testing opinion. Otherwise, ask kids questions as they do their homework. Ask their teachers. Ask their parents. React to obvious interests (Internet training, sports card/comic book collecting, etc.). Be ready to capitalize on a hot topic.

Be mindful of creating programs on perceived notions of teens. Not all eyebrow-pierced teens like Marilyn Manson; they might be opera fans. The hazards of basing programs on stereotypes are numerous. The teens will continue to think that librarians and libraries are clueless and nerdy, respectively. They won't attend programs. Or they will attend programs, be severely disappointed, and never return. I made the fatal error of collecting prizes for the library's first young adult summer reading program based on nothing but my own idea of 1990s teenagers. Instead of being delighted to win a prize, some of the ''winners'' actually whisked their prize away as if they were embarrassed to pick it up. These very prizes that bombed in Ohio might have thrilled a teen in another state. My lesson was learned; for the second summer reading program, I asked teens for good prize ideas. The response? Restaurant and music store gift certificates.

A common concern about library programs is finding the tie-in to the library. When teens suggest weird programs, the lack of tie-in can be a barrier to bringing such an idea to fruition. Stop worrying about being relevant! The justification is bringing the public in. In the ''why'' portion of this chapter one of the reasons for doing programs is giving the program attendees a positive library experience. Anything is library-related when you consider the breadth of a library collection. Sucking Jell-O through crazy straws could be some kind of physics experiment in a program on doing science projects. At my former library, we did a kind of Nickelodeon *Double Dare* takeoff. How is that different from doing the perennial *Jeopardy* takeoff? The kids answered different trivia questions based on the summer reading theme, and if they couldn't answer, they could accept a physical challenge—stuffing Jell-O into mini-Coke bottles, for example.

3. *What somebody else did.* Steal from others. Stealing and modifying ideas are skills that, once developed, will serve you extremely well. If an idea is published or presented, those colleagues want you to say, ''Good for you,'' then wonder if you could do the same thing at your library. Too often, admittedly, we read these articles and say, ''Jolly for them, but that would never work here.'' Stop doing that. Scan professional literature for articles on programs done by colleagues. The best sources to thieve from are *VOYA, School Library Journal,* and church youth group books such as *Junior High Game Nights: Wild and Crazy Outreach Events for Junior-High Ministry* by Dan McCollam and Keith Betts. Join a listserv like PUBYAC for tons of unique ideas. Call your local consortium or state library group and find out if there's an existing compilation of youth programs. Go to programming-related programs at ALA and your state

and regional professional conferences. Share your enthusiasm with some teens. If they agree that the idea is good, modify the program for your community and go to it.

Promotion

Name the program. Do not use dorky program names. I truly believe that vague is better because people have to ask about the program. If the title were very specific, they might too easily say, "Nope, that's not something I'd like." Ask YAs if they'd rather attend "Halloween Stories for Teens" or "The Blood and Guts Horror Hour." Which do you think they are more likely to consider attending?

Once the title of the program is set, create eye-catching signs with whatever resources are available to you, from cut-and-paste to fancy desktop software. Don't post the signs too early. Many times spontaneous attendees will outnumber those who registered. The flyer must include the program title, time and date, where to meet, and how/if to register. Lengthy explanations of program events take up too much room, plus you want them to approach staff for more information. It's a flyer, not an agenda!

To register or not? Registration is absolutely necessary when there are craft or other supplies involved. Otherwise, registration is optional. People who sign up won't show up, and people will show up even if they haven't signed up. If you feel you must have an estimate of attendees, *recommend* registration for all your programs, but stay flexible.

Put the programs in the children's and library newsletters if you have them, especially if YA programs are a new addition to library services. Folks are used to picking these up and will see the programs listed. A separate YA list is important, too, but piggybacking on established methods is a good start.

Having a core group of teen contacts helps mightily with promotion of programs. They will bring friends and relatives and neighbors to programs they helped plan. They will hand-deliver signs to teachers and school librarians they know are receptive and most likely to post or even announce library programs. If such a group is not available, do a mailing to school librarians and/or teachers in the area middle, junior, high, and private schools serving secondary students. Post flyers around the library in odd places so they are not lost in the sign sea that is a library bulletin board. For big programs, use tempura paint or static cling letters and shapes on library windows.

Promotion does not stop until the program begins. If your library allows announcements, do a couple of them before the starting time. If you cannot make announcements, prowl around the library for people who look between 10 and 18 years old and encourage them to attend. At my urban library, this technique has worked well. Five young women spontaneously took a break from their homework and got their nails done at a beauty program. Two 13-year-old boys won candy bars at a Choco-Bingo event for which they would not have dreamed of registering.

All the glamorous public relations in the world cannot overcome bad timing. If no one shows up for a Tuesday night Star Wars party, change it a little (broaden the scope to science fiction films, acquire a life-size cardboard Darth Vader), and try it again on a Thursday afternoon.

The Execution

Basically, this is just the carrying out of all your planning. Try not to make the program like school. If your signs have been inviting and exciting, kids will be disappointed if they find that the Horror Hour will be spent sitting in rows listing to a librarian spout about Stephen King's *Green Mile* series and its marketing strategy. Actually *doing* a YA program is a chance to be youthful in a way not unlike getting to color with small children. Dance around if there's music involved. They'll laugh, but you can handle it. If there's food involved, eat some. Facilitate, but join in. Young people will have to reconsider the librarian stereotype burned into their brains thanks to television commercials. Remember, some of the young people at your program could be *your* future librarian!

If possible, involve a lot of your library's staff. This involvement works wonders, especially if YA programming is a new concept at your library. The staff will feel more comfortable with teens. They will discover that those shaven-headed boys who make them uneasy are actually pretty darn witty when pursuing a hidden library artifact for a scavenger hunt. At the same time, the teens are getting used to approaching library staff all over the library. The kids, therefore, will be less likely to leave the library empty-handed the next time they need homework information. Other times, of course, involving other staff is a necessity. You can't manage 50 sixth graders throwing water balloons by yourself. Get some help or do something with less frenzy.

Execute a program with as many bizarre props as possible. Kooky toys will quickly erase the kids' idea that libraries are just about big, fat, dusty books. Polaroid cameras work really well with self-absorbed teens (instant gratification, complete with pictures of *me* to show my friends!). A murder mystery is made more fun if there are Polaroid pictures of the suspects posted around the library. With a handful of cameras, participants can photograph clues and meet to put their cases together. That one added element can bring a "handout program" to life. Real kitsch can be added to a program with the inclusion of green Jell-O. Somehow that special green gelatin is both gross and fun at the same time. Other wacky food to include might be edible gummy boogers, tongue-shaped lollipops, and Pop Rocks (candies that sizzle on your tongue).

The wackiest, most prop-involved summer (outside) program I ever did was stolen from *More Junior High Game Nights* and required wet sponges and legs cut off pantyhose. Cut the legs off cheap pantyhose (bright colors are great if you can find them). Put a wet sponge in the foot of the stocking and put the other end over your head. Have a partner do the same. If you can stop laughing, move your head and neck around to get the sponge swinging and try to tangle it with your partner's sponge. When one of you successfully removes the stocking from the other guy's head, you win. You will whack each other in the face with the wet sponge a few times, but there's the hilarity!

Where to hold the program depends on your library and the program itself. Summer programs are great to take outside, weather permitting. Always have a Plan B in case of rain or 100+ temperatures. Some of the best programs I've hosted have no one location. They require the participants to wander around the library. Having no perfect space is no excuse to pass on a potentially exciting YA program. Sitting on the floor in the mystery section is a great starting-off place for a mystery program. Community rooms are grand, but they can also alienate a program. The teens may enjoy themselves, but they don't necessarily feel as though they were at the library.

Try to learn participants' names, but use name tags only if program-appropriate. Badges for detectives and suspects work fine at a murder mystery, but little bats for a horror book discussion would be patronizing.

When the program is over, be sure to tell the attendees about the next program and thank them for coming.

Evaluation

There are whole books on the subject of this admittedly very important (especially to library boards and administrators) but rather tedious topic. Evaluation, in most cases, means statistics. Statistics for young adult programs can (especially to boards and administrators used to seeing three-figure children's programs numbers) look bad. Do not feel bad about low attendance. Go ahead and do a program with five registrants unless you are told not to. An intimate program is a good experience for everybody.

As much as we might hate numbers, accountability is not an option. Instead of a dry numbers report, write a brief YA services monthly, bimonthly, or quarterly report. This textual information can show how a mere "7" for a book discussion and a "43" for a sports card swap can be equally valuable to the library and attendees. This text can also become your article in a professional journal from which others can borrow.

If you are really having to defend services to young adults, always keep in mind that success is measured in different ways. If stats and stats alone drive a program budget, be creative with numbers. Count all middle, junior, and high school tours as programs. Boost circulation statistics by making sure you have books, or at least a booklist, available at every program. Teens and their parents will check out materials after seeing their interests spelled out so handily on that list. Circulation numbers will go up, and voilá, justification numbers for the big guys. Ask your system administrator (computer person) how to gather as many numbers as possible. If patrons are coded as juvenile, young adult, and adult, surely reports can be generated based on those categories and their use of library materials.

Sometimes it seems silly to a nonnumbers person to go through all this rigmarole to justify something that is so obviously necessary. You and I both know that meaningful feedback is a parent's genuine thank-you, a teen's telling her friend she had a good time, and repeat attendees.

CONCLUSION

My daily goal is that library customers, teenagers especially, will either find what they are looking for or have a good library experience, preferably both. Many days this is a simple goal; some days it isn't that easy. I have found that planning and executing young adult programs seem to give all parties involved (librarian, library staff, library administration, parents, educators, teens, and sometimes their young siblings) an overall good library vibe.

When I take my job too seriously, I remind myself that I am neither a doctor nor a social worker. We are not in the business of saving lives, but we are in the business of filling a need. Sometimes people, especially teenagers, have to be convinced that we're here to provide services they need rather than to collect fines or shush them. A trip to the library should be as routine as a trip to the grocery store. If a goofy YA program makes a teen think good thoughts about the library, an idealistic goal becomes real. What more could we possibly ask for?

Lastly, to assist you in developing those ideas, the following is a very short list of possible programs: library tours; booktalks; school visits; young adult advisory councils; writing contests; dramas/reader's theater; demonstrations (karate, rollerblading, etc.); job-hunting skills; baby-sitting clinics; cartooning; vehicle maintenance; jewelry making; Halloween makeup; games (Dungeons and Dragons, Magic the Gathering, chess, etc.); car-buying tips; multigenerational reading programs (seniors and teens, children and teens); T-shirt/sneaker art; fashion and beauty tips; comic book exchange; sports card trading; author visits; scavenger hunts; letter writing (to celebrities, grandparents, etc.); overnights; or, anything with off-beat, zany appeal.

NOTES

1. Margaret A. Edwards, *The Fair Garden and the Swarm of Beasts* (1969; reprint, with a foreword by Patty Campbell, Chicago: American Library Association, 1994), 88.

2. Carolyn Caywood, "To Linger in Good Company," *School Library Journal* (March 1996): 138.

3. Mary K. Chelton, "We Don't Want You—We Want Your [Dumb] Friends!" *Voice of Youth Advocates* (October 1994): 187.

4. Jane Pratt, *For Real: The Uncensored Truth about America's Teenagers* (New York: Hyperion, 1995), xiv.

5. Ibid., xv.

19

Long on Enthusiasm But Short on Ideas? An Annotated Bibliography on Young Adult Programming

Sean P.S. George

A vital component of excellent service in any young adult department is programming—planning events and activities to organize and motivate teenagers. While collection development and basic reference services are usually the highest priority for youth librarians and deservedly so, effective programming is important for promoting and improving these two traditional functions in addition to providing benefits of its own. The value of programming is widely recognized now more than ever, with increasing attention being drawn to the destructive lifestyles teens can pursue in the absence of better alternatives. Public libraries can offer occasional events that attract young people with specific interests, as well as ongoing programs that give them an opportunity for organizational experience and leadership. Working professionals, however, novice or veteran, who have decided to make programming a priority in their service to young patrons may be uncertain where to begin. This chapter is intended as a guide to available resources that will help librarians who want to add programming as a new service or need new ideas to revitalize existing programming efforts.

FINDING A FORUM FOR PROGRAMMING IDEAS

Most of the literature discussed in the following bibliography was published from 1990 through 1996 in journals and books indexed by the *Library Litera-*

ture, ERIC, and *LISA* databases. Journals such as *Voice of Youth Advocates, School Library Journal,* and the *Journal of Youth Services in Libraries* consistently address this topic. Occasional articles also appear in other national journals like *Public Libraries, American Libraries,* and, in retrospect, *Wilson Library Bulletin.* State library organizations may also feature youth programming in their journals from time to time, and some even compile handbooks or manuals on the subject. In the interest of brevity, only one example of each of these state-specific resources is annotated in this bibliography (citations 2 and 33). A selected list of other citations from state and regional journals indexed in the aforementioned sources follows the annotations.

Another viable and valuable forum, which does not fit neatly into bibliography format, is the Internet. Although Internet access is not yet universal, it is already a staple for many information professionals, and the field of youth services is no exception. PUBYAC, for example, is an e-mail listserv dedicated to issues concerning public library service to young adults and children, with frequent discussions of programming ideas, successes, and warnings.[1] Questions to the group are always welcomed and usually get timely and enthusiastic response from other working professionals, students, and professors, many of whom are cited in this chapter. Several World Wide Web and Gopher sites devoted to young adult library services also include helpful programming information. The Young Adult Librarian's Help/Homepage,[2] originally created by Patrick Jones and now hosted by the Kansas City Public Library, is an excellent example of such a resource. Whether electronic or printed, there is a variety of resources available for the youth librarian who has the will and is looking for a way.

BIBLIOGRAPHY

The publications collected and annotated here are limited to those that concentrate on proactive public library programs that seek out and address the needs and interests of community teenagers and promote the library. Whether such activities are worthwhile or appropriate for the public library is not the primary focus of the literature presented, but rather assumed as an important component of public library service. Among the types of youth programs described are organized group activities for library planning, opportunities for creative expression, and scheduled events or programs that meet some educational or recreational need. In addition to sound advice and valuable guidelines, many of the authors present the real difficulties involved in undertaking programming projects. Throughout their discourse, they convey their enthusiasm and dedication to their young adult patrons, often with anecdotes and humor familiar to anyone working with teenagers.

The citations are numbered consecutively and arranged thematically in four major sections based on the primary thrust of the article. The first section, "General Programming Guidelines," contains articles that discuss considerations common to any programming venture, with a few also giving brief synopses or simple listings of some specific activities. "Involving Youth in Library Operations," the second section, presents programs in which, regardless of other features, the planning and/or execution is largely performed by youth advisory boards or volunteer groups supervised by a youth librarian. Section 3 focuses on gearing summer reading programs, a traditional mainstay of children's service, to the teenage population. "Other Events and Activities," the final section, is a miscellaneous array of program descriptions that do not fit into the second or third sections but are valuable ideas year-round. Articles designated by an asterisk in the left margin contain their own bibliographies that provide some selective access to the pertinent literature prior to 1990. Most of the articles describing the execution of specific programs, however, are entirely a product of the authors' personal experience and ideas.

General Programming Guidelines

1. Black, Nancy. " 'Lasers in the Jungle': Programming Tips, Techniques and Ideas for Young Adults." *Emergency Librarian* (May–June 1992): 16–19. Reading somewhat like a "book of lists" for YA programming, this article starts out with a list of nontraditional programming activities to spark the reader's interest. With a few paragraphs of explanation here and there, Black goes on to list some criteria for successful programming, reasons for "instigating" YA programming, examples of guidelines from two Canadian public libraries, and elements of a useful YA service philosophy. The bulk of the article is composed of ten effective YA programming tips, followed by ten PR hints, a column full of inexpensive program ideas, and finally a list of advice.

2. Boyce, Judith. "Programming for the Public Library." *LLA Bulletin* (Spring 1995): 203–7. This is a representative example of a state-specific publication, in this case the bulletin of the Louisiana Library Association, more of which may be found listed at the end of this chapter. "Motivating youth to read" is the reason Boyce cites for offering special library programs and activities, and she begins with an argument for the library's responsibility to offer such programs, along with several goals to guide program development for children and young adults. The article goes on to discuss some sample programs, fund-raising efforts to support programming, the development of a "program resource list," and effective marketing for the activities developed. In describing sample programs, she breaks them down into five distinct groups, Razzle/Dazzles, Beginnings, Mind Benders, Troubadores, and Academics, and offers examples that readers can adapt in their own libraries.

3. *Jones, Patrick. *Connecting Young Adults and Libraries: A How-to-Do-It Manual.* New York: Neal-Schuman, 1992. Jones uses a detailed approach throughout this book to address every element of young adult programing. The eighth chapter, "Programming," follows suit, starting with a brief argument on its importance and purposes. Jones describes the planning process as a series of questions, namely, Why? What (type)? Who does it? How often? What format? Who plans? What topic? What will it cost and who will pay? Will it work? and How will it get done? He gives practical examples of how to answer each of these questions

and safeguards against how they should not be answered. He stresses the importance of effective promotion, especially contacting other YA agencies, enlisting
the support of other library staff, creating hype, and encouraging repeat business.
Following the general guidelines are some more specific suggestions for running
advisory groups, book discussion groups, summer reading programs, and literary
magazines. Throughout the chapter Jones provides examples of forms for planning, documenting, and evaluating projects, as well as valuable resource lists of
possible agencies and organizations for partnerships and programming "round-
ups" in previous publications.

4. Jones, Patrick and Anne Prusha. "Young Adult Programming: Identifying the Elements of Success." *Voice of Youth Advocates* (June 1991): 83–85. Here Jones
and Prusha encourage young adult librarians to overcome their fear of failure in
programming by identifying 25 factors that can multiply one's chances for success. The two writers present a wide variety of ideas, some self-evident, others
less likely to cross the reader's mind, as well as warnings against common mistakes that can doom a program. They present their suggestions with a healthy
dose of humor but seriously acknowledge that situational circumstances can always interfere, arguing that a good YA librarian is the ultimate factor for success.

5. Wallace, Mildred G. "Tips for Successful Young Adult Programming." *Journal of
Youth Services in Libraries* (Summer 1993): 387–90. With only a brief paragraph
of introduction Wallace presents a straightforward and concise collection of tips
for effective young adult programming based on her experience. Her dozen main
headings start with "Study the Literature" and proceed through to "Evaluate
Every Program," elaborating several points under each heading. The first three
headings deal mainly with information gathering from different sources. The next
five focus on different types of support that will strengthen programming activities, and the final four address miscellaneous but essential items to remember
throughout the process.

6. *Wilson-Lingbloom, Evie. *Hangin' Out at Rocky Creek: A Melodrama in Basic
Young Adult Services in Public Libraries*. Metuchen, NJ: Scarecrow Press, 1994.
Throughout this book Wilson-Lingbloom presents aspects of young adult service
by identifying challenges present in a hypothetical library scenario. In Chapter 8,
"Involving Youth in YA Programming on a Limited Budget," she speaks specifically to the problem of redirecting the disruptive activities of a sizable group
of teens regularly present at the library. After discussing YA programming as a
"service priority," she shares some ideas for "simple informational programs"
as an alternative to more intensive, ongoing programming. A particularly strong
element of this chapter is the author's attention to intergenerational involvement
and its benefits, complete with examples of successful programs across the country and contact information for national organizations. In the process of elaborating on the strategies needed to involve YAs in ongoing library programming,
she comes down firmly on the side of youth participation in planning to ensure
success. The sections on facilitating and reviewing the success of youth participation groups offer valuable insight and give thirteen examples of effective implementation, some of which have their own citations later in this bibliography.
Wilson-Lingbloom then outlines some general program-planning steps and ends
with several suggestions to consider when bringing in visiting YA authors,
gleaned from experience and the authors themselves.

Involving Youth in Library Operation

Volunteer Groups and Advisory Boards

7. *Broderick, Dorothy M., ed. *The VOYA Reader*. Metuchen, NJ: Scarecrow Press, 1990. This book is a compilation of articles previously published in *Voice of Youth Advocates* that provide, among other things, a wealth of information on involving youth in the planning and delivery of library services. Lynn Eisenhut takes a comprehensive look at the development of a strong volunteer program that involves teens in the children's summer reading program at the Orange County (California) Public Library. Nearly half of the article is devoted to the process of program implementation, with sections outlining how to plan ahead, recruit, train, monitor, and reward. Chris Piatelli's "Youth Helping the Handicapped" introduces a project that involves youth volunteers, recruited from another community agency, in planning and presenting library activities for their mentally disadvantaged peers. The scope and general structure of the activities generated by the youth volunteers are valuable on their own and could also be effectively applied in other situations. Terry Stevens, a teenage member of the Spokane Public Library's Young Adult Advisory Committee (YAAC), describes in her article the evolution and operation of their successful Golden Pen Awards. In the process she gives a brief history of how the YAAC began, including the development of a constitution to establish important administrative policies for the group. Evie Wilson in "The Young Adult Advisory Board: How to Make It Work" shares "some practical suggestions . . . for making legitimate youth participation a reality." Among these are pointers on recruiting members, suggestions for the new board's first meeting, a section on ensuring repeat attendance, and an admonition against undertaking a YA advisory board without full support from library administration. The Youth Participation Project of the Nassau County (New York) Youth Board contributes their "Youth Participation Guidelines," which presents a specific and definitive example for youth involvement on planning committees. Pragmatic rationale supports each of the eleven guidelines, which primarily focus on the selection, expectations, and empowerment of the youth members to ensure effective participation rather than a token presence.

8. *Caywood, Caroline A., comp. and ed. *Youth Participation in School and Public Libraries: It Works*. Chicago: American Library Association, 1995. A combined and revised edition of *Youth Participation in School and Public Libraries* and *Youth Participation in Libraries: A Training Manual*,[3] this handbook is the comprehensive guide to giving youth a role in designing the programs that impact them. The first section addresses how this involvement can meet the needs of young adults and simultaneously benefit the library, presents YALSA's "Guidelines for Youth Participation in Libraries," and summarizes the elements and procedures of implementing this concept. The chapter on implementation begins with seven commonsense planning points from the National Commission on Resources for Youth, goes on to describe the roles of the adult facilitator, administration, and staff, and briefly discusses the processes of recruitment, training, evaluation, and reflection. Section II is devoted to "Training for Youth Participation," including some tips for preparation and a detailed guide on how to conduct a workshop. To encourage by example, Section III is a directory of youth

participation groups arranged by state and describes some of their activities. Moving to the national level, the fourth section introduces the YALSA, outlines the benefits of membership, and provides a membership form. The final section contains four appendixes: (1) an extensive bibliography of "Resources on Youth Participation," (2) camera-ready handouts for the training workshop, (3) over 50 programming ideas to help youth participation groups get started, and (4) a script for a dramatic presentation on intellectual freedom written by YAs for YAs (see citation 11).

9. *Finney, Kay and Kim McCombs. "Teenagers Work Well in the Berkeley Public Library." *Voice of Youth Advocates* (April 1994): 11–14. In response to an extensive needs assessment funded by the California State Library's "Youth at Risk" grant, the Berkeley Public Library created three paid library positions for youth. Finney and McCombs discuss the needs assessment process and the library's collaboration with community youth and youth-serving agencies to reach the decision to provide employment. She offers an important perspective on the concept of "youth at risk" and then describes the four facets of the jobs that were created: public service, clerical work, computer literacy, and outreach. One rough spot she addresses is the amount of supervision that may be required for some teens who are less autonomous. To counter that drawback she provides an array of advantages the program provides for the library and the youth involved. Attesting to its success was the decision of library administration to allocate funds to continue the positions after the grant money ran out. Finney and McCombs' article is an excellent profile of this innovative approach to youth library service, full of details on the program's planning and operation.

10. *Herald, Diana Tixier. "Buy More Books! and Other Bright Ideas from a Teen Advisory Board." *School Library Journal* (July 1996): 26–27. Originally suggested as a forum "to talk about books without being considered strange . . . [and] a way to meet boys from other schools," Herald reveals the early stages of Mesa County (Colorado) Public Library's Teen Advisory Board (TAB). With sections devoted to the group's summer reading game, best books list, and TAB's outreach activities, this article also gives an anecdotal account of the fluctuating membership and interests associated with a crew of teen advisers. Two useful insets, "TAB Meetings: Books + Cookies" and "8 Tips for Running a Successful Teen Advisory Board," distill some of the essentials of this activity, and the author cites other successful examples of YA participation councils.

11. MacRae, Cathi Dunn. "Watch Out for 'Don't Read This!': How a Library Youth Participation Group Was Silenced by Schools Yet Made Its Voice Heard." *Voice of Youth Advocates* (June 1995): 80–87. While this article might be considered most valuable in a bibliography on intellectual freedom, MacRae gives enough attention to the planning and mechanics of this controversial youth participation project for it to be useful as a programming resource as well. A play conceived, written, and produced by Boulder (Colorado) Public Library's Young Adult Advisory Board (YAAB), *Don't Read This!* began as a rather elaborate endeavor and grew to enormous proportions. Tucked into her narrative of this challenging venture are details on editing the script, managing rehearsals, scheduling performances, and building associated activities out of the spontaneous energy generated by the original project. Successfully managing potential and actual conflicts and increasing media attention are among several important lessons in this article that

serves as both an inspiration and fair warning for any librarian leading a strong youth participation group. Intrepid YA librarians can find the script of this play included in *Youth Participation in School and Public Libraries: It Works* (see entry 8).

12. Maggio, Mary. "Romancing the Young Teen." *Voice of Youth Advocates* (February 1996): 360–62, 367. Concentrating on service to early adolescents, an age group frequently avoided or omitted, Maggio examines the initial steps in cultivating a Young Teen Advisory Board (YTAB) at the Mastics-Moriches-Shirley Community (New York) Library. From dances that garnered only lukewarm response, to the highly popular *Win, Lose or Draw*-style game show, Maggio describes the progression of activities planned and sponsored by the YTAB. Winnowing the group to a manageable size and tempering the young teens' "grandiose" ideas are two of the challenges she discusses in the course of building success and support for this frequently ignored age range. Details of the decoration and furnishing of a new dedicated room for this segment of patrons crown Maggio's efforts and conclude the main body of her article, before a few closing remarks.

13. Sprince, Leila J. "For Young Adults Only: Tried and True Youth Participation Manual." *Voice of Youth Advocates* (October 1994): 197–99. In her discussion of the Young Adult Library Advisory Board (YALAB) at the North Regional/Broward Community College Library in Florida, Sprince focuses attention on the active and enthusiastic recruitment of teen volunteers as the first step in getting youth involved in library program planning. As part of this program, recognized in *Excellence in Library Services to Young Adults* (see entry 32), teen library volunteers eventually earn the opportunity to be selected for the YALAB. She emphasizes personal contact and outlines the "Teen Volunteer Guidelines" that she presents to her new recruits. Next she lists eighteen steps to develop a library's first corps of teen volunteers and create from them a working YALAB. She suggests some long-range and short-range goals to focus the group's energy and ends with five basics to remember when contemplating this type of ongoing project.

14. Sprince, Leila J. "Whose Teen Advisory Board Is This, Anyway?" [Focus on Youth Volunteers]. *Journal of Youth Services in Libraries* (Spring 1996): 247–50. In this latest publication of Sprince's experience with teen advisory groups, she discusses her "most valuable experience" in this arena. Possibly the best lesson in this article is that one should never assume that all YAs are the same, a point driven home to her when her most recent TAB ignored the ideas she brought from her past successes and came up with an array of completely new activities on their own. To her credit Sprince allowed the group to chart its own course, and she reports on several original programs that they brainstormed and implemented, including OPAC instruction for other patrons, discussion groups on teen problems, a multicultural community fair, and a "Teen Cafe" to showcase local youth musicians. Common sense should tell us all to answer this article's title question the way Sprince has, that it belongs to the teens.

Young Adults Working with Children

15. Baldwin, Liz. "A Summer Lesson in Service" [Practically Speaking]. *School Library Journal* (May 1993): 40. Not enough library staff to put together a summer program for both children and teens? Baldwin's article suggests solving this problem efficiently by recruiting teen volunteers to help run the children's summer

reading program. She explains how the 30 teens who participated benefited from the opportunity to develop their skills in organization, communication, technology, and creativity through the experience. The library in return gained 411 hours of assistance in producing a fine summer reading program. The author briefly describes the recruitment, orientation, and performance of the youth volunteers and enthusiastically asserts the program's success.

16. Baldwin, Liz. "It All Started in the Summer . . ." [Focus on Youth Volunteers]. *Journal of Youth Services in Libraries* (Spring 1996): 250–52. Actually, according to Baldwin's most recent account, she begins her recruiting in early spring to effectively redirect the energy of many community teens, for their own benefit and the library's. She tells more of the group's orientation to library procedures that they perform to facilitate the summer reading program, including OPAC instruction and other ways of helping children find books, as well as program paperwork. From this summer volunteer pool, Baldwin also highlights a few participants who remain active in the library's operation the rest of the year, leading to an interest in library careers for some.

17. Coleman, Yvonne K. "Teen Corps Reaches Out with Pride" [Focus on Youth Volunteers]. *Journal of Youth Services in Libraries* (Spring 1996): 243–47. Coleman's offering brings to life the activities of the young adult Reach Out and Read (ROAR) Corps, designed to reach preschool and school-aged children in a variety of settings. Coleman talks about recruiting and training corps members in the art of picture book reading and other more mundane procedures involved in the corps' operation, as well as the library's cooperation with a community bank that provided the impetus and funding for the program. The evolution of corps members' storytelling skills and the variety of venues for their performances, such as supermarkets, local parks, town parades, and nursing homes, are especially interesting elements of this intriguing program report.

18. McGrath, Marsha and Jana R. Fine. "Teen Volunteers in the Library." *Public Libraries* (January/February 1990): 24–28. McGrath and Fine explain all of the important elements of their successful Teen Volunteers program in the Clearwater (Florida) Public Library System, beginning with the four guiding goals for the project. These two librarians devote most of their attention to promotion techniques, the orientation procedure, and the training and responsibilities of the young volunteers. As a companion program the authors discuss the puppetry troupe, also entirely composed of teen volunteers, which performs for children at each library branch and other community venues. The youth participants are evaluated on their performance, and the program itself is also evaluated to identify areas for improvement. In closing the article provides several frequently omitted details of staffing and funding and summarizes the success and effectiveness of the program.

19. Speight, Jean J. "Pulling a Few Strings: How to Start a Volunteer Puppet Troupe." *School Library Journal* (May 1994): 24–27. As a response to her own difficulty in starting a youth volunteer puppet troupe, Speight elucidates the vital elements of planning and executing this activity. She covers the acquisition of material necessities, the process of recruiting and screening teen volunteers, the agenda and progression of the group's first meeting, and subsequent rehearsals, finishing with an overview of performance-day activities. A helpful inset provides guidelines for selecting and adapting stories for performance, addressing script length,

props, characters, dialogue, and stage directions. The straightforward nature of this step-by-step guide should encourage YA librarians to try this program as a way to serve multiple purposes in a comprehensive youth services department.

Young Adults Working with Special Populations

20. Bern, Alan. "What We Did Together over Their Summer Vacation: Reading Buddies in the Children's Room of the Oakland Public Main Library." *Voice of Youth Advocates* (February 1996): 357–59, 367. Young adults helping young children with learning disabilities is the subject of this thorough program report. Bern starts with the impetus for this activity and several reasons for his reluctance to approach it, then discusses the specifics of the program that produced repeated success, giving due praise to the program's volunteer coordinator, a local learning disabilities and reading specialist. Though recruitment receives only cursory attention, scheduling sessions, training teen reading buddies, and the teens' planning of creative activities for the children are all well articulated. Information on the program's evaluation and improvement for its second year is also particularly helpful.

21. Karpas, Beth. "Sidekicks: An Intergenerational Program" [Need a Program Idea? Try These . . .]. *Voice of Youth Advocates* (April 1995): 12. Karpas gives a brief overview of this example of a relatively rare program type, born out of a continuing cooperation between the Clermont County (Ohio) Public Library and Clermont Senior Services, Inc. Her summary mentions the annual training for the young adult participants, some of the activities that these teens plan and attend with their senior counterparts, and the benefits of the program for both age groups. Karpas unfortunately omits the mechanics, but, as with any successful intergenerational program, it is obvious that both groups gain from the experience.

22. Union, Bunni. "Reading to Seniors" [Focus on Young Adult Programming]. *Journal of Youth Services in Libraries* (Summer 1996): 381–84. Showing another successful example of young volunteers' serving the older population, this offering gives ample information on the operation of an intergenerational program. Initial fears, exciting results, preparations, group composition, materials, and activities— all of these are present in Union's account. Comments from both groups of participants, parents of teen volunteers, and the community are also mentioned, unanimously praising this effort that "combine[d] the elements of educational, social, and informational needs and fulfillment into an intergenerational program involving the library, books, and reading."

Summer Reading Programs

The Mystery Genre

23. Brown, Marilyn and Anne Merkle. "Bibliothecam Amissam Inveni! (I Found the Library)" [Need a Program Idea? Try These . . .]. *Voice of Youth Advocates* (April 1995): 10–11. This inventive summer reading program, the Archaeological Dig Reading Club, gives an interesting twist to the mystery genre by building on the premise of David Macaulay's *Motel of Mysteries*. Adapting this concept of a humorous speculation on how future archaeologists would interpret today's material culture, Brown and Merkle tell how they enticed junior and senior high

school students in Holland (Michigan) to keep reading over the summer. An introductory story provided the imaginative framework, and teen reading was rewarded with the opportunity to identify artifacts, which, in turn, accumulated to earn a registration for the grand prize drawing. Details of the program's operation are accompanied by a retrospective look at its best and worst features.

24. Graham, Kent W. and Gail Roberts. "Murder, They Read: YA Summer Reading Success." *Voice of Youth Advocates* (February 1992): 363–64. Combining elements of the board game Clue, the name from a popular television show, and a variety of other creative ideas, this mystery-oriented program encouraged long-term independent reading by participating youth. Almost 200 YAs participated, writing short book reviews, or "investigation reports," in return for clues that they could use to solve the fabricated mystery and be registered for the grand prize drawing. In addition to describing the structure of the game and the culminating party, Graham and Roberts address the elements of staff involvement and publicity, providing all the necessary evidence for any YA librarian to run a similarly successful program.

Computer-Based Programs

25. Makowski, Silvia A. et al. "Computer Pix: A Computerized Summer Reading Program for YAs." *Voice of Youth Advocates* (August 1994): 132–36. The philosophy behind this program is similar to that of a computer dating service, matching books with prospective young adult readers based on a reading interest form. Makowski and her colleagues trace the fourteen-year history of Computer Pix, the bibliographic selection software designed for reader's advisory to teenagers, as a central part of summer reading programs in several Michigan libraries. Throughout the article they address many issues, such as book selection, marketing strategies, accompanying graphic design, usage trends, and planned improvements. In light of the continuing effectiveness of Computer Pix in these library systems, any YA librarians or consortia that have a computer programmer on hand may want to consider a similar project.

26. Olson, Renée. "Young Adults Read Year 'round in Reading" [Youthreach]. *American Libraries* (June 1994): 579–80. Placing heavy emphasis on the collaboration between school and public libraries, Olson describes a perpetual reading program that combines computer quizzes and an incentive system. The central element of the program is a commercial software package that generates questions on over 500 novels. Young readers are rewarded during the school year with small prizes from their school librarians and in the summer with "dollars" issued by the public library to be used in a culminating auction. Olson explains that the challenge to beat the computer motivates the youth to read, as much as the prizes they might win, and the continuity of the program helps to promote lifelong reading habits.

Other Programs

27. Krahnke, Kitty. "Ripples on the YA Pond: The Library Lottery Is Born." *Voice of Youth Advocates* (August 1992): 161–62. Krahnke tracks the collaborative development of a YA summer reading program modeled after typical state lotteries that provide opportunities for both "instant wins" and big "jackpot" prizes. From creating the reading list, writing questions for each title, soliciting prize

items, and advertising the program, to establishing procedures and finally carrying out the plans, the process took an entire year. Fortunately, Krahnke doesn't end the article with the success of the first year's program but goes on to tell how the program was improved, expanded, and transmitted to other libraries.

28. Olson, Betty. "Auction Climaxes YA Summer Reading Program." *Voice of Youth Advocates* (June 1991): 86–87. In this article Olson describes the planning and execution of the auction that was the last part of the Mishawaka (Indiana) Public Library YA summer reading program. To promote the program and encourage participation, they adopted a celebrity theme and contacted over 100 entertainers, sports figures, and YA authors for prize donations. Olson details the procedures she followed for soliciting prizes, promoting the auction, and carrying it out. With the consistent participation and impressive final turnout, Olson looks forward to repeating and improving the program and suggests that other libraries do the same.

29. Reich, Carol and Lynn Brady-Tompkins. "Jump Right In." *Voice of Youth Advocates* (June 1990): 87–90. Although the first part of this story recounts the evolution of an Oregon librarians' network to improve YA service throughout the state, the larger second part focuses on the development of a successful summer reading program. Reich and Brady-Tompkins describe the adaptation of an eclectic incentive system for Hillsboro (Oregon) Public Library's first summer reading program for young adults. They give plenty of details on implementing the system, which rewarded a variety of activities, including novel reading, reference work, and reading aloud to younger children, with prizes donated by local businesses. Other useful features of this article are the longitudinal look at the program's evolution from one year to the next, examples of the flyers and quizzes used, and the affirmation that programming efforts need not be perfect on the first try but often develop over time.

30. Shama, Carol and Lindsay Ruth. "The Empire Summer Puzzler." *Voice of Youth Advocates* (August 1994): 140. Shama and Ruth describe their concoction of a New York state trivia game, the Empire Summer Puzzler, to lead teens to selected reference sources. These two librarians focus on the time-intensive process of writing the 104 questions and 300+ corresponding clues, also mentioning publicity strategies and their initial feelings of uncertainty. While the time-consuming work of creating conundrums may not appeal to every YA librarian, this article shows that the product can successfully motivate teens to use the library.

Other Events and Activities

Comprehensive Works

31. *Broderick, Dorothy M., ed. *The VOYA Reader*. Metuchen, NJ: Scarecrow Press, 1990. This aforementioned volume (see entry 7) also contains a wealth of ideas for miscellaneous activities that public librarians can initiate. In "Youth Helping Youth," Dolores Maminski outlines the organization of a volunteer tutoring service, in which teens tutored their peers, at Baltimore's Enoch Pratt Free Library. Kathi Moeller-Peiffer's article "After-School Programming: You Can Do It Too!" gives extensive information on the planning and implementation of a series of weekly afternoon programs developed through collaboration between the Or-

ange County (North Carolina) Public Library and the local 4-H office. Joanne Petrick and Janice Hummel describe several activities that grew out of their Young Adult Reading Club (YARC), including a book review newspaper, literature-based board games, and a sweepstakes-format YA summer reading program. *The VOYA Reader* also provides a thorough treatment of pen pal programs, with a detailed article by Diane Tucillo explaining the development of a pen pal network of six libraries across the United States and a follow-up article by Pam Spencer giving lively and humorous anecdotes that inspire and motivate.

32. Chelton, Mary K., ed. *Excellence in Library Services to Young Adults: The Nation's Top Programs*. Chicago: American Library Association, 1994; Chelton, Mary K., ed. *Excellence in Library Services to Young Adults: The Nation's Top Programs*. 2d ed. Chicago: American Library Association, 1997. With insightful introductions from Mary K. Chelton, these slim volumes execute a simple but excellent idea, recognizing and describing the 50 most effective examples of library service to young adults in the United States. For the first edition, programs and services voluntarily submitted by librarians throughout the United States were evaluated by the ALA President's Committee on Customer Service to Youth, and the most outstanding services were published here. The first section presents the top 10 services overall, and the remaining 40 are divided into sections on "Collaborative Efforts," "Education Support," "Information Services," "Programs and Services," "Reading Promotion," "Special Needs Populations," and "Youth Participation." Each entry includes the idea, target audience, brief descriptions of the community setting, and the program as it was designed and executed, as well as the amount and source of funding and contact information for the librarians responsible.

33. *Fairbanks, Gretchen, ed. *Book Beat: A Young Adult Services Manual for Louisiana's Libraries*. Baton Rouge: State Library of Louisiana, 1992. Another type of state-specific publication, this handbook has counterparts outside Louisiana. Librarians should always remember to contact their state-level support agencies to see if a resource like this exists or to motivate them to produce one. Two sections in particular, "Activities" and "Workshops," provide excellent information and ideas on proactive young adult services. The first contains ten specific activities with step-by-step instructions for carrying them out: a murder mystery party, dinner theater, summer entertainment troupe, sleep-over, scavenger hunt, fashion show, library club, teen magazine, auction, and a black history program. The second section of interest serves as a guide for conducting young adult workshops and provides 47 workshop ideas on which to build. Out of the 47 ideas listed, the first 6 (tutoring, papier roulé, baseball cards, car audio, snack cooking, and summer self-employment) are developed into step-by-step guides, including a sample PR notice. Thirteen more workshop topics, from the Iberia Parish Library, are described in short paragraphs, and the remaining 28 are simply listed and left up to the reader to develop.

Creative Arts Programs

34. Rome, Linda. "Creative Writing Programs, YAs, and Libraries." *Wilson Library Bulletin* (October 1992): 48–51. Through a dialogue with other public librarians, Rome examines several different types of creative writing programs in public libraries across Ohio and in the Boston Public Library. Among these are Boston Public Library's annual young adult author workshop, a quarterly newsletter pro-

duced as a forum for young writers at the Henderson (Ohio) Memorial Public Library, an annual literary magazine by youth at Mayfield Regional branch of the Cuyahoga County (Ohio) Public Library, and an author visit at the Geauga (Ohio) Public Library that drew many teen writers interested in career possibilities and the technical side of writing. Rome's survey of successful programs shows the range of ideas that a YA librarian might use to address and encourage an interest in creative writing among library teens.

35. Morgan, Nola. "Teen 'Express-Ways.' " *Voice of Youth Advocates* (October 1991): 217. Showcasing local YA writing and art is a great way to simultaneously encourage creativity and library involvement. Morgan tells of the writing and art contest that the Kalihi-Palama (Hawaii) Public Library sponsored for intermediate and high school students in the community. Although it was the brainchild of the Teen Library Council, Morgan was initially hesitant about attempting such a program in an area with a low literacy rate. Trusting her teen council members, though, she supported the idea and was pleasantly surprised at its success. The article provides a great programming idea and attests to the benefits of YA involvement in program planning.

36. Williams, Sheila. "Making Books" [Focus on Young Adult Programming]. *Journal of Youth Services in Libraries* (Summer 1996): 384–86. Williams describes this "Journalmaking" course as one example of the Lincoln (Massachusetts) Public Library's involvement in the public school system's middle school elective offerings. Tantamount in this program's rationale are the observations that it reaches students that normally have no access to the public library and that it fosters relationships between the librarian and youth that can reach beyond the classroom. Included here are some of the procedures students learn in manufacturing their journals and the methods of creative expression demonstrated as appropriate entries once they have made their own blank books. Comments on evaluation, staffing, and materials wrap up this enthusiastic account.

The Mystery Genre Revisited

37. Gorman, Nancy. "The Body in the Library: Who Dunnit?" *Voice of Youth Advocates* (August 1994): 191. Playing on teenagers' taste for intrigue, Gorman's version of the murder mystery theme actively engages teens in nonprint information seeking and deductive reasoning skills. By interviewing staff members and piecing together the clues, 40 middle school-aged youth worked in teams to solve the staged "murder" of a local librarian. For librarians with creativity and a theatrically inclined staff, this article should provide enough information to perpetrate a similar "crime."

38. Knieriem, K. Lesley. "Murder in the Library!" [Practically Speaking]. *School Library Journal* (April 1994): 48. Knieriem adapted an actual unsolved murder mystery to attract YAs to this summer afternoon library program. Focusing on reference and research skills as the means of solving the puzzle, this librarian modified a historical murder case for the basis of the game and generated 20 partial clues that required the teen sleuths to consult important reference sources for key facts. Despite a few problems, which she addresses, the event succeeded in drawing many older teens to the library and into the reference collection. If the article is not descriptive enough for the reader to create a similar activity,

Knieriem gives her contact address and offers to send interested librarians a full copy of the program materials.

39. Plesser, Frances. "Programs with Boys and Girls Together" [Need a Program Idea? Try These . . .]. *Voice of Youth Advocates* (April 1995): 11–12. A continuing series of mystery oriented activities accomplished the seemingly impossible goal named in this article's title. Plesser explains the somewhat serendipitous sequence of events that sustained the first year of East Meadow (New York) Public Library's ongoing Detective Club program for young adolescents. Activities, planned all year long, included a mystery writing contest, a series of movies and theatrical performances that involved the young audience in solving the mystery, and other opportunities for young sleuths. Plesser gives information on each activity and the competition and recognition that kept the young detectives coming back.

Sports-Based Programs

40. Kaplan, Paul. "Take Me Out to the Library: It's Baseball Season." *School Library Journal* (July 1994): 40–41. Although this article deals with collection development and reference services associated with the program's subject, it also contains some good tips for holding a workshop for young baseball card collectors. The suggestions for this event, as well as those for connecting this hobby to reading and other information skills, could also be adapted to other collecting hobbies. Kaplan's report is just one example of a good strategy for attracting youth who might not normally patronize the library.

41. Ruth, Lindsay D. "Rebound and Read" [Practically Speaking]. *School Library Journal* (July 1994): 46. An original idea to attract reluctant readers, the program described in this article combines basketball and books to show YAs how reading can relate to every interest. Ruth explains how, with grant funding, she developed a basketball and reading camp for over 70 teenagers in the Geneva (New York) Free Library's community. She addresses the problems of staffing, recruiting participants, and transportation, as well as describing the activities and structure of the two-week summer program. This innovative integration of information seeking and sports activities is as impressive as the positive response from the youth who attended. Ruth closes her article with the obvious but important comment that this type of program can be adapted to fit any sport and any community to hook reluctant readers and at-risk youth on the advantages of the library.

42. Quatrella, Laura and Barbara Blosveren et al. "Sweat and Self-Esteem: A Public Library Supports Young Women." *Wilson Library Bulletin* (March 1994): 34–36, 139. A nontraditional program like this one proves that the library is not just for homework anymore. Recognizing the dynamic role of their young adult department, these YA librarians put together a support group and aerobics class for 24 young women at the Stratford (Connecticut) Library. The authors review their planning process carefully, from the initial contact with the leader of a similar program in a neighboring city, through the recruitment and training of five teen library volunteers to be peer counselors, to the structure and evaluation of the eight weekly sessions. Funding was supplied by a grant, allowing the library to offer this program at no charge to area teens. Using this article as a guide, other motivated YA librarians could begin to transform their own departments from the

familiar homework station into a center for teens to nurture their bodies as well
as their minds.

Other Programs

43. Auerbach, Barbara. "Hangin' at the Library" [Practically Speaking]. *School Library
Journal* (June 1996): 60. If you are looking to promote the recreational role of
the library among your teenage patrons, you may want to try the type of "just-
for-fun" program that Auerbach describes here. She summarizes the bare-bones
preparation she does in her library but maintains that young adults' tastes differ
from one community to another. Sections on how to know your audience and
make sure that the word is out round out this overview of a simple, sure-fire
recreational program.

44. Conant, Cynthia and Natalie Weikart. "Life Skills Grant Introduces Young Adults
to the Rest of the Library." *Public Libraries* (July/August 1990): 215–19. This
article provides a fine example of responsible outreach programming to those
teenagers least likely to use the library's resources out of ignorance or apprehen-
sion. Conant and Weikart give a step-by-step explanation of Prince George
County (Maryland) Memorial Library's "Life Skills" presentations for young
adults, which was financed by an LSCA grant and supplemental funds from the
library system. Taking their target audience into careful consideration, they designed a classroom presentation with multisensory appeal, introducing job-hunting
materials, consumer information, community referral services, and recreational
media. The two authors describe the components of each presentation, including
video clips, "survival kits," library card applications, discussion of library materials and services and hands-on demonstrations of some of those services, followed by library tours. The coordinating staff developed a training package so
that other libraries could duplicate and adapt the concept, which garnered positive
feedback from both the teens it reached and their high school administrators.

45. Hultz, Karen and Lisa C. Wemett. "A Dozen Ways to Reach Young Adults When
You Are Short on Space, Staff, and Time." *Voice of Youth Advocates* (December
1991): 298. These twelve quick suggestions are somewhat lower-profile than
events like a summer reading program or an author visit. They are, nonetheless,
proactive programs that can greatly improve young adult involvement in the library. Each idea is accompanied by a brief paragraph description, leaving readers
to tailor each idea to their specific circumstances.

46. Mediavilla, Cindy. "Books in the Hood" [Practically Speaking]. *School Library
Journal* (May 1994): 40. While many public libraries may find it difficult to
finance the elaborate event Mediavilla describes, the core concept of this project
is worth the effort of adapting it to fit one's resources. As an emphatic response
to the self-destructive lifestyle of drugs and violence that beckons so many inner-
city youth, Mediavilla and cartoonist Phil Yeh orchestrated "Books in the Hood."
For this event the Downey (California) City Library hosted an impressive array
of authors, musicians, and actors recognized and respected in their young Latino
community who emphasized the importance of reading, education, and libraries.
Mediavilla reports all the details of the successful event, which drew over 2,500
people, describing its conception and some of the unexpected challenges involved and offering suggestions for improving the next "Books in the Hood"
program.

47. Union, Bunni. "Pizza and Politicians" [Focus on Young Adult Programming]. *Journal of Youth Services in Libraries* (Summer 1996): 378–81. One of the two elements from this article's title formed the central focus for teenage participants in the political awareness program that Union recounts, though which element was more important was uncertain at the outset. Union tells how she cooperated with local high school teachers and contacted every pertinent elected official to provide this forum for young adults to have input and get information on the issues that affect their community. Concerns about the potential for protests, adult domination of the event, and lack of teen involvement are all presented, along with the actual outcome of the program. Using this concise article as a guide, other YA librarians may be pleasantly surprised at how many teens pay as much attention to the politicians as they do to the pizza.

48. *Wilson-Lingbloom, Evie. *Hangin' Out at Rocky Creek: A Melodrama in Basic Young Adult Services in Public Libraries*. Metuchen, NJ: Scarecrow Press, 1994. Generally regarded as a staple of library service to children, storytelling receives relatively little attention as an effective program idea for young adults. Chapter 7 of this previously mentioned book, "Storytelling Teenage Folklore: A Basic Library Program for Young Adults," builds on the concept of urban legend or teenage folklore and the narrative propensities of many teenagers to develop a young adult storytelling festival at her hypothetical library. She reviews some familiar urban legends and reasons for their popularity among young people and discusses the oral tradition of storytelling as a natural and valuable foundation for adolescent programming. After establishing storytelling as a creative, expressive, and confidence-building experience for youth, the author turns to the selection of appropriate stories. She suggests factors to consider when preparing for the presentation and gives practical approaches to maintaining a good progression during the program. Finally, she reviews some of the possible results of a successful adolescent storytelling program, benefiting both the teen participants and the library's image.

NOTES

1. To join this listserv, send your subscription message (subscribe PUBYAC Your Name) to majordomo@nysernet.org.

2, To access this site, point your Web browser to http://www.kcpl.lib.mo.us/ya/.

3. *Youth Participation in School and Public Libraries* was a product of the 1983 Young Adult Services Division, now the Young Adult Library Services Association (YALSA), of the American Library Association; *Youth Participation in Libraries: A Training Manual* was produced by YALSA in 1991.

20

You Don't Have to Do It Alone: Young Adult Partnerships in the Public Library

Diane Stine

INTRODUCTION

Public libraries form partnerships on a formal and informal level with many different types of organizations. Almost all public libraries have some type of cooperative involvement with local schools, including community colleges. In "Rural Libraries and Partnerships" Cary Israel writes that the partnerships formed between community college, school, and public libraries provide access to valuable resources for the residents of his state.[1] He goes on to say that community college partnerships with rural school and public libraries could develop activities as simple as recycling reference books or as ambitious as establishing the community college as a regional interlibrary loan center to provide direct loans.[2]

In recent years public libraries have sought to reach out to a broader constituency by forming working relationships with bookstores and other types of community businesses. They have begun to collaborate with other nonprofit agencies such as museums. In addition they have sought to cooperate with governmental, social services, and other types of community agencies that also provide services to the young adult community.

Many libraries have begun to get involved with intergenerational programming, which can involve people of all ages and all types of agencies. In "Interagency Cooperation" Joan M. Wood describes a grant project, Life Spectrum Programming, that the Pekin (Illinois) Public Library developed. They hold a workshop to make local service providers aware of their intergenerational efforts and to encourage them to consider initiating programs. Representatives attend their workshop from the city's park district, office of economic development, the YWCA, nursing homes, schools, the county health department, the Salvation Army, Head Start, the local literacy office, and several other libraries. As a result of the workshop, one high school vocational teacher creates and carries out a three-week intergenerational curriculum plan that involves teens, elders, and toddlers.[3]

THE PUBLIC LIBRARY AND THE SCHOOLS

Partnerships between schools and public libraries run the gamut from very simple to quite complex. A procedure as straightforward as advertising YA public library activities in the school or PTA newsletter can be beneficial to both groups. Public libraries reserve materials for school projects when school liaisons contact them and often will even send books for a particular project to the school. Libraries visit their neighborhood schools to promote summer reading programs or send flyers to the schools to distribute to the students. Many libraries will display books suggested on their schools' summer reading lists.

Most public libraries offer library tours for schools in their community focusing on resources related to a specific research topic. These sessions are most beneficial when planned jointly by teachers and librarians. This type of experience broadens the students' and the teachers' knowledge of library resources. To supplement these visits, YA librarians will often prepare bibliographies. Sometimes the YA librarian will go into the schools to teach reference skills. To encourage reading, librarians offer booktalks for young adults and also for school faculty. Public libraries and school districts hold monthly meetings where they discuss items of joint interest. Some even have cooperative collection development policies to make the most of their resources. Libraries often have authors speak and lead writing workshops in conjunction with writing projects in the schools. With the increase in families' choosing home schooling, some libraries have extended outreach to these groups.

Many public libraries allow schools to access their on-line catalogs and CD-ROM products through dial access and may even provide training to schools to enable them to take advantage of this resource. States such as Illinois encourage partnerships between schools and libraries by offering grants to support such activities.

It is common for libraries and schools to join forces in a "Battle of the Books" program. Students read books from a specified list and then compete in teams. The competitions consist of answering questions related to the books being read. The schools and public libraries both make copies of the books available and collaborate on the questions. Often the "battles" are held at the public library.

As part of their relationship with schools, libraries may offer family night programs where families participate in tours, learn about library services and resources, and register for library cards. Illinois has a night in November declared as Family Reading Night by the state library. Public libraries have involved other agencies as well, including the mayor's office.

Schools often require volunteer service, particularly for membership in the National Honor Society. Many young adults fulfill this requirement by working at the public library. A popular use for teen volunteers is in teaching Internet skills to the general population. Libraries recognize that young adults today are computer-literate, and many are quite adept at "surfing the Net." Pairing teens with senior citizens for computer training has become popular in public libraries. Other teens help with story times for younger children, book processing, and other duties.

The Bettendorf (Iowa) Public Library and Information Center has established several projects involving the public schools in their city. The first project involves establishing a new position for a librarian to work part-time in the elementary and middle schools and part-time in the public library. Resulting from this collaborative effort, the library and school have increased communication. More teachers are using assignment alert forms, and teachers have become more aware of library resources. The public library becomes more effective in helping students with research skills and homework assignments. The partnership eases staff shortages in both locations. In addition, summer reading program participation increases.[4]

In Illinois students in grades four through eight are given an opportunity to vote for their favorite book from a list, and the book with the most votes receives the Rebecca Caudill Young Readers' Book Award. The students are usually registered through the school. Public libraries serving students whose schools have not registered can also participate. Public libraries and schools have developed partnerships to promote participation in this activity. YA librarians and school librarians work together to develop quizzes for each of the 20 books and booktalk the books. The public library also participates in the voting and culminating party festivities.

Many of the public library/school partnerships involve other agencies as well. The Bettendorf Public Library has a partnership called Project Civics. The project involves local government agencies working with the library and the schools. Sixth, seventh, and eighth graders are introduced to areas of local government and learn about civic responsibility. As a result of this partnership these students have an opportunity to identify, research, and suggest a solution to a local problem. In addition to meeting community leaders, students learn to use research tools and presentation technologies. The library increases communication with local government agencies, and government officials learn more about library resources.[5]

In the Seattle area, the Seattle Public Schools, the Seattle Public Library, and the King County Library System issue the Sonics & SeaDogs Read to Succeed Challenge. Children completing the required amount of reading receive a Sonics or SeaDogs prize. Reading more books qualifies kids for a raffle to win a chance to watch a Sonics or SeaDogs practice or memorabilia signed by the Sonics or SeaDogs.[6]

Eastland High School (Illinois) Student Council members entertain residents of the Gordon Jones Home at the Lanark Public Library as part of National Library Week activities. The students interview the residents and help them make booklets about themselves. They color door posters and sing songs and play games.[7]

THE PUBLIC LIBRARY AND LOCAL CORPORATIONS

Many partnerships between public libraries and local businesses are formed through the local chamber of commerce. Sometimes local businesses are used as the basis of a Friends of the Library support program to raise money for the public library. Many libraries seek donations from local businesses as prizes in their summer reading programs. These donations can be gifts of money to purchase prizes or gift certificates or actual prizes. For this age group restaurant coupons, movie coupons, CDs, vouchers from hair salons and camera stores, and concert tickets are particularly appreciated. Some creative librarians have local banks provide cash and savings bonds as awards. Often librarians will become involved with the local chamber of commerce to plan joint activities and encourage support for the library.

The North Suburban Library System (NSLS) is a multitype consortium of libraries in the north and northwest suburbs of Chicago. The Chicago Wolves Hockey Team, the North Suburban Library System, and Jel-Sert, makers of Wyler's and Mondo Fruit Squeezers, sponsor a Read to Succeed Program designed to enhance the winter reading programs of the NSLS public libraries. Wolves' game tickets, hockey pucks, and banners are given to participants as incentive prizes. In addition, a hockey player is available to visit each library for a program. This enhancement to the winter reading programs has increased participation by students in the YA age group and has also increased the participation of boys in the programs. Other libraries partner with local minor league baseball teams for similar types of programs.

KidStar Interactive Media is an organization with the mission "to provide a wholesome, engaging entertainment choice that embraces all that is creative, curious, and imaginative in kids. The company is deeply committed to making a difference in children's lives." [8] KidStar is sponsored by numerous corporations in Washington state and has plans for national expansion. KidStar asks kids to register by filling out a membership form and by having parents sign a permission slip allowing kids to use the PhoneZone to enter contests and record messages that may be heard on KidStar Radio.

The King County (Washington) Library System incorporates KidStar programs into their summer reading programs. KidStar provides a radio campaign that includes creative writing, production, and broadcast of spots for eight weeks that promote participation in the summer reading program. The radio station is directed toward kids and their families.

They also use a phone line where kids can leave messages about their favorite books and hear how to participate in the summer reading program. The organization publishes a magazine that promotes the summer reading program and stimulates kids' interest. The King County Library and Parks distribute membership forms at park-sponsored events, distribute the magazine at the branch libraries, and use the company logo on summer reading program materials. The partnership has increased participation in the library's summer reading program as well as increased children's interest in reading and lifelong learning. The partnership has benefited KidStar by increasing the children's and parents' awareness of the corporation.[9]

THE PUBLIC LIBRARY AND OTHER NONPROFIT AGENCIES

Museums donate passes for use as individual prizes for library summer reading programs. In Seattle, the Museum of Flight partners with the King County Library System and the parks. The museum leads presentations at the libraries and parks, such as one that focuses on aviation of pioneers in Alaska before statehood, including a hands-on balsawood glider workshop. By having these presentations, the museum expands its audience, encourages the use of museums as a learning resource, and extends community outreach outside the traditional visitation area. This is a chance for families to participate in a museum activity free of charge, therefore extending its services to people who would not otherwise be able to attend. The program also encourages exploration of science and the humanities through reading.[10] Libraries prepare exhibits of books to tie in to themes featured at the local museum.

In the Chicago area the Ravinia Music Festival provides lawn-seating tickets for classical and jazz concerts to public libraries in the North Suburban Library System. Libraries arrange for some of these tickets to be given to YAs involved in band, orchestra, or choir.

THE PUBLIC LIBRARY AND GOVERNMENT AGENCIES

Library–government agency partnerships often begin with requests from these agencies for information. The library serves as a resource point. As the parties involved get to know one another, and communication is established, partnerships are formed. Government agencies that provide job training often place teens in public libraries where they receive on-the-job training as well as instruction in job seeking. Many public libraries have partnerships with local fire and police departments to support educational programs on topics such as babysitting, bicycle and boating safety, and fire safety. Students in court-supervised community service programs are sometimes used as library volunteers. Police departments often cosponsor community gang awareness and substance abuse information programming with the library.

Park districts are likely partners for public libraries. The parks donate passes to park district events and to swimming pools as prizes for summer reading programs. The King County Library System has two partnership programs with the King County Parks that involve young adults. During the summer, the library system delivers the summer reading program and boxes of books to King County Parks locations, as well as other school-age outreach sites. This program extends their usual summer reading program to children who would not otherwise be able to participate. The library is thus able to reach more children using the same library staff. The program raises the library's visibility to children, parks staff, and the community in general. Library and parks staff have also jointly planned a Summer Antics series of concerts and events in the parks. The two agencies work together to develop cooperative logos, plan the curriculum for summer programs, and share staff development. Besides providing local access to library materials and resources, these partnerships teach reading as a life skill and provide an economic benefit to the county.[11]

THE PUBLIC LIBRARY AND LOCAL COMMUNITY AGENCIES

Some YA librarians teach Red Cross baby-sitting classes at the library. YA librarians work with Teen Support Groups and arrange visits for teens from group homes and shelters. The local chapters of the Moose Lodge and the American Legion are supportive of public library reading programs and often offer their halls for programs. In communities where there is a large migrant population public libraries cosponsor events with agencies serving these people. Some communities choose an activity in the public library for a merit badge for local Scout groups.

CONCLUSION

Public libraries form partnerships to serve their YA community in many different ways. Some partnerships are common to all libraries, including those that seek to increase communication between local schools and the library or those in which libraries seek donations from local businesses as incentives for reading programs. Other library partnerships are varied and creative. All of these various programs involve libraries working with other agencies to expand and increase use of their services. By joining forces with other agencies, libraries expand and enhance the services and programs they can offer to young adults and teens in their communities.

NOTES

1. Cary Israel, "Rural Libraries and Partnerships," *Illinois Libraries* 75 (January 1993): 22.

2. Ibid.

3. Joan M. Wood, "Interagency Cooperation: Benefits of Intergenerational Programming," *Journal of Youth Services in Libraries* 9 (Spring 1996): 237–43.

4. Faye Clow, Tami Chumbley, and Maria Wegscheid, "Public Library/School Partnerships: Six Ideas That Work," presented at the Public Library Association Sixth National Conference, Portland, OR, March 1996.

5. Ibid.

6. King County Library System, Children's Services Department, "Rockets, Boom Boxes and Kids in the Nineties: Partnerships Recreating Communities," presented at the Public Library Association Sixth National Conference, Portland, OR, March 1996.

7. Photo caption in *The Prairie Advocate Today*, May 1, 1996, sec. A, 2.

8. King County Library System.

9. Ibid.

10. Ibid.

11. Ibid.

21

Serving Underserved Populations: Reaching Out to Young Adults in Need

Diana Tixier Herald

Who are the underserved? In one sense of the word they are all young adults, a population that makes up approximately 25 percent of people who use public libraries but that is served by YA librarians in only 11 percent of public libraries.[1] Great numbers of teens, though, never use the library or, in fact, may have never even been in one. For some teens, going to the library is not an option, so to serve them the library may have to go to them. Homelessness, incarceration, institutionalization, and hospitalization are just some of the factors that preclude a great number of youth from using libraries. YALSA recognizes the need for library services to underserved youth in the charge of its Outreach to Young Adults with Special Needs Committee.[2]

Why should access to public library services by adolescents be important to us? It is not just because they are members of the communities for which we provide services. It is not just because they need libraries to fulfill their information and recreational needs. It is not just to help build an informed populace in a democracy where one is essential for the well-being of the nation. In a high-tech world where some question the future existence of libraries, it is important that we woo and court future voters and taxpayers. Why should citizens vote to fund entities that shunned them in their teens? Public libraries across the nation perform an exceptional service in providing programs and materials for children, but to keep the goodwill and respect engendered by those successes we need to continue on through the teens. Underserved teens are often a group that is just easier to avoid.

All teens, not just the underserved, can be scary. They are adult-sized but without the constraints learned by adults through the years. They are also volatile and energetic. Underserved teens may be even scarier than other teens. Teens in runaway or homeless shelters may dress and talk street-tough. Teens who are incarcerated may in all reality have killed or raped, or their crime may have been as unthreatening to society as running away from unlivable home lives.

Underserved teens may be the ones who need library service and access to books the most. The phrase "Libraries change lives" is really true. Through reading a youth can discover the world outside his or her narrow confines. Youth without access to television or video games can find that books and reading become very important in their lives. Many institutionalized and homeless youth find they have nothing but time on their hands. Library services and resources are a constructive way to fill that time.

I was inspired to work with the incarcerated teens in my community by a speaker at a YALSA program one year at an ALA annual conference. She related the story of a wealthy businessman who made large contributions to a juvenile correction facility library because as a teen he had been incarcerated in that facility and had discovered books and reading, inspiring him to turn his life around.

Transitioning from realizing the need to serve the underserved to actually putting programs into place poses several difficulties. Practically speaking, it is hard to come up with funding for programs to these young people, whom society would rather ignore. There are many obstacles to overcome. The first one may be locating the youth in the first place. Even if your community does not have a youth correctional facility, it may have a homeless shelter. Some communities have family shelters. Orange County in California has a large shelter for children and teens. Our community has a very small teen shelter that most people in the community don't know about. There are also group homes and staff-secured homes in the community. The easiest way to find out about these, if one's library has not already identified them, is by contacting someone at social services. A general caseworker will probably not be aware of all the different institutions where underserved youth can be found, but most departments of social services have someone who works exclusively with teens. In our community it is the person in the Independent Living department who works at the Transitional Living Center. This social worker probably knows most of the facilities and institutions in the area.

The next obstacle may be the managers of the facilities or institutions. I had worked with one halfway house, a home for boys released from the corrections facility working to reintegrate into the community, whose director thought the library the best resource around for his youth. The teens came to the library at least once a week in a group, and several of them came in when they were out on day passes. That director left the position, and suddenly those teens weren't seen in the library. When the new director was called after several months, she stated that this kind of kid "didn't need libraries"! I have worked in a very

successful program providing monthly booktalks to inmates in our youth correctional facility for eight years. Suddenly the person in the facility who acts as
the liaison with the public library was switched to a different position. Her
successor doesn't want to be bothered by actually going to the public library to
submit book requests made by the inmates or to pick up the filled requests, so
eight years of positive library experience for youth is coming to an end. On a
more positive note, the homeless shelter for youth is thrilled at the idea that its
teens can be given a library tour and orientation, and since they have an address
at the shelter, they can even get library cards.

Library staff and administration may throw up barriers. The administration
may need to be convinced that providing library services to underserved youth
is a legitimate use of staff time. Obstacles may come from unexpected sources.
In one library it was from the circulation clerk, who refused to issue library
cards to teens who listed the address of a group home, since in the past, some
residents did not return books. Policies should already be in place to deal with
this sort of problem.

The issue of books not coming back is a real concern for many libraries. For
some underserved youth, the whole idea that someone cares enough about them
to bring books or programs to the facility will encourage them to be responsible.
One day at the information desk I was approached by three teen boys. They
asked if I remembered them and told me that they were at the library because
they had just been "sprung from jail" and wanted to find more books similar
to those that had been booktalked when they were in the institution. When they
were arrested for a new offense, they were very adamant with the facility staff
that their library books must be returned right away to the public library.

One way to deal with the problem of a high rate of lost books checked out
to underserved youth is to limit the number of items to be checked out at one
time. In situations where the material is taken to a facility, it is easy to take
lower-cost paperbacks and magazines to minimize losses. These formats are
more popular with teens, anyway. Even though, when dealing with underserved
youth, you may lose a few books, you also may be surprised by the responsible
attitudes of many.

There does not seem to be a concerted effort under way to provide library
resources to underserved youth, but across the country individual librarians and
libraries have developed innovative programs to provide these services.

At Contra Costa County Juvenile Hall in Martinez, California, a YALSA/
Econo-Clad Award-winning program called "The Late Show" was developed
by a volunteer and staff from the Contra Costa County Library. Trained volunteers read stories, play music, and chat for a weekly in-house audio show.
The programs are 30 to 45 minutes long and presented at bedtime. A very similar
program is in place in Kalamazoo, Michigan.

The Allen County Public Library in Fort Wayne, Indiana, developed TAP,
the Teen Agency Program. They identified six agencies in their community that
serve teens, including correction facilities, a shelter, and a school for emotionally

troubled teens. Deposit collections of paperbacks and magazines were distributed to the agencies and are supplemented each month.

Orange County, California, has a library staffed by a full-time, on-site librarian at the Orangewood Children's Home. It serves the homeless youth as well as incarcerated youth at a nearby facility. Originally, the program "Library STARS" was a one-year LSCA grant-funded project to establish library services for children between the ages of 5 and 12. With the advocacy of shelter staff, programming was extended to the teens. The program has been so successful that it has continued beyond the grant period with library funding. Pam Carlson said, "The goal for all of us is to get the kids to see the library as a good place to be, a place to get information and to get materials to read for fun."[3] They keep on hand a good selection of magazines and paperbacks for their teen patrons.

"Leap Ahead," a project of the Cuyahoga County (Ohio) Public Library, puts together thematic kits including a variety of library materials: books, videos, cassettes, posters, games, pamphlets, and booklists. The kits are checked out by youth agencies for three weeks at a time and cover practical issues as well as other areas of interest to youth.[4]

The DeKalb Public Library placed computers in homeless shelters serving families through their "Project Horizons." One teen who discovered he was a computer whiz through the program decided to stay in school and ended up being offered a scholarship.[5]

Mesa County Public Library District (Colorado) provides monthly booktalks to incarcerated youth, as well as an opportunity to read and evaluate books eligible for the Best Books for Young Adults list. Teens from the facility also participate in a special version of the library's teen summer reading game.[6]

CONCLUSION

The successes of working with the underserved may come one at a time: the homeless teen who decides to stay in school because of discoveries made through library programs, the incarcerated youth who decides to turn his life around after reading a novel that touches his life, or another teen's untold story. By serving underserved youth, we can enrich and broaden the lives that possibly need libraries the most.

NOTES

1. Department of Education, National Center for Education Statistics Survey Report, *Services and Resources for Young Adults in Public Libraries* (Washington, DC: Government Printing Office, 1994).

2. The charge reads: "address the needs of young adults who do not or cannot use the library because of socioeconomic, legal, educational, or physical factors; to serve as a liaison between these groups and their service providers, and to identify and promote

library programs, resources, and services that meet the special needs of these populations.''

3. Pam Carlson, ''Books, Books, Books—Let Us Read,'' *VOYA* (August 1994): 137–39.

4. Cynthia Glunt, ''Guidance to Go,'' *School Library Journal* (October 1995): 56.

5. Sherry Des Enfants Norfolk, ''Project Horizons: A Closer Look,'' *Youth Services in Libraries* (Spring 1994): 269–78.

6. Diana Tixier Herald, ''Booktalking to a Captive Audience,'' *School Library Journal* (May 1995): 35–36.

22

Young Adults and Intellectual Freedom: Choices and Challenges

Nancy Kravitz

Intellectual freedom is a major concern in many libraries, but materials made available to young adults in libraries tend to be particularly susceptible to being challenged. We live in a time when challenges have increased involving removing or restricting access to classic literature, sex manuals, and popular YA books.

Young adults live in a changing world—a world of new technology, changing values and mores, increased violence, illegal use of drugs, and AIDS. They live in the information age, where they have access to information through a variety of formats on the adult level at home and elsewhere. The public library stands at the forefront of trying to provide this access to information for minors while respecting the wishes of parents. The viewpoint of librarians is that only parents or guardians, not librarians, have the responsibility to restrict the reading, viewing, and listening experiences of their children as well as their children's access to library resources. Libraries do not want to act in loco parentis. Intellectual freedom provides all patrons with freedom of expression, freedom of choice, freedom of independent decision, and freedom of access to all ideas. All sides of a suggestion, cause, or movement and all examinations of a theme may be explored. The library is a viewpoint-neutral institution.

ALA AND INTELLECTUAL FREEDOM

The basic policy of the American Library Association that upholds the principle of intellectual freedom for minors is incorporated in the Library Bill of

Rights, Article V. In 1967, Article V was amended to include "age" following the recommendations of a preconference on "Intellectual Freedom and the Teenager." The right to use a library includes "free access to and unrestricted use of all the services, materials, and facilities the library has to offer. Every restriction of access to and use of library resources, based solely on the chronological age, violates Article V of the Library Bill of Rights."[1]

Three interpretations of the Bill of Rights concern young adults in libraries. These interpretations, which are now ALA policies, are:

1. Access for children and young people to videotapes and other nonprint formats: "Policies which set minimum age limits for access to videotapes and other audiovisual materials and equipment, with or without parental permission, abridge library use for minors."[2]

2. Restricted access to library materials: "Because materials placed in restricted collections often deal with controversial, unusual, or sensitive subjects, having to ask a librarian for them may be embarrassing or inhibiting for patrons, especially minors."[3]

3. Access to electronic information, services, and networks: "Users, including minors, have the right to be free of unreasonable limitations or conditions set by libraries. They have the right of privacy and confidentiality. Electronic information, services, and networks provided directly or indirectly by the library should be equally readable and equitably accessible to all library users."[4]

Intellectual Freedom—The Past

Historically, librarianship's position on censorship has paralleled public opinion, tastes, mores, and social issues. As a result, there has always been a protectionist attitude toward YA literature.

Nineteenth-century literature for young people reflected popular culture with books such as those by Horatio Alger. However, even the most liberal librarians drew a line of exclusion that readers could not cross. Libraries did not allow immoral literature and bought only materials that would not provoke objections. Libraries had many restrictions—age limits, deposits on borrowed books, restricted circulation, closed shelves, and different circulation rules by type of user.

The first major censorship issue concerning libraries came in 1880, when James H. Hubbard, a former minister and cataloger, claimed that Boston Public Library was buying "vapid and sensational" books that were read by well-to-do people and their children.[5] He made four proposals to protect youth: a board of censors to screen material, a special children's card (children younger than 14), the labeling of harmless books, and a separate children's collection and catalog. At first, the library trustees and the examining committees defended their selection choices, but the library retreated and by 1885 met all of his demands.

In the late 1880s Anthony Comstock headed the Society for the Suppression of Vice in New York. He confiscated and destroyed "bad" literature and imprisoned "evil" authors and publishers. In the title of his most famous book, *Traps for the Young*, Comstock meant the devil's work for young people: dime novels, newspapers, advertisements, saloons, and such vices as playing pool and free love. Comstock was convinced that any young person was doomed to hell and to a life of crime and degradation who shot pool, smoked tobacco, drank, or read dime novels.

In the 1890s, patrons had limited freedom in libraries. There were open shelves for most material, but restricted shelves still existed. One could check out more than one book at a time, but the second book could not be a novel. During that era, books challenged old values. There were such authors as Stephen Crane, Rudyard Kipling, and Mark Twain. However, a professional consciousness made librarians even more decisive as guardians of the young. Stephen Crane's *The Red Badge of Courage* was considered "unrealistically profane." In Philadelphia, books by Kipling were pulled from the shelves. *The Adventures of Huckleberry Finn* was widely censored. The Brooklyn library kept it off its shelves on the grounds that "Huck not only itched but scratched and that he said sweat when he should have said perspired."[6] Books were usually banned for three reasons: vulgarity, sex, and being a menace to the social structure.

By the 1920s, the mood in librarianship began to change. Nationwide, librarians began to object to censorship issues such as labeling, restrictive shelves, and community censorship. Library journals and trustees began to support this movement. The younger generation began to insist on the newest and most radical authors who represented new values, such as F. Scott Fitzgerald and Upton Sinclair. Unfortunately, the ALA leadership still remained very conservative, refusing to make a statement against the burning of books in Germany or joining with other groups on anticensorship issues.

Finally, in the 1930s, ALA began to change. Librarians nationwide demanded that their organization take a stand against censorship. In 1939, ALA adopted the Library Bill of Rights. This document focused on unbiased book selection, balanced collections, and open meeting rooms. It did not mention censorship or the removal of materials by community groups; instead, it confirmed consensus rather than neutrality. In both 1948 and 1980, the Library Bill of Rights was completely revised into what we know today. Also in 1944, the ALA Committee on Intellectual Freedom was created.

INTELLECTUAL FREEDOM AND THE LAW

There have been several court cases that affect censorship. The oldest is *Queen v. Hicklin*, L.R.3 QB. 360 (1868), which tried to define "obscenity." According to the "Hicklin test," anything is obscene if the tendency of the material is to deprave or corrupt the minds of those open to immoral influences. The Hicklin test held until 1957.

In *Roth v. US*, 54 US 476 (1957), the Supreme Court said, "Obscenity in itself is not within the area of constitutionally protected speech and press." A new test evolved, saying that "whether or not the average person applying contemporary standards, the dominant theme of the material, as a whole, appeals to the prurient interest." In the case *A Book Named John Cleland's Memoirs of a Woman of Pleasure, et al., Appellants v. Attorney General of the Commonwealth of Massachusetts. No. 368*, 86 S. Ct. 975 (1966), the Supreme Court expanded the protection of the Roth case by adding another test—whether or not the work is "utterly without redeeming social values." In *Smith v. California*, 361 US 14 (1959), the Court ruled that one had to have knowledge of the content of the book. In *Redrup v. New York*, 84 US 916 (1966), the Supreme Court concluded that everything has some social value to someone.

A new test was created for obscenity in 1973. In *Miller v. California*, 413 US 15 (1973), the Supreme Court held three main principles: (1) whether the average person applying contemporary community standards will find the work taken as a whole appeals to his prurient interests; (2) whether a work depicts or describes sexual conduct in an offensive way that is specifically defined by state law; and (3) whether the work as a whole lacks serious literary, artistic, political, or scientific value. Thus the prosecutor no longer has to prove the material has redeeming social value.

A famous censorship case that involved libraries was the *Board of Education Island Trees Union Free School District no. 26 et al. v. Pico*, 457 US 853 (1982). It concerned a school library in New York where three members of the school board tried to remove certain objectionable books. According to Justice William J. Brennan:

[The] First Amendment rights of students may be directly and sharply implicated by the removal of books from a school library. . . . Petitioners possess significant discretion to determine the content of their school libraries but that discretion may not be exercised in a narrowly partisan or political manner. . . . Our Constitution does not permit the official suppression of ideas.[7]

A recent Court decision in November 1995 in Kansas City involving the book *Annie on My Mind* was based on the *Pico* case. The book was returned to the school libraries after the school board and the superintendent tried to remove it.[8]

THE CENSOR

A censor is defined as "A person authorized to examine books, films or other material and to remove or suppress what is considered normally, politically or otherwise objectionable."[9]

Who are would-be censors? Concerned parents are by far the largest group. Their concerns center around materials that contain profanity, pornography, and sex in an explicit or realistic manner. They protest teens' access to certain books they fear will lead to antisocial or antifamily behavior. Some parents are threatened by changes in the traditional way of life. They often see one particular lifestyle, homosexuality, as immoral and antifamily, rather than an alternative lifestyle. Religious groups object to books on moral or sexual grounds. They may also reject satanic material and books that depict religion in a negative manner. Political groups complain that their viewpoint is not represented fairly in libraries. Minorities object to materials that they consider racist or that stereotype their culture or history. Patriotic groups protest anti-American material. School and library personnel also may challenge certain materials.

Whether on the Left or the Right, censors have similar fears—fear of the unknown, change, the future, losing control, and other people and ideas they disapprove of or know little about. Censors believe that if the book is removed, then the ideas in the book also are gone. Censors usually use three words to describe objectionable works: filthy, obscene, or vulgar. They also describe material as anti-Christian, un-American, immoral, satanic, antifamily, pornographic, racist, profane, and indecent.

WHAT THEY CHALLENGE

Almost any kind of material is being challenged today, including books, movies, videos, magazines and, most recently, computer software.

The present realistic YA novel depicts life as it is. Young adults understand that literature and life are different, that the representation of reality through fiction is not the same as reality itself. The teenage novel developed to reflect adolescent concerns and attitudes and to help them mature by indicating to them that their individual anxieties are not strange aberrations that mark them as some kind of freak but truly part of the growing-up process. Many young adults learn through reading realistic fiction not to make the same mistakes that the characters in the books make.

One of the topics of YA literature is violence. As the rate of violence in society accelerates, sensationalism in television, movies, and magazines accelerates. With some amount of violence socially acceptable in these other media, it is not surprising that young adults read books containing violence just as adults do. Fortunately, there is little evidence of a connection between reading and violent behavior.

The newest subject to be tackled in young people's literature is homosexuality. *Daddy's Roommate* by Michael Willhoite and *Annie on My Mind* by Nancy Garden are the most recent books concerning this topic. *Daddy's Roommate* is about a boy who adjusts to his father's new male companion after his parents' divorce. By describing the family activities in a normal and affectionate manner, the book delivers the message that alternative lifestyles can be as nurturing as traditional ones. *Annie on My Mind* is a love story between two young women who discover their homosexuality and the joys and problems it incurs.

Many YA books, fiction and non-fiction, contain references or information on sexuality. Parents are embarrassed and uneasy when their children ask them questions about sex. They are often unable to answer those questions, especially those concerned with the physical and emotional changes that occur during puberty. Many parents come to the library to find these books so they can explain this subject to their children.

The public library remains a safe haven for young adults to find books on such subjects as sex, drugs, AIDS, and homosexuality, as well as other self-help books. When teenagers or their friends have a problem or a question, they need somewhere safe to go for the answer. Kids worry about their friends and want to know how they can help them cope with their problems. It is better that they visit a library for unbiased, correct information than to get that information on the streets or in adult bookstores.

Many of Judy Blume's books deal with questions of a sexual nature. Her books *Are You There God? It's Me Margaret* (menstruation), *Deenie* (masturbation), and *Forever* (explicit sex) have all been banned sometime, somewhere. Some adults call her books "pornographic trash," despite the fact that they provide valuable information/insight to readers.

Some challenges have been against such classics as *Of Mice and Men* and *Catcher in the Rye*—two mainstays of high school reading lists.

Of Mice and Men, written in 1937 by John Steinbeck, has earned a host of awards while leaving a trail of controversy. In making it the second most challenged book of the 1990s, some people claim to be protecting the young from crude heroes who speak vulgar language within a setting that criticizes our social system. This is unfortunate, because Steinbeck was a deeply Christian person who purposefully used Christian themes in his book. He had a desire to see people love each other.

Over 10 million copies of *Catcher in the Rye* by J.D. Salinger have been published since 1951. Challenges center around its use of profanity and obscenity as well as its references to premarital sex, alcoholism, and prostitution.

Most contemporary students are able to discover the theme of a novel despite the use of certain "objectionable" vocabulary. When characters in fiction use obscenity or profanity, this does not mean that the author advocates the use of such language. It is the author's attempt to add a sense of realism to the characters in the book.

Mark Twain is a good example of an author who does not agree with the vocabulary he uses in his writings. He may be the least "racist" of all major writers of his time. However, because of his depiction of the character Jim as a "Nigger," his book *The Adventures of Huckleberry Finn* has been called a "grotesque example of racism." Having Huck use another term would really be a grotesque misuse of language. Huck was an unlettered boy from the lowest class of the South, using normal language common to the Mississippi Valley 30 years before emancipation. *The Adventures of Huckleberry Finn* is a historical novel of its time, not a 1990s non-fiction work. It teaches young adults that they can rise up against ignorance and bigotry to make something of their lives. It is a book about hope, not racism.

LIBRARY POLICIES AND INTELLECTUAL FREEDOM

Some library procedures and practices effectively deny minors' access to certain services and materials available to adults. Restrictions are often initiated to avoid controversy with parents or groups that might think certain materials are harmful to minors.

Restrictions based on age include:

1. Restricting access to reading or reference rooms or open stack areas.
2. Issuing limited-access library cards or otherwise restricting the circulation of materials.
3. Assigning materials to special collections.
4. Using manual or computerized registration or circulation systems.
5. Sequestering or otherwise restricting access to material because of its content.
6. Requiring or soliciting written permission from a parent or guardian to gain access to materials.
7. Restricting access to interlibrary loan, fax, and electronic reference services.
8. Restricting access to materials because of their format or their cost.
9. Charging fees or requiring deposits to gain access to services, materials, or facilities.
10. Refusing to process interlibrary loans, reserves, or reference requests for materials classified as juvenile.
11. Restricting access to public facilities, such as meeting rooms and bulletin boards.[10]

In 1994 *Library Journal* conducted a survey among the top 20 public libraries in the country concerning their circulation policies dealing with age. City systems that have policies of unrestricted access to all print materials for all ages include Los Angeles, Chicago, Baltimore, San Francisco, Oakland, Boston, Detroit, Dallas, Houston, Miami, Seattle, Atlanta, Cleveland, Minneapolis, Pittsburgh, and Phoenix. None of these libraries have provisions allowing parents to limit their children to age-specific print materials. Some do, however, require a parent's signature on a child's library card application. None restrict children's browsing inside the library.

In the Free Library of Philadelphia, there are some restrictions up to age 14. A child may be issued either a "children's card" or an "adult card" (unrestricted) depending on the request of the parent or guardian. Parents or guardians must give their written permission for a child to have an adult card. A child who is unaccompanied by a parent or guardian and has a children's card who wishes to check out adult material needs an "adult materials request slip" from the children's librarian. A child accompanied by a parent or guardian who approves of the adult material or book for use by the child may charge out a book without an adult materials request slip with no argument or discussion.[11]

St. Louis Public Library has a very restricted policy that states that ''parents of a child applying for a card may indicate whether they wish the card to be restricted or unrestricted.'' With an unrestricted card, the child has access to the collection (except adult videos). The child's borrowing privileges are limited to the juvenile collection until age 18 if the card is restricted.[12] This policy makes it very difficult to meet the needs of high school students who write countless term papers. They require analytical information that can be found only in adult material. Children's books are usually written at a reading level below seventh grade and are relatively useless for high school research.

INTELLECTUAL FREEDOM TODAY

Today, challenges to library materials for young adults that discuss sexuality, the supernatural, or controversial topics continue to increase, according to annual figures released by ALA's Office of Intellectual Freedom. There were 664 reported challenges to library and school materials in 1996.

The most challenged were *Daddy's Roommate* by Michael Willhoite, *Impressions Reading Series* by Harcourt Brace Jovanovich, *The Adventures of Huckleberry Finn* by Mark Twain, *Goosebumps* series by R.L. Stine, *More Scary Stories to Tell in the Dark* by Alvin Schwartz, *Bridge to Terabithia* by Katherine Paterson, *Scary Stories to Tell in the Dark* by Alvin Schwartz, *I Know Why the Caged Bird Sings* by Maya Angelou, *Forever* by Judy Blume, *Heather Has Two Mommies* by Leslea Newman, *The Chocolate War* by Robert Cormier.

Most challenges involve schools and school libraries, but some do involve public libraries.

In March 1995 three trustees of the Marshfield, Vermont, Public Library quit over a book about gay teens called *Two Teenagers in Twenty*.[13] This is a collection of essays by teenagers trying to come to terms with their homosexuality. The issue revolved around free speech, family values, and local control of the public library. Books about the opposite viewpoint were purchased to solve the concerns. In May 1995 an incident occurred in Corvallis, Oregon, where almost a dozen sex education books were vandalized in the Corvallis-Benton County Public Library. [14]

In Clifton, New Jersey, sexually explicit material is now limited to patrons over 18 years of age. Six books, including *The Magic of Sex, More Joy of Sex*, and *The New Joy of Gay Sex*, are now held behind the circulation desk. Adults must request them to be able to check them out.[15]

One of the hottest issues concerning censorship concerns the access to R-rated videos for minors. Across the country, this debate is intensifying as library video collections expand and include R-rated titles. Video collections now account for an average of 20 to 30 percent of library circulation.

At the Cragin Memorial Library in Colchester, Connecticut, in April 1996, a parent insisted that the library enforce the Motion Picture Association of America (MPAA) rating system after her 11-year-old son checked out the movie *True Lies*.[16] In response, the library reaffirmed its open-access policy to all library materials.

In a similar challenge to videos in the Watertown, Massachusetts, Public Library, some adult patrons wanted to restrict access to R-rated videos in libraries to those over 16. The board of the Watertown Library, however, voted to retain its current open-ended purchasing and circulation policies, citing, in part, a state law that prohibits policies contrary to the Library Bill of Rights.[17]

Libraries like the William K. Sanford Town Library in Loudenville, New York,[18] and the Grafton Public Library in Wisconsin[19] have parental responsibility policies that restrict young patrons from obtaining R- and PG-14-rated films. Parents can use published reviews of films and videos and/or reference works that provide information about the content, subject matter, and recommended audiences to choose appropriate nonprint material for their children.

Some state legislatures have entered the debate by trying to legally restrict access. In New York and Tennessee, state laws would penalize libraries for circulating R- or NC-17-rated videos to minors.[20]

These laws would oppose the Library Bill of Rights by setting age limits for access to videotapes and/or other audiovisual material and equipment with or without parental permission. As a result, library use for minors would be restricted. These laws also require the adoption of the MPAA rating system which is, in reality, a very vague advisory system. As such, MPAA ratings have no legal basis. For a public library to enforce such guidelines would probably be a violation of the First Amendment.

Some people and groups have gone further than just challenging books. They now seek to change the fundamental premises and policies under which libraries operate, which include equal access to all patrons and providing information on all sides of different issues.

Two newly appointed board members of the Prince William County Library Board in Virginia are attempting to limit young people's access to inappropriate books, either by removing them from the collection or by creating an "Adult-Only" section of the library. They want a review of the library's guidelines for buying books, and they favor requiring patrons younger than 18 to have parental permission to check out any book from the "Adult-Only" section.[21] Similar situations have recently occurred in Medina, Ohio, and Oklahoma City.

There has been a long-running battle concerning the Gwinnett-Forsyth Regional Library System in suburban Atlanta. In May 1995 a conservative member of the library board introduced a plan called the "1995 Library Contract with Gwinnet."[22] This plan would label "explicit" library materials, restrict them to readers over age 17, place them in a separate book section, and give the community more control over book selection.

One group, called "Family Friendly Libraries," has started a national campaign to spread such a contract throughout the entire country. This group originally tried to create an "Adult-Only" library section in the Fairfax County Library System in 1994 in Virginia.[23] This would have restricted books on sexuality, the occult, suicide, homosexuality, and other controversial subjects to an area that minors would not have access to without parental consent. Fortunately, the library board voted to continue providing free access, regardless of age, to all library books, although it did make one concession—parents of children under the age of 12 have the option of restricting their children's borrowing to the juvenile collection.

Family Friendly Libraries met in Cincinnati in October 1995 to lay out a national campaign to bring libraries back to traditional family values and the local community. To promote formation and survival of those values, this group has issued a charter for use in local communities emphasizing these values, as well as initiating restrictions for minors and more local control over library policies, including book selection for minors.[24]

To counteract Family Friendly Libraries, librarians need to reclaim the "family friendly" label. Libraries have always had materials and programs for traditional families. The needs and the desires of the community and patrons have always been considered when selecting library materials. Librarians are willing and able to offer guidance to young adults and their parents in selecting and using materials that are both entertaining and age-appropriate.

One positive step that libraries are taking to promote the concept of intellectual freedom is to involve young adults in the debate.

In 1991 the Young Adult Advisory Board of the Boulder County (Colorado) Public Library produced a play called *Don't Read This!: A Dramatic Presentation for Teens by Teens to Raise Awareness of Censorship Issues*. The play included sketches on history, religion, and sexuality; booktalks on banned books; and a narrator and questioner to help the audience consider the issues that were presented. At first, schools were hesitant to present the play, but eventually the group was able to present it at a number of schools, bookstores, and churches. They managed to enlighten themselves and hundreds of other teens and adults about the issue of intellectual freedom.[25]

There is an annual essay contest for young adults at the Dorchester Road Regional Library of Charleston, South Carolina, called the "Freedom to Read Essay Contest." The contest tries to meet three goals: (1) promote the discussion of, and interest in, intellectual freedom among young adults; (2) bring the library to the attention of schools and the students; and (3) bring young adults and their families to the library. Young adults learned that advocating limited access is quite different from actually implementing it.[26]

In one fictional book, *The Day They Came to Arrest the Book*, a group of high school students defends *The Adventures of Huckleberry Finn* when it is challenged by some parents. In real life, often students stand up to defend books being challenged in their schools and libraries.

CONCLUSION

There has been a long relationship between intellectual freedom concerns and young adults. Starting with the 1880s and the Society for the Suppression of Vice to Family Friendly Libraries in the 1990s there have always been groups attempting to deny information to teens. Not much has changed. The same books are being challenged by the same kind of people for many of the same reasons.

Fortunately, ALA stepped in to protect the rights of minors, and some courageous librarians and teachers have stood up to the censors. Numerous challenges have involved YA literature in which the books were retained.

Parents do not understand what we are making available to young people today, because libraries have changed so radically over the years. Now libraries have on-line catalogs and access to the Internet. Libraries must bring parents or guardians into the library and help them understand how they can begin to rely on librarians to help them guide their children With books and other materials, libraries are helping young adults grow intellectually. Libraries open new doors to new ideas to help them cope with a changing world.

NOTES

1. American Library Association, Office for Intellectual Freedom, *Intellectual Freedom Manual* (Chicago: American Library Association, 1996), 84–85.

2. Ibid., 2–22.

3. Ibid., 103–4.

4. Ibid., 24.

5. Evelyn Geller, *Forbidden Books in American Public Libraries 1876–1938* (Westport, CT: Greenwood Press, 1984), 32–33.

6. Ibid., 86.

7. Alleen P. Nilsen and Kenneth Donelson, *Literature for Today's Young Adult*, 4th ed. (New York: HarperCollins, 1993), 480.

8. Randy Meyers, "Annie's Day in Court," *School Library Journal* 42, no. 4 (April 1996): 22–25.

9. *American Heritage Dictionary of the English Language*, 3d ed. (Boston: Houghton Mifflin, 1992), 310.

10. ALA, *Intellectual Freedom Manual*, 93–94.

11. Registration, Free Library of Philadelphia. Policies and Procedures, PS #12, March 20, 1980, 1–36.

12. Michael Sadowski, "New St. Louis Policy Raises Questions of Parental Control," *School Library Journal* 40, no. 5 (1994): 10–11.

13. "Book Sparks Resignation," *Newsletter on Intellectual Freedom* 44, no. 2 (1995): 37.

14. "Censorship Dateline 'Libraries—Corvallis, Oregon,' " *Newsletter on Intellectual Freedom* 44, no. 3 (1995): 67.

15. "Censorship Dateline 'Libraries—Clifton, New Jersey,' " *Newsletter on Intellectual Freedom* 45, no. 4 (1996): 117.

16. "Success Stories 'Libraries—Colchester, Connecticut,' " *Newsletter on Intellectual Freedom* 45, no. 4 (1996): 133.

17. Marilyn Gardner, "Push for V-Chip on Library Videos, " *Christian Science Monitor* (February 29, 1996), 1, 12.

18. Ibid.

19. "Success Stories 'Libraries—Grafton, Wisconsin,' " *Newsletter on Intellectual Freedom* 45, no. 5 (1996): 169.

20. Randy Myers, "Furor over R-Rated Videos Sparks Library Legislation," *School Library Journal* 40, no. 4 (1996): 11.

21. Ann O. Harlen, "2 on Library Board Call for Restrictions," *Washington Post* (September 28, 1996), sec. B, 1, 5.

22. "Gwinnett County's Library Contract,' " *Newsletter on Intellectual Freedom* 44, no. 4 (1995): 91.

23. Eric Lipton, "Fairfax to Consider 'Adult-Only Library Section,' " *Washington Post* (September 15, 1994), sec. D, 1, 9.

24. Jessea Greeman, "FYI: Right Wing Plan to Infiltrate Libraries," cited 11 November 1995, Internet.

25. Ingrid Ulrich, "Don't Read This!" *School Library Journal* 42, no. 1 (1996): 46.

26. Mary Cockrell and Cheri Estes, "Freedom Writers," *School Library Journal* 42, no. 3 (1996): 136.

23

Getting Started on the Right Foot: The Training Needs of Young Adult Staff

C. Allen Nichols

The issue of training in a public library brings to mind a broad range of competencies, educational levels, and job responsibilities. Some public libraries take the issue of training quite seriously, establishing weeklong orientation centers for new employees, while others are not nearly as formal with training situations. Many use shadowing and trial-by-fire to teach and indoctrinate new employees.

Training is particularly difficult when approaching it from the YA department's point of view. This is especially so in smaller libraries that only have one YA staff member, and that person is the new employee. Unfortunately for that new employee in this environment, the position is usually entry-level, and the person rarely has any practical library experience, much less any experience working with teens. In a smaller setting no one is around to teach booktalking, YA collection development, or the importance of a positive attitude toward YAs.

SOURCES/OPPORTUNITIES FOR TRAINING

YALSA Speaker's Database

The Young Adult Library Services Association can assist with training in two ways. The division maintains a YA speaker/trainer database that library organizations may use to find staff day speakers or workshop instructors. Information about the speakers includes areas of expertise, ability to travel to various regions of the country, and fees for speaking or conducting training workshops. Contact the YALSA office for more information and assistance.[1]

Serving the Underserved

The Serving the Underserved workshops were designed by YALSA to train participants to conduct workshops for library generalists in public libraries to help them provide services to young adults.[2]

Participants were taught the basic techniques of planning and running a workshop, including effective openings and closings and active learning approaches. Time was also spent learning the "YA substance," which covered the foundation of YA library service, knowing the YA customer, and the basics of YA library service.

As a result of the Serving the Underserved workshops (held at ALA in Miami, 1994, and in San Antonio at ALA, midwinter 1996), the workshop participants now constitute a core group of knowledgeable individuals who are trained and ready to spread the word regarding young adult library services. These trainers are in the YALSA Speaker's Database. YALSA encourages libraries and library staff to take advantage of these qualified trainers to assist with any YA training effort.

Practicums

Another training tool that is extremely beneficial is the practicum or college co-op experience, available to library school students. The practicum traditionally involves 100–150 hours of real-life practical experience by the student in a library setting.

The setting is chosen depending on the student's desired career/education goals. For future young adult librarians, it is vital for them to experience working with young adults in a public library or media center.

In the host library, the practicum student becomes a kind of apprentice, learning library routines, customer service skills, and the actual day-to-day operations of the library. Young adult practicum students interact with teenagers and assist with programs, collection development, reference, and reader's advisory.

One also hopes the students exhibit a positive YA attitude from the beginning of the experience or learn the trait before embarking on their first professional position after graduation.

Melanie Rapp, a 1996 library school graduate from Kent State University and practicum participant, had this to say about the experience: "It was the most valuable experience I had in graduate school. I could listen to 'what to do' in class until I was blue in the face; but it was when the first reluctant young adult confronted me desiring help that I became educated."[3]

A practicum experience should be required of all library school students at some point during their graduate school enrollment. This is especially important for students who desire a career serving young adults in libraries—because theory and class work are one thing, but the two cannot replace a firsthand opportunity to actually work with teenagers.

MENTORING

Mentoring is another wonderful source for training for young adult staff members, whether new on the job or ready to retire, especially for those in one-person YA departments in smaller libraries. Benefits for both participants can be derived. The mentee can receive guidance in relationship to professional development, learn more about professional concerns, and establish networks with others who share career interests. Mentors also benefit. They are able to refresh their own professional commitment and reevaluate their beliefs and practices, all while contributing to the good of their profession.

The Cleveland Area Metropolitan Library System (CAMLS), a consortium of multitype libraries in the northeastern Ohio area, as a part of its strategic plan, developed a mentoring program for employees of its member libraries. Its Young Adult Services Committee was chosen to design the pilot project in this ambitious plan.[4]

A basic definition of mentoring was developed as a "deliberate pairing of a more skilled or experienced young adult librarian with a less skilled or experienced one, with the agreed upon goal of having the lesser skilled librarian grow and develop specific competencies."[5] Volunteers are selected to serve as mentors, and committee members who feel they need assistance in certain areas of young adult service apply to become mentees. A committee meets to pair the volunteers, who then meet and agree to work together up to a year to fulfill the needs of the mentee.

Lastly, mentoring is inexpensive and can serve to start forming a network of YA librarians to use for further assistance for the future. The difficulty, of course, is getting a group of individuals together to use as a pool of prospective mentors and mentees. Everyone has a few friends and acquaintances here and there in the profession. Use each other to mentor/mentee if no formal opportunity is available as in the CAMLS program.

TRAINING CENTERS

The Cuyahoga County (Ohio) Public Library has decided that the entire concept of training deserves special attention. Through the library's training coordinator (a part of the Human Resources Division staff) a weeklong Training Center is held monthly for all new library employees, regardless of position held.

The mornings of the training week are spent in the system's administration building. Participants tour the administrative departments, learning what each does in support of the library's mission, completes necessary paperwork, receives basic instruction in using the automated catalog/circulation system, and reviews the history and structure of the library.

Afternoons are set aside for training in specific job duties by a group of trained volunteers from around the system. Young adult librarians learn the basics of booktalking, customer service skills, YA collection development, specifics in using the on-line materials ordering system, and other necessary bits of information that will prove beneficial on the job.

To facilitate training, the library's regional young adult services managers developed a number of Training Breakdown Sheets. Tables 23.1–23.6 are used to take new YA librarians through each step of a particular job responsibility. Obviously, these are not going to be specific to every library situation, but you could use these as a basis of developing your own training sheets, which could then be used to train a substitute for when you go on vacation or your replacement when you move on to another position. (*Note*: references in tables to ''attached lists'' refer to additional training materials provided to new employees of the Cuyahoga County Public Library.)

CONTINUING EDUCATION

State Library Associations and/or State Libraries

Continuing education courses are another source for training opportunities. State library associations and state libraries are excellent sources for such workshops. These are normally accessible and moderately priced. In YA services, workshops are often presented by ''local experts'' who present ''this is how we did it''–type programs. During statewide conferences young adult offerings should be readily available and an integral part of conference programs. If not, ask for them.

Library Cooperatives

Multitype consortia/cooperatives also host training workshops for their members. Not only are these geared toward specific competencies or problems, but they are also fairly inexpensive for participants.

Library Schools

Lastly, there are the workshops and classes offered through the graduate library schools, if you happen to have access to one. These one- to two-day courses are extremely important in filling the gaps in competencies and experience.

VOLUNTEERING

For those who are interested in breaking into YA services but who have not worked with teens previously and have completed their formal education requirements, I would strongly recommend becoming a volunteer. Find a willing host and work with teens in a library setting. I cannot stress enough the impor-

Table 23.1
CCPL Training Procedures
Job Breakdown Sheet—Position: PSL I Young Adult; Operation: Reader's Advisory

IMPORTANT STEPS IN THE OPERATION: An important step is any major, logical segment or sequence of the operation which must be done to ADVANCE the work.	KEY POINTS: A key point is any element or stage of the operation which might make or break the job, a special **knack** for making the job easier, etc.
1. Acquire reader's advisory skills by interviewing the patron to determine reading interests.	Use good communication skills—greet patron, listen, ask leading questions, determine interests. Approach patrons in fiction area and ask if they are finding what they want.
2. Acquire background on reader's advisory.	Read reviews. Be aware of new materials as they arrive at the branch. Talk with co-workers and regular patrons who read.
3. Design a personal reading file.	Read extensively and create personal reading records on 3" x 5" cards. Read at least three books in each genre.
4. Consult with supervisor on training opportunities.	Take advantage of local training opportunities in readers guidance, i.e., CAMLS or Kent State University.
5. Become familiar with basic resources.	Be aware of basic resources. See attached.
6. Be aware of local resources at the branch.	Branches often have notebooks of genre lists, "If you like this author, try these . . . ," or files on note cards of staff/patron favorites.
7. Set up displays.	Set up displays—i.e., "Books you may have missed . . ."—in high-traffic area. Take cues from books at hand where patron is in the stacks. Offer a range of choices.

tance of having that experience under one's belt. It is a positive addition to a resumé, is a strong talking point in an interview, and more important, will tell you if you are able to work with teens. Not everyone can, and it is fine if you can't, but find out first.

TRAINING OBJECTIVES

While there are some specific competencies that should and can be learned in any of the aforementioned training opportunities, some other issues need to be addressed as the focus and reason for any training of young adult librarians. These are more philosophical, and some cross age-level boundaries but are equally as important as the competencies.

Political Skills

I have always believed that librarians are not political enough. While this is changing in order to provide visibility and security to the profession, it is in-

Table 23.2
CCPL Training Procedures
Job Breakdown Sheet—Position: PSL I Young Adult; Operation: Book Talk

IMPORTANT STEPS IN THE OPERATION: An important step is any major, logical segment or sequence of the operation which must be done to ADVANCE the work.	KEY POINTS: A key point is any element or stage of the operation which might make or break the job, a special **knack** for making the job easier, etc.
1. Schedule engagements far enough ahead to allow for thorough preparation.	Obtain details of the group—size, age, interests—to ensure audience interest. Also find out how long you're to speak.
2. Read the book(s) and make notes of key points. DO NOT BOOKTALK BOOKS THAT YOU DON'T LIKE.	Pick books that you can be enthusiastic about. Be creative in your approach if you want to tempt the audience to read it.
3. Outline or write out your booktalk.	Rehearse it so that you can do it from memory or notes, and to time your presentation.
4. Call to reconfirm the day before to reassure your host.	
5. Arrive early to familiarize yourself with the facility, make any necessary changes, check setup, and use the washroom.	
6. Booktalk.	Do not give away the ending.
7. Answer any questions from the audience. Promote library services.	
8. See attached list for additional resources.	

cumbent upon all librarians to gain political skills. These skills must be mastered to bring the spotlight to teens and the services young adult librarians provide for them.

While the phrase ''political skills'' is often thought of in relationship to governmental bodies, those skills must be used with other youth-serving agencies and in your own library. Having been the ugly stepchild for far too long, young adult services must push ahead to reap the rewards for the services they provide.

Networking. Librarians must learn the skill of networking, not as it relates to computers but as it relates to people. Don't be afraid to meet new people and talk about YAs to anyone and everyone.

Self-promotion. The only way your community, your coworkers, or your peers are going to learn about what you are trying to do in the YA department is to tell them. But do not stop there; call the local media, send letters to your governmental representatives, send press releases to *American Libraries*, and so on. Spread the word.

To train yourself in political skills, learn as much as you can about public relations and become involved not only in the professional organizations, locally and nationally, but also in your local chamber of commerce or Kiwanis.

Table 23.3
CCPL Training Procedures
Job Breakdown Sheet—Position: PSL I Young Adult; Operation: Reference Interview

IMPORTANT STEPS IN THE OPERATION: An important step is any major, logical segment or sequence of the operation which must be done to ADVANCE the work.	KEY POINTS: A key point is any element or stage of the operation which might make or break the job, a special **knack** for making the job easier, etc.
1. Greet teens as they enter; smile and establish eye contact.	Look up frequently to check for patrons needing help; canvass area regularly.
2. Demonstrate a willingness to help patron by exhibiting supportive, helpful behavior.	Listen actively to patron's questions, giving full attention to patron.
3. Determine actual information needs. Many times the first question does not reflect the actual need. ("Where are the dog books?" can become "I want to train my dog" or "I have a science project to do based on Pavlov's work with dogs.")	Question the patron to determine purpose, deadlines, format and amount of materials needed and what patron already knows about the subject.
4. Be alert to those with special needs e.g. hearing difficulties, non-English speaking, shy, indecisive.	Exercise patience. Talk slowly and clearly. Bring in another librarian if you find it impossible to understand the request/need.
5. Draw out monosyllabic responses.	Use open-ended questions, such as what, where, when, why, how, in what manner. Avoid questions that can be answered with a grunt or nod.
6. Repeat patron's query to make sure that you both agree.	Paraphrase and repeat.
7. Keep the patron informed as to where you are in the process of finding the information needed.	Let patron know what you're doing and where you are going before you walk away or place a call on hold.
8. Accompany him/her to the source or location.	Demonstrate how the source (print or electronic) is used. Remind patron to ask if more help is needed.
9. When working with a teenager/child accompanied by a parent who is speaking for the student, try to engage the **student** in the interview process.	Look at the student. Direct comments to him/her to determine the teacher's assignment or the young person's preference.
10. As much as possible try not to let the patron leave empty-handed. Make referrals when appropriate.	Use basic sources, such as encyclopedia, almanacs. Be aware of resources available at other branches, regionals and ILL. Ask co-workers for help.
11. With reference interviews conducted on the telephone follow the same procedures being sure to keep the person informed as you are proceeding.	Be sure to cite the source used for the answer. This is especially important when the patron is not there to see.
12. Provide closure to the interview.	Use questions such as "Does this answer your question?" or "Did you find what you were looking for?" Ask if the patron needs help with anything else.

Table 23.4
CCPL Training Procedures
Job Breakdown Sheet—Position: PSL I Young Adult; Operation: Dealing With Misconduct

IMPORTANT STEPS IN THE OPERATION: An important step is any major, logical segment or sequence of the operation which must be done to ADVANCE the work.	KEY POINTS: A key point is any element or stage of the operation which might make or break the job, a special **knack** for making the job easier, etc.
1. Do not anticipate negative behavior based on appearance (clothing, hairstyle).	Greet all teens courteously and respectfully.
2. Control yourself first, then control the situation.	Your anger adds fuel to the fire and clouds judgment. Less emotion is more effective.
3. Ask another staff member to accompany you for support if you feel it is necessary.	There is safety in numbers and you will have a witness if you need one.
4. State the undesirable behavior in a calm, factual manner without accusing.	"I noticed you shooting paper clips at the posters."
5. Emphasize what is in the person's best interest.	"I'm sure you don't want to be responsible for blinding someone."
6. Give the consequences. Don't make threats.	"If you do that again, you will be asked to leave." Say what you're going to do and DO what you say.
7. Do not engage in back and forth verbal battles.	Teens have more practice and it prolongs the situation unnecessarily.
8. Do not single out one in a group if you are not positive of his/her guilt.	Address misbehavior and consequences to the entire group. "All of you will be asked to leave. . . ." This eliminates "It wasn't me. It was him" or "You told her to stop, not me."
9. DO NOT tolerate verbal or physical abuse of staff or customers.	This is cause for immediate dismissal from library premises. Accept apologies, if offered, but be firm about dismissal. "You are welcome to come back tomorrow but that's all for today."
10. Always make the person responsible for his/her behavior.	"You put yourself out by behaving in that manner. I would like for you to stay but you made that impossible."

YA Attitude and Advocacy

A YA attitude is exhibited by showing an interest in, and having a concern for, the young adults you work with. It is being willing to go the extra mile when the assignment is due tomorrow. It is having the young adults seek you out for assistance because they know and trust you. A YA attitude is much more than all of this, but one way to acquire this trait is to shadow a fellow YA librarian or attend a workshop or two made up of only YA staffers.

Thus the development of a YA attitude is important. True YA librarians are youth advocates who happen to work in a library. Advocacy is extremely im-

Table 23.5
CCPL Training Procedures
Job Breakdown Sheet—Position: PSL I Young Adult; Operation: Pen Pal Program

IMPORTANT STEPS IN THE OPERATION: An important step is any major, logical segment or sequence of the operation which must be done to ADVANCE the work.	KEY POINTS: A key point is any element or stage of the operation which might make or break the job, a special **knack** for making the job easier, etc.
1. Display pen pal application forms in a high traffic area.	1. All pen pal materials are available from Supplies. Order by the form number. Applications - #3393 Record card - #3391 Post card - #3390
2. Check all turned in forms for legibility, accuracy and general content.	2. Be sure to stamp or write the branch code in the space provided in the lower right-hand corner.
3. Complete two pen pal record cards for each applicant. One gets attached to the application; the other is filed in the branch.	3. Send the completed form to the branch currently handling applications. That branch is _____.
4. Two files of cards need to be kept—one for matched participants and one for unmatched.	4. As matches are made, date the cards and move them to the matched file.
5. Matches will be returned to the branch on slips of paper via interoffice mail.	5. Always record the match on the pen pal record card.
6. Fill out a pen pal notification postcard and send it to the applicant.	6. Always proofread and double check the information before it is sent to avoid errors and delay.
7. Participants can submit application for more than one pen pal at the discretion of the librarian.	7. Sometimes the applicant's match does not respond or stops writing. Additional applications from an individual can be held, sent in or investigated.
8. Applications from youngster under 12 years of age can be accepted but should not be encouraged.	8. Under age matches are handled separately when they are matched nationally. Attach a note to indicate that the applicant is under 12.
9. **Legibility and accuracy are very important.**	9. Be sure to check all information before sending it in or out.

portant because YAs have no one else in the library setting to provide and promote services to them, except YA librarians. This is not a trait that can be taught but must be learned by example or brought with new librarians to the profession.

Change

Constant change is a scary thought for most individuals, especially in a work environment that is so stereotypically inflexible. YA librarians are at the forefront in this area as a result of working with teens and never knowing what is going to happen next. With the advent of the Internet and World Wide Web, the whole perception of a library has changed, as well as a number of jobs within the library. The ability to adapt, learn new skills, and accept the changes

Table 23.6
CCPL Training Procedures
Job Breakdown Sheet—Position: PSL I Young Adult; Operation: Ordering Using Library Material Order Slips (LMOS)

IMPORTANT STEPS IN THE OPERATION: An important step is any major, logical segment or sequence of the operation which must be done to ADVANCE the work.	KEY POINTS: A key point is any element or stage of the operation which might make or break the job, a special knack for making the job easier, etc.
1. Select/find an appropriate source for the information needed to complete the form.	Reviews, copy being discarded, Books in Print, Forthcoming Books in Print, Ingram's fiche, CLIO are the most commonly used to verify order information.
2. Be sure to type or write legibly.	If you are writing use a ballpoint or hard-tipped pen to make a clear copy.
3. TITLE Fill in the name of the item, leaving off "A," "AN" or "THE" if it is the first word.	When ordering series it helps to include the series title. Subtitles are not necessary.
4. AUTHOR Author/artist/composer's name is written last name first.	
5. PUBLISHER Publisher's name can be written fully or abbreviated.	Abbreviations are often found in reviews. Be sure to use one that is accepted/recognizable.
6. PREPUBLISHED DATE used only if the book is coming out more than two months in advance of the current month.	It is recommended to hold items not coming out for more than two months in the branch and to send them in closer to the release date.
7. VENDOR CODE is not used.	
8. ISBN # is the international standard book number, which is used to identify a particular title, or the order number indicated by the vendor for the item to be purchased should be written here.	This is essential information and should be checked for accuracy. A mistake here could get the order returned or the wrong item received. Almost all items ordered will have an ID number of some sort.
9. SOURCE/DATE should indicate where you found the information (VOYA, PW, BIP, etc.) and the date of the issue (9/94).	If you are replacing a title and using the discarded copy for information write "REPL" in this space.
10. LIST PRICE is the cost of the item.	The list price and actual cost of an item often differ because the library receives discounts for volume ordering. Occasionally the price may be higher reflecting an increase by the publisher.
11. SPECIFY FUND is the area used to designate the account to which the material will be charged.	Ask your branch manager for the young adult print and audiovisual account numbers.
12. MEDIA TYPE is self explanatory. Mark the box for the type of material being ordered.	If the material ordered does not fit any of the categories indicated, use OTHER and briefly describe what is being ordered.
13. The four boxes below MEDIA TYPE are seldom used.	SHOW AT . . . is outdated. MATL EXAM no longer exists for YA. BIND is to indicate paperback materials to be bound in hardcover. PAY . . . means that the publisher indicated will not bill CCPL and that payment should accompany the order. ORDER . . . tells ORD that holds exist for this item.
14. COLL. DIST. indicates collection for which materials are being ordered.	On the line following Y write the number of copies being ordered.
15. REORDER . . . if marked tells ORD to submit this order again if it is not filled.	This is used for items that are currently in print or known to be available.

Table 23.6 (continued)

IMPORTANT STEPS IN THE OPERATION: An important step is any major, logical segment or sequence of the operation which must be done to ADVANCE the work.	KEY POINTS: A key point is any element or stage of the operation which might make or break the job, a special **knack** for making the job easier, etc.
16. AGENCY is the branch for which the materials are being ordered.	
17. REQUISITIONER'S . . . is where the person ordering or approving the order places his/her initials.	Check with your branch manager to find out who initials orders for the department/branch.

taking place in the profession is a must—not only to help one's self but to provide the highest level of service possible to your teenage patrons.

Creating Alliances

An extension of political skills is the trend of partnering and developing coalitions with community organizations, business, and government. As of this writing, the Library Administration and Management Association (another ALA division) is focusing on this by providing a number of workshops across the country to help libraries develop a partnering action plan that can be implemented from the libraries' perspective. This has tremendous potential for YA librarians.

From my experience, children's departments are able to get enormous amounts of money for programming and other activities, while young adult departments often get the short shrift. If YA librarians have learned the appropriate political skills, then they need to go in search of a partner to help promote and subsidize a YA project or day-to-day activities. Appropriate partners could be the local YMCA/YWCA (Young Women's Christian Association), the parks and recreation department, a bookstore, or fast-food restaurant. Not only will the partnership benefit the library, but your young adult patrons will benefit as well.

CONCLUSION

Training is essential. How else will YA librarians be able to keep up with current trends and new services? There are plenty of opportunities available for YA librarians to receive the necessary foundation to provide services to teens and then to build upon the foundation. Regardless of the format training takes, it is vital for the YA librarian to take advantage of whatever training opportunity that presents itself. Whether as a refresher or to acquire a new skill, training can serve to enliven and revitalize one's self and the services provided to young adults.

Do not limit yourself to library-related training opportunities. The more you can learn, the more you bring to your job, your employer, and your teen patrons. This will make you invaluable to your employer and could make you the hero of your library's YA service program. The successful YA librarians I have met are the ones who have mastered the skills and have taken advantage of all sorts of training. That is why training is essential. Take part and become a success yourself.

NOTES

1. Young Adult Library Services Association, 50 East Huron Street, Chicago, IL 60611, 1–800–545–2433.
2. C. Allen Nichols, "Get on Board the YA Train," *Voice of Youth Advocates* (February 1995): 333.
3. C. Allen Nichols, e-mail interview with Melanie Rapp, September 6, 1996.
4. Cleveland Area Metropolitan Library System, 20600 Chagrin Blvd., Suite 500, Shaker Heights, OH 44122, 1–216–921–3900.
5. Mary Huebscher, "Young Adult Librarian Mentoring Program," *CAMLS News* 18, no. 1 (Spring 1996): 7.

24

Professional Resources: An Annotated List

Don Kenney

Bibliographies provide a rich, varied source of information for librarians and staff members working with young adults. Familiarity with bibliographical sources in the field of YA literature can provide a gateway for enhancing a library staff's ability to better serve young adults. Knowledge of bibliographic sources and tools is essential for providing meaningful programming, reader's advisory, and informational/reference assistance for a library's YA clientele.

THE COMING-OF-AGE OF YOUNG ADULT LITERATURE AND SERVICES

Within the last ten years, more and more bibliographic tools have been published exclusively devoted to YA literature and services. Previously, young adult librarians and staff members had to rely on those guides and tools generally labeled *children's literature*. With the evolution of a body of literature primarily intended for middle and high school students, library services and programs likewise evolved to meet the needs of these age groups.

Young adult literature has long had an identity crisis, as evidenced by the fact we have called it so many different names. In its evolutionary days, when Felson was writing hot rod novels, and Betty Cavanna romance novels, educators and librarians called them juvenile or junior novels; when they decided that this term had negative connotations, they decided to call it adolescent literature (notice how the term ''literature'' sneaked in to give it respectability). When the term "adolescent" was also derided and considered politically incorrect, educators and librarian professionals switched to "young adult literature," hoping that the words "adult" and "literature" would somehow lend greater credibility to this body of literature.[1] However, whatever librarians and educators choose to call it, YA literature is a growing body of literature. It is becoming respectable and accepted by educators, librarians, parents, and literary scholars.

Disciplines by nature evolve, and they evolve primarily once the *literature* of that discipline becomes codified, that is, indexed and abstracted. Through codification, it develops a history of its own, a body of works, books, journals, reports, conferences, workshops, and meetings that disseminate information about the discipline and research findings and, finally, canons. For example, the types of reference books published over the last few years that focus specifically on YA literature attest to the recognition of young adult literature as a serious field of endeavor. Recently, St. James Press' *Twentieth-Century Young Adult Writers*[2] and the *Index to Literary Criticism for Young Adults*[3] and *Olderr's Young Adult Fiction Index*[4] are just a few examples of titles that provide useful referencing for the field that previously was not available or was accessible only through limited resources in the general field of "children's literature." In the area of critical literature, of which English teachers are so fond, the Twayne series on young adult literature now includes a growing number of young adult writers such as Sue Ellen Bridgers, Robert Cormier, and Judy Blume, just to name a few.

This codification tells us a lot about the evolving discipline of YA literature. It tells us it is maturing and gaining acceptance as a worthy, serious area for scholars to examine. The fact that this bibliographical chapter list has some 100 items exclusively devoted to YA literature is further evidence that YA literature has come into its own.

CRITERIA FOR SELECTION

These bibliographies are intended to assist all library staff, especially those working with young adults, in introducing and supporting the reading needs of young readers. Too often children in their middle and teen years are left to struggle on their own to find reading material that is engaging and relevant. Many of the items in this listing are primarily reader's advisory sources— sources that the YA librarian and staff can use to place the right books at the right time in the hands of an adolescent. Second, the sources will be useful for collection development tools, and a select few are books on programming and issues appropriate to the teen years that will assist the library staff in better understanding the needs of the young adult client.

This bibliography of bibliographies is grouped into four categories: general bibliographies, subject/topical bibliographies, journal sources for bibliographies, and electronic sources on the Internet. Full bibliographic information is provided, along with a brief description of each item. I have attempted in the description to inform the user of the scope of the bibliography as well as the major access points, that is, indexing tools to fully utilize the source. I have, in most cases, refrained from making judgmental comments but instead have allowed the user discretion in deciding how to use the sources and place a value on them. What is a useful, favorite source for one librarian may not be for someone else.

Initially, I set out to provide a more detailed division of the bibliographies in terms of subject coverage. However, that proved impracticable since, in some instances, only one or two bibliographies exist on any one subject. In each annotation, I have indicated the arrangement of the bibliography. Some are arranged by genre and/or topics that we know from research studies match the reading interest of young adults. I did not establish a cutoff publication date for inclusion of a bibliography. This would have meant excluding a few earlier works in the field and some works that contribute to the historical body and understanding of YA literature. Finally, these are tools that are simply launching pads. Librarians and library staff in the field need to stay abreast of new publications through traditional review sources and, most important, connecting with each other to exchange ideas and information on new tools.

GENERAL

Anderson, Vicki. *Fiction Sequels for Readers 10–16: An Annotated Bibliography of Books in Succession.* Jefferson, NC: McFarland, 1990. Lists and provides short annotations for some 1,500 series books published for children and young adults.

Association for Library Services to Children. *The Newbery and Caldecott Awards: A Guide to the Medal and Honor Books.* Chicago: American Library Association, 1997. Annotated list by year, starting with the latest year, of the Newbery and Caldecott Awards. Indexed by author, illustrator, and title.

Barker, Keith, ed. *Information Books for Children.* Brookfield, VT: Ashgate, 1992. The arrangement of the titles in this source follows the Dewey classification for school libraries, starting with genre works to history. Each entry includes basic bibliographic information, the reviewer of the book, and age range.

Baskin, Barbara H. and Karen H. Harris. *Books for the Gifted Child: Serving Special Needs.* 2 vols. New York: R.R. Bowker, 1980. Annotated bibliography of recommended books for gifted children. Essays on topics relating to gifted children.

Beetz, Kirk H. and Suzanne Niemeyer, eds. *Beacham's Guide to Literature for Young Adults.* Washington, DC: Beacham's, 1989. This five-volume set is arranged alphabetically by title. Each entry includes an extensive annotation and lists additional books by the same author and author biographical information. Two appendixes are helpful in using this multivolume set: Newbery winners and titles grouped by themes such as death, father–son relationship, and war.

Bodart, Joni Richards. *Booktalk! Booktalking and School Visiting for Young Adult Audiences.* New York: H.W. Wilson, 1980.

———. *Booktalk! 2 Booktalking for All Ages and Audiences.* 2d ed. New York: H.W. Wilson, 1985.

————. *Booktalk! 3 More Booktalks for All Ages and Audiences.* New York: H.W. Wilson, 1988.

————. *Booktalk! 4 Selections from the Booktalker for All Ages and Audiences.* New York: H.W. Wilson, 1992.

————. *Booktalk! 5 More Selections from the Booktalker for All Ages and Audiences.* New York: H.W. Wilson, 1993. The initial volume discusses booktalking and how to do one. Arrangement is by title of the book with an informative synopsis. Indexing in each book of the series provides cross-references, and the theme/ genre index is particularly valuable.

————. *100 World-Class Thin Books, or, What to Read When Your Book Report Is Due Tomorrow.* Englewood, CO: Libraries Unlimited, 1993. A quick reference guide to 100 short novels under 200 pages arranged from *thin* to *thinnest*. Each entry includes the subjects the novel deals with, major characters, a booktalk synopsis, major themes, and book report ideas. An appendix includes tips on writing effective booktalks. In addition to a subject index there is a genre and curriculum area index.

Caroll, Frances and Mary Meachan. *More Exciting, Funny, Scary, Short, Different, and Sad Books Kids Like about Animals, Science, Sports, Families, Songs, & Other Things.* Chicago: American Library Association, 1992. This bibliography of fiction and non-fiction works is unusual in that it is arranged in divisions that reflect the way children and young adults request books: "I want a book about . . ."; "I have read . . . and want another one like it." Annotations are written in a brief and popular style that appeals to young adult and children audiences. However, the upper reading range is only eighth grade.

Cart, Michael. *From Romance to Realism: 50 Years of Growth and Change in Young Adult Literature.* New York: HarperCollins, 1996. Traces the history of the YA novel beyond the formula-written novels of the 1960s and early 1970s to the more recent realistic developments in the publishing of young adult novels.

Carter, Betty. *Best Books for Young Adults: The Selections, the History, the Romance.* Chicago: American Library Association, 1994. Includes interesting history of the annual Best Books for Young Adults list now sponsored by the Young Adult Library Services Association of ALA. Other chapters include issues related to this list, authors' repeat appearances on the lists, and the selections of the books for each year's list. The culminating section is the Best Books for Young Adults list, 1966 to 1993.

Caywood, Caroline A., ed. *Youth Participation in School and Public Libraries: It Works.* Chicago: American Library Association, 1995. This revised, updated edition of two earlier publications, *Youth Participation in School and Public Libraries* (1983) and *Youth Participation in Libraries: A Training Manual* (1991), provides guidelines for implementing a youth participation program. Appendixes include a list of resources and camera-ready handouts. It is a very practical guide for the novice YA librarian.

Christenbury, Leila, ed. *Books for You: An Annotated Booklist for Senior High Students.* Committee on the Senior High School Booklist of the National Council of Teachers of English. 12th ed. Urbana, IL: National Council of Teachers of English, 1995. This latest edition of a standard, annotated bibliography includes 1,000 titles published between 1990 and 1994, though there are some titles from many years ago. The books are grouped under the usual popular genres and themes, from adventure and survival, to sports and war. In addition, several new categories serve as timely guides to what many teens are reading now for curriculum support and for recreation. There are sections on the Holocaust, on religion and inspiration, and on self-help; a multicultural list includes 150 books that are also listed in other sections. Indexed by author, title, and subject.

Criscoe, Betty L. *Award-Winning Books for Children and Young Adults: An Annual Guide.* Metuchen, NJ: Scarecrow Press, 1989. This planned annual publication brings together 227 awards given internationally for achievement in literature for children and young adults. Awards given to individuals for their body of work (e.g., the YASD/SLJ Young Adult Author Award) and to individuals for research or service in the field (e.g., ALSC's Arbuthnot Award) are also included. The main part of the book is an alphabetical listing of awards, with the chosen winners for 1989. Each listing gives the name and address of the sponsoring organization, information about the award and its history, an annotation of the book or description of the individual's achievements, and a picture of the book's cover or of the award winner (in the case of individuals). Indexes including age/grade preference and genre are included. An excellent book for collection development, reading guidance, and research.

deVos, Gail. *Storytelling for Young Adults: Techniques and Treasury.* Englewood, CO: Libraries Unlimited, 1991. Includes an Honor Title of the Storytelling World Awards for 1995. Discusses storytelling techniques, how to pick a good story, and storytelling extensions before introducing an excellent bibliography of 120 stories suited to young adults ages 13 through 18. The stories are summarized, timed, and arranged by subject: folktales and fairy tales; myths and legends; ghost, horror, and suspense tales; urban belief tales; tales of love, romance, and sexuality; and twists, satire, and exaggeration.

Drew, Bernard A. *The 100 Most Popular Young Adult Authors: Biographical Sketches and Bibliographies.* Englewood, CO: Libraries Unlimited, 1996. Featuring 100 favorite YA authors, from Joan Aiken and Lloyd Alexander, to Jane Yolen and Paul Zindel, this book provides information about fiction writers for research papers and reports. Objective biographical sketches provide an evaluative treatment of the author's publications. Arranged alphabetically by author name, each is accompanied by a complete list of the writer's works, critical comments from a variety of sources, and suggestions for further reading. The book focuses on individuals writing in the 1990s but also includes twelve classic authors (e.g., Mark Twain, Louisa May Alcott, J.R.R. Tolkien) who are still widely read by teens. It also covers some authors known primarily for adult literature (e.g., Stephen King) and some who write mainly for middle readers but are also popular among young adults (e.g., Betsy Byars). This book makes a great collection development tool and resource for author studies.

Gillespie, John Thomas. *Best Books for Junior High Readers.* New Providence, NJ: R.R. Bowker, 1991. Lists materials for students in grades seven to nine, or ages 12 to 15. The listing of some 6,800 titles gives full bibliographic information as well as citations to reviews of each book. Fiction categories include "Contemporary Life and Problems," "Fantasy," and "Sports Stories."

————. *Best Books for Senior High Readers.* New Providence, NJ: R.R. Bowker, 1991. Includes 5,000 books recommended for senior high school arranged by popular subjects such as sports, science, fiction, ecology and environment, and adventure and exploration.

Gillespie, John Thomas and Corinne J. Naden. *Juniorplots*. New Providence, NJ: R.R. Bowker, 1967.

————. *More Juniorplots: A Guide for Teachers and Librarians*. New York: R.R. Bowker, 1977.

————. *Juniorplots 3: A Book Talk Guide for Use with Readers Ages 12–16*. New Providence, NJ: R.R. Bowker, 1987.

————. *Juniorplots 4: A Book Talk Guide for Use with Readers Ages 12–16*. New Providence, NJ: R.R. Bowker, 1993. The *Juniorplot* series are divided by subjects and genres popular with adolescent readers, such as "Teenage Life and Concern," "Developing Values," and "Adventure and Mystery Stories." Individual titles in each series are analyzed under six categories: plot summary, thematic material, booktalk material, additional readings that explore similar themes of the book that is annotated, listing of review sources, and autobiographical information. Author, title, and subject indexes provide easy cross-referencing; *Juniorplots 4* has a cumulative subject index for all series.

————. *Seniorplots: A Book Talk Guide for Use with Readers Ages 15–18*. New York: R.R. Bowker, 1989. Like the *Juniorplot* series, this companion volume extends coverage to senior high years. It is divided into twelve subject/genres representing a variety of reading areas popular with late adolescents: "Growing Up," "Interpersonal Relations," "Challenging Adult Novels," "Stories of Other Lands and Times," "Possible Worlds" (science fiction), "Fantasy," "Adventurous Stories," "Suspense and Mystery," "Sports in Fact and Fiction," "Interesting Lives and True Adventures," "The World around Us," and "Guidance and Health."

Haviland, Virginia. *Children's Literature: A Guide to Reference Sources*. Washington, DC: Library of Congress. 1966. Supplement 1, 1972; Supplement 2, 1977. Annotated bibliography covering history, criticism, authorship, illustration, bibliography, books and children, the library and children's books, international studies, and national studies. This bibliographic source is considered a standard in the field of children's and YA literature.

Hearne, Betsy. *Choosing Books for Children: A Commonsense Guide*. New York: Delacorte Press, 1990. Includes over 300 annotated selections that can be used for selecting books for children and young adults. There is an author-illustrator and subject index to facilitate the use of the book.

Helbig, Aletha and Agnes R. Perkins. *Dictionary of British Children's Fiction: Books of Recognized Merit*. Westport, CT: Greenwood Press, 1989. Contains some 1,626 entries of outstanding British children's fiction. Annotations are not included. A comprehensive index and a system of asterisks provides cross-referencing between various entries for each book.

————. *Phoenix Award of the Children's Literature Association 1985–1989*. Metuchen, NJ: Scarecrow Press, 1993. The Phoenix Award of the Children's Literature Association is given to an author, either living or dead, of a book published 20 years earlier that did not win a major award at the time of its publication but that, over time, has received recognition for its high literary quality. Each winning title includes acceptance speech (if author is living), biographical sketch, bibliography of author's works, and critical essays on known works by the winning author. Includes such notables as Rosemary Sutcliff, Leon Garfield, and Milton Meltzer.

Herald, Diana Tixier, ed. *Genreflecting: A Guide to Reading Interest in Genre Fiction.* 4th ed. Englewood, CO: Libraries Unlimited, 1995; Herald, Diana Tixier, ed. *Teen Genreflecting.* Englewood, CO: Libraries Unlimited, 1997. These titles cover such popular genres as crime, adventure, romance, science fiction, fantasy, and horror, defining each along with its many subgenres and listing books in each category. Subject, author/title, and series character indexes provide easy access to the seven genre categories.

Hicken, Mandy and Ray Prytherch. *Now Read On: A Guide to Contemporary Popular Fiction.* Brookfield, VT: Ashgate, 1994. Focuses primarily on British authors of popular contemporary fiction. As outlined in the introduction of the bibliography: "[T]he purpose of this book is to answer the question so often put to staff public libraries and bookshops—'I've read all Catherine Cookson's or Wilbur Smith's books. Does anyone else write like ... ?'" Arranged by broad genres such as adventure stories, gothic romances, and war stories. Two indexes—author index and series and character index—provide acess to the listings. Each author listing has a brief biography.

Immell, Myra and Marion Sader, eds. *The Young Adult Reader's Adviser.* New Providence, NJ: R.R. Bowker, 1992. The two-volume set consists of subject bibliographies augmented by profiles of famous authors and historical figures. Volume 1 includes literature on language arts, math, and computer science; volume 2, the social sciences, history, science, and health.

Jensen, Julie M. and Nancy L. Roser, eds. *Adventuring with Books: A Booklist for Pre-Kindergarten—Grade 6.* Committee on the Elementary School Booklist of the National Council of Teachers of English. Urbana, IL: National Council of Teachers of English, 1993. A booklist for prekindergarten–grade six, listing and annotating alphabetically by author under such categories as "Basic Concept Books," "Science Fiction," and "Contemporary Realistic Fiction." Includes both fiction and non-fiction.

McElmeel, Sharron L. *Educator's Companion to Children's Literature, Volume 1: Mysteries, Animal Tales, Books of Humor, Adventure Stories, and Historical Fiction.* Englewood, CO: Libraries Unlimited, 1995. Five popular genres—mystery, animal tales, humor, adventure, and historical fiction—are explored to promote learning in the library and classroom. After an introductory discussion of each genre, the author recommends a title, gives a list of related titles, and provides a variety of ideas for genre-related activities.

———. *Educator's Companion to Children's Literature, Volume 2: Folklore, Contemporary Realistic Fiction, Fantasy, Biographies, and Tales from Here and There.* Englewood, CO: Libraries Unlimited, 1996. McElmeel examines five genres— folklore, contemporary realistic fiction, fantasy, biography, and tales from here and there—to demonstrate ways to use them in the library and classroom. This book includes an overview of each genre with title listings and a list of related titles. This bibliography is a very useful reading promotion tool.

———. *Great New Nonfiction Reads.* Englewood, CO: Libraries Unlimited, 1995. More than 100 of the best non-fiction reads published in the five years before 1995 are included in this source. Selected for their accuracy, authenticity and appeal, these books cover topics from adoption, African Americans, and automobile racing, to bats, cats, and dinosaurs. The author provides thorough guidelines for choosing and using information books to promote literacy and learning through inquiry. Complete bibliographic information, grade and age levels, and series information are given for each title, with suggestions for related sources (both fiction and non-fiction) and learning connections. A useful selection, collection development, and reading promotion tool, the book will also help librarians advise readers making the transition from fiction to non-fiction with books that have story lines and appealing characters.

————. *The Latest and Greatest Read-Alouds*. Englewood, CO: Libraries Unlimited, 1994. This book supplements Jim Trelease's *Read-Aloud Handbook* and covers more recent titles. One hundred of the best and most exciting reads for elementary and middle school students have been selected. Each title is categorized by general reading and listening levels according to both grade (for librarians and classroom teachers) and age (for parents and grandparents). Annotations summarize the plots and provide concise book information to aid selection.

Meacham, Mary. *Information Sources in Children's Literature*. Westport, CT: Greenwood Press, 1978. Bibliography of bibliographies and finding tools for the field of children's literature. Useful in finding books dealing with such broad topics as American history in juvenile books, the black experience in children's books, and storytelling.

Moir, Hughes, ed. *Collected Perspectives: Choosing and Using Books for the Classroom*. Boston: Christopher-Gordon, 1990. Five hundred of the best K–12 books from 1984 to 1989 are reviewed with suggestions for using them in the classroom.

Montgomery, Paula Kay. *Approaches to Literature through Subject (Oryx Reading Motivation Series, Vol. 3)*. Phoenix, AZ: Oryx Press, 1993. Although the bibliography is intended for teachers, the sources included can be used in a variety of reader-advising techniques. Focus of subjects is arranged around four categories: people, places, things, and events. A serious shortcoming of the bibliography is the lack of annotations.

New York Public Library. *Books for the Teen Age*. New York: Office of Young Adult Services of the New York Public Library, 1996. An annotated list of some 1,200 books arranged by broad subjects. The list has been produced since 1955 and is considered a traditional standard for librarians in young adult service.

Pellowski, Anne. *The World of Children's Literature*. New York: R.R. Bowker, 1968. International in scope, covering more than 30 countries; includes monographs, series, and multivolume works relating to history and criticism of children's literature; national book clubs; reading circles; subjects such as storytelling and folklore; reading interests; national bibliographies; and lists of recommended books. Arranged geographically with a general index.

Pelton, Mary Helen. *Reading Is Not a Spectator Sport*. Englewood, CO: Libraries Unlimited, 1993. This books offers numerous ideas and activities for creating an environment that leads to children's reading success. The author discusses incentives, events, and programs that promote reading and what administrators and national organizations can do to support reading. Reading centers, cooperative learning and literature, and thematic units with bibliographies are just a few of the topics covered.

Peterson, Linda Kauffman and Marilyn Leathers Solt. *Newbery and Caldecott Medal and Honor Books: An Annotated Bibliography*. Boston: G.K. Hall, 1982. Lists and annotates by year the Caldecott (1938–1981) and the Newbery (1922–1981) awards. Appendixes include the honor books by year; terms, definitions, and criteria for each award; distribution by types of literature such as fantasy, historical, or animal stories. Indexed by author, illustrator, title, and subject.

Phelan, Patricia, ed. *High Interest—Easy Reading: An Annotated Booklist for Middle School and Senior High School*. Urbana, IL: National Council of Teachers of English, 1996. Some 300 titles are arranged into nineteen chapters, each indicating a central idea or theme, such as "Adventure," "Dealing with Death," "Sports," and "Science." A chapter entitled "Issues of Our Time" includes books that consider such controversial subjects as violence, bigotry, and child abuse. Standard topical chapters on such areas popular with teenagers include fantasy, mystery, and the animal world. Full bibliographical information is included, and following each annotation is a listing of any national award that the book has been given. Multicultural books are identified by cultural traditions such as African American or Hispanic American. Indexed by author, title, and subject.

Reed, Arthea J.S. *Comics to Classics: A Guide to Books for Teens and Preteens*. New York: Penguin Books, 1994. Consisting of three parts—"Teens and Preteens," "Sharing Books," "Books for Teens and Preteens"—this book is aimed at teenagers, teachers, librarians, and parents. The third part of the book is an annotated bibliography by genre and is divided into fiction and non-fiction chapters. Includes many early works such as *Johnny Tremain* and Steinbeck's *The Pearl*.

Roginski, Jim, ed. *Newbery and Caldecott Medalist and Honor Books Winners: Bibliographies and Resource Materials through 1991*. 2d ed. New York: Neal-Schuman, 1992. Arranged by author, each entry includes the award (Newbery or Caldecott); bibliography, which lists all other printed material by the author; listing of libraries or museums that retain original manuscripts by the author; exhibitions; and background reading related to other readings about the winner or works. Indexed by author, artists, and titles.

Rosow, La Vergne. *Light'n Lively Reads for ESL, Adult, and Teen Readers: A Thematic Bibliography*. Englewood, CO: Libraries Unlimited, 1996. This annotated bibliography of high-interest, low-reading-level materials is arranged by themes that will appeal to young adults—from sports and the arts to money and U.S. history. A variety of resources from books and chapters of books, to magazine articles and letters is included.

Samuels, Barbara G. and G. Kylene Beers, eds. *Your Reading: A Booklist for Junior High and Middle School*. Committee on the Middle School and Junior High Booklist. 9th ed. Urbana, IL: National Council of Teachers of English [NCTE], 1993. Like the other NCTE bibliography series, this annotated bibliography includes fiction and non-fiction arranged topically. One appendix lists 100 books from 25 years of YA literature, 1967–1992. Indexed by author, title, and subject.

Sharkey, Paulette Bochnig. *Newbery and Caldecott Medal and Honor Books in Other Media*. New York: Neal-Schuman, 1992. The text of this book is arranged by award year, with the Newbery or Caldecott Medal book listed first, followed by the Honor Books in alphabetical order. An alphabetical arrangement of media by type (filmstrip, video, etc.) is used within each award-winning title. Particularly useful are the media, "large print" and "talking book." A separate "About the Book" section lists analytical treatments of the titles.

Shapiro, Lillian L. and Barbara L. Stein. *Fiction for Youth: A Guide to Recommended*

Books. New York: Neal-Schuman, 1992. Alphabetically by author, annotations are thorough and objective. An excellent subject index provides good access to books about such topics as abortion, death, fathers and sons, and the West and western stories.

Spencer, Pam. *What Do Young Adults Read Next? A Reader's Guide to Fiction for Young Adults.* Detroit: Gale Research, 1994. The volume includes some 1,500 books published from 1988 to 1992 aimed at YA readers. Entries are alphabetized by author with standard bibliographical information and a plot summary. Also each annotation includes review sources for each entry, other books by the author, and other authors who write on a similar theme or in a similar style. Indexes include "Award Index," "Time Period Index," "Geography Index," "Subject Index," "Character Name Index," "Character Description Index," "Author Index," and "Title Index."

Spirt, Diana L. *Introducing Books: A Guide for the Middle Grades.* New York: R.R. Bowker, 1970.

———. *Introducing More Books: A Guide for the Middle Grades.* New York: R.R. Bowker, 1978.

———. *Introducing Bookplots 3: A Book Talk Guide for Use with Readers Ages 8–12.* Rev. ed. New York: R.R. Bowker, 1990. The *Introducing Book* series is designed to assist educators and librarians to give booktalks, read aloud, or engage in other types of reading guidance. Each volume in the review is arranged around topics and genres relevant to YA audiences. Each entry includes a plot summary, thematic analysis, discussion material, and listing of books and audiovisual material on similar themes or topics.

Trelease, Jim. *The New Read-Aloud Handbook.* Rev. ed. New York: Penguin Group, 1989. Trelease describes with contagious enthusiasm the reading-aloud experiences he has had with his family and with students in classrooms. An annotated, graded list of recommended read-alouds is appended.

Yaakov, Juliette, ed. *Children's Catalog.* New York: H.W. Wilson, 1991. Comprehensive, annotated bibliography of children's books and books about children's literature, with non-fiction arranged by Dewey classification, 000–999. Fiction and short story collections are alphabetized by author. Updated by annual supplements.

Young Adult Library Services Association. *Best Books for Young Adults.* Chicago: American Library Association, 1998. The annual publication list annotates fiction and non-fiction works for young adults ages 12 to 18. Selected on the basis of each book's proven or potential appeal and value to young adults, the titles for the 1998 list were published from 1996 through 1997.

Young Adult Library Services Association. *Quick Picks for Young Adult Readers.* Chicago: American Library Association, 1998. Annotated list of fiction and non-fiction works. Selections of popular titles were published in 1996 and 1997 and are intended to stimulate interest in reading.

SUBJECT/TOPICAL

Adamson, Lynda G. *Recreating the Past: A Guide to American and World Historical Fiction for Children and Young Adults.* Westport, CT: Greenwood Press, 1994.

The 970 works selected for this bibliography are arranged within historical time periods such as "Prehistory: Greece and Japan: before 1199." Within each section, entries are arranged alphabetically by author. Seven very useful appendixes and an index of authors, titles, and illustrators follow the bibliography.

Azarnoff, Pat. *Health, Illness, and Disability: A Guide to Books for Children and Young Adults*. New York: R.R. Bowker, 1983. Categorizes and annotates some 1,000 works of fiction and non-fiction books for children and youth about health and illnesses, disabilities, and dysfunctions. A detailed subject index leads the reader to books on such subjects as "fear and phobia," "freckles," and "leukemia." Annotations are brief.

Barron, Neil. *Fantasy Literature: A Reader's Guide*. New York: Garland, 1990. An annotated bibliography of fantasy literature from its early conception of 1988. A chapter, "Modern Fantasy for Young Adults, 1950–88," is included. A section on research aids is very helpful in providing critical sources and teaching ideas.

Baskin, Barbara H. and Karen H. Harris. *Notes from a Different Drummer: A Guide to Juvenile Fiction Portraying the Handicapped*. New York: R.R. Bowker, 1977. This annotated guide of 311 books includes juvenile fiction portraying the handicapped, 1940–1975. Each annotation, arranged alphabetically by author, includes bibliographic information, reading level, and the disability portrayed in the book. Plot descriptions are detailed, followed by an analysis that encompasses both interpretive and literary aspects of the work. Although somewhat dated, this source provides an excellent guide to many early works dealing with disabilities. Indexed by title and subject.

Bernstein, Joanne E. and Marsha Rudman. *Books to Help Children Cope with Separation and Loss: An Annotated Bibliography*. New York: R.R. Bowker, 1989. Titles are arranged in categories by the primary loss experience dealt with in the work. Examples of categories are "Loving a Pet," "Prisons," and "Serious Illness." Each entry includes the full bibliographic citation and interest level or intended reading age. An "Interest Level Index," which categorizes the loss faced by the main character in the book, is especially useful.

Bishop, Rudine Sims, ed. *Kaleidoscope: A Multicultural Booklist for Grades K–8*. Multicultural Booklist Committee of the National Council of Teachers of English. Urbana, IL: National Council of Teachers of English, 1994. Annotations of nearly 100 books published between 1990 and 1992, featuring photographs of the covers of many annotated books; focuses on people of color, especially African Americans, Asian Americans, Hispanic Americans/Latinos, and Native Americans. Chapters group books by genre or theme rather than by cultural group. A detailed subject index, listing books pertaining to various cultural groups and to the distinct sociocultural groups, will prove invaluable to librarians in locating specific books. Also included are a list of resources pertaining to multicultural literature, a directory of publishers, and indexes of authors, illustrators, and titles.

Blake, Barbara. *A Guide to Children's Books about Asian Americans*. Hantz, England: Scolar, 1995. Entries are arranged by author within each grade-level section. Titles were published between 1970 and 1993; most have received favorable reviews in one or more standard journals. Each entry provides standard bibliographical information as well as the particular culture covered by the book, a descriptive annotation, a list of reviewing journals (but no date of reviews), and subjects (e.g., calendars, internment camps, adoption). Appendixes include alphabetical lists of authors and titles and lists by culture, category, and grade. There are no subject index and no index by culture; for instance, one cannot look up all the titles on friendship for the Vietnamese.

Carlin, Margaret F., Jeannine L. Laughlin, and Richard D. Sanja. *Understanding Abilities, Disabilities, and Capabilities: A Guide to Children's Literature*. Englewood, CO: Libraries Unlimited, 1991. The bibliography includes more than 40 disabling conditions. These include books in print, films, and other nonprint media currently available. Annotations are lengthy and may be used as the basis for booktalks; each includes age level and discusses readability and whether or not the author has written appropriately about the disability.

Carter, Betty and Richard F. Abrahamson. *Nonfiction for Young Adults: From Delight to Wisdom*. Phoenix, AZ: Oryx Press, 1990. Examines non-fiction works and the general neglect of informational books in teacher and librarianship training. Discusses such aspects of non-fiction as interest, accuracy, content, style, and uses. The extensive bibliography includes monographs and journal articles pertinent to the promotion of non-fiction for young adults.

Cordier, Mary Hurlburt and Maria A. Perez-Stable. *Peoples of the American West: Historical Perspectives through Children's Literature*. Metuchen, NJ: Scarecrow Press, 1989. Divided into two main parts—analysis and bibliography—this book provides a helpful guide to those looking to purchase and use historical fiction about the American West. Part one includes an introduction and examination of the genre, while part two is made up of more than 100 books, separated into grades K–3 and 4–9. Individual annotations provide imprint information, geographical setting, time period, and main characters in the book.

Dale, Doris Cruger. *Bilingual Books in Spanish and English for Children*. Littleton, CO: Libraries Unlimited, 1985. Annotated bibliography of bilingual books in Spanish and English for children published or distributed in the United States since the 1940s. Arranged by decade with various indexes to provide ample access.

Davis, Enid. *The Liberty Cap: A Catalogue of Non-Sexist Materials for Children*. Chicago: Academy Press, 1977. Short review articles on topics relating to nonsexist children's books and reviews of nonsexist books. Two sections include works of fiction and non-fiction for grades 3–10. Another section, "Adult Books for Young Adults," is brief.

Dreyer, Sharon Spredemann. *The Bookfinder: A Guide to Children's Literature about the Needs and Problems of Youth Aged 2–15*. Circle Piner, MN: American Guidance Service, 1977–. Each volume has annotations of books alphabetically arranged by author. The subject index is very useful and comprehensive, spanning the subjects of "abandonment" to "youngest child."

Dwyer, Jim. *The Earth Works: Recommended Fiction and Nonfiction about Nature and the Environment for Adults and Young Adults*. New York: Neal-Schuman, 1996. Nearly a quarter of the books annotated are appropriate for both adults and young adults and are identified with a pound (#) sign; "OT" is used to designate for older teens at the high school level. The bibliography is in two sections: fiction and non-fiction. Each section lists works under broad subject areas such as "environmental nature writing," "animals," and "ecofeminist fiction." Annotations are well written and brief.

Fakih, Kimberly Olson. *Literature of Delight: A Critical Guide to Humorous Books for Children*. New Providence, NJ: R.R. Bowker, 1993. Over 700 annotations organized according to seventeen categories of humor provide a good representation of humorous material for children and young adults. Included in the categories of humor are "Bonk! Physical Humor," "Nothing Is Sacred: Irreverent Humor," and "Goose Bumps and Chills: Gothic Humor." Annotations are perky and include grade level.

Field, Carolyn W. and Jacqueline S. Weiss. *Values in Selected Children's Books of Fiction and Fantasy.* Hamden, CT: Library Professional Publications, 1987. Over 700 annotations of books for children from preschool to eighth grade are categorized by the values they represent or reinforce. The selections demonstrate or project values that help children develop skills for decision making and problem solving.

Friedberg, Joan B., June B. Mullins, and Adelaide W. Sukiennik. *Accept Me As I Am: Best Books of Juvenile Nonfiction on Impairment and Disabilities.* New York: R.R. Bowker, 1985. Arranged topically, including such disability topics as deafness, speech impairments, and mental retardation. Excellent annotations include a brief critical analysis at the end of each annotation.

———. *Portraying Persons with Disabilities: An Annotated Bibliography of Nonfiction for Children and Teenagers.* New Providence, NJ: R.R. Bowker, 1992. Lists books in four problem categories: physical, sensory, cognitive and behavior, and multiple/severe and various disabilities. Each entry, in addition to a complete bibliographic citation, includes reading level, specific disability with which the book deals, meaning of the book, and a critical analysis that suggests specific errors of the book, as well as its strengths and weaknesses.

Helbig, Alethea and Agnes Regen Perkins. *This Land Is Our Land: A Guide to Multicultural Literature for Children and Young Adults.* Westport, CT: Greenwood Press, 1994. Contains books of fiction, oral tradition, and poetry published from 1985 through 1993. It is divided into four major ethnic groups in the United States: African Americans, Asian Americans, Hispanic Americans, and Native-American Indians. There are 570 entries arranged alphabetically by writer within each ethnic group, subdivided by fiction, oral tradition, and poetry. Full bibliographic information is provided. Each entry includes summary incorporating major themes, critical comments, and other pertinent books by the writer. Cross-references direct reader to books with similar themes or works by the writer in other genres. Indexes of titles, writers, titles by grade level, and subjects provide multiple access points.

Jenkins, Esther C. and Mary C. Austin. *Literature for Children and Young Adults about Oceania: Analysis and Annotated Bibliography with Additional Readings for Adults.* Westport, CT: Greenwood Press, 1996. Arranged geographically. Australia, New Zealand, Melanesia, Micronesia, and Polynesia annotations are divided by two headings: "Folk Literature" and "Contemporary Literature." Within each section, entries are arranged alphabetically by author and numbered in sequence for easy reference in the indexes. Full bibliographic information is included. Indexed by name (author, illustrator, translator, editor, reteller), title, and subject.

Kaywell, Joan F. *Adolescents at Risk: A Guide to Fiction and Nonfiction for Young Adults, Parents, and Professionals.* Westport, CT: Greenwood Press, 1993. This book is divided into fourteen chapters dealing with such problem areas as teenage pregnancy, AIDS, and stress and suicide. Each annotation includes bibliographic detail and a summary that focuses on a problem area dealt with in the novel or work of non-fiction. Each chapter also includes information on what to do and when to go for help, including addresses and toll-free numbers. Indexed by author and title.

Kennemer, Phyllis K. *Using Literature to Teach Middle Grades About War.* Phoenix, AZ: Oryx Press, 1993. The wars included in the bibliography are the Revolutionary War, the Civil War, World Wars I and II, the Vietnam War, and the Gulf War. Selections are both fiction and non-fiction. Annotations give concise book summaries and provide some indication of the tone of the writing. Although primarily intended to assist teachers in preparing thematic units, it is an excellent source for reader's advisory to assist young adults who may be interested in one of the wars or doing school-related research.

Kenney, DayAnn M., Stella S. Spangler, and Mary Ann Vanderwerf. *Science and Technology in Fact and Fiction: A Guide to Young Adult Books.* New York: R.R. Bowker, 1990. This annotated bibliography is an excellent source for locating titles related to the physical and earth sciences. The book is divided into two sections, "Science" and "Technology," each again divided into "Fiction" and "Nonfiction" and organized alphabetically by author. Each entry has a summary, complete bibliographic information, age and grade levels, series, and whether or not a title received any rewards.

Khorana, Meena. *Africa in Literature for Children and Young Adults: An Annotated Bibliography of English-Language Books.* Westport, CT: Greenwood Press, 1994. This annotated bibliography of English-language books set in Africa lists books dating from 1873 to 1994. Nearly 700 entries are arranged in six chapters according to region: "General Books," "North Africa," "West Africa," "East Africa," "Central Africa," and "Southern Africa." Each chapter is subdivided by genre. Full bibliographic information is provided as well as grade level. Indexed by author, title, and subject.

―――. *The Indian Subcontinent in Literature for Children and Young Adults: An Annotated Bibliography of English-Language Books.* Westport, CT: Greenwood Press, 1991. This bibliography examines literature in English for young people concerning the Indian subcontinent and associated areas. An introductory essay traces the development of children's literature about the subcontinent. Annotations provide plot summary, thematic analysis, literary evaluation, and international concerns. Indexed by author, title, and subject.

Kies, Cosette. *Supernatural Fiction for Teens: More than 1300 Good Paperbacks to Read for Wonderment, Fear, and Fun.* 2d ed. Englewood, CO: Libraries Unlimited, 1992. Annotates 1,300 supernatural fiction paperbacks with entries arranged alphabetically by author. Annotations are brief, but assigned subject headings such as paranormal abilities, horror, or vampires are listed. If part of a series, series titles are listed. The subject index is very useful in accessing the guide.

Kruse, Ginny Moore and Kathleen T. Horning. *Multicultural Literature for Children and Young Adults: A Selected Listing of Books, 1980–1990, by and about People of Color.* 3d ed. Madison: Cooperative Childrens Book Center, University of Wisconsin–Madison, 1991. The bibliography by and about African Americans, American Indians, Asian Americans, and Hispanic Americans includes children and young adult books with multicultural themes and topics. The annotated bibliography is arranged under sixteen different categories, including "History, People

and Places," "The Arts," "Issues in Today's World," and "Fiction for Teenagers."

Kuipers, Barbara J. *American Indian Reference Books for Children and Young Adults.*
Englewood, CO: Libraries Unlimited, 1991. This non-fiction bibliography can be
useful to librarians working with young adults for both readers advisory assistance
as well as collection development purposes. The bibliography is arranged alphabetically by authors under the Dewey decimal classification areas. Annotations
are extensive and include subject headings.

Kutzer, M. Daphne, ed. *Writers of Multicultural Fiction for Young Adults: A Bio-Critical
Sourcebook.* Westport, CT: Greenwood Press, 1996. A bibliographical source that
includes many well-known young adult writers, such as Paula Fox, Rosa Guy,
Robert Lipsyte, and Lawrence Yep. Although the primary thrust of this tool is
biobibliographic and critical analysis, each author entry has an excellent bibliography of books by the author and works about the author.

Lynn, Ruth Nadelman. *Fantasy Literature for Children and Young Adults: An Annotated
Bibliography.* 4th ed. New Providence, NJ: R.R. Bowker, 1995. This annotated
bibliography of fantasy novels and story collections for children and young adults
in grades three to twelve also has a research guide on the authors who write in
the genre. In part one, the annotated bibliography, the books listed are novels and
story collections published in English (including translations) between 1990 and
1994. In part two, the research guide, almost 4,000 new books, Ph.D. disserta-
tions, and articles are included. These references are divided into four areas:
"Bibliographical and Reference Sources," "Critical and Historical Studies,"
"Educational Resources," and "Fantasy Literature Author Studies." An excellent
introduction to fantasy literature covers definitions, classification, use with children and young people, criticism, and historical overview. The bibliography is
indexed by author and illustrator, by title, and by subject.

Makino, Yasuko, comp. *Japan through Children's Literature: An Annotated Bibliography.* 2d ed. Westport, CT: Greenwood Press, 1985. The annotated bibliography
is topically arranged and includes both fiction and non-fiction. Each book was
evaluated in terms of context and accuracy in portraying Japan and its culture
and people.

Manna, Anthony L. and Carolyn S. Brodie. *Many Faces, Many Voices: Multicultural
Literary Experiences for Youth: The Virginia Hamilton Conference.* Fort Atkin-
son, WI: Highsmith Press, 1992. In addition to the variety of essays by such
notables as Arnold Adoff and Virginia Hamilton, the appendixes are extremely
valuable. Appendixes include a listing of trade books for children and young
adults, sources of multicultural materials, and an inventory of the Virginia Hamilton Papers at Kent State University Libraries.

Miller-Lachman, Lyn. *Our Family, Our Friends, Our World.* New Providence, NJ: R.R.
Bowker, 1992. An annotated guide to the best fiction and non-fiction, focusing
on the cultures, identities, and histories of minority groups within the United
States and Canada as well as native cultures in Asia, Central America, Africa,
and others.

Moss, Joyce and George Wilson, eds. *From Page to Screen: Children's and Young Adult
Books on Film and Video.* Detroit: Gale Research, 1992. A guide to 1,400 film,
video, and laser disc adaptations of 750 literary works for children age five

through high school. Organized alphabetically by book title, each entry includes basic bibliographic information followed by a listing of the cinematic adaptation.

Olexer, Marycile E. *Poetry Anthologies for Children and Young People*. Chicago: American Library Association, 1985. The major portion of this book analyzes some 300 volumes of children's poetry. It is arranged in three parts to correspond to the suggested audience: part one, "Preschool through Grade Three"; part two, "Grades Four through Six"; part three, "Grades Seven through Nine." Each entry provides purpose and scope of the book of poetry. The author-title and subject indexes are crucial to the use of this tool.

Osayimwense, Osa, ed. *The All-White World of Children's Books and African American Children's Literature*. Trenton, NJ: African World Press, 1995.

Povsic, Frances, comp. *The Soviet Union in Literature for Children and Young Adults: An Annotated Bibliography of English-Language Books*. Westport, CT: Greenwood Press, 1991. This bibliography annotates 536 books written in, or translated into, English and published from 1900 to 1990, portraying the lives of Soviet peoples in their homelands or as immigrants in Europe or North America. Annotations include plot summary, literary and artistic analysis, and information about awards; reading levels are noted with citations.

Robertson, Debra E.J. *Portraying Persons with Disabilities: An Annotated Bibliography for Fiction for Children and Teenagers*. New Providence, NJ: R.R. Bowker, 1992. Includes works of fiction divided into four problem categories: physical, sensory, cognitive and behavior, and multiple/severe and various disabilities. Like its counterpart for non-fiction (see Friedberg and Mullins, *Portraying Persons with Disabilities*), each citation includes the specific disability the book deals with.

Rochman, Hazel. *Against Borders: Promoting Books for a Multicultural World*. Chicago: American Library Association, 1993. The bibliographic essays cover seven themes: "The Perilous Journey," "The Hero and the Monster," "Outsiders," "Friends and Enemies," "Lovers and Strangers," "Family Matters," and "Finding the Way Home." Woven within each thematic essay are works of fiction and non-fiction with full bibliographic citations provided for each source in the margin. Part Two, "Resources; Going Global," is arranged within three categories: "Racial Oppression," which includes work on the Holocaust and apartheid; "Ethnic USA"; and "The Widening World."

Rollock, Barbara. *The Black Experience in Children's Books*. New York: New York Public Library, 1974. Contains more than 450 recommended fiction and non-fiction titles divided into geographical areas.

Schon, Isabel. *Books in Spanish for Children and Young Adults: An Annotated Guide*. Metuchen, NJ: Scarecrow Press. Series I 1978; Series II 1983; Series III 1985; Series IV 1987; Series V 1989; Series VI 1993. This annotated series, arranged geographically, identifies books for children and young adults that highlight the lifestyle, folklore, heroes, history, fiction, poetry, theater, and classical literature of Hispanic culture. The appendix, which includes bookdealers in Spanish-speaking countries, is an excellent collection development aspect of the series.

———. *A Hispanic Heritage: A Guide to Juvenile Books about Hispanic People and Cultures*. Metuchen, NJ: Scarecrow Press. Series I 1980; Series II 1985; Series III 1988; Series IV 1991. This series of bibliographies is much like the *Books in Spanish for Children and Young Adults* by Schon. Arranged geographically, they cover all types of books dealing with the history, culture, and literature of Hispanic countries. Within each geographic section listings are alphabetical by author. Each entry includes bibliographic information and a summary. Noteworthy books are indicated with an asterisk. Indexed by author, title, and subject.

———. *A Bicultural Heritage: Themes for the Exploration of Mexican and Mexican-American Culture in Books for Children and Adolescents*. Metuchen, NJ: Scarecrow Press, 1978. The bibliography is designed to expose children and young adults to customs, lifestyles, heroes, folklore, and history of Mexican and Mexican-American cultures. The bibliography is arranged by theme areas: customs, heroes, folklore, and key historical developments, and each theme divided by grade levels: K–2, 3–6, and 7–12. Not all books included are annotated. Indexed by author and title.

Sinclair, Patty K. *E for Environment: An Annotated Bibliography of Children's Books with Environmental Themes*. New Providence, NJ: R.R. Bowker, 1992. This source includes a variety of topics related to the environment, including fictional works dealing with environmental themes. Each chapter, such as population and food supply and garbage and recycling, includes annotations of books on that topic. Annotations often include suggestions for use in the classroom.

Slapin, Beverly and Doris Seale. *Through Indian Eyes: The Native Experience in Books for Children*. 3d ed. Philadelphia: New Society, 1992. Includes essays, stories, and poetry. The selected bibliography included provides one of the few available sources of books by and about Native people. An additional bibliography, "American Indian Authors for Young Readers: An Annotated Bibliography," compiled by Mary G. Byler, limits selection to American Indian authors appropriate for young adult readers.

Stephens, Elaine C., Jean C. Brown and Janet E. Rubin. *Learning about the Holocaust: Literature and Other Resources for Young People*. North Haven, CT: Library Professional Publications, 1995. An overview of the Holocaust and a rationale for using its literature provide the framework for the annotated plot summaries and listings of works on the Holocaust for young people. Each chapter is organized thematically by genre and by grade level. Indexed by author and index of book titles by chapter and genre. A concluding section lists organizations and institutions, curriculum guides, journals, and media resources related to the Holocaust.

Sullivan, C.W., ed. *Science Fiction for Young Readers*. Contributions to the Study of Science Fiction and Fantasy, No. 56. Westport, CT: Greenwood Press, 1993. Although not a bibliography, the bibliographies at the conclusion of each chapter are exhaustive. Part II is divided into author studies and includes such favorites of young adult science fiction fans as Alan E. Nourse and Monica Hughes.

Van Meter, Vandelia. *World History for Children and Young Adults: An Annotated Bibliographic Index*. Englewood, CO: Libraries Unlimited, 1992. Arranged geographically, by continent and country; includes annotated titles, both fiction and non-fiction.

———. *American History and Young Adults*. Englewood, CO: Libraries Unlimited, 1990. Annotated bibliography of fiction and non-fiction books related to U.S. history for students K–12. Arranged chronologically beginning with 1600. Included are works on immigrants, inventions, and the growth of the labor union, along with traditional works on explorers, wars, and presidents. Also works on the social life and customs of each period are included.

Wilkin, Binnie Tate. *Survival Themes in Fiction for Children and Young People*. Metuchen, NJ: Scarecrow Press, 1978. Listing of fiction to help children and young adults deal with issues such as sexuality, identity, self-image, peer pressure, and loneliness.

Zvirin, Stephanie. *The Best Years of Their Lives: A Resource Guide for Teenagers in Crisis*. Chicago: American Library Association, 1992; Zvirin, Stephanie. *The Best Years of Their Lives: A Resource Guide for Teenagers in Crisis*. 2d ed. Chicago: American Library Association, 1996. Annotated bibliographies of self-help fiction and non-fiction for adolescents, age 12 to 18, arranged under such topics as "Family Matters," "Wellness," and "Sex Stuff." Indexed by author, title, and subject. Appendixes, "Filmography," list current videos available to young people facing personal challenge.

PERIODICAL SOURCES

Several periodical sources regularly publish bibliographies related to YA literature and issues/problems in working and developing programs for youth. Obviously, searching various printed index and electronic sources such as ERIC and *Library Literature* is certainly a strategy to use if one is attempting to find sources. However, the journals in this list are certainly among the key journals that should be consulted.

The ALAN Review. Assembly on Literature for Adolescents, National Council of Teachers of English. Quarterly. The journal is one of the key journals in the field of YA literature and publishes a broad scope of articles, author interviews, and bibliographical essays related to YA literature. Issues have bibliographical essays on the literature of Vietnam and Afghanistan, a bibliography on multicultural literature, YA literature about AIDS, and homosexuality in YA fiction and non-fiction.

Booklist. American Library Association. Published twice a month (September through June and monthly in July and August). Although primarily a book and multimedia review journal, the occasional bibliographies published by the Books for Youth section are excellent. Some examples of those bibliographies include "The Asian American Experience: Nonfiction"; "The African American Journey: From Slavery to Freedom"; "By Gays and Lesbians, for Every Library"; "Growing Up Male: Boys in Love," and these are just a sampling of published bibliographies. In the August issue an index is published to provide easy access to the retrospective bibliographies and features published by the Books for Youth section. The March 15 issue of each year features the Best Books for Young Adults and Quick Picks for Reluctant Young Adult Readers.

Journal of Youth Services in Libraries. American Library Association. Published quarterly. The journal is the divisional publication of the Association of Library Service to Children and Young Adult Libraries Services Association. The journal publishes research studies, critical/analysis, author interviews, and bibliographical essays related to children and YA library services and literature.

School Library Journal. R.R. Bowker. Published monthly except June and July. The journal focuses on school librarianship and publishes various articles dealing with young adults. Bibliographies published in the last few years have dealt with cultural diversity, mathematics, and women authors, to name just a few of the topics covered. Each year *SLJ* selects the best books and multimedia for young adults selected from among the books, videos, tapes, and CD-ROMs reviewed in the journal. In each March issue the notable books for children and best books for young adults are listed.

WORLD WIDE WEB SITES AND INTERNET SOURCES

With the advent of electronic communications and publications, numerous listservs and World Wide Web pages are available on YA literature and issues related to providing a broad range of library services for YA populations. An excellent article, "Young Adult Literature on the World Wide Web" by Betty Carter, published in *The ALAN Review* 23, no. 2 (Winter 1996): 46–48, gives an excellent overview of what is available on various Web sites. Some of those listed in that article are included in the following listing. While listservs have multiple functions, primarily chatting and exchanging information, some of the listservs devoted to children and YA literature often include bibliographical information. Librarians and teachers often are looking for a book or books on a particular topic/theme, and responses can provide useful guidance and information to those who are willing to devote time to perusing these avenues of information exchange.

Kid-L@Bingvmb.cc.Binghamton.Edu. A listserv that allows users to exchange a wide variety of information related to children's and YA literature and library services. Information can range from inquiries or readings on the Civil War for eighth graders to discussion on parental involvement on Web sites.

http://ipl.sils.umich.edu/youth/. Internet Public Library Youth Division. Includes book-talks, book reviews by kids, and author interaction.

http://www.parentspace.com/readroom/childnew/index.html. *Children's Literature: A Newsletter for Adults*. To help parents find the best children's books.

http://sunsite.unc.edu/cheryb/nancy.drew/ktitle.html. A home page devoted to in-depth study, critical analysis of the Nancy Drew series.

http://members.aol.com/biblioholc/bseries.html. Overview of series books for boys.

http://members.aol.com/biblioholc/gseries.html. Overview of series books for girls.

http://www.city-net./~lmann/awards/hugos/index.html. Listing of the Hugo Awards from 1953 to 1995.

http://www.city-net.com/~lmann/awards/nebulas/index.html. For young adults who are science fiction/fantasy readers, this site includes all the Nebula Awards from 1965 to 1994.

http://edfu.lis.uiuc.edu/puboff/bccb. The review journal *The Bulletin of the Center for Children's Books* is available at this address.

http://scholar.lib.vt.edu/ejournals/ALAN/alan-review.html. *The ALAN Review* is available full text beginning with the winter 1994 issue.

http://www.cs.cmu.edu/Web/People/spok/most-banned.html. Listing of the most frequently banned titles.

http://www.cs.cmu.edu/Web/People/spok/banned-books.html. Web site devoted to intellectual freedom issues.

http://www.bookwire.com/PW/bsl/bestseller-index.html. Current best-sellers reported by *Publishers Weekly*.

http://www.scils.rutgers.edu/special/kay/100list.html. Comprehensive recommendation of
     100 YA novels.

NOTES

1. Kenneth L. Donelson and Alleen Pace Nilsen, *Literature for Today's Young Adults*,
3d ed. (Glenview, IL: Scott, Foresman, 1989), 13.

2. Laura Stanley Berger, *Twentieth-Century Young Adult Writers* (Detroit: St. James
Press, 1994).

3. Nancy E. Shields, *Index to Literary Criticism for Young Adults* (Metuchen, NJ:
Scarecrow Press, 1988).

4. Steven Olderr, ed., *Olderr's Young Adult Fiction Index* (Chicago: St. James Press,
1990).

Selected
Bibliography

CHAPTER 1

Came, Barry. "Young, Gay, and Alone." *MacLean's* (February 22, 1993).

Eagle, Carol J. and Carol Colman. *All That She Can Be.* New York: Simon and Schuster, 1993.

Fenwick, Elizabeth and Tony Smith. *Adolescence: The Survival Guide for Parents and Teenagers.* New York: Dorling Kindersley, 1994.

Haffner, Debra W. "Facing Facts: Sexual Health for America's Adolescents. The Report of the National Commission on Adolescent Sexual Health." *SIECUS Report.* New York: Council of the United States, August/September 1995.

Knight, Sophie. "Indigo 101." *Seventeen* (May 1997).

CHAPTER 2

Broderick, Dorothy M. and Mary K. Chelton. *Librarian's Guide to Young Adult Paperbacks.* 3d ed. New York: New American Library, 1986.

Chelton, Mary K. "Unrestricted Body Parts and Predictable Bliss: The Audience Appeal of Formula Romances." *Library Journal* (July 1991): 44–49.

Estes, Sally, ed. *Genre Favorites for Young Adults: A Collection of Booklist Columns.* Chicago: American Library Association, 1993.

———. *Popular YA Reading: A Collection of Booklist Columns.* Chicago: American Library Association, 1996.

Herald, Diana Tixier. *Teen Genreflecting.* Littleton, CO: Libraries Unlimited, 1997.

Jones, Patrick. *Connecting Young Adults and Libraries: A How-to-Do-It Manual.* New York: Neal-Schuman, 1992.

Kies, Cosette. *Young Adult Horror Fiction.* New York: Twayne, 1992.

Leonhardt, Mary. *Keeping Kids Reading.* New York: Crown, 1996.

Lukens, Rebecca. *A Critical Handbook of Children's Literature.* 3d ed. Glenview, IL: Scott, Foresman, 1986.

MacLeod, Anne Scott. "Nancy Drew and Her Rivals: No Contest." The *Horn Book Magazine* 63 (May/June 1987): 314–22.

Makowski, Silk. "Serious about Series." *Voice of Youth Advocates* (February 1994): 349–51.

Nilsen, Alleen Pace and Kenneth Donelson. *Literature for Today's Young Adults.* 4th ed. New York: HarperCollins, 1993.

VanVliet, Lucille W. *Approaches to Literature through Genre.* Phoenix, AZ: Oryx Press, 1992.

CHAPTER 7

Bold, Rudolph. "Trash in the Library." *Library Journal* 105, no. 11 (May 15, 1980): 1138–39.

Felder, Deborah. "Nancy Drew: Then and Now." *Publishers Weekly* 229, no. 26 (May 30, 1986): 30.

Huntwork, Mary M. "Why Girls Flock to Sweet Valley High." *School Library Journal* 36, no. 3 (March 1990): 137–40.

Lynch, Chris. "Today's YA Writers: Pulling No Punches." *School Library Journal* 40, no. 1 (January 1994): 37–38.

Peck, Richard. *Love and Death at the Mall.* New York: Delacorte Press, 1994.

Pollack, Pamela D. "The Business of Popularity: The Surge of Teenage Paperbacks." *School Library Journal* 28, no. 26 (November 1981): 25–28.

Shapiro, Lillian. "Quality or Popularity: Selective Criteria for YAs." *School Library Journal* 24, no. 9 (May 1978): 23–27.

CHAPTER 14

Barteluk, Wendy D.M. *Library Displays on a Shoestring: Three-Dimensional Techniques for Promoting Library Services.* Metuchen, NJ: Scarecrow Press, 1993.

Dimick, Barbara. "Marketing Youth Services." *Library Trends,* 43, no. 3 (Winter 1995): 463–77.

Display and Publicity Ideas for Libraries. Jefferson, NC: McFarland, 1985.

Heath, Alan. *Off the Wall.* Englewood, CO: Libraries Unlimited, 1987.

Jones, Margaret. "Facing Up to Fewer Faceouts: Merchandising More with Less." *Publishers Weekly* (September 7, 1992): 22–25.

Kohn, Rita and Krysta Tepper. *You Can Do It: A PR Skills Manual for Libraries.* Metuchen, NJ: Scarecrow Press, 1981.

Walters, Susan. *Marketing: A How-to-Do-It Manual.* New York: Neal-Schuman, 1992.

CHAPTER 15

Anderson, Mary Alice. *Teaching Information Literacy Using Electronic Resources for Grades 6–12.* Worthington, OH: Linworth, 1996.

Baule, Steven M. *Technology Planning.* Worthington, OH: Linworth, 1997.

Beasley, Augie. *Making It with Media.* Worthington, OH: Linworth, 1992.

———. *Looking Great with Video.* Worthington, OH: Linworth, 1994.

Ensor, Pat, ed. *Cybrarian's Manual.* Chicago: American Library Association, 1996.

Farmer, Lesley S.J. *Training Student Library Staff.* Worthington, OH: Linworth, 1997.

Kyker, Keith and Christopher Curchy. *Video Projects for Elementary and Middle Schools.* Littleton, CO: Libraries Unlimited, 1995.

LaGuardia, Cheryl. *The CD-ROM Primer.* New York: Neal-Schuman, 1994.

Mason-Robinson, Sally. *Developing and Managing Video Collections in Libraries.* New York: Neal-Schuman, 1996.

Metz, Ray E. and Gail Junion-Metz. *Using the World Wide Web and Creating Home Pages.* New York: Neal-Schuman, 1996.

Pappas, Marjorie L., Gayle A. Geitgey, and Cathy A. Jefferson. *Searching Electronic Resources.* Worthington, OH: Linworth, 1996.

Ross, Calvin. *The Frugal Youth Cybrarian: Computing for Kids.* Chicago: American Library Association, 1996.

Simpson, Carol Mann. *Internet for Library Media Specialists.* Worthington, OH: Linworth, 1995.

Walker, H. Thomas and Paula K. Montgomery. *Media Production and Computer Activities.* Santa Barbara, CA: ABC-CLIO, 1990.

CHAPTER 17

Adamec, J., "Homework Helpers: Making Study Time Quality Time." *Wilson Library Bulletin* 65 (1990): 31–32.

Alesandrini, B. Letter to author, June 13, 1995.

———. "PASS!—Partners for Achieving School Success." Photocopy, 1995.

———. "PASS!—Partners for Achieving School Success: Annual report." Ethical Strategies Committee, photocopy, July 1995–June 1996.

Allen, S.G. Telephone conversation with author, June 13, 1995.

Davis, V. "Homework Center—Textbooks in the Library." *School Library Journal* 33, no. 7 (1987): 52.

Dunmore, A.J. and K.C. Hardiman. " 'My Turn' Boosts Teen Self-Esteem." *American Libraries* 17 (1987): 786–87.

Harper, E. Telephone conversation with author, June 13, 1996.

Ivens, B. "No 'Quiet Please.' " In *The Public Library Plans for the Teen Age.* Chicago: American Library Association, 1948.

Mondowney, J.G. "Licensed to Learn: Drivers' Training for the Internet." *School Library Journal* 42, no. 1 (1996): 32–34.

News brief. *Library Hotline* 24, no. 31 (1995): 7.

Wagner, M.M. and G. Wronka. "Youth Services Policies and Procedures." In *Youth Services Librarians as Managers: A How-to Guide from Budgeting to Personnel.* Chicago: American Library Association, 1995.

CHAPTER 22

Caywood, Carolyn. "The Courage to Trust." *School Library Journal* 41, no. 8 (1995): 43.

"Censorship Dateline 'Libraries—Clifton, New Jersey.' " *Newsletter on Intellectual Freedom* 45, no. 3 (1996): 83.

Fine, Sara. "How the Mind of a Censor Works." *School Library Journal* 42, no. 1 (1996): 23–27.

Foerstel, Herbet N. *Banned in the U.S.A.* Westport, CT: Greenwood Press, 1994.

Free Library of Philadelphia. *Use of Adult Materials by Children.* PS #52 (May 3, 1966): 1–3.

———. *Use of Adult Materials by Children.* AG #71–109 (September 24, 1971): 1.

Garden, Nancy. *Annie on My Mind.* New York: Farrar, Straus, Giroux, 1982.

Gerhardt, Lillian N. "Restricted Borrowing." *School Library Journal* 40, no. 5 (1994): 4.

Glick, Andrea. "Groups Work to Restrict Kids'Access." *School Library Journal* 43, no. 3 (1997): 86.

Goldberg, Beverly. "On Line for the First Amendment." *American Libraries* 22, no. 8 (1995): 774–78.

"Gwinnett County 'Contract' defeated." *Newsletter on Intellectual Freedom* 44, no. 5 (1995): 123.

"Gwinnett Turmoil Continues." *Newsletter on Intellectual Freedom* 44, no. 6 (1995): 180–81.

Harlen, Ann O. "2 on Library Board Call for Restrictions." *Washington Post* (September 28, 1996), sec. B, p. 1; sec. B, p. 5, col. 2.

Harmon, Charles. "But We're Family Friendly Already—How to Respond to the Challenge." *American Libraries* 27, no. 7 (1996): 60–62.

Hentoff, Nat. *The Day They Came to Arrest the Book.* New York: Delacorte, 1982.

Lee, Earl. "On My Mind." *American Libraries* 27, no. 1 (1996): 51–52.

Lipton, Eric. "Fairfax to Consider 'Adult-Only' Library Section." *Washington Post* (September 15, 1994), sec. D, p. 1; sec. D, p. 9, col. 4.

———. "Fairfax Opens Book on Censorship Issue." *Washington Post* (September 16, 1994), sec. B, p. 1; sec. B, p. 6, col. 3.

———. "Adult-Only Library Debate Starts." *Washington Post* (September 17, 1994), sec. A, p. 1; sec. A, p. 6, col. 1.

———. "Fairfax Library Panel Rejects Restricting Minors' Choices." *Washington Post* (October 25, 1994), sec. B, p. 1; sec. B, p. 3, col. 1.

National Coalition Against Censorship. "Censorship News 60" (cited May 22, 1996). Available from http://www.ncac.org/cnold.html.

Reichman, Henry. *Censorship and Selection: Issues and Answers for Schools.* Chicago: American Library Association; Arlington, VA: American Association of School Administrators, 1988.

Rogers, Jo Ann V., ed. *Libraries and Young Adults.* Littleton, CO: Libraries Unlimited, 1979.

Settoff, Rebecca. *Adolescence.* New York: Chelsea House, 1990.

St. Lifer, Evan and Michael Rogers. "Family Friendly Libraries Attacks ALA in Cincy Meeting." *Library Journal* 120, no. 19 (1995): 12–13.

Whitiwell, Stuart C.A. "Special Report: Christian Conservatives Organize to Criticize ALA." *American Libraries* 26, no. 10 (1995): 983–84.
Woodworth, Mary L., ed. *The Young Adult and Intellectual Freedom: Proceedings of an Institute*. Madison: University of Wisconsin Library School, 1977.

Index

About the Contributors

MARY ARNOLD is a Young Adult Librarian with the Medina County (Ohio) District Library and is a member of the Young Adult Library Services Association Board of Directors.

BARBARA AUERBACH is a librarian in the Youth Services Division of the Brooklyn (New York) Public Library.

JERI BAKER is a Young Adult Librarian with the Dallas Public Library.

MICHAEL CART is the author of *From Romance to Realism: 50 Years of Growth and Change in Young Adult Literature* and is the 1997–1998 president of the Young Adult Library Services Association.

LYNN COCKETT is a former YA librarian.

JAMES COOK is the Young Adult Services Coordinator at the Dayton and Montgomery County (Ohio) Public Library.

AUDREY EAGLEN is retired from the Cuyahoga County (Ohio) Public Library and is a past president of the Young Adult Services Division of the American Library Association.

LESLEY FARMER is the author of seven books and is a librarian at Redwood High School in Larkspur, California.

SEAN P.S. GEORGE is the Youth Services Coordinator for the St. Charles Parish (Louisiana) Library.

DIANA TIXIER HERALD is the author of *Genreflecting* and *Teen Genreflecting*.

PATRICK JONES is the author of *Connecting Young Adults and Libraries: A How-to-Do-It Manual.*

DON KENNEY is the past coeditor of the *Journal of Youth Services* and is the Associate Dean of Administrative Services for the Virginia Tech University Libraries.

RICK KERPER is an Assistant Professor at Millersville University, Millersville, Pennsylvania.

NANCY KRAVITZ is a librarian with the Free Library of Philadelphia.

ELAINE MCGUIRE is the IMC Director for the Ida Weller Elementary School, Centerville, Ohio.

CINDY MEDIAVILLA is a former YA librarian.

C. ALLEN NICHOLS is Director of the Ella M. Everhard Public Library in Wadsworth, Ohio.

MARY ANNE NICHOLS is School-Age and Young Adult Librarian at the Akron–Summit County Public Library in Ohio.

MELANIE RAPP is a Young Adult Librarian with the Cuyahoga County (Ohio) Public Library.

TOM REYNOLDS is a Young Adult Librarian with the Edmonds Public Library, Edmonds, Washington.

CATHERINE RITCHIE is a librarian with the Decatur (Illinois) Public Library.

ANN SPARANESE is a former member of the YALSA Best Books for Young Adults Committee and is the Head of Adult and Young Adult Services for the Englewood Public Library, Englewood, New Jersey.

DIANE STINE is the School and Youth Consultant for the North Suburban Library System, Wheeling, Illinois.

SUSAN WEAVER is an Assistant Professor and Director, Library Services, for the Kent State University East Liverpool Campus.